MW01698009

THE FUNDAMENTALS OF GENERAL TREE WORK

25th Anniversary Edition

THE FUNDAMENTALS OF GENERAL TREE WORK

25th Anniversary Edition

Gerald F. Beranek

H.A.F.
Publishing

The Fundamentals of General Tree Work
25th Anniversary Edition

High Angle Forestry Publishing

www.hafpublishing.com
email: patrick@hafpublishing.com

PO Box 340
Rodney, ON, Canada
N0L 2C0

DISCLAIMER

Tree work is inherently dangerous. Be advised that this book is intended for informational purposes only, and cannot be substituted for professional, in-person instruction. Serious injury or death could result from the use of techniques and equipment described in this book. It is the reader's responsibility to seek qualified instruction on the techniques and safety protocols of tree climbing, tree felling, and general tree work. Every person involved in any type of tree work should exercise patience, good judgement, and an abundance of caution while practicing new techniques. Unfamiliar techniques should be practiced in a controlled environment before they are incorporated into everyday work procedures. If you have not been properly trained, or you have any doubts as to your ability to safely complete any type of tree work task, especially those involving climbing and/or chainsaws, please do not attempt it. This book is sold with no liability to the author, editor, or publisher, expressed or implied, in the case of any injuries, death, or damages resulting from the use or misuse of the information contained herein.

Layout and design produced by Mendocino Lithographers and High Angle Forestry Publishing.

Special thanks to Gileno Rego and Patrick Donoahue for their help and patience in restoring "The Fundamentals" to a physical book once again.

25th Anniversary Edition
High Angle Forestry Publishing © 2021

1996

This book is dedicated to Phil Sharples. Though I've only known him a few months, he showed me the way through the publishing jungle and took personal interest in my project to make it a book that I'm proud to present to you.

2021

My, how things have changed since 1996. In 2005 I published another book all about local logging history called 'High Climbers and Timber Fallers'. In 2006 I married the daughter of a local fisherman, Terri Carpenter, now Mrs. B. Thank you!

In 2007 I was injured and put out of work. Which wasn't all bad actually, as I suddenly had all the time needed to complete a video series I started about tree-work called 'Working Climber'. Which basically is this book in video format. Over 20 hours long! In 2012 I published yet another book called 'Coast Redwood', and from 2013 to 2016 I published 4 more titles about our California Old-growth Redwood Parks.

In latter 2016, after 20 years running, I opted to let the Fundamentals of General Tree Work go out of print, because I felt the chapters on climbing tools and technique were outdated, and Jeff Jepson already had that covered very well in his Tree Climber's Companion series, which he did beautifully. So why bother updating the Fundamentals? It would be timely, costly, and plus I wasn't getting any younger.

Not to throw the baby out with the bathwater, on an internet forum called Butch Ballow's Tree House, I offered any member there the opportunity to take this book and keep it going, if any one of them had a mind to. Months went by, no takers. But then I received a personal message from a member who said he would take it on. Enter: Patrick Masterson of Ontario, Canada. www.EducatedClimber.com. Thank you, Patrick!

Patrick has done an outstanding job. Starting with scanned pages, he published the Fundamentals in PDF format for electronic download. Then he revamped the cover, typesetting, and images, and republished the Fundamentals in book format again!

On the back cover are supporting reviews from top tradesmen in the industry: Reg Coates, Lawrence Schultz, August Hunicke, Don Blair, Jeff Jepson and Buckin' Billy Ray Smith. And don't forget my original supporters: Bill Bailey and Charly Pottorff.

Today, The Fundamentals of General Tree Work 25th Anniversary edition, is dedicated to all of these people who gave their support and sought to keep it going. Thank you all!

Gerald F. Beranek.
July 12, 2021.

Publisher's Note

Here it is folks, the Bible of Tree Work from the legend himself, Gerald "Jerry" F. Beranek! Within these pages you will find the most comprehensive reference work in our field, the go-to resource for professionals in the industry for over 20 years.

Jerry Beranek - climber, timber faller, photographer, writer, and educator - worked for 18 years to produce this incredible resource, to pass along his knowledge to future generations. Sadly, his book went out of print in 2016. With no plans to do a re-print, I contacted him about bringing it back. After several failed attempts at a paperback copy, we finally compromised and put it out as a digital edition PDF. This version of The Fundamentals was the only way for people to get their hands on this knowledge from November of 2017 until mid 2021. But now, finally, The Fundamentals is back in print for good!

This is the book that started it all for me and countless others. I remember in my first term of apprenticeship school, the Sherrill dealer stopped in to take orders for climbing gear. This book is what I ordered. Everyone else was getting ropes and saddles. When the order finally came in, I can just remember the other guys looking over and rolling their eyes, like to say, who orders a book? ... this guy, that's who!

My hope for you, whether you are just starting out in tree work or you are a seasoned veteran, is that this timeless classic will touch you as it did me. This book connected a lot of dots in my head, and I am so, so grateful to Jerry for writing it all those years ago. The Fundamentals played a vital role in my personal journey to becoming an 'Educated Climber', a journey that continues to this day. As Ernest Hemingway once said, "We are all apprentices in a craft where no one ever becomes a master..."

Climb high, Work smart, Read more.

Patrick Masterson

H.A.F. Publishing and EducatedClimber.com

January 2021
Somewhere in Canada

Table of Contents

Photographs and Illustrations

Foreword

Choosing to go into tree work is choosing to go into battle. Don't be like some, and go into battle without basic training. This book is a guide for basic training. "Basic" is a modest description considering that the era and dynamic skills of the author, show him going into more advanced scenarios (especially with tree felling) than most tree workers will ever find themselves. I am not suggesting the book should be skimmed because there is something for everyone in all the contents. Consider this book to be wise reconnaissance of the jobs ahead. Although your battleground might not have an adversary scheming to get you, the worksites of the vocation will have nearly as many ways to wreck you as a field of war. It does not suffice to just, "be safe," you need to know the "fighting arts" of the tree craft. They are in this book. Please read the author's preface of the book for more on this subject. If you are new, start with this book, if you're not, take advantage of Jerry Beranek compiling all this knowledge in one place. Brush up on what you know, and pass your skills on to those who come after, as he has done.

I was one of those that went into battle without basic training. It was before the incredible power of Google allowed us to instantly search any subject under the sun from our smartphones, and before YouTube tradesmen both good and bad, were uploading their work to the web. It wasn't that I didn't want training, I was hungry for it. No! I was starved for it! It's just that good teachers are very rare. I worked on crews that were driven by expediency. Immediate production always ruled the day. This meant that regardless of my longing to climb or cut, time was rarely taken to teach me. Worse than that even, I've noticed that no matter the trade, those with skills are usually more interested in showing them off than in teaching them. Their arrogance not only makes them lousy teachers, but it stifles their own growth. One might think he has 20 years experience, when really he has just one year, repeated 20 times. Business models like this are often the norm, because production does occur. The problem is, the greenhorns stay green and even the company as a whole is held back from greater potential by it's constant focus on the ever present now.

Not all the experts of my young career were condescending. I did pick up things from a few but there is a difference between knowing how to do something and knowing how to teach something. Jerry Beranek has the heart of a teacher. It shows by how simply he breaks complex principles down to "Fundamentals" for the reader's advantage. It also shows by the fact that to make it simple for us, he took eighteen years to compile and arrange it! That's the heart of a teacher!

A lack of mentorship, coupled with my own insane fascination with the work, spelled trouble for me. I went on my own. If no company had time to get me cutting, I'd start my own business. I enrolled in the school of hard knocks. Twelve years went by and the knocks came. The stories of pain and victory would require their own book but in 1998 I got my hands on Jerry's book, the original release of the very book you now hold.

I had done it backwards. I went to basic training after many battles and wounds. But I read his book with the enthusiasm and awe of a person called to the work; a person "Made for This" Tree Life. The Fundamentals book rounded me out and though I already had much hard-won experience, I learned and was able to apply so much more. And even now, in the year 2021, with 34 years at my career and the respect of many colleagues, I've not come near the magnitude of experience in this book. Like many people, I revered Jerry for his work and wanted to tell him so. In 2014, I finally got the chance via an internet forum for tree workers called, "The Treehouse."

The following is an excerpt of what I told him on the forum:

> "Mr. Beranek, just so you know... your book 'The Fundamentals of General Tree Work', I bought in 1998, 12 years into my career. Those 12 years prior to the book were painful ones. I have always been resourceful but I won't say I wasn't dumb. I needed a teacher but I was almost completely self-taught and well acquainted with a salty mix of injury, ambulance, glory, and embarrassment. In 1998 your book became my teacher. It was gospel. It was a holy vocational bible of skill, teaching, experience, and tactful objectivity. I saw the Jedi-level moves and knowledge I wanted to have. I also saw so many things spelled out play-by-play that I understood but couldn't explain prior to your book. I don't know how many times I exclaimed, 'Wow, there's a name for that!'

"Terms like, 'trunk drag', and 'salami cut', and even, 'nervous tension', (which, because of you is where I begin when I train someone). So many times over the years I've wanted to somehow call you up and thank you for working so hard to share your knowledge. I never dreamed I'd be able to just chat it off to you instantly in such a place as a 'Tree House!' But I can, so, Thank you! Your diligence, passion, humility, and skill-on-loan from God have played a huge part in my development. I wish I had found your book many years (and injuries) sooner than I did, and because of that I've loaned it to many young woodsmen under my care since. You have the heart of a teacher and the knowledge, skill, and diplomacy to back it up. I've been a grateful student and have attained many victories as a result of it. Also, your dedication to documenting your experience has rubbed off on me, and now in this media-gadget splendor-land of the 21st century I can take viewers places I always wanted to, but never dreamed I'd be able to. Thanks for the book. I'm sure it is just a snapshot of your depth but wow! What a picture! It should have a $1000.00 price tag on it, after all, that's probably the minimum cost to get in an ambulance." -August Hunicke

Jerry and other colleagues responded on the forum. Jerry wrote:

"Thank you all so much! Your support is so over-whelming. I never ever considered myself any more than just part of the backbone of hard working people that makes up this industry. An industry I chose to make a career of, after spending 9 years in it. Today I am truly honored to receive the accolades that have come from my efforts over the years. Hey, when I started in this business I had absolutely no idea where I was headed. That is the truth.

"August, your love of trade and professionalism transcends through your videos. Of which rank up with the best arb videos I've watched on the world-wide-web. The message in your videos pulls my heart-strings. Like Reg C, I can't help but think you're a cool guy. Your actions reflect it. Thank you for being you, and all the kind words and appreciation!"

- Jerry and Terri B

Amazingly, not long after this correspondence, I was able to interview Jerry on my YouTube channel. It was surreal that the mentor I'd never met was coming to see me. My success and my survival had, in many ways, been unknowingly built by him and it was proof of his artful teaching that the occasion was even happening. Life can really take some poetic turns.

The sincere hard work and value of 'The Fundamentals' book was discussed in the interview and I promoted it much. Ironically, I discovered the book was just then going out of print, and that the $1000 price tag I mentioned in 2014 could soon become a reality for the book on Ebay. How could that be? Had the book really run it's course?

Well, as it turns out, NO! Thanks primarily to the timeless value of the book, and the efforts of Patrick Masterson at H.A.F. publishing (aka The Educated Climber), the book is now back in print.

If you are reading this, you are now in possession of the most concise and comprehensive library of tree work knowledge and technique that's ever been written. It's here in one spot, prepared for you. Take it into battle, and enjoy the success it brings you. Be like Jerry, take full advantage of his knowledge, but share it also.

Be deliberate...

August Hunicke

August Hunicke Arborists Inc.

and

MonkeyBeaver.com

January 2021
Grant's Pass, Oregon

Author's Preface

I began climbing power poles in 1968 while I was with the U.S. Army Combat Engineers in Vietnam. In 1969, I got a job climbing and trimming trees for a small line clearance contract company in Santa Rosa, California. I spent the next six years working and attending Santa Rosa Junior College, where I studied plant sciences. I was fortunate to live and work where Luther Burbank did his research, and I learned a great deal about ornamental trimming and detailed pruning.

In 1975 I moved to Fort Bragg, a small logging and fishing town on the north coast of California. I continued to trim trees for line clearance, but my ornamental and pruning work came to an end. Because there's practically nothing but indigenous forest trees around Fort Bragg, I started to work in the woods climbing a lot of big timber for the loggers and timber fallers. The heavy work fascinated me, so after eighteen years of line clearance trimming I then began working steadily in the woods.

The idea of this book came to me in 1978. At that time I was a foreman for the Sohner Tree Service, and I had nine years of line clearance experience and nine years of breaking in new climbers at a rate of about two a year. The employee turn-over in line clearance work was high back then and it still is today. Only about five percent of the people that get into the business ever make a career of it and those few that do are in the same predicament that I was in with the Sohner company: breaking in new people all the time! It was the same with the Davey company. There were no books or manuals on tree climbing technique or its associated tree cutting practices. There were plenty of safety manuals though. But they never really tell a person how to do anything, but be safe! As a result, every practical thing a new employee learns, good or bad, is passed on by their foreman, many of whom have only a few years experience themselves. From my own experiences with these matters in the line clearance business I found much complacency in craft and management. Not on safety matters, everybody's hell on safety, but on proficiency and expertise! I've never seen any emphasis put on either craft or management. I was told many times, "What can you expect? Just make sure they do it safely!" With that attitude there's people doing tree work that don't even know their basic knots and splices let alone the physics of what they're working with. This is why I decided to write a book; a book on practical techniques, ideas, theories, and practices used in tree work. I really didn't think it would take eighteen years to do it though. Looking back now, I realize that it was me that had to learn about tree work in order to become qualified to pass it on. It's July 1996 right now, and this book is just weeks away from going to press. It's finally done. What I included in this book related to tree climbing and timber falling I could have covered in much greater detail. It is not definitive by any stretch of the imagination. It is though, a good introduction for the beginner to the wide world of practical tree work. I'll be starting a new book soon about my logging and climbing experiences over the last 25 years in the big timber. Lots of great photographs and stories! It's going to be a good one.

About the photographs in this book. The ones contained herein were selected out of more than five thousand in my collection. In the last eighteen years I shot more than ten thousand Kodachromes all together. I have a series of photographs to go with everything I talk about in this book, but I couldn't include them all as it would have made the book way too expensive. About a dozen photos in this book are generic and placed with illustrations in chapters 13 and 26. These few don't depict entirely what's being illustrated and should not be confused as such.

I really must thank all the people that put up with me during the work and photo sessions. It was, at times, most trying for them to follow my instructions, hold still long enough for me to focus, compose, set exposure and finally take the picture. More than once they told me, "Hurry up Jer, I'm getting tired!" Most of the pictures of myself were taken by myself using an infrared remote control and motor drive camera that could be operated up to 200 feet away. I've been told my photographs do not reflect adequate use of personal safety equipment and are not correct to use in this kind of book for that reason. Well, my book wouldn't be what it is without these pictures, and I can't go back and do it all over again. You'll see in the text that I do promote the use of personal safety equipment and cite its importance in the situations where it's most needed.

In this book I recommend no procedure that is unsafe; my intent is to present insights into the practical applications and techniques used in tree work. But this work is full of contingency and an accident is possible throughout everything discussed. Remember, when you walk up to a tree - to climb it, to work in it, to fall it - you are betting your knowledge, experience, and common sense that you'll accomplish your goal without an accident. This is the lore of tree work that makes it exciting for some and fearful for others.

Climb and work safely. G.F.B.

Acknowledgments

Thanks to the climbers, timber fallers, loggers and individuals for their cooperation and assistance. Without their help many of the pictures in this book would not have been possible.

THE CLIMBERS

Keith Anker, Tom Alger, David Rexrode, Dwayne Slaven, Anthony Potter, Tom Clifton, John Ramsey, Vince Hoffman, Gene Potter, Andy Augustinovich, Tim Cook, Walley Shattock, Mike Rantala, Bruce Sheltron, Wess Burns, Stan Richards, Dwight Ramey.

THE TIMBER FALLERS

Dave DeConti, Mike Davis, John Ciro, Jon Taylor, Bob and Chip Defer, Mike Manus, Bruce Ingram, Gilbert Coleman, Jim Saldani, Larry Galliani, Mike Bennet, Fred Shuler, Stewart Titus, Gary Peeler, Steve Van Horn, Rocky Bakalino, Gordon Sipila, Jim Grey, Steve Coverston, Rick Rial, Gary Roach, Don Stanton, Les Giacomini, Leroy Kindal, John Welch, Pete Ensalada, Dave Pronsolino, Ron Pronsolino, Harry Spencer.

THE LOGGERS

Benedetti Logging, Sunstrom Custom Logging, Anderson Logging, Philbrick Logging, Pronsolino Logging, Giacomini Logging, Manus Logging, Columbi Logging.

THE INDIVIDUALS

Charly Pottorff, Mike Oxman, Steve Foster, Jim Ponce, Roy Stockton, Rocket Ron, Herb Walters, Charly and Mitch White, Chris Van Peer, Steve Mokma, George Stephen, Dean Quaid.

Special thanks to the editors who worked with me to make the manuscript a professional presentation: John Fremont, senior editor QED Press; Sal Glynn, associate editor QED Press; Helen Stone, editor Arbor Age magazine; John Welsh, the Print Shop; Philip Sharples, Mendo Litho.

The photographic, illustrated and written material in this book is the cumulative effort of twenty five years work by G. F. Beranek.

Introduction to Tree Climbing

There are many differences between tree climbing and the work done in the tree. Many people confuse the two, thinking them the same. But climbing and working in the tree are two distinctly different activities. A person can learn how to climb a tree in a relatively short length of time, but working in the tree takes much time and is a "never ending" learning process.

FEAR AND NERVOUS TENSION

Fear of heights is one of the biggest obstacles that new climbers have to overcome. It can overwhelm them and distract them from what they are doing.

The classic signs of fear and nervous tension are common when a new climber starts working at greater heights. Some people work fine at moderate heights and begin slowing down their productivity the higher they work. Being nervous is okay to a point. Nervousness can make you cautious and more alert. You check your lines, snaps, knots, and cuts more frequently when you are nervous. It can be considered a safety factor that keeps you careful and attentive. But nervousness can also become a nemesis and keep a person from being productive if it occurs frequently. It is distinctly different from fear but a very fine line divides the two as nervousness can easily turn into fear. When fear takes over a new climber it can strike in a bad way, and that person will need help immediately. This is why it is important that a qualified climber be present on any job that has beginners at work. The presence of an experienced climber on the job can bestow confidence during a trial situation. All people are different and the amount of time it takes for each to overcome the fears and anxieties they may encounter is also different. Fear and nervousness are expected, and the beginning climber should not become too discouraged by it.

PHYSICAL FITNESS

One of the basic requirements to become a good climber is fitness. Some of the work is very demanding of one's strength and endurance, even as simple a task as getting over to the top side of a single limb. Such obstacles can be beyond a person's physical capabilities if they are not in shape. In many trees, a number of obstacles may have to be overcome just to get to the actual work. Knowing the tricks will save a lot of work in the climbing of any tree, and being in good shape can make it a whole lot easier and bail you out of many tough situations. One good aspect of tree work is that it will keep you in pretty good physical condition.

A climber must also set a pace that befits their strength while they climb and work. A good pace will increase your endurance and keep you productive for longer periods. It will also keep a climber from becoming unduly fatigued while working and climbing, with enough reserve strength to use as an important safety margin. If you become too fatigued while climbing or working, you may not be able to pull yourself out of a tight spot. So it is important to maintain your fitness for this kind of work and set a safe working pace.

STATURE

One of the great misconceptions in tree climbing is that a person's physical size and reach can make them a better climber. This is not true in the broad spectrum of climbing, though it may be cited in a particular situation. Overall, anyone's size or reach will not make them a better or worse climber. When a limb is beyond any climber's reach, it doesn't matter that one climber may have a shorter reach than someone else. What matters is knowing how to get to the limb and this goes for just about any obstacle you may encounter in tree climbing. A few inches more height or reach will not get you there any quicker than knowing the tricks involved to reach the limb. Climbing requires more brains than physical stature. One's own good physical health combined with a rounded knowledge of climbing techniques will always be of more benefit than an extra couple inches of reach.

POSITION AND STANCE

Many of the positions and stances a climber assumes to do the work will never be required in their regular climbing, but specific positioning is required to manage the work properly. This is the sacrifice a climber must make to do the work, and it's the distinguishing difference between the tricks you must know to climb the tree and what you need to know to do the work. The so-called "best" position or stance to use is not always comfortable, but these events are usually short-lived and last not much longer than it takes to complete a certain cut. Knowing the proper position and stance and how to set the lines to assist you will come easier as you learn how certain cuts work, where you want them to work, and how to keep yourself out of harm's way.

REQUIREMENTS OF A CLIMBER

As you learn to climb and cut trees, you'll also learn many other aspects of the trade. A good climber must have a thorough knowledge of the business. You must learn the fundamentals of tree falling and the many varied cuts that are used for specific purposes. A good climber must also know a lot about rigging with ropes, fasteners, cables, straps, chokers, blocks, and brakes, plus the runs of rigging, the angles and dangles, and the tension and vectors. A climber must also know a fair amount about how trees grow and how to control that growth with their trimming and pruning. There is much prestige in the business when you are regarded as being knowledgeable as well as being able to do it well. A climber must also be good in public relations and be able to answer the many questions about a tree that the customer may have. In this requirement there are many legal aspects a climber should know to keep their liabilities to a minimum. A climber must also be a good estimator of time, cost, and the right personnel to do the work. To estimate work takes much experience and a wide eye to take into account all that has to be considered for any job. Underestimating work has cost people a lot of money in more ways than one. It often results in hurrying to finish a job (a major cause of accidents) when you realize you underestimated it. It takes much experience to accomplish the rank of a good climber. It is not learned in a minimum of time. Just remember, if climbing and cutting trees appeals to you, you should know all the things that are included in this book.

Chapter 1

Splices, Knots and Fasteners

For the beginner, it is necessary to learn a certain amount about the splices, knots, and fasteners used in tree work. While people use many different types of knots, you only need to know a handful to get by adequately in this line of work. Along with the basic knots, there are some variations on each that may be better suited for certain situations. Splicing is somewhat essential to know how to do, but it seems that only a small percentage of people in the business know how to do it. All persons in the business should develop a working knowledge of knots and splices within their first few months in the business.

Fasteners can be used in place of certain knots and splices. A person can gather together a nice collection of fasteners; whether or not they're

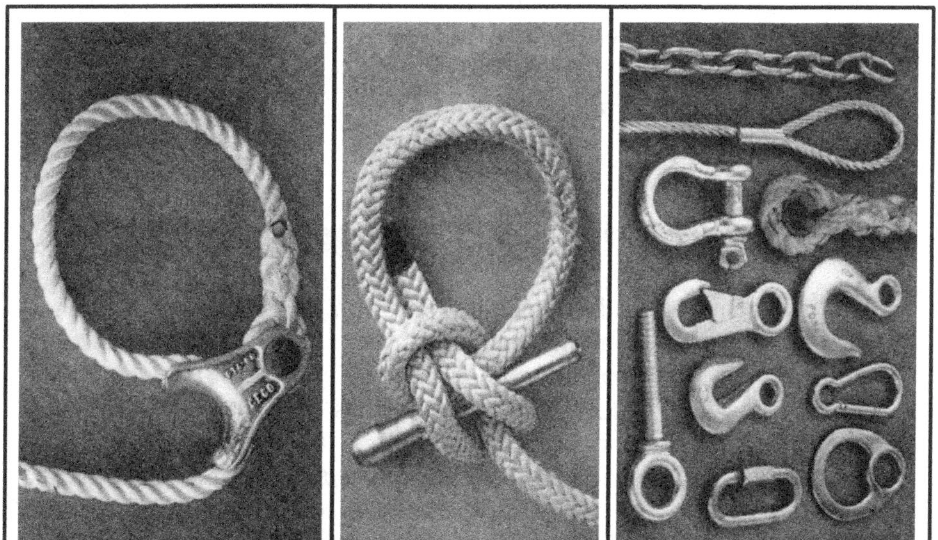

all really necessary is a matter of opinion and practicality. Some fasteners - like snaps, eyes, and links - can save a considerable amount of time by eliminating tedious knot tying and untying. Other fasteners - like thimbles, pins, grips, and shackles - can even spare a rope the gruel and grind of biting, seizing, and cutting into itself. This makes them a particularly valuable item to have. Throughout the book, you'll see where fasteners and their counterparts are used in rope and rigging schemes.

In all knots and splices, proper forming and snugging of the line is vital to the performance of the knot or splice. Many knots can slip, creep, work loose, cut, or seize into themselves if they are not formed, set, or snugged up properly. You must realize also that the proper forming and snugging of the line is a highly variable factor in knot tying. At times it is appropriate to have some of your knots tied loosely and some of them tied snugly. Thorough knowledge of tying comes after seeing and experiencing knot seizure and failure. The best thing you can do in the beginning is choose the proper knot to use and weigh the impact, load, and angle factors the knot and line are expected to take. Consideration of these last three things will give you a good indication of how the knot you've chosen should be formed and snugged. The work itself, be it a limb, top or length of wood, is another important consideration that can influence the effectiveness of the knots you choose to use. Slipping bark particularly, dead or alive, can nullify the grab or hold power of a knot on the work. During active growth in the spring, a "grabbing knot" such as the clove hitch or running bowline, can strip off the bark and you can lose the load if there's not a crotch or stub to hold the knot in place. If the shape of the work tapers too quickly, like some crotch cuts often do, any knot can slip off the work for the lack of positive taper to secure or snug the knot to. The way the work settles into the line and tightens a knot can result in some slipping before the knot actually holds. In either of these situations, you might consider using some kind of fastener to help secure the line to the work.

COILS, WRAPS, AND TUCKS

Whether you are handling, working with, or storing synthetic lines, you need to know something about coils, wraps, and tucks. Regardless of size, lines can be wrapped in random or progressive coils. Random coils are prone to line tangles. Progressive coils consist of a pattern or arrangement that can assume several forms. In one form, coils begin large and end up small. In another, they are arranged, or stacked, on the ground so one end of the line pulls off the top. Either form results in

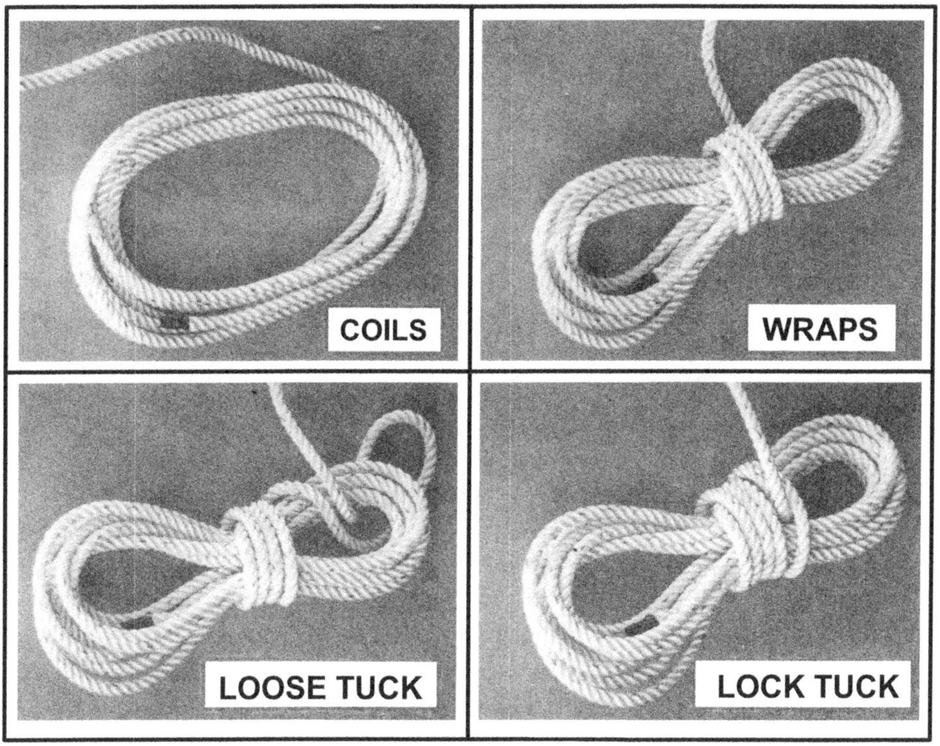

fewer tangles when the line is run or pulled from the coil.

Wraps are used to bind coils. Proper wrapping will prevent coils from shifting during storage or handling and ensure fewer tangles when the rope is used.

Tucks are used to lock the wraps. After wrapping, the line is doubled and tucked through the coils. The loop that's formed is then drawn over the coils and pulled tight. These are locking tucks. Two is all that are needed.

A loose tuck is one that will pull through and allow the wraps and coils to release. This is used by a climber to heave and set lines in remote places. See "throwing knot."

THE CHAIN OF COILS

The burden of coiling together a long or heavy line can be eased by coiling it into two or three parts. For example, instead of forming a 300 foot line into one large bunch of coils for storing, coil up a third, wrap and lock tuck, repeat, and repeat again. Lines of six hundred feet or more can be easily managed by a single person this way. What's more, with a chain of coils you can use what you need without disturbing the rest, so you end up with a lot fewer line tangles in spite of moving and working with such a long line.

FISHERMAN'S KNOTS

The main trick to know about these knots is that they consist of a number of wraps around themselves and then the end is tucked under the wraps. The nice feature about them is that they form permanent, secure bonds to whatever they're tied to. These knots are reserved to the finer lines, like the throw line.

CLINCH KNOT

The clinch knot is a common fisherman's knot and is used to join the throw line to a throw-weight eye, which is the same as tying a fishing line to a hook.

BLOOD KNOT

Another fisherman's knot; the blood knot can be used for joining two throw lines together.

NAIL KNOT

A good fisherman's knot to know. The nail knot is excellent for joining a throw line to a climb line for the purpose of pulling it through a crotch, or bull line through a block. It's sometimes called the serving knot, of which is used to hold the end of a larger line from unraveling. It's unobstructive and strong holding.

BOWLINE KNOT

The bowline knot is one of the more frequently used knots of many trades. It's very adaptable and has a lot of variations suitable for different applications.

SIMPLE BOWLINE

The simple bowline forms an eye in the line that can be tied around anything or used as an attachment loop. When pulled on tightly, the

Simple Bowline

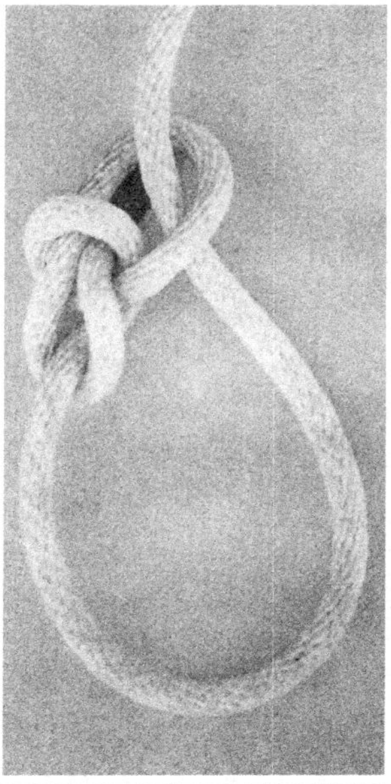

Running Bowline

Attachment Bowline

bowline can seize on itself and make untying difficult. To lessen the problem of seizure from hard pulls, leave the top loop a little loose; in other words, don't form the knot too tightly. A plastic or metal tapered pin can be inserted where the top loop forms around the line. After the knot is used, the pin can be removed, thus introducing slack in the knot and making it easier to untie after a hard pull. Such use for a tapered pin can be applied to many knots.

RUNNING BOWLINE

The running bowline makes an adjustable loop that can be set around, or tied on to, anything you would like the line to cinch around, or grab hold of. It's a very handy knot for bunching and holding limbs or brush together. It can be tied loosely around an object, but it will tighten the harder the line is pulled. Be cautious of the running bowline though, the line's strength is greatly reduced because it cuts into itself where it runs through the eye. A thimble can be used in place of the bowline to achieve the same effects of the running bowline without losing the line strength. The running bowline is an excellent knot though because it can be remotely set and fixed around limbs that are afar, but only in cases where you can retrieve the end of the line after setting it afar.

ATTACHMENT BOWLINE

The attachment bowline is quick and useful for joining lines together. It only takes a second to tie and can hold a fair load without seizing.

THE CLOVE HITCH

The knot proper is tied with two hitches, although it can be tied with more than that. It is an excellent knot as it holds onto smooth surfaces well. One very important thing to know about this knot is that it will untie itself if the loose end is not securely finished. This is an unforgiving trait of loose hitches. Don't ever trust a single half hitch to finish the knot; at least two or three very snug half hitches are required to secure it. The better way to finish the knot is with a bowline finish. With the bowline finish, both hitches in the clove hitch are pulled on evenly. This is not so when finishing the clove hitch with regular hitches.

TAUTLINE HITCH

Sometimes called the climber's knot, monkey fist, and wrongly, the prusik. The main feature of the tautline hitch is its ability to bite and hold on to a line carrying a load, and still be able to slip on command.

The tautline hitch can creep to the end of its tail while in use; more easily on certain kinds of rope than others. Many braided varieties creep and slip notoriously until they're formed and snugged securely. Keep your tautline hitch snug at all times; however, too firm or too tight of a knot can seize on the line and make its control difficult. Creeping of the knot can be controlled by tying a half hitch on the tail end. This hitch on the end of the line is often referred to as a security knot.

THE BLAKE'S HITCH

The Blake's friction hitch is a recent development in the world of climbing knots. It has solved many of the problems encountered with the tendencies of braided lines to creep at the tautline hitch. For this reason you may prefer to use it. It's a bit clumsy to tie at first, but, as with all new knots a person learns, in time it will become second nature. On firm twisted rope this knot doesn't appear to have an advantage.

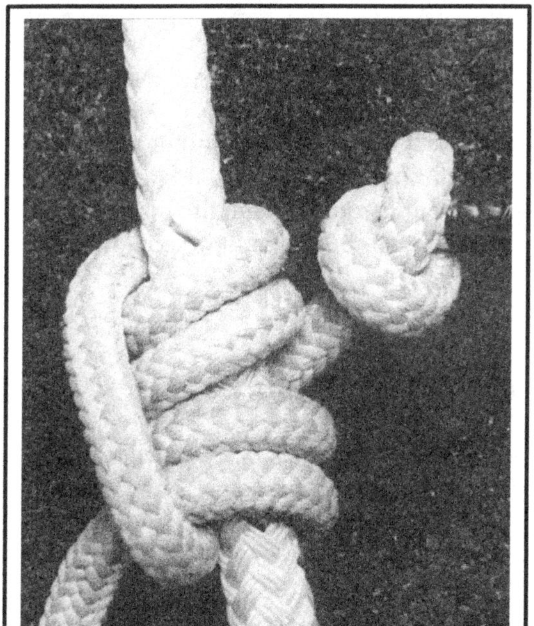

The Blake's Hitch-right hand version. Like the tautline hitch and other knots, it can be tied right or left hand.

THE CAT'S-PAW

Sometimes referred to as the Stilson hitch. The cat's-paw is a good rigging knot for fastening the line to hooks, pins, shackles, and tow balls. It's most frequently tied mid-line to the implement and is a knot you can tie quickly on any hook or hitch it can be placed over after it is formed. Forming the knot is done by holding the line in both hands and then rolling your wrists together. The two loops that are formed are then placed on the implement. Seizure from heavy loads seldom binds the knot tightly; for this reason it is preferred over other knots.

Timber Hitch

Overhand Loop

Figure Eight

TIMBER HITCH

The timber hitch cannot be excelled for its ease in untying, even after a heavy load lays into it. Like the running bowline, it can develop the tendency to cut into itself where the line runs through the formed eye. When setting a sling using the timber hitch, be sure it's long enough to secure properly.

OVER HAND LOOP

A mid-line knot used for attaching snaps and fasteners. It's intended for light use; for example, snapping on the power saw mid-line for a climber to haul up. On hard pulls this knot seizes badly.

FIGURE EIGHT

A simple and effective knot for terminating the end of a line in order for it to act as a stop or attachment. It is the best knot to use to tie off the ends of the pull rope on power saws. The figure eight is used to attach steel cable to a bull hook or shackle. Tied mid-line it is a good attachment loop.

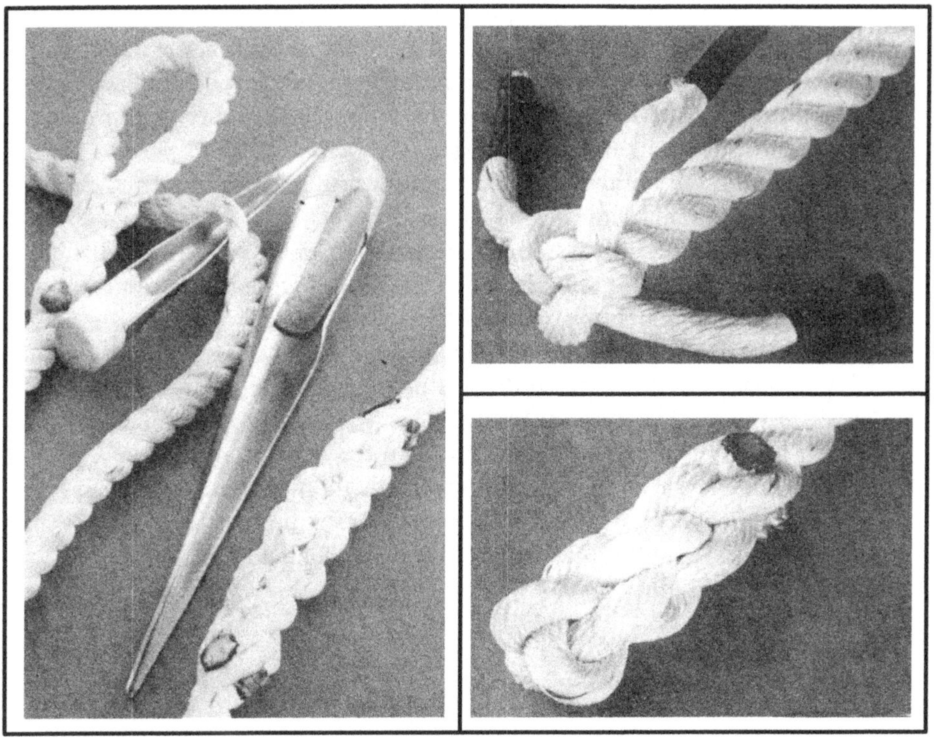

Twisted Rope Splices and Back Splice

THROWING KNOT

Simply a number of short coils in the end of a climber's line held together by a couple of wraps and a loose tuck. After the knot is thrown to a target limb or crotch, it's possible to have these coils release themselves by giving a smart jerk on the line. Thus, the knot can serve to get a specific length of rope to a remote location.

TWISTED ROPE SPLICES

In any twisted rope, the number of strands doesn't really matter; the splicing technique remains the same. The only difference, excluding the number of strands, is how each splice is started. The pattern for all twisted splices described here is "over one and under the next."

BACK SPLICE

On most twisted rope, the ends of the strands will need to be taped to keep them from unraveling. The rope itself is held with one hand about three to four inches from the end by the thumb and forefinger. The strands are separated down to where the thumb and forefinger have them pinched together. Next, lay each strand over and under one another in the same direction as the twist, or lay in the rope. In the proper configuration they will be symmetric and hold themselves together. Any other configuration will unravel as you attempt to snug up the beginning of the splice and the ends may become considerably longer. The start of this splice is called the crown, and it seems to be one of the more difficult things for some people to learn. The pattern for tucking the strands in the rope after this is much the same as the start of the crown. Each strand is pulled over one strand and tucked under the next. This results in an intersecting cross-hatch pattern or braid. Any deviation will show as a break in the pattern. Back splices are not a critical splice, but they look good when done right. Two tucks are all that's needed in firm rope. Limp or soft rope may need more. Pull the strands tightly to snug up the splice, then roll it between your palms or on the floor with your foot. This evens the tension of the splice. Next, cut the ends with a hot knife.

EYE SPLICE

Here again, the ends of the strands must be taped to keep them from unraveling. The rope itself should also be taped about six or eight inches farther down from the ends. Both hands are needed to start the splice, so the tape serves to hold the rope together in place of the thumb and forefinger. The taped portion of the line is pulled over and placed in the location for the desired size of eye. Spread the lays there so that a strand can be inserted and pulled through. The strand must enter in the opposite direction as the twist of the rope. Firm or hard rope will have to be spread open with a fid to do this. A fid is a hollow, tubular prod that simplifies the process of inserting and pulling the individual ends through the lays. After tucking one strand through, spread the lays again where the first strand comes out. Then tuck the second strand through. The second strand would be the neighbor to the first as they lie in sequence. Repeat with the third strand. Snug up the start and observe. When done properly, each strand will be separated by those in the main part of the line. After this, the tucking of the strands, over and under the next, is the same. Eye splices experience loads and stress; you should make at least four tucks in hard rope and more in soft rope. Finish by cutting the ends with a hot knife.

STRAIGHT SPLICE

Used for joining lengths of twisted rope together. Place the two ropes together and alternate the placement of the strands between the two lines. It's best to tape the loose ends of one of the ropes out of the way so at least one tuck can be made without everything coming loose. Begin on one side tucking the strands over and under one another. Snug up and repeat on the opposite side. After snugging up the start, the splice is finished by the regular pattern. In a straight splice, there should be at least four tucks on each side. In a tapered straight splice, a third of the strand is removed after the fourth tuck and a second third again after the fifth. This makes the splice not as abrupt in the line. Straight splices tuck easily because everything is so loose at the start. But after snugging up the start and after each tuck is made, the splice will become firm and a fid may be needed to finish it.

SPLICING BRAIDED LINES

The splicing of braided rope will not be discussed in this book, because there are so many different kinds and so many specifications on how each is spliced. Booklets on splicing braided roped are available from the Samson Rope Company.

WRAPPING ROPE AROUND A STEEL CORE

The mystery of getting a steel cable in the core of a twisted rope is no secret after you start doing it. Spread the lays open in the rope and lay in the cable to start. Continue opening the lays and forming the rope around the cable. In short lengths it's easy to do.

WILD-EYE SPLICE IN STEEL CABLE

Unwrap half the strands in the cable; at least eight turns for a small eye and more for a larger one. Align and bow both sets of strands towards one another so their lays will intersect in the middle. The natural set in the cable strands will allow them to mate and wrap back together forming the eye. A simple procedure once it's started.

Steel Cable

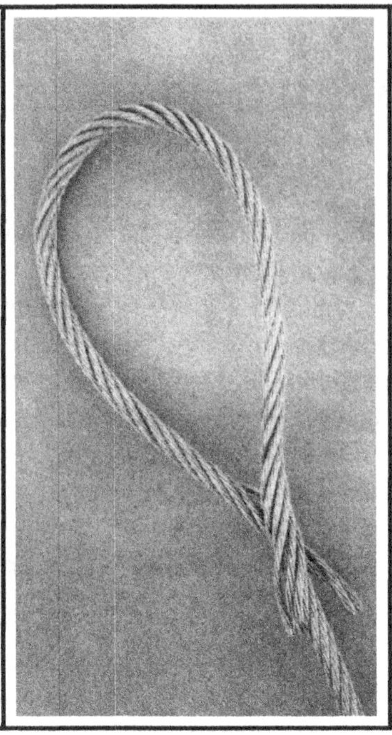

Wild Eye

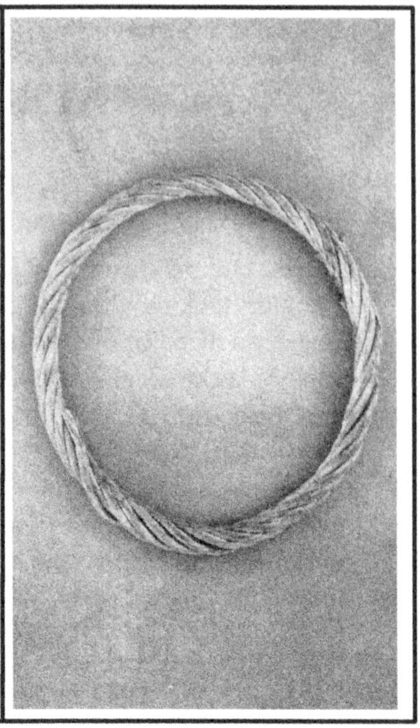

Molly

Knowing how to make a wild eye and wrap rope on cable is all you need to know to make your own steel core safeties. Wrapping the rope around the wild eye, through a snap, and finishing with a twisted rope splice takes a little time and practice. The beginner must learn to ignore the cable and carry on the twisted rope splice as usual. In this application only two tucks are needed in the twisted splice, since the cable is what secures the snap.

THE MOLLY

This is a wire rope ring fashioned out of a single strand of steel cable. Useful in many applications, it can be made of a single strand whose length is twenty times the diameter of the ring size you desire. A four-inch ring made out of quarter inch cable would require about eighty inches of strand. Some excess will be left to trim. When applicable, include a circumference length of core. Pull one or both ends around to mate them; then it's a simple matter of wrapping. Eye protection is important because the end of the strand whips around a lot during the wrapping procedure. Mollies can also be formed out of stiff poly rope, and it takes only half as much strand to make them, plus there's no core in the poly.

Chapter 2

Rigging Tools

BULL LINES

The ropes used for rigging work are commonly referred to as bull lines. The majority of the time you will use nylon bull lines. Nylon lines do not conduct electricity when clean and dry, making them safe to use in the vicinity of power lines. The quality of a nylon line varies depending on how firm the strands are laid in it. A firm rope will always be stronger and less apt to lose its diameter when it's stretched. This is important to

Bull lines

know when using a rope come-along, or similar grip, on the line. Because, when pulled tightly, the limp rope will shrink in diameter to the point where it'll slip through the come-along, the sheaves of a puller, or the jaws of a grip. Nylon line is very elastic in long runs. It can act like a large rubber band. Be wise to this fact when tightening up the line to pull or tension a load. Long runs of twisted line will cause loads that are freely suspended to rotate. Braided lines do not have the tendency to rotate the load and they can be obtained in a near static (nonstretching) construction.

TERMINATING THE BULL LINE WITH AN EYE

For efficient use and minimum wear on a bull line, it should terminate in a spliced eye. The advantages are many. For one, it eliminates knotting the bull line to the work. Most of the wear on a bull line occurs as a result of the way it is knotted to the work. An eye on the end allows easy attachment and the use of various fasteners and other sorts of rigging. Slings, straps, chokers, snaps, shackles, lags and chain can all be utilized to take the wear and tear. The opportunity to incorporate various rigging into a scheme can greatly improve the productivity and safety of a job.

REELS AND SPOOLS

For convenient use and storage of your bull lines, they should be kept on the spools they were shipped in. This has many advantages over coiling the line: spools can store the line with a lot less bulk; the line stays cleaner on a spool and is better protected. When the spool is mounted on a reel shaft, you can 'pull off' or 'spool on' a long bull line in a matter of seconds. Hand coiling a long bull line can be a painful task. Spooling the line on also eliminates the inherent twist that is a common problem that comes from hand coiling it. Inherent twist is evident in many line tangles. The core on most shipping spools that rope is bought on is cardboard. It doesn't last long before collapsing and rendering the spool useless. This is easily remedied by replacing with schedule 10-20 PVC or equivalent in pipe or tubing.

WEB GEAR

The use of nylon web straps and slings is becoming more commonplace in tree work. It's amply strong, and for its size it can exceed the strength of its comparable weight in rope. Nylon web items can be special-ordered or made to suit specific needs. But the convenience of having more rope on hand to use as slings and straps makes it more practical for the tree worker.

STEEL CABLE (HARD RIGGING)

Steel cable, or wire rope, is the best thing to use for heavy ground work. Synthetic lines just can't take the beating that steel can in the heavy work, like pulling logs and stumps. Steel is static and positive when pulled on or when holding a load. Steel makes the heavy work safer, too. But steel is hazardous to use around power lines. Wear gloves when handling it because any pulled strands in the cable, called jaggers, can rip your hands terribly. You can obtain steel products in a variety of forms: bull lines on winches, straps, and chokers. You can get these

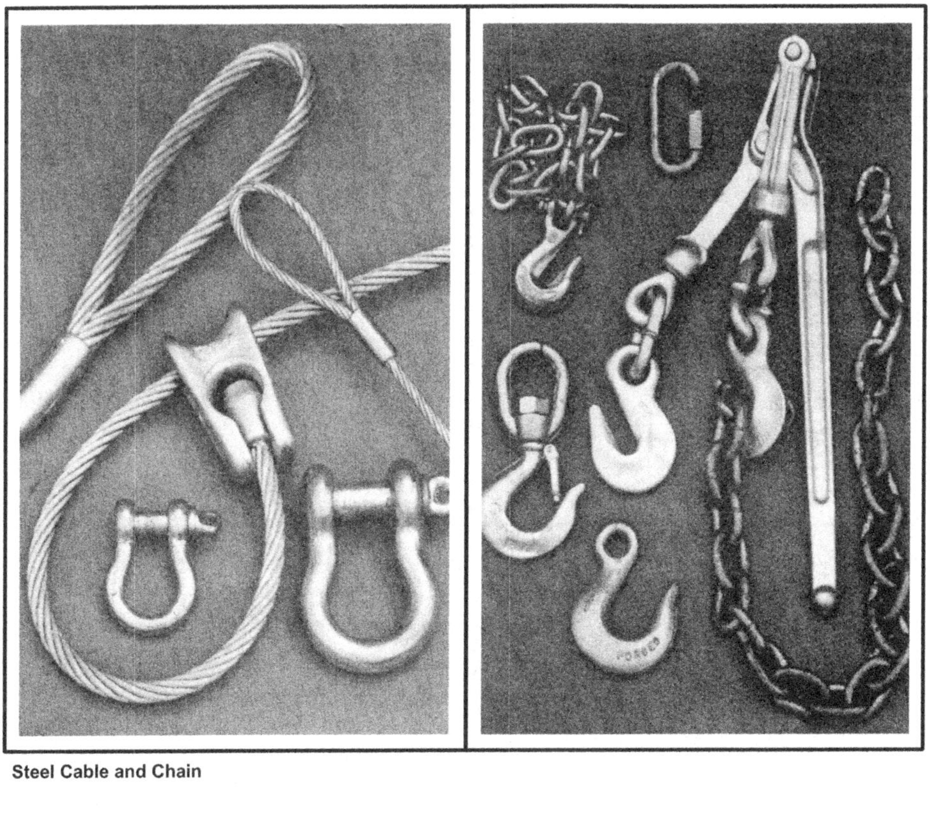

Steel Cable and Chain

made up in any size and length through logging supply outlets. The chokers and straps are ideal for setting or tagging blocks. They are easy to set and they're strong.

CHAIN (HARD RIGGING)

In spite of its weight and the fact that it's cold in the mornings, chain cannot be beat for setting a hold in a tight spot. It's infinitely adjustable. You can easily set a block or hook right up against a stump or tree with it, whereas with web gear, cable, or rope, you may be left with slack in the line and not be able to do the same thing. Along with the chain, there are a variety of specially designed fasteners: grab hooks, slip hooks, link connectors, and binders.

SAFE WORKING LOADS

The working load of a line is usually rated at one-fifth of its breaking strength. This is a good margin of safety to work with and you shouldn't take advantage of it. Even staying within the recommended working-load range of a line can still break it if the load is dropped into it too hard.

DYNAMIC LOADING

A so-called safe load can still break a line if the load falls hard into it. For example, take a two hundred pound piece of wood and drop it ten feet. By the time the load is caught in the line, it can increase its weight by five to ten times, exceeding the safe working-load range of a half-inch nylon line. You can draw up on, pull, tether, and lower loads like that all day long with a half-inch nylon line. But start dropping and jerking on them and you'll break it, even if the breaking strength is five thousand pounds. You'll find that the type of knot you use or the way the line is fastened to the work is the weak link during dynamic loading; thus, it is also the cause of most broken lines.

LENGTH OF A LINE'S RUN

The length of a line's run affects how it works. Short runs are the most positive and easiest to work with, making pulling and tensioning easy. Long runs of synthetic line are quite stretchy and can be compared to working a load on a bungee cord. If you're pulling a heavy load on the end of a long run, you may pull fifteen to twenty feet of line before you even pick up the work. So, determining the accurate tension in the line can be difficult to estimate in long runs. To make a long run, you may have to splice or knot two or more lines together. Twisted rope is most easy to straight-splice. Braided rope is not routinely spliced in the field; if you want to build a long run out of it you can knot it together. Keep in mind, though, knots can be a problem if they have to run through any blocks.

BALANCING THE RIGGING

As a firm rule, you should use stronger slings, straps, chokers, fasteners, and blocks than the bull line you're using. If they're not stronger, they'll fail first. This can create more harm than just the line breaking. If you tool up and get a five-eighths-inch bull line, it would be best to use one-inch slings and straps. The line used to make them should be firm to hard. Remember, keep the rigging balanced.

RECOIL AND LINE OF BITE

Recoil from a synthetic line breaking can cause cuts, bruises, and broken bones. If you're near a pulling implement and the line is starting to twitch and make funny sounds, you had better stand aside. Such sounds are peculiar to a line getting ready to break. When it does it can recoil and shoot to each end or corner in its run. Even steel cable can recoil, and it's a sure source of injury or death if you get hit by it.

The "line of bite" refers to the area of recoil that rigging can fly through. You must stay outside of this line; there are no exceptions to this rule. As a climber working in the tree, though, this can be difficult to do. Inside corners are the most hazardous area of coverage that the rigging can fly through. Always stay on the outside of any corners when the rigging is working.

Blocks—Be sure the block you use is stronger than the line and load it's meant to bear.

BLOCKS

The simple block is used extensively in tree work. It serves as an axis point when changing the angle of pull in a line. The block is especially effective when the line running through it is used for pulling loads. The pulling power is not lost in the line the way it is when run through or over a crotch. Likewise, the line is not subjected to the wear and tear of running over a stationary or rough object.

There are many kinds of blocks available. The ones preferred most in tree work are the snatch blocks. They're easy to open and lay in the line without having to run to the end of the line each time. Blocks with a hook should be secured to their slings with a workable keeper. A hook without a keeper can be secured with a number of wraps of vinyl tape. This is especially important if the block is used for a tail hold, because any block used as such will raise, drop, and flop around as the load changes in the line. If there is not a keeper on the hook the block may come loose. For the same reason, you should always keep an eye on any tail-hold block to make sure that the bull line doesn't jump the pulley and get fouled in the housing. If this happens, it can result in the bull line getting cut. The duty ratings on blocks vary quite a bit. Be sure to use a block that is known to have a duty rating greater than the line being used for the pulling and lowering.

SPAR BLOCKS

Any block set overhead in the tree can be called a spar block. Generally speaking, the higher you have the block set over the work, the better your line angles will be. Good line angles make tree work much safer.

TAIL-HOLD BLOCKS

When a block is rigged to the butt of the tree, or on a stump, it is referred to as a tail-hold block. In rigging work, the tail hold can serve to improve the line angle to a pulling source. It can also keep the running part of the line out of the way of the work and allow you much better control when tensioning, holding, pulling, or lowering.

BLOCK ON A TAG

At times you'll have to use a tag line to set a block to a remote anchor. Having a block on a tag may be the only way to get it positioned past obstacles and still have a good anchor angle. In certain rigging schemes, a block on a tag is useful for changing the angle of pull in the bull line. In this case, the tag line itself can be adjustable. A block on a tag can also make use of a short run of line, which it couldn't if the block was remotely anchored. Always check your tail hold and tag blocks for line fouling. They raise, drop, and can flip-flop while the line is working between slack periods and loads. The bull line can get fouled in the block housing and get cut by it, a shackle pin can drop out, the gate on a snatch block can be tripped open, etc. Keep your eye on them.

PASS BLOCKS

These are usually small, light-duty blocks which a climber sets in the tree for pulling up tools and heavier rigging. They are sometimes referred to as hand-line blocks. In the normal course of events, a climber will ascend to the work area and set a pass block and line. The ground crew will do the hauling on the line and send the heavy stuff up to the climber.

HOIST AND HOLD BLOCKS

In nautical applications, hoist and hold blocks are called fiddle blocks. They hold the line as you pull it, using an integrated cam lock that the rope runs through. For pulling overhanging limbs, they come in handy for the climber and ground man. You can fashion one by incorporating a spring-loaded ascender on the block you run the pull line through.

PULLING AND TENSIONING

It is not always necessary to tension or pull the line with anything other than what you can pull and hold by hand. After working in this business for a while, a person is able to judge their limits pretty well in this regard. Pulling the bull line is simple in most cases, but tensioning a line is much different. Setting tension in a line is nearly an art form. You have to consider the length of a line's run, the size of the line, how many blocks the line is running through, and the weight of the work. They each affect one another and together determine the accurate setting of tension in a line.

At a certain point in pulling and tensioning lines, you'll begin needing a mechanical advantage. The means by which you pull or tension a bull line depends on the amount of line to be pulled, the pulling power necessary, and the speed at which it needs to be pulled. The tools used for pulling or tensioning are simple come-alongs, block and tackle, a variety of winches, and even a vehicle equipped with a pulling eye or hook.

COME-ALONGS

These are lightweight, portable hand winches, ranging in their power from one-quarter of a ton to several tons. They're slow and their pulling range is limited by the amount of cable or chain with which they're spooled. On long runs of line, they can bottom out before the rope is even tight enough to pull or hold the load. This is because they may only have the pulling range to take out the stretch in the line before any actual pulling on the load is done. However, the rope come-along can pull as much line as the length of rope with which they are set up. If you use a rope come-along, be sure to spool it with firm rope. Limp rope can slip through the sheaves of the come-along in a hard pull.

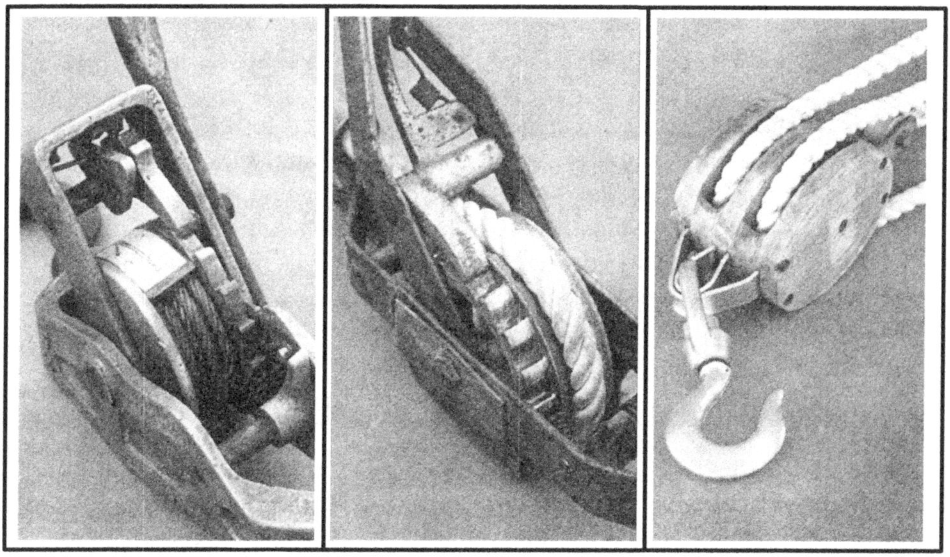

BLOCK AND TACKLE

This application of pull is ages old, but of great utility in tensioning and pulling a line. The power of a block and tackle is governed by the amount of pulleys in the blocks: the more pulleys, the more power. These are called gang blocks; they can be two, three, or four gang. The power of a block and tackle can be lost if the runs of line between the gang blocks cross over and drag against one another. Keep an eye on this as you work with the block and tackle, and periodically straighten the runs if they cross. The "pulling range" in block and tackle can be increased by using longer lengths of rope.

CABLE WINCHES

The small electric bumper-mounted winches are commonly used in tree work. They supply ample power, and most are equipped with enough steel cable for a good working range. But they are slow in pull, speed, and pay-out. If you use one, make sure the vehicle is anchored securely. Note, too, that steel cable is more awkward to work with in the tree than rope and it can be hazardous to use if the tree is close to power lines. Power takeoff (PTO) winches and those on heavy logging equipment should be considered for the heavy work.

CAPSTAN WINCHES

The capstan rope winches are ideally suited for tree work. They can handle almost any size and length of line, and they offer a very precise control over the take-up and payout of the line. Their maximum take-up speed is sometimes not as fast as you might like it, though. There are many hand powered capstan winches available through arborist tool suppliers and marine catalogs. The PTO operated capstan winch is the optimum to use where you can get a truck to, or near the work.

PULLING WITH A VEHICLE

A vehicle with a pulling eye, hook, or tow ball is the most efficient means of pulling, tensioning, and lowering with a line. They are powerful enough for most of the trees in which you'll ever work, providing that the terrain allows them the range and traction they need. It's best that you run the bull line through a tail-hold block when pulling with a vehicle. This keeps the run of line close to the ground and provides better traction for the vehicle. Use a heavy vehicle; three quarter ton or better, four wheel drive, loaded down for improved traction and use low gears where applicable.

Vehicles are fast in their take-up and payout of the line, which make them an ideal source of power for pulling in many jobs. Communication and understanding with the operator is critically important; they can't always see what's going on and rely on signals most of the time. Radios can remedy this complication.

FASTENING THE BULL LINE TO THE IMPLEMENT

With all the different tools to pull and tension the bull line, there must be at least one common way to fasten the two together. Actually, there are quite a few. Different kinds of knots can be used, depending on the type of hook, eye, or hitch you're fastening it to and the amount of load or strain the knot is expected to take. The cat's-paw is probably one of the easiest knots to use when fastening to a hook, hitch, or pin. The bowline and figure eight are also satisfactory in light to moderate pulls. But remember, some knots can cut into themselves or seize badly if they are wrongly chosen or used. Review **Chapter 1** on knots, splices, and fasteners.

LINE GRIPS

Many problems associated with knotting a line to an implement can be solved with the aid of a line grip. These grips are used extensively in the lineman's trade for pulling and tensioning a wide variety of wires, guy lines, and cables. This one tool can save a mega-amount of time and hassle because it allows the rope to be connected to any pulling implement, and it can be connected or disconnected in an instant, anywhere on the line, under load or not. There are many different kinds of grips available, but the only one that should be used on rope is the smooth, serpentine-jawed Chicago grips made by Klein tools (501 Easy Dr, Mansfield TX, 76063). There are different sizes of these grips available. Each one has a maximum and minimum diameter capacity. Never use the line that is the minimum the grip is designed to grab, and don't use limp line either. If you do, the line will start slipping through the jaws after a certain point of tension is reached. This also happens in the sheaves of rope come-alongs spooled with limp rope. The best you can do with either tool is to use firm to hard rope near the maximum size the mechanism is designed to handle.

BRAKING AND EASING DOWN THE LOAD

Once a portion of the tree has been cut and is hanging in the line, it must then be lowered down. If a capstan or cable winch is being used, all that must be done is to pay out the line. When a vehicle is used, the brakes can be eased off and the pieces lowered, but when a person is holding the line and the load is heavier than them, they must use something as a brake. One of the oldest ways of doing this is to take a couple of wraps with the line around the trunk of the tree. The friction created by the line being wrapped around the tree will act as a brake. This way a person can hold and ease down pieces much heavier than themselves. This method works, but if there are a lot of pieces to lower, it can be very awkward for the ground man. There are a few other factors against this method: the line biting around the trunk of thin-barked trees can strip it off, or if the bark is particularly rough, the wear and tear on the line is increased, and line control can be uneven and jerky.

LINE BRAKES

These steel spool devices greatly simplify the procedures of braking and lowering a load. There are many different kinds of line brakes, each with its own features and brand names. Common trade terms are capstans and bollards. Some brakes feature racheting devices that allow you to tighten and pull as well as brake and lower a load. Without these devices, tree work would be more timely and laborious. Anyone in the business should have at least one, but a couple would be better because brakes vary considerably in practicality, duty and load requirement. There are a lot of them around. The real value of these items comes from knowing how to anchor and use them. Improper anchoring or use can result in malfunction and loss of load, so before investing in one model, check out its features very carefully.

LETTING THE WORK RUN

This technique, and often used phrase, can be better understood by the layman if they consider how a fisherman utilizes the drag on a fishing reel to let a fish run. There are times when you must tether and let the line run, much the same as the fisherman does. One reason why would be for the safety of the climber. Particularly in those situations where the work swings away and then back towards them. By letting the line run a little before putting the halt on it, you can prevent a collision between work and climber. This technique can significantly reduce the amount of swing the work will take. Also, by applying drag while letting the line run, you can ease the momentum of the work, and by it, greatly reduce the dynamic loading forces on the line. How this technique is applied in any situation is highly variable and worth a volume of discussion by itself.

Unfortunately, it can't all be elaborated on here. What can be said about it is, it must be clearly understood by the ground person on exactly how much line is allowed to run, when to apply the brake to it, and when to let it go. The type of brake or drag being used will greatly determine how each is done. During this procedure, the ground person must make accommodations to see that there is no chance of the line becoming fouled in their hands or feet. Other applications utilizing the theories of this technique are discussed elsewhere throughout the book.

ANCHOR POINTS

Whenever you're without a suitable anchoring spot for a pulling implement, block, or brake, you can position a truck or vehicle and use it for an anchor. When doing so, chock the wheels, set the brake, and park in low gear. If you cannot get a vehicle in the desired location, a ground anchor should be set. Ground anchors can be obtained through line distribution companies and utilities departments, or you can make your own. Light-duty anchors can hold up to one thousand pounds, depending on the ground in which they're set. The heavy-duty screw and expanding ground anchors are the only safe way to hold heavy loads. The expanding type requires a sufficiently deep hole to be dug with an auger or posthole digger. Once set, their anchor plates are not retrievable, but the rod is easily removed by unscrewing it.

STATIONS

Your station is located where your pulling implement and brake are located. Be careful! Your station can be right under the tree and loads where you are working. For obvious reasons, being right under the work is not always safe. A so-called "remote station" can offer you greater safety. The worth of a remote station depends on a number of things, including its distance. If your station is too far away, this might prove a disadvantage. Its strength or security is another. A good strong anchor is absolutely necessary for a safe station. Your rigging scheme is another consideration. Will you be using ground runs or aerial runs, or both? Will you swing loads from more than one spar? Will the loading be static or dynamic? The ability to set up a remote station as a safe place to work is limited only by your imagination.

GROUND RUNS VERSUS AERIAL RUNS

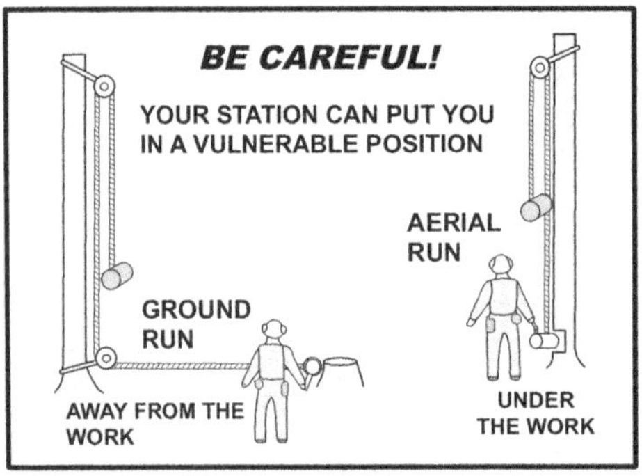

Tethering or working a line that runs diagonally or straight up the tree can be considered an aerial run. It's the most usual way for a ground man to manage light loads in a line by hand. With an effective braking surface, heavier loads can be held and lowered. Ratcheting bollards and capstans enable you to pull and increase the tension with an aerial run. However, if you have neither implement, your ability to pull on the line using an aerial run becomes quite limited. By placing a block at the base of the tree for the line to run through, you can change to a "ground run" in which the line runs closer to the ground. With a ground run you are not necessarily limited by the choice of implement to pull on the line. Common items like the block and tackle or come-alongs can be utilized, but only as long as you have a suitable anchor to pull from. Aside from the options for pulling a line, you can also utilize a greater variety of brakes as well as less expensive types of brakes. A ground run also allows you to work out from under the tree. Not all rigging schemes that utilize aerial runs can offer you that safety margin, for aerial runs can leave you vulnerable. For example, pulling with a ratcheting bollard under the main spar and block where your work is overhead could be hazardous.

WORKING THE HOLE

As a ground man working the hole, your duties will include the tending of the lines: pulling, holding and lowering. You will also have to clear the hole so more work can come down, an arduous task in tight quarters. You'll also have to refuel, sharpen and maintain the power saws. You'll use knots and fasteners, and you may even be required to do some "on the spot" splicing to keep the job going. You'll be in the position to call how large a cut the climber takes, and the climber will be relying on your good judgment to manage it after it has been cut loose. Working the hole can be fun and exciting, but it can also be difficult and dangerous. To keep it safe, remember to have a good plan, adequate tooling, and training in the procedures of working the hole.

DEAD ENDING A LINE

"Dead ending" refers to the task of "tying off" the end of a line that may have a load bearing in it. The most frequent way of dead ending is by wrapping the end of the line around an object, usually a tree, stump or

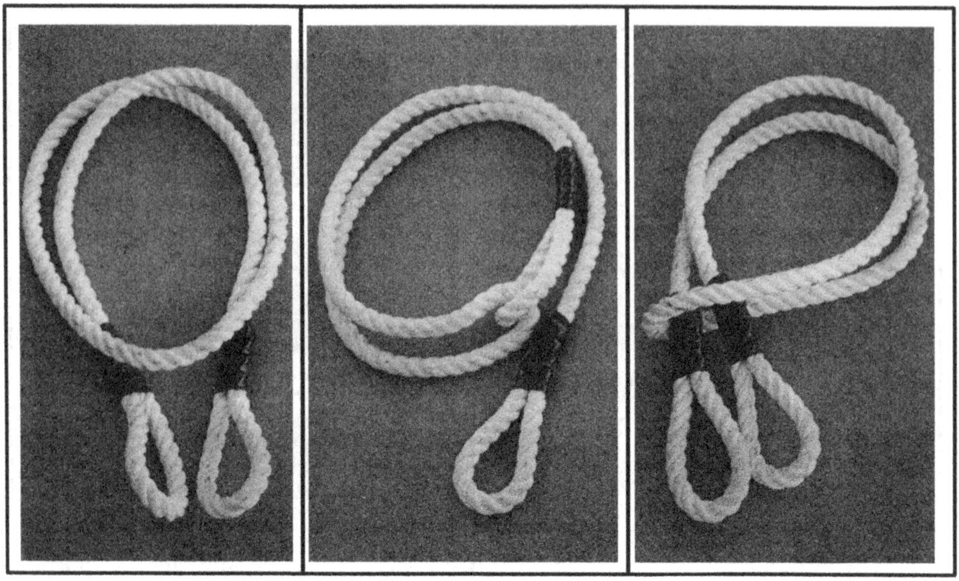

limb, and then tying a number of hitches with the end over the main part of the line. This is not always an easy task. One problem comes from having to take the wraps and hitches with a doubled line around the tree or other anchor and finishing the end off with a rough form of mid-line knot. Adding to the difficulty is having to do it with one hand while the other is holding the tension or load from slipping. Practice the procedure to achieve proficiency with dead-ending.

SHORTENING A SLING

A common difficulty in rigging work is shortening an overlong sling or strap. There are several ways to shorten a sling. One is by doubling the sling and setting it in a bite. Another is by wrapping and bringing the eyes together. And a third is by setting the sling in a bight first and then finishing with the required wraps necessary to properly position the eye. Using a chain with the appropriate fasteners you will not have a problem shortening a sling.

SLIDING TAG LINE

In many rigging schemes the bull line will run through a block that is set in a remote location, tree, or spar. Retrieving the line without losing it through the block can pose a big problem for the climber. The sliding tag line can solve this problem. The slide can be a shackle, thimble or snap. Whatever slide you use, make sure that it is smooth inside where

the bull line will run. The particular tag line you use will depend on whether it will be used to control, aid, or slow the movement of the work. For bull line retrieval purposes only, the tag line does not have to be substantial. It can be allowed to run loose. In the case of load bearing, a climber should consider using a half inch line and running it through a figure eight descender or other suitable light weight braking device at or near the work point. The climber should observe carefully how this tag line is set, for it may become fouled in the work if it is not set properly. The tag setup may not slide and the line could be lost.

THE SPEED LINE

When it can be used, what is called the "speed line" can ease and hasten the movement and disposal of the trimmings during tree removal in cramped quarters. The scheme resembles a pulley clothes line, but it works more like the "shotgun" yarders used in logging. The rigging consists of a static line that spans between the tree and a tail hold, on which a block or "carriage" runs. Positioning and movement of the block is controlled by a "haul back" line. This traveling block carries the loads from the tree to the tail hold, which can be some distance away, but the haul back line is not always necessary. You can attach the work directly to the speed line with snap-on gear and let it run (slide) down the line.

A speed line can be set up to work in many different ways, but certain criteria must be met. The spar and tail hold must be substantial enough to hold the working system, so you must be able to appreciate how much stress is involved. Any unconsidered element of the system may cause it to fail. Guy lines and anchors can bolster the spar or tail hold.

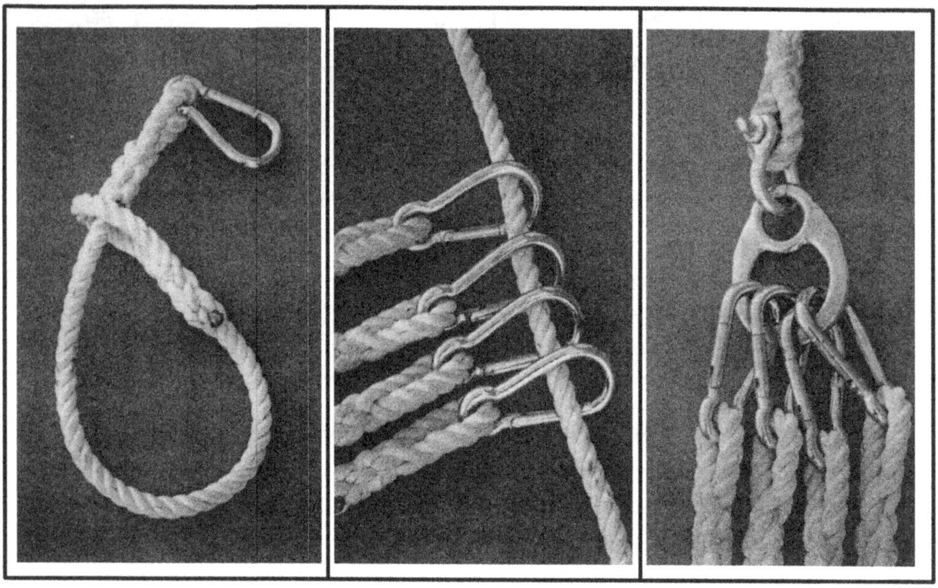

SNAP-ON GEAR

For attaching multiple pieces of work to the bull line, use snap-on gear. These short slings can save a lot of time by allowing a climber to cut numerous pieces, usually limbs, at one time (See Chapter 3—Multiple Sets).

Chapter 3

Angles and Dangles

ANGLE OF PULL (LINE ANGLE)

The angle of pull in the rigging greatly influences the action the work will take after it's cut free. Whenever possible, it's best for the bull line to run through a block located above the parts of the tree that need to be worked off. Remember, as different parts of the tree are worked in, the line angle will change and so must a climber's tactics.

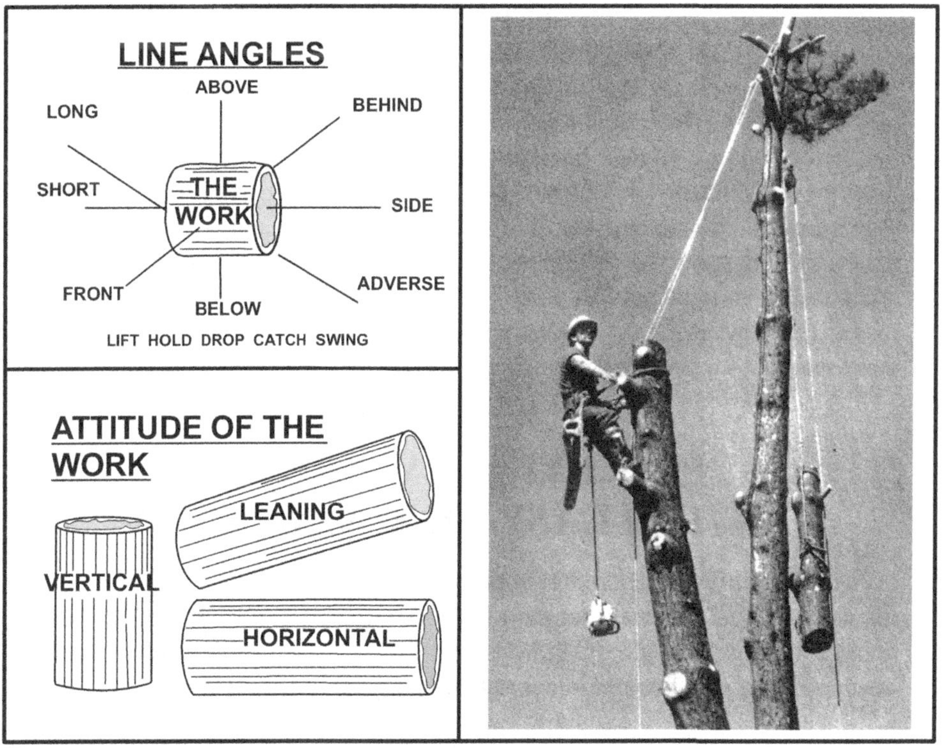

Line Angles Attitude of the Work

ACCOUNTABLE FACTORS

Besides line angle, a climber must also account for the tension or slack in the line; the length of its run; the size, weight, and balance of the piece they're cutting loose; the attitude of the piece; and their position to do the work. Even as simple a thing as which side of the work the knot is fixed can matter a great deal! These accountable factors will be discussed.

WORK ATTITUDE

The attitude of the work refers to the angle at which it stands, sticks out, or hangs. The piece in question can be a limb, top, or length of wood. The attitude plays a key role in deciding where the line is best tied and how it is best cut. By working with the line angle in relation to the attitude of the work, you can tie and cut the piece in question to make it raise, hang, drop, tilt, fall, or swing. The action that the work takes should be as easy as possible, with no unnecessary drops, jump, jerks, or other surprises. All of this means that you must have a plan; in other words, you must know what's going to happen before it happens.

EASY LINE ANGLES (OVERHEAD)

An overhead angle in the rigging is one of the better with which to work off different parts of a tree. The chief advantage of an overhead angle is that the line can be tensioned to compensate for the weight of the work without causing it to drop off the tree or swing away. A nice feature. This line angle also allows for the safe handling of pieces within the line's maximum recommended load range. But dynamic loading can still occur. Estimating the tension the line must have to hold the work takes a little experience. So until you become good at it, start with small pieces and then work up to the larger or heavier ones. In this way you'll develop a feel for working with an overhead angle.

VERTICAL WORK WITH EASY LINE ANGLES

The line must be fixed to the work at a very specific location. As in the case of a tall, vertical length of wood, the line should be tied at its top quarter or third to make it butt-heavy and keep it upright after the cut is made. Fixing the line any lower than that puts it dangerously close to the work's center of gravity, or balance point. The work may roll over as a result. If you're in the way of a piece that flips over, regardless of whether the line is properly tensioned or not, one end or the other could strike you. With the line properly fixed the work will stay up. Keep in mind that the work, even with the line fixed properly, will still tilt over to a minor degree. The line is tied to its top but it also comes off the side of the work, which will come to be the high side when the work is being held by the bull line. Cut through tall lengths like these with a single straight-through crosscut entering from the side opposite the direction the work will leave the cut, or from the side that will lift first. Observe the work while you cut it and have the ground worker adjust the tension of the line if necessary. The reason why an undercut isn't used is because it makes the work leave the cut abruptly. You cannot monitor the tension in the line as well with an undercut. With a straight-through crosscut you can observe the work for any indications that the line is too tight or not tight enough as you near the finish.

Short rounds cut off a vertical trunk will be quite stable and sit on the cut if they're kept shorter than twice their diameter. Here, the cut can be made all the way through and then the work can be lifted off the cut. There is no need to pre-tension the bull line. In the tall lengths, pre-tensioning is necessary to keep it upright. Not so in the short rounds. Pay particular attention to this fact because these short rounds can flip, or turn over. The side the line is fixed on will come to be the high side. So lift these short sections off easily after the cut is completed. Because of the way the line is fixed to the work, this situation will always be a factor to deal with. If you fix the line to the top of the work with a lag eye, these short rounds will lift straight off the cut without turning over. The lag can save you a considerable amount of time because there is a lot of repetitive and awkward knot tying on these short rounds, especially if they're large. Make sure you use only the forged lags with the solid eyes. Don't use the cheap, mild-steel bent-eye lags. They'll straighten out in the heavy work. It's also necessary to drill a pilot hole for large lag sizes. The pilot hole should be two-thirds the diameter of the lag size. Thus, a one-inch lag would have a five-eighths-inch pilot hole. But this will vary, depending on whether the wood is sound or punky, hard or soft. The use of lags to fasten the bull line offers you the chance to fix the line to the work in ways that ordinary knot tying cannot.

LEANING OR HORIZONTAL WORK WITH EASY LINE ANGLES

The line must be fixed to cradle the balance point of the work. This is so it won't turn, or roll over after the cut is made, unless of course you specifically intend it to. Again, the idea is to neutralize the weight and balance of the work with this line angle. To cradle the balance, you have to approximate where the center of gravity is and tie a spread clove hitch over it. This is done by spreading the hitches apart after forming the knot. Tension the line. Cut through the work with a single, straight-through crosscut without an undercut. Progress the cut and observe the work for telltale signs of incorrect line tension. The cut opening or closing, the work raising or dropping. Have the ground worker make the necessary adjustments to correct the tension if necessary. If you're at all close to the balance point with the clove hitch the work shouldn't tip or roll much when it's finally free of the cut.

MODERATE LINE ANGLES (DIAGONAL PULL, MORE ABOVE)

With this line angle, everything you cut will swing to the direction the line is coming from. Keep this in mind and adjust your position, gearing the cuts and rigging for this inclination to swing. Since the angle comes more from above, it is still safe and practical in most cases to tension the line in order to compensate for the weight of the pieces being cut. However, also keep in mind that since the pieces will swing, further tensioning of the bull line will enhance this tendency. Keep yourself and your lines out of the path that the bull line and the work will take.

VERTICAL WORK WITH MODERATE LINE ANGLES

Tall lengths should be undercut to prevent splitting or wood pull. For most, you can safely use kerf undercuts. Regular face cuts may fail to close and break the hinge if the line is keeping the work from tipping over enough; then you will have to nip the hinge wood to get the work to leave. This may not be a bad thing in itself with a moderate angle of pull. Be cautious if the work leaves the cut quickly, it can gain enough momentum to reach you on the back swing if there is nothing to prevent it. So, as a rule, get the work to leave the cut easily and use a tag line now and then to control it.

With short rounds that are stable enough to sit on the cut, fix the line on the side of the work from which the bull line is angling. The tendency for the rounds to lift or roll over when they're pulled from the cut is still a probability. In either situation, position yourself to the side or the back of the work as it leaves. And be ready for back swing if the work is moving fast.

LEANING AND HORIZONTAL WORK WITH MODERATE LINE ANGLES

In leaning work there are more coordinations due to the relative angle of lean, the relative line angle, and your position. Sometimes, you can get caught between the work and where it's directed. If you're working from the high side of a lean and pulling all the pieces back, it could become dangerous. In this case, secure a tie-in that will afford you the support for a position to work off the side of the lean. This will often put your climb line and the bull line coming from the same direction much of the time. Try to keep your climb line coming from a position over the bull line if they share a common spar or top. This will keep the heavy work below your support. Setting it the other way will put your

Pulling the Work Back Against a Lean

line and support under the rigging, giving it more chance to catch your line.

If the bull line is directing the work other than behind the lean, it will be safe to position yourself to do the cutting from the high side. You can take heavier pieces more safely in this situation. Remember that the work is going to swing away. It exerts centrifugal force on the rigging and spar, which increases the weight of the work. Tag lines can help minimize centrifugal forces and momentum.

HARD LINE ANGLES (FROM THE SIDE)

At hard angles, the distance between the work and the spar becomes a very important factor. An increase of distance causes a marked increase in the centrifugal forces exerted on the rigging and spar. Therefore, it's neither safe nor practical to cut anything near the maximum recommended load range of the bull line being used. All pieces cut should be at the minimum, because very little can be done to compensate for the weight of what's being cut. Trying to do so by tensioning the line will result in what's being cut to break or pull away more violently. Unless the line is actually meant to pull what's being cut, it shouldn't be tensioned any more than it takes to get the sag out of it. It's best to use a line that is static, or nearly so. Long runs of synthetic line are very dynamic and allow the work to drop quite a bit before the line actually holds it, an undesirable effect in many situations.

VERTICAL WORK WITH HARD LINE ANGLES

Tall sections with hard line angles should be face cut. On rare occasions you can get by with kerf undercuts. You have several choices as to how you can fix the line to the work. Fixed at the top, the work can be pulled if needed. Fixing the line in the middle, the work is held, to an extent, by its balance point as it leaves the cut. Which in some circumstances can give a certain margin of clearance for the work. However, the work will tend to spin during its departure and travel. With the line fixed at the bottom of a vertical section, not always your best option, the work can be cut and felled in the line as if no line was tied to it at all. In this situation you have a degree of flexibility in the angle you fall the work into the line.

LEANING AND HORIZONTAL WORK WITH HARD LINE ANGLES

The discussion earlier about your safety and pulling the work back behind its lean, and your position to do the work, is emphasized here. If there's no lift in the line, trying to pull the work back against a lean of more than forty-five degrees is downright dangerous. The work can jump or fly off the cut. If it drops off the cut, the bull line could catch you or your lines. If this is a possibility, change your plan. Consider maybe using the level cut if pulling the work back against the lean. Or consider using bottom rigging to butt-tie and lower the work.

If the line is directing the work in any direction other than behind its lean, much of what has been discussed when working with moderate line angles will apply here, too. But use more undercuts, to keep splitting to a minimum, and cut lighter pieces. The frequent use of tag lines is necessary to slow the work down if it can collide with something during its travel; if it can reach you on the back swing; if it will stress the rigging; and just to stop its swing, so it can be lowered to the hole. If none of these things poses a problem, then tag lines may not be needed. In fact, in situations like this, you can release the bull line and let the work fall during a certain part of its swing. Especially the last part, where it stops going forward and begins to swing back. A smart release of the bull line can drop some sections cut out of a tree in the exact spot you want them. However, accurate release of the line is critical. If the line becomes

fouled, the section could fall during a back swing, damaging something in its path. This maneuver is risky for that reason alone. But in some situations it's more of a convenience than a necessity that it works out as planned.

DOUBLE BULL LINES

When it's not desirable for the work to drop or swing at all, it may be possible to rig a second bull line opposite the first to neutralize the tendencies of a hard side-angle pull. Do not confuse this with using tag lines. Tag lines are only used to slow or control the motion of the work, not to actually support it. If there's any upward angle between the two lines, some deflection will result. Good deflection is much the same as having an overhead line angle. The run of the two lines may be out of lead from the work, though. If so, there will be some line angle to consider. In spite of it, the chance to do this can change a difficult and time consuming job into a relatively easy and faster one because it allows you to take larger pieces where you couldn't before, plus it extends the location of the hole by allowing you to lower the work anywhere between the two runs of line. One bull line should be fixed directly to the work according to how it is to be supported by the line. The other line should be tied fast to the first a foot or two out from the work.

A tautline hitch works well to attach a second bull line to the first. But be sure to secure the loose end. This makes it possible to accurately determine the proper tensioning of the two lines. If one line is tighter than the other, it will show in the angle of that portion of line between the work and where the lines are knotted together. This portion of line will point to where the most tension is, and thus, to the direction in which the work will leave the cut. When both lines are tied to the work, it is difficult to determine which line is pulling harder than the other. It's even more difficult when one run of line is longer than the other because more stretch will have to be taken out of the longer run to equal the tension of the shorter. A substantial amount of rigging is required to properly set up a double bull line.

LINE ANGLES BELOW THE WORK

This kind of work is often called butt-tying or tailing. The rule here is to keep the pieces light, since the work will fall hard into the line. It's easy to do in small trees, but in large ones even a small section can weigh a lot, so use heavy rigging when butt-tying and tailing in large trees.

VERTICAL WORK

Secure the block to the trunk just below the point where the cut will be made. Secure slings used to hold the block with a bite to keep them from slipping down. This may not be necessary if the slings are held by a crotch or stub. Another alternative is to use chain with a slip or grab hook to set the block. A length of line fastened to the block and set as a timber hitch around the trunk will also work. However you set the block, keep it simple, because you'll be resetting it for every cut you take out of the tree. Keep the block close to the work to minimize the shock absorbed by the rigging. The shock will be greater the farther away it is.

On tall vertical work, face up the section first, tie the line to the butt with a clove hitch or other suitable grabbing knot, and then put in the back cut. If you're in a swaying or limber tree, use the hand saw to place or finish the back cut. Be cautious, the work can carry over to the back side when it's caught in the line, with the possible result of injury to you. Take this into account and adjust your position and lines to accommodate it. Consider "letting the work run."

In this kind of work you have to mind your lines more. They will tangle frequently if they drape or mingle with the rigging and the loads.

CROTCHING THE LINE

Much of this butt tying and tailing can be done without a block if there is a suitable crotch, stub, or surface to wrap the bull line around and get the bite necessary to brake the load. Here, the climber will often tether the line and lower the loads. A stub or limb is often needed in the vicinity to tie off or "dead end" the line. This allows the climber to use both hands to cut and trip the work loose.

SETTING THE WRAPS

The irregularities in the crotches of a tree can afford you many unusual ways to crotch the line for braking and lowering. How it's done exactly is often beyond description, as each is unique to the situation. But one thing that need be mentioned is how the wraps are laid in relation to the free end and the load end. Never set the wraps in a crotch so the load end rides over the free end. The line will seize on itself, preventing your ability to lower the load. When you set the line, look at the way it will be when the load is in it; do not take for granted that the

Crotching the Line—Consider a light weight brake in lieu of an undesirable crotch.

way you set it is the way it will stay. The line can change in a couple of ways: a half to full wrap may be taken out by the way the work carries the line.

When fixing the line to a stub, put the load end on the inside and the wraps on the outside whenever you can. This way you can add or remove wraps, the other way you can't. And don't set the line on a pendent or drooping stub unless there is something on it to prevent the line from crawling off. You just have to imagine how the load will make the line run to keep from losing wraps. As the work falls over, it can throw slack in the configuration. Falling off one side or the other can add half a wrap. It usually doesn't take more than two full wraps to crotch hold any heavy load. However, two full wraps is too much on light loads; the load can stall. It can be a nuisance because you have to force-feed the line to lower the load. On light loads you can often get by with half to one full wrap. The lighter loads will pull the line themselves, this way.

RETRIEVING A LINE

If you make wraps around a full limb or crotch, pull them all at once when hauling the line back. But first, introduce enough slack into each wrap to grab them all. If you don't, you will have to pull the line off the limb one wrap at a time. This means pulling two or three times as much line just to get the end. For example, if you lower a load fifty feet with two wraps around a limb, you would pull back one hundred feet of line if you pulled the line off the limb one wrap at a time. Pulling the proper way, all you would pull back is fifty feet plus the length of one wrap. If you are using eighty feet of line, it is most practical to start retrieving the shorter end to use. This way, you will be able to retrieve the short end, reset it, and be ready. If you do it the other way, you will have to wait for the ground worker to untie the long end of the line, haul back the long end, and then repeat the procedures. You can save a mega-amount of time when crotching a line if you think carefully about these two things.

MULTIPLE SETS

If you have a lot of individual limbs or small pieces to lower out of a tree, it is more practical to lower down several at a time. This can be done by setting hitches on the butts of the limbs with the bull line or by using slings (snap-on gear) to fasten each limb to the bull line. The use of slings is the fastest, easiest, and the safest. Hitches work satisfactorily, but you can lose one or more of the limbs if any slack is introduced into the line before they reach the ground.

This method of taking multiple limbs in one setup can be used in any limb configuration. In the forest trees, you can lower out as many limbs as you have room and rigging to manage it. In the broad trees, you can reduce the substantial size of some spars into a mere bundle of limbs hanging on the bull line, and the use of snap-on gear dramatically reduces the dynamic loading in the rigging.

Chapter 4

The Throw Line

The throw line, or heaving line, is widely used in tree work. Most people in private tree work know how to use throw lines fairly well and they are known for always having these lines on hand. The uses of the throw line are numerous. They are especially good for setting rigging in trees where the line can be thrown as well as retrieved; they are useful for pulling out "hangers," limbs that were cut out of the tree but never fell to the ground; they are useful to the climber for setting other lines in regular climbing and work; and as a safety tool the throw line cannot be excelled for getting lines to a climber who may be out-of-reach of the ground with their own lines.

TYPES OF LINES USED FOR THROWING

Throw lines can be made of anything, but they are best made of one-eighth to one-quarter-inch firm polypropylene. Firm to hard is preferred because it slides over branches with less resistance. The diameter of the line greatly influences its handling and throwing characteristics. Fine diameters can be thrown greater distances because of their lightness and wind resistance. Heavy commercial types of braided fishing line throw the farthest, but they are of fine diameter and hard on the hands if you have to throw or pull hard on them. Limp line, no matter what kind, is undesirable for a throw line. Unless of course that's all you have. But try to obtain a stiff type over a limp type; the limp line drags and tangles too easily.

THE WEIGHT

The throwing weight can be made out of just about anything. You can obtain a foam-rubber-covered throw weight through any outlet that carries tree work supplies. It's a pretty good weight but a little expensive. The foam-rubber covering is a safety feature in case you hit yourself with it, but it also causes the weight to bounce quite a bit in the tree. The ability of a weight to bounce is not always a negative thing; it may offer you the chance to fix the line in some obtuse places. Small lead fishing weights work satisfactorily and they aren't expensive, but they aren't cushioned either. Don't get in the way of a fishing weight when pulling it out of the tree, and by all means be sure to wear a hard hat.

The best weight on the market at this time is the lead shot or gravel-filled nylon bags with a ring eye. They're a good weight and they don't bounce. But the manufacturer has yet to come up with a small one that is suitable for climbing situations. In climbing you can get by quite well with one-eighth-inch lines and three to four ounce weights.

COILING THE LINE

One factor affecting the accuracy of a person's throw is the way the line is coiled. New line takes a little stretching to get any undesirable set out of it so it will coil neatly. Most stiff line will develop set, which makes it difficult to coil the line without a lot of twists and tangles. If knots form in the line, they should be taken out, as they will hamper the ability of the line to slide over limbs and through crotches. Knots that are drawn tightly can form permanent set where they occur in the line, thus making a neat coil job impossible. If the line has developed set from being coiled too tightly it can be removed by working with it for a while or stretching it out between trees for a while. It'll come out very straight and coil neatly.

When coiling the throw line, you must remove any possibility for it to twist or tangle in the coils. As with most lines, this is done by imparting twist as the coils are individually formed and bunched together. For every loop formed in the coils, a third- to half-twist is needed to form a neat set. If you don't impart a twist to the line, you'll get a set of coils with hitches and figure eights in it, which is no good for serious throwing. While coiling the line, the twist you impart to it will gather on the free end. Periodically shake the line to get the twist to run out the free end. This applies mostly when the line is lying on the ground.

The size of the loops in the coils affect the throwing performance of the line and how much set it will attain while it's stored. Small coils as a rule tangle less and are preferred whenever throwing the line within the confines of a tree. However, storing the line in small coils will put more set in it. Large coils tend to tangle more amongst themselves and have a tendency to bungle more shots.

Progressive coils should be used for most long throws. Progressive coiling starts with large loops and ends in shorter, or smaller, loops at the weight end. This eliminates a lot of bad throws as a result of loops tangling. Loops of all the same size will cross each other when they are coiled or bunched and cause tangles when the line is thrown. In progressive coiling, the loops can mesh together in the hand and not catch on one another.

When working on a smooth surface such as a roadway or on short grass, ground coils are an effective and quick way to retrieve the line and be ready for another throw. This eliminates the need and time it takes to hand coil the line. Retrieving the line and making ground coils can take only seconds. Ground coils can be laid on the ground in large loops one over the other or even in a progressive fashion. They do not work well in brush or ground that has a lot of sticks and debris lying about. Also, make sure that you are not standing on one of the loops. With long throw lines it's best to leave the bulk of the line on the ground and coil up only what you need to make the throw. For example, if you have sixty feet of line and you're throwing to a limb twenty feet up, leave most of the line on the ground and coil up only what you need to reach the limb. This saves a lot of time and unnecessary tangle-ups.

STYLES OF LAUNCHING THE LINE (OVERHAND THROW)

There are different ways to throw the weight and line. For accuracy at short distances, the overhand or sidearm throw is best. This is the very same way you would throw a baseball in the overhand or sidearm tradition, and it's the best way for many a climber to throw it within the confines of a tree. It is very accurate over short distances and the trajectory is very straight. Straight shooting is ideal for shots that are tight where you do not want the line over other limbs in between. Climbers are often restricted to the overhand or sidearm throw anyway. Small to medium coils are best for this kind of throw because they peel off and travel straighter than large ones.

UNDERHAND LOB

On the ground, the underhand lob is probably the most common way to launch the throw line. Vertical throws up to fifty feet with good accuracy are not uncommon. The weighted end is allowed to dangle and swing from the hand as you line up for the shot. Often, people swing the weight back and forth a number of times before launching it. This swinging of the weight is a manner of lining up for the shot, although some people launch the weight directly without any prior aiming or lining up. The amount of line between your hand and the weight bears some influence over the distance and accuracy you have with this throw. The usual distance to let the weight dangle from the hand is from twelve to twenty inches, depending on the individual and the situation.

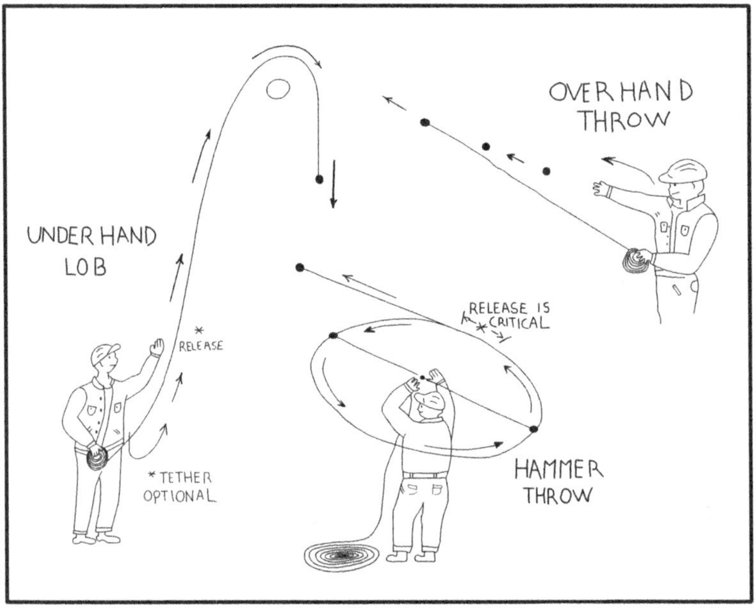

Long throws require some room to wind up and launch the weight, which makes them difficult to do up in a tree. The trajectory of this shot is not always as straight as the overhand throw; it is lobbed-in more often than shot straight to the target. On hard throws of this kind the proper release can be difficult if the line is wet and of fine diameter. It tends to slip or creep out of the fingers just a microsecond before the actual or intended release; it becomes too much for the skin to hold and release at the proper time. Instead, a little line pulls out from the fingers just prior to the intended release, which bungles the shot. It can actually take skin off the fingers when you're heaving the weight with a lot of force. To avoid slippage and possibly burned fingers, try doubling the line in a loop and hold the loop instead of a single strand. It takes a little practice to accustom yourself to this release.

HAMMER THROW

The hammer throw is one of the more uncommon ways to launch the throw line. This throw covers a distance unachievable with other throws for horizontal shots, such as throwing the line across a draw or ravine. Swing the line and weight over the head in an arc, allowing it to extend outward by releasing a little bit of line as the weight picks up centrifugal force. The hammer throw consists of about a half dozen windups. People standing by should take cover, especially when a novice is throwing the line. Here again, the moment of release determines the accuracy of the hammer throw; it can be difficult to gauge that moment in the beginning. Until you get accustomed to it, some bad throws are to be expected.

Ground coils are the only way to set the line up for the hammer throw. A special line made from ten feet of one-quarter-inch polypropylene for holding on, knotted to one hundred-plus feet of eighty to one-hundred-pound test monofilament, is a good line for the hammer throw. The monofilament is best nail-knotted to the polypropylene.

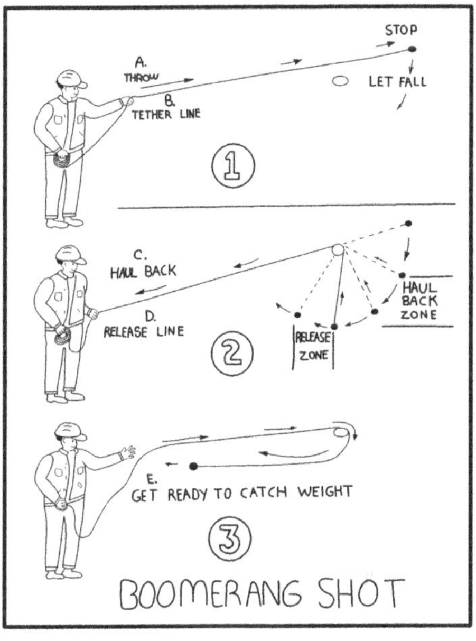

BOOMERANG SHOT

The boomerang shot is a method of retrieving the throw line weight over horizontal distances. With this method, it's possible to shoot the weight and line back to yourself from a limb some thirty horizontal feet away. The boomerang shot is useful in the tree and on the ground. Many factors, though, may influence the outcome of the shot; for example, the presence of other limbs and brush can foil it. When the line and weight are thrown over the target limb two, three, or more feet, and then stopped, the weight will drop and swing down to the underside of the limb. As it swings downward, you must haul back on the line for an instant—long enough to increase the speed of the weight—and then instantaneously release it at the time the weight reaches approximately bottom center, or just a fraction after. Hauling back on the line like this while the weight is dropping and circling around the limb increases its speed dramatically. If you're too late or slow with the release, the weight and line will wind or wrap itself around the limb very tightly, making it nearly impossible to unwrap in some instances. This is a common goof-up of many other throws besides the boomerang shot. When the haul back and release is timed perfectly, the weight and line can swing back to you faster than it was thrown to the limb. If you're not ready to catch it, you can get bopped pretty hard by the weight. Performed correctly, the boomerang shot is very impressive. There are a number of variations that you'll discover while practicing it.

A little note here: use the finger and thumb to tether the line so that you can control its speed, distance, and approach to the target limb. This is the same hand that performs the haul back and release. The other hand holds the coils. It's a good idea to fix the end of the line to a belt ring or snap to keep from losing it. In many throws, especially the boomerang shot, it's easy to lose the end.

RETRIEVING THE WEIGHT

Over smooth limbs, or crotches, the weight will usually pull the line over without any problems. But whenever the weight of the line exceeds that of the actual throw weight, you must throw slack or rolling loops upward to relieve the burden on the throwing weight. This will get many a weight to lower to the ground. If the line is dragging through twigs or brush, repeat this technique with subtle jerks and releases on the line. If that doesn't work, you may have to shoot for another limb or try the shot again and hope the line isn't carried through as much brush. After going over the target limb, sometimes the throw weight will drop onto another limb and not be able to drop to the ground. Here the remedy is to pull back smartly on the line and then let it drop back down. This technique will often get the weight to swing a little bit and when it does drop back down it will miss the crotch or limb it was caught on. You may also have to repeat this technique until you are successful.

A lot of times you'll miss your target limb or crotch and the weight will carry the line over or through an unchosen limb, or crotch. Pay close attention here. You often have the option to pull the line and weight out either way. That is, you may choose to let the weight pull the line out of the tree rather than pull the line to get the weight out. When pulling the weight back through there is more chance of it getting stuck or tangled in the unchosen crotch or limb. This is ever so important if the line is carried over any power lines. Trying to pull the weight back over power lines will get them to shake, cross or break. Don't do it. Let the weight come down and pull the line instead.

THE STUCK WEIGHT

In the event your line gets stuck in a tree, there are several ways to get it down. One way is to pull, jerk, and throw slack in the line to unwrap, or drop, the weight from the crotch or limb. The timing of these movements can make a big difference in your ability to be successful getting a line and weight out of a tree. You have to experiment. If the first method doesn't work, you can pull on the line until something breaks. But a word of caution: if the weight flings back to you while the line is stretched to its limit, it can reach speeds in excess of one hundred miles per hour! This is fast enough to kill you and if it hits you in the head it can break bones and induce internal injuries. Even the recoil of the line can break the skin, causing a bad cut. Remember these facts before pulling on a line so hard as to break it. Most of the time it's best to leave the line and weight where it is and try again with another line. It is prudent to have a couple of lines available.

Chapter 5

Lines Used in Tree Climbing

The climber's ropes are the most important part of their climbing gear. When I first started climbing we used Manila rope for both our climb lines and safety lines. It was "Tubbs" brand, half-inch, three and four strand, firm lay Manila that was of very good quality for its day. It was also stiff as cable when it was new and left us with many splinters in our hands until it softened up. About three months, or halfway through its life, we would turn it around and use the tail end until both ends were worn about the same. Nowadays there are many varieties and types of synthetic lines to choose from. Deciding which of these synthetic lines to use depends a lot on your own personal preference. The new synthetics will last a climber several years depending on how hard they use and take care of them.

TWISTED ROPE

A good twisted climbing rope should be firm, but not hard. Lesser quality rope will be loosely laid and limp, or soft. The difference in quality is in how the fibers are laid down in the rope during its manufacture. While the layman will be inclined to believe that the soft rope will be easier to work with, it's actually more of a problem in the long run. Soft rope tangles more readily during handling and use. Although it's easier to splice, it will not hold its splices well, and in use the splices can even work out. Also, the soft rope does not wear as well and knots can cut and seize into it more readily.

All twisted rope, firm or soft, has the tendency to untwist, or rotate. This is most noticeable when a load is suspended freely by it. If you're suspended on a long run of twisted rope, you'll spin around by the rope's natural tendency to rotate. It can make you dizzy enough to get sick if there's nothing around to grab ahold of and stop it. Another

disadvantage of twisted rope is that it tends to wad, or tangle, at the tautline hitch during descents. This will be more of a problem on long runs when the running part of the line is not hanging free. All of these tendencies come from the twist inherent in the construction of this type of rope. Not a whole lot can be done about it, although there are ways to deal with it as you climb and work, and in time keeping it under control can actually become second nature.

BRAIDED ROPES

There are two kinds of braided ropes, the single braid and the double braid. Both single and double braided ropes will exhibit similar qualities characteristic to the firmness and construction of their lays, although the single braid is preferable for tree work, as the outer sheath of the double braided rope has some annoying traits. It tends to wad or bunch up at the tautline hitch which can make climb-line control difficult.

Braided ropes are very good ropes. They are not prone to the rotation tendencies of twisted rope unless a twist has occurred from the way the rope was coiled prior to use. Braided ropes will not stretch excessively as compared to equal lengths of twisted rope. Some braided varieties can be obtained which are of a near-static (non-stretch) quality, although stretch in a line is not always an undesirable feature. Not all braided ropes can be easily spliced. Knotting is a more widely used means of joining them together, or to certain fasteners.

The disadvantages of braided ropes are that they are notorious for creeping at the tautline hitch and prone to slippage if the knot is improperly snugged or set. The tendency of braided ropes to creep or pull through can put you out-of-reach of your tautline hitch. It can even pull the end through the hitch if there isn't a security knot to prevent it.

One thing common to all synthetic ropes, twisted or braided, is that they are not resistant to heat and will melt if they come in contact with a hot muffler on the chainsaw. They can even fuse when too rapid of a descent is taken out of the tree. The fusing will occur at the tautline hitch. Synthetic lines other than nylon, Dacron, or poly-Dacron should be avoided for use as climbing or safety lines. The types to avoid include the polypropylene and plastic varieties.

STRETCH

Twisted rope will stretch more than braided rope. Finer diameter lines will stretch more than heavier diameter lines. Lines that stretch are called dynamic. Lines that don't stretch, or that stretch very little, are called static. Stretch in a line is not always a disadvantage; it offers some cushion and it can give you that extra distance to reach parts of the tree, or the ground, that a static line won't, particularly in long runs. The static line is more suitable for use in the rigging of fixed lines and bull lines where stretch cannot always be tolerated.

CLIMB LINES

The climbing lines used in tree work are a standard half-inch in diameter, whether twisted or braided. This diameter is long wearing and amply strong for tree climbing. The breaking strength of the half-inch lines varies according to the firmness of the lays, or braid. The firm, or hard rope, will always be the stronger. When the rope is new it will have a slick finish that can make it difficult to hold onto (such as hand-over-hand pulling yourself up the line) for extended periods of time, but after some use the rope will develop a nap finish that is much more comfortable and easier to hold onto. While the half-inch line is the

Climb Lines – Tall trees require long lines.

proper choice for most tree work, there are times when a lighter gauge line is more suitable. This is particulary true if you are climbing or rappelling out of very tall trees. The three-eighths-inch lines, while not recommended for tree work, are the cat's meow for tall timber, where rappels over two hundred feet are not uncommon. Working with this much half-inch rope can be a burden on a climber, but if the thought of climbing with a three-eighths-inch line bothers a person, they can settle on an intermediate sized line like the seven-sixteenths-inch.

CLIMB-LINE LENGTHS

The standard length of most climb lines is 120 feet. A 120 foot, half-inch climb line will give you a little more than sixty feet of drop, scope or working line. But only if the line is stretchy. There are times when you need more than sixty feet of drop and times when sixty feet is too much. I personally have a collection of lines that range in 20-foot increments up to 120 feet. In small trees the short lines are an advantage; for the tall trees I have lines in lengths from 200-300 feet in fifty-foot increments. Though most climbers will never need as many lines as I use, this should impress upon you that one line is usually not enough. Setting and using the climb line is discussed in depth later.

COILING THE CLIMB LINE

For proper storage of the climbing line, the new climber must learn how to coil it. It's simple enough, but many climbers are picky about how their lines are coiled and seldom are content with someone else's method. Coiling a climb line is somewhat of a personal thing. What can be said about it is that the coiled climb line should lend itself to easy uncoiling during the line's next use. Any coil job that tangles the line when it's used again is not a good job. Short climb lines seldom pose a problem even if some of the coils tangle; it's the long lines that can become a problem. Firm rope will tangle less than limp rope. In either limp or firm rope though, how the line is coiled will affect its ability to uncoil without tangling. Avoid random or overlapping loops. It's best to build the coil with consecutive loops in which one end of the line is separated from the other by the rope in between. It takes a little bit of thought. After the line is coiled, it is held together by a few tight wraps and a tuck or two through the bunch to lock it together, another personal thing about which each climber will have an opinion.

The climb line can be coiled and stored in a canvas or nylon bag, which keeps it clean and dry. The bag can even be used to hold the bulk of the climb line on the ground while a climber ascends or works in the tree. This will greatly reduce the chance of tangles occurring from sticks or limbs falling on the rope.

THE SAFETY LINES

These are the most specialized, personal, and variable of lines a climber will use; most climbers will have at least a couple of safety lines. Although most of the safeties you'll ever use will be made of rope, some are fashioned out of steel cable and chain. Your average tree diameter usually determines the lengths of your safety lines. The common safety line is five-eighths to three-quarters of an inch in diameter. On the finer side, do not go less than one-half inch.

The large diameter is preferred because it's easy to hold on to and to work with for long periods. Long length safeties are used primarily to scale the trunks of big forest trees such as the redwood. The technique of working a long safety line is called fliplining, and such safeties are

Fliplines and Safety Lines

frequently referred to as "fliplines." Fliplines can be over forty feet in length and inlaid with a steel core.

Standard safety lines are made primarily of twisted rope and come equipped with a snap end and an adjustable end. The old safeties were made of Manila rope and were splintery when new. You rarely ever see any Manila safeties anymore; however, in the logging industry, the one-inch Manila steel-core fliplines are still available for the hard-core climber. If you are working in trees that are in the vicinity of power lines, the steel-core line is extremely dangerous to use. Most safety lines, especially the Manila ones, are short-lived; they get more abuse than any other line you'll use. They often get nicked by the hand saw and even by the spurs on occasion. Safety lines will become impregnated with resin and pitch when working in young conifers which essentially ruins them by making them difficult to work with.

Other materials and combinations of materials have been used for special adaptations of safety lines. The lineman's safety strap has been used by some tree workers, though it is not well suited for tree work. Stiff steel cable has been used as a core in short racing safety lines for competition pole climbing. Such safety lines are also not suited for tree work. Steel chain has been used by some climbers but I can't see where it is of any advantage unless for its durability.

THE SNAP END

The snap end on the safety can be fixed onto either the right or the left side depending your preference. Traditionally, the snaps are eye-spliced to the rope with at least three tucks in the hard rope and four or more in the soft rope. The safety snap should have a good firm spring in the keeper. This is most important, as snaps can be tripped by line and hardware entanglements. Should you ever hear a snap keeper click, make no other move other than to secure your position. Snap failure is more common than people might think, so you should always keep an eye on them. But they are a necessary evil and tree climbing would be difficult and probably more dangerous without them. I do not recommend the locking type of snap for use on the safety line because they require a special grasp to trip them open. This can hinder your ability to fix the snap in a difficult situation. I've seen the locking parts on these snaps themselves be the cause for snap failure; their dual mechanical feature is more susceptible to being damaged, particularly so on the climb lines when pulling the snap end out of the tree. Even bits of bark, sticks and leaves can become jammed in the mechanism and be the cause of failure. Always check them.

TAUTLINE HITCH TAILS

The tautline hitch tails are used to adjust the slack, tension, and working length in the climb line and rope safeties. On climb lines the hitch can be fashioned directly by using the end of the line. Knot the line to the belt ring with a cat's-paw or bowline. Run enough line through the knot to fashion the tautline hitch; this eliminates any need for a snap connector on the climb line. This is a plus in some cases and a disadvantage in others. Eliminating the snap on a climb line is a definite safety advantage but it's time consuming in terms of set up and takedown time when you're tying in a lot, like when you're working in hedgerows. Using the end of the climb line for the hitch works fine, but you may prefer to use a separate piece of rope for it instead. This way, you do not have to cut off the ends of the climb line to renew the tail after it's worn, which in time shortens the climb line. Separate tails can be made from a stock of other line considered suitable for such use. The tail should be long enough to tie the hitch within easy reach and no further

Tautline hitch tail on the climb line.

Tautline hitch tail on the safety.

than that. Tautline hitch knots tend to creep out if the free end of the tail is not fixed back or secured. As mentioned previously, this trait is more commonly associated with braided ropes, although it can also occur with twisted rope. But twisted rope will readily develop more set after it's used for a while, which will remedy the problem. To prevent line creep in the tautline hitch, use a back splice or security knot to jam the hitch. This may only be necessary if you're putting a working load in the line. In regular descents it's not always required. The tail ends on the climb lines wear out relatively quickly and they must be replaced or renewed when wear becomes obvious. Look for fusing and abrasion, and spread open the lays to inspect twisted rope.

The adjustable tail ends used on the safety lines last considerably longer than those used on the climb lines. This is because descents are never really made out of the safety line; primarily just slack and length adjustments are. But a great deal more pressure may be exerted on the safety and tail which makes it almost mandatory to fix the loose end back. There are also many more ways to rig the adjustable tail to a safety. Some safety tails are spliced or knotted directly to the saddle dee ring and you'll see some fastened to the dees with a snap or connection link. If a snap is used on the tail end it should be of the locking type, but only on the tail. I would also not recommend using carabiners unless they are of the heavy-duty locking type and are used only as a fastener for the tail end. Rated quick-links for connecting chain offer a cheap and strong connection for the tail ends. Whatever kind of fastener you prefer, remember that all are mechanical and subject to failure in more ways than you might think. Always double-check them.

On the long fliplines, thirty to fifty feet, it's desirable to have an adjustable tail on each end. This way slack and length adjustments can be worked out on either end without requiring a climber to pull their slack all the way around the tree to do it. An adjustable tail on each end also gives the climber the opportunity to work around the trunk by letting out slack on one side and taking it up on the other without having to scooch the line around the trunk to do it. This feature is indispensable because it greatly reduces the chance of the line becoming fouled in the bark of big trees.

MAKING ADJUSTMENTS

With tail ends it's easy to make adjustments. To gain slack, or let out line, all you have to do is grasp and pull on the knot. This releases the bind in the knot, easing its bite on the rope. Slack will now feed through the knot. To take up line requires two hands. The safety must be grasped and drawn up on, so as to slacken the hitch. While holding on to the safety like this, the hitch is then pushed up the line with one hand. The overall length of the tail has a lot of bearing on the ease with which you can take up slack in either the safety or climb line. You can suck up, or draw, a lot of slack with a long tail but not with a short one. The exact length of tail after the knot is formed is a matter of personal preference but falls somewhere between twelve and eighteen inches for most people.

Some climbers fix their safety directly to the dee ring with a cat's-paw or figure-eight knot. With this method, adjust the length of the safety by loosening the knot and pulling the slack in the desired direction. This can be rather cumbersome and requires the use of both hands whether you're letting out line or taking it up.

There are numerous bite and bind devices with which to make adjustments in the safety line. These devices are crude at best and, again, often require the use of both hands to make any kind of adjustment to the line's working length. Bite and bind devices are fastened to the dees by snaps or links.

POWER SAW ROPES

All power saw rope should be made of half-inch firm Manila because it's heat resistant and not at all likely to melt through if it comes in contact with the muffler on the power saw. The diameter of the line is somewhat important; any smaller than half-inch can be rough on your hands managing a large saw by it. Traditionally, there's an eye spliced on one end and a snap on the other, with an overall length to suit your reach. The snap is most practical as you often have to disconnect the saw for various reasons. The snap, or connector, should be of the locking type; I've seen a few saws take a fall from snap failure. The snap should also distinguish itself from your own safety and climb-line snaps. This prevents confusion should all the snaps get bunched together on one ring, which happens from time to time. Some climbers prefer a lighter gauge line for the powersaw rope, with its lower breaking strength, because some have managed to get their saw stuck in a cut and get the heck jerked out of them. This does happen but it's more due to operator error than anything else. If you feel it's necessary, you can splice a lighter gauge of line to the end of the saw rope and have the benefits of a heavy line for handling and a lighter one for a break away.

Incorporating a short 6 inch piece of stout bungee in the saw rope acts as an efficient shock absorber when tethering the saw by it.

HAND SAW ROPES

Hand saw ropes, though not essential, are very valuable at times. You can get by quite well with quarter- or eighth-inch line for a hand saw rope. The ends can be spliced, knotted, or have little snaps. Just make the line long enough so that your reach is not hampered. The main purpose of the hand saw rope is to tether the saw in situations where you'll have to let go of it. There are times when this is necessary and having the saw tethered saves losing it. Don't make a practice of using hand saw ropes all the time because they're just another line to get tangled up. Don't use bungee cords here; hang-ups with them result in the hand saw winging back to you with undue force.

INSPECTION OF YOUR LINES

Wear and deterioration can occur throughout, or in localized areas of the lines you use, so you must be able to evaluate it to know when to scrap or "down-grade" a line. Common sense dictates this more than anything else. If a line looks bad, cut it or scrap it. Obvious defects where strands are cut, fused or pulled loose are cause for a discriminating look. Inspect the end of a climb line that is used to fashion the tautline hitch. Extreme wear and fusing can occur there. Carefully inspect where your line is subject to an "impact". A line can become smashed or crushed at an impact point. Also consider fungal, chemical and ultraviolet deterioration in the older lines you acquire. These factors do not always give noticeable indications of deterioration to the untrained eye. Run the line through your hands; spread the lays; bend the line sharply. A deteriorated line will often feel rough, and crack or "pick" the fibers upon such an inspection. If it does, it may not be safe to use for climbing purposes. Even for use as a ground line, you should "pull" or "knot test" a suspected line before using it.

Chapter 6

Using the Climb Line

In selecting a limb or crotch to run the climb line through, certain factors should be considered.

THE STRENGTH OF THE LIMB OR CROTCH USED

The limb or crotch must hold your weight plus any binds you'll put in the line while working. The binds a climber may put in the line while

The position and height of a tie-in.

working can more than double the force exerted on the limb or crotch they're tied into. In simple rappelling, a climber will seldom throw the load of an added bind in the line and the crotch chosen will not necessarily have to be as strong as one the climber is working out of.

THE BITE OF THE LINE IN THE CROTCH

This is an important factor to consider because certain bites can make the line run smoother and easier. A climb line that runs too tightly through a crotch is of no benefit to a climber. However, it is desirable to have a certain amount of bite or drag in a crotch as it eases the pull on the running part of the line and the tautline hitch, which in turn makes working the tautline hitch and making adjustments in the line much easier. Experience will dictate decisions. So remember, careful observation of the limb configuration is important in choosing how the line will run through it and the degree of bite it should have.

THE RELATIONSHIP OF CROTCH ANGLE TO WORKING ANGLE

The relationship between these two angles is important. In simple rappels where a climber is descending straight down, the line angle seldom, if ever, changes and is usually not a major concern unless the line can slide or work out of the crotch during the descent. But while working, angles change a lot. This can cause the line to slip or crawl out of a crotch if the way the line runs through or in it is poorly chosen, especially in situations when you are working over your tie-in height.

THE POSITION AND HEIGHT OF THE TIE-IN

This determines the angle from which you'll have to work out of the line. In a nutshell, the higher you tie in over the work area, the more mobility you'll have to cover a larger area and to do your work in relative comfort. With high tie-ins, the line supports the majority of a climber's weight, and the climber can often work in the outer reaches of the smallest limbs without putting any significant weight on them.

TYING AROUND THE TRUNK

Tying in around the trunk of the tree is generally accepted as being the safest way for a climber to rig their climb line. It is undoubtedly the strongest tie-in a climber can get anywhere in the tree, with few exceptions. The diameter of the trunk, its relative angle, its bark, and choice of available limbs to use as stoppers (limbs intended for the line to ride on or against) can make a lot of difference in how safe and efficient the tie-in will be. An increase in the diameter of the trunk will accordingly increase the amount of friction on the rope and the bite it can attain. Around small trunks or tops, the friction will be minimal and the line will usually run smoothly. As a rule, larger diameter trunks or tops will have more friction and much more drag on the line will be experienced. The type of bark in the tree can add to or decrease the friction and bite around the trunk. Any bark that the line wears or cuts into can increase the friction and bite. This can seize a line, rendering it useless. Certain types of trees are known for this tendency, one way to get around it is to remove some of the outer layers of bark where the line will be fixed. In young conifers, the line can cut a groove through the bark and cause it to bleed pitch. The combination of rope, groove, and pitch can cause seizure and make climb-line control quite difficult. Smooth and hard bark that shines up after the line wears on it can actually decrease the friction on the line.

THE LIMB CONFIGURATION

Both the limb configuration and the way the line runs over, around, and through it can influence the amount of bite the line has on the trunk. The limb configuration will also determine the relative safety of the bite and the desirable or undesirable factors governing climb-line control. As a rule, you do not want to choose a configuration that will increase the bite of the line around the trunk. Using a single limb for the line to ride over will make for a minimal bite around the trunk. The limb must be amply strong if it's the only one used, and it must have an angle that will keep the line against the trunk. If the limb droops, it is likely that the climb line will creep or crawl away from the trunk over it. When using a single limb on the back side of a trunk, the climb line will run on the side of the trunk as you descend. This is of no consequence in simple descents, but whenever you move to one side or the other to do some work, the far part of the line will drag or catch on the trunk. This has been referred to as "trunk drag." It can greatly hinder the virtue of a high tie-in. Ideally, a good configuration would bring the static and running parts of the line together on the same side of the trunk. This increases the bite dramatically if the line circles around a large trunk. To reduce the bite in such a configuration, the line should be in an elliptical rather than a circular run around the trunk. Thus, a limb on the back of the trunk for the line to ride over, and two position limbs on the working side a little farther down that the line will run between, will reduce the bite and eliminate trunk drag on the side of the tree where you are working.

LIMBS AS TIE-INS

Using limbs as tie-ins for the climb line is often more practical than fixing the line around the entire trunk of the tree. However, some people contend that a person should never tie into a limb, for safety reasons. Such a statement may be true for those who don't know better and might choose a limb to tie into that isn't safe. There are lots of situations and conditions that undoubtedly make some limbs the wrong choice for a tie-in. By the same token, there are just as many, if not more, reasons why a person should tie into a limb rather than the main trunk. A seasoned and experienced climber can distinguish the difference and give many reasons why any one limb is a better or worse choice than another.

When choosing whether to tie into a limb, there are a number of things you should consider. Is the limb strong enough to hold your weight to do the work you need to do? In simple rappelling you do not exert much more than your own weight on the line unless the descent is jerky. But when you're working, the binds and angles you get in can exert much more force on the tie-in and limb. The species of the tree will determine the strength of its limbs and will be a big factor in deciding whether to use a limb as a tie-in. Species will also determine how far out on the limb is safe to go. Right up against the trunk, even a small limb or stub can bear a heavy pull. But a foot or two out can snap the same limb. The angle of the limb in relation to the angle that the line and load will run is also a big consideration. You should never tie into a limb that will cause the rope to creep farther out as you descend or move to the work. A limb whose angle will naturally draw or force the line against the trunk or crotch is the best choice to use. But working angles change and the line may creep or walk out the limb whenever you begin to exceed certain limits or angles. When working even with or over the height of the tie-in, the line is highly susceptible to sliding or creeping out a limb. Particularly

Limbs as Tie-ins

when the limb you're tied to angles to the same side that you're working. So, if you choose a single limb to tie into, try to pick one that will run at least at a right angle to your work. The advantages of using a limb as a tie-in are many. Large limbs that branch out over other parts of the tree can offer much better tie-in points for position. Climb-line position is the all-important factor that makes the work easy or difficult. If a limb's position is good but its strength is questionable, you may rig the limb to strengthen it so that it can be used as a tie-in. Limbs are not prone to the friction and drag forces on the line because they have considerably less surface area for the line to dig into. This makes managing and working the line much easier. Also, being smaller, a limb will not spread the line apart as it is when it's around the trunk. A climber can take full advantage of the height of their tie-in without trunk drag distracting from it. A limb may be the only logical choice of tie-in when the diameter of the trunk makes it difficult or impractical to get the line around it. So, when deciding to use a limb or go around the trunk, you must look at the situation and make the best available choice of tie-ins. You can save yourself a lot of extra work and time by choosing the proper tie-in for each situation, whether it be a limb or trunk.

SLINGING THE CLIMB LINE

This is the method used to set the climb line in a far limb or a crotch. First double the end of the climb line two, three, or four feet depending on the situation. Then sling it toward the far limb or crotch to catch it. By doubling the end of the line, you give it more momentum to travel greater distance; whip around a limb or through a crotch; and make its way through minor twigs and brush. The doubled end is easy to snare from a reach with the tip of the handsaw or whatever you have to reach it. In clear open shots you can allow the doubled portion of the line to straighten out when you sling it. This can present the end of the line within easy reach from a far crotch. This technique is very similar to slinging a safety (See **Chapter 12**).

SLACKING OFF

Upon reaching a tie-in point you should be secure. Your security at a tie-in point is or should be the result of the safety. While supported by the safety, fix the climb line. After tying in and before releasing the safety entirely, slack off on the safety until your weight is in the climb line and it is taut and holding you. Then remove your safety support. This procedure is mandatory in the fixing and reliability of most climb-line tie-ins. This applies also to when you swing to a spar you're tied into. In many situations you would prefer to slack off a line to get there rather than risk swinging and crashing into it (See **Chapter 12— The Short Traverse**).

ROLLING OVER

At times you'll tie to a spar or limb that you're straddling. This unique circumstance requires you to roll over the limb or spar to gain the climb-line support. You usually have the option to fix the climb line before or after you roll over. In either case, follow the rule of slacking off the safety to gain the support of the climb line. Upon rolling over a limb or spar to reach the low side, clinch the safety taut to a bite and with your legs clinched, ease yourself over. For the beginner this maneuver can be a trial. But after you have done it a few times, it will feel more natural. The saddle or belt you use can make a big difference in the difficulty of the procedure. Note that rolling over can cause the belt to shift over your waist and inch up to under your arm pits, leaving you in a stressful situation. Make sure your belt is fitted properly before rolling over. With the leg type climbing belts that will be no problem.

IMPROVISING A TIE-IN

There are times when a suitable tie-in is not available and you have to improvise a solution. Tying into a drooping limb is a good example. As a rule, you should never tie into a drooping limb because the line tends to crawl down if there is no suitable lead or lateral to prevent it. The solution is rather simple. All you need is a spare piece of line to tie on the limb; this acts as a stop for the climb line to ride against. The spare piece of line can be anything you can come up with, be it a safety tail, safety, or even part of the climb line. It must be knotted, with a couple of very tight wraps, to the limb. This alone can be sufficient for the climb line to ride against. However, sometimes it isn't, and a loop may need to be formed with the line that will catch the climb line if it slips over the stopper wraps. Drooper limbs can be relied on as a tie-in point to set your climb line but remember there must be no possibility of the line creeping, crawling, sliding or working its way down or out on the limb.

Tying to a stub is another example where a short piece of line can be wrapped or knotted to prevent the climb line from working off it. Tying in where there are no limbs or crotches can be done if a line, like your safety, is fixed around the trunk and set with a bite so it won't slip. In a "do or die" situation, the safety line itself can be used as the tie-in, but the wear from the climb line in such a configuration *will cut through it,* especially upon a burnout. Use a thimble device in this situation to ensure a safe descent.

TIGHT CROTCHES

One type of crotch that most climbers agree not to tie into is a tight crotch. A tight crotch is one that causes the climb line to become bound or pinched when you put your weight into it, or shortly thereafter. Sometimes you won't have much choice in the matter if there are no other available crotches. But there is an easy way around this problem. Observe the angle of the crotch carefully and then cut a small wedge off a limb or stub closest to the angle of the crotch, but thicker than the width of your rope. Insert this little wedge of wood into the crotch and drive it into place with the back side of your hand-saw. If it's cut out at the right angle and is the proper thickness, it will seat itself tightly in the crotch. You can then use the crotch as a tie-in without the fear of the line working itself in and seizing up. Keep in mind that the crotch may still be too tight to pull a splice, knot, or snap through. A thicker wedge will allow them through. The fact that the wedge is round will give a nicely curved surface for the line to run over, making the crotch totally desirable to use. In large crotches, a couple of wedges may have to be used side by side. Any loose or soft bark should also be cleaned out so the wedges will seat positively and not be likely to shift or work loose.

Improvising a Tie-in

Tight Crotches

Multiple Tops as Tie-ins

MULTIPLE TOPS AS TIE-INS (CODOMINANT)

In many small trees and in the tops of many large trees, a climber will not always find a single good top strong enough for a tie-in. But when there are a number of tops in a tree, their combined strength may offer you a tie-in position. Running the climb line around a multiple top will draw all of its parts together, substantially increasing their strength. This is an important consideration as many multiple tops will split or pull apart at the crotch union if only one is used as a tie-in, particularly if the one used is on the same side that the load you're bearing is pulling it. If a single top is chosen from a number of tops, it should either be the strongest one or the one that will be drawn into, rather than away from, the rest by the force of the climb line. This applies especially to sucker tops. Sucker tops are notorious for splitting off the trunk and being a major cause of bad falls out of a tree. Slings or straps can be used to draw the tops together and a thimble fixed for the tie-in.

DOUBLE TIE-INS

In some situations, back pull, or inadequate support from the climb line, can cause you to lose your balance or make it difficult to work; it can cause small trees to bow over; and it can put excessive strain on dead trees. By using two different tie-in points, you can turn many difficult or dangerous situations into relatively safe ones. But the work will have to fall somewhere between the two tie-in points.

The lines themselves can be two individual lines from two tie-in points, set in a conventional double-line manner. You can change your position and height by letting out or taking up on either line. To capitalize on the length of a single run of line, the climb lines can also be set single-line with adjustable tails. You can, in effect, double your reach. In some work or traverses, a single line can be used in a double tie-in configuration, but only if it's long enough. Although there is just one line, it is set like two. Any line pulled from one side can be tethered back to the other and the work or traverse accomplished. At times, spanning a static line between tops of trees and fixing a thimble at the preferred location on the line may prove to be a better way to position your tie-in.

Double Tie-ins

MINDING YOUR LINES

This phrase is not used much, but it means pay attention to your lines and know where they are.

In any horizontal movement through the tree, a climber's lines should usually precede them. If you are going over some limbs to get to a particular one, you should coil up the line and throw it ahead of you. Don't drag them behind because they will catch, slowing your movement. The running part of the climb line is particularly susceptible to this. If you're toting long safeties and moving a lot, they should also precede you. Short safeties can be dragged behind you without too much difficulty. Sometimes you will have a lot of lines to mind; for example, two safeties, a climb line, and maybe some rigging such as straps, slings, and bull lines. This can be a lot to carry around without it tangling or getting caught on something.

After you're tied in, you'll seldom need a double safety, so one of them can be removed. Using the climb line for support or for movement will often eliminate the need for any safeties during the movement. To keep from dragging them, they can be coiled into a compact size and fastened to the dee ring, out of the way. This is also the best way to carry any long safeties during rappels or descents as they often tend to wrap and tangle in the running part of the climb line.

The usual way of following your lines is to coil and then throw them ahead to where you're going. This may not always be practical if you're climbing over a lot of different obstacles; it can mean having to repeat the procedure many times. This is common in hedge rows. In such situations, it's best to carry the running part of the climb line as coils and let them out as you cover the course. When working over roadways, never let your lines hang so low as to catch in traffic. Any excess line you are not using should be coiled and draped over a suitable limb or in a crotch. When cutting and dropping pieces of the tree, make sure your lines are not under where the pieces will fall. They can catch the line and give you a heck of a jerk. When rigging sections of the tree that will swing away from your position, watch that your lines do not tangle in the rigging or become fouled when pieces are being lowered. This can create a wicked mess. When cutting with the power saw or even with the hand saw, make sure your lines are not in the path of the cut or the follow-through of the saw when it finishes a cut.

There are quite a few methods for keeping the lines out of the way while climbing and working, but it takes keeping your mind on them. This is ever so important when you're working near the ends of your lines. Over the years, many a climber has run off the ends of their climb line and taken a bad fall. You can prevent this by back splicing your twisted line or tying a security knot in your braided ones. While either method will ensure your safety, many climbers don't use them because of their tendency to catch or hang up in tight crotches. This is something else you must keep in mind. If you use a security knot, untie it before pulling your line out of the crotch or tree. It's hard to live with the end of the line getting hung up in a crotch because you forgot to untie the security knot; but you really can't live without it either. In some of the taller trees, a climber may tie in six or seven times before reaching the ground and it's reassuring to see that security knot at the end of the line.

If you're topping a tree out, after you've worked in its top, make sure you're not tied into it when you cut it out. It sounds pretty stupid but it's happened before to experienced climbers. Sometimes you'll climb to the top of a tree to cut a few limbs off one side, then rappel down to a lower point and cut the top out. Remember to take your climb line out first.

When pulling your climb line out of the tree, there are a number of things to consider. Don't pull it out if there's a knot or snap on the end that will run through the crotch. A knot or a snap can hang up in many a crotch, requiring you to climb back up to get it out. Also, the fall out of the tree is damaging to the keeper mechanisms on snaps and fasteners. On long runs of line, pull the line out gently so it falls out of the crotch on its own. If you jerk it out of the crotch, the end can whip out instead of fall out, and in the course of falling to the ground, wrap around an incidental limb. Again, this can require a climb back up to free the line. In some cases, it may behoove you to tie a fishing line to the end of the climb line, thus tethering it. This can totally control the fall of the climb line and prevent any possible hang ups. Don't stand under the line when you pull it out, and advise others to do the same. The line can come down with considerable force, causing a welt on your head or shoulders.

A climber must mind their lines at all times to make the climbing and the work easier and safer. At first, the beginner is thinking about other things and tends to forget where their lines are. This results in tangle-ups. I've seen some tangle-ups cause the new climber much frustration and anxiety because they didn't mind their lines. Keep it in mind, especially when working with a lot of rigging: mind your lines.

LINE ANGLE

It is important for the beginner to know the relationship between the angle of their tie-in and the amount of weight borne by any part of the tree they're working on. A direct overhead tie-in can support all of a climber's weight and there will essentially be no weight-bearing factor on the limb the climber is standing on. But, as a climber moves outward on the limb or other structure, the angle in the line changes. The amount it changes is determined by how far away the tie-in point is above the climber. The farther away the tie-in point is overhead, the less the line angle will change during any movement. The actual weight put on the limb one is standing on increases with the angle of the tie-in and can be decreased by moving the tie-in farther up the tree. There is a natural tendency for a person to be pulled back by the line as they move out on the limb and away from the overhead position if they are safetied to the limb. This tendency can nullify the amount of weight you bear on any ascending structure (the limb) that you are climbing out on. This is because the line angle is pulling both the climber and that part of the tree to which they are safetied back towards the tie-in point. On any drooping, or descending limb, there are no nullifying effects, so the back pull force of the climb line and the relative weight of the climber will be brought to bear on any descending limbs. Thus, drooping limbs are difficult to work with.

To sum up, the actual weight you bear on any part of a tree changes dramatically by the angle of the tie-in, its length of run, and the attitude of the structure you're in. The amount of tension in the climb line can also affect weight-bearing factors considerably. As a climber moves around the tree, they pay out and take up slack in their climb line almost continually, unless the parts of the tree they're on are strong enough to support them. If they are not strong enough, the climber must keep the line taut and their weight in it at all times.

Chapter 7

The Tree Climber's Belt

Most climbers will only have one belt and use it through the better part of their career. More times than not, it is the same belt they learned on and were broken in on. Once a person breaks into a particular climbing belt, every other belt after that will feel different and usually uncomfortable to them. As funny as it seems, it's actually the climber who breaks into a belt rather than the belt breaking into the climber. For this reason, many climbers are reluctant to give up an old belt and often swear that theirs is the most comfortable anybody could wear or use. But even the belt you're used to can eventually become uncomfortable after enough hours of rigorous climbing and working.

There are four major kinds of climbing belts. They are the back belts, the butt belts, the seat saddles, and the leg saddles. These four categories are based on the suspension characteristics of each type of belt. Construction of the belt, regardless of which kind, affects how the belt wears on a person, how long it will last, and its true utility.

THE BACK BELTS (BODY BELTS)

These are a simple type of belt used by many linemen. The main feature of the back belt is its back support. Although the back belts are not well suited to general tree work, they are perfect for climbing poles or trees in which no climb-line work will be necessary. They are good for simple climbs with the safety line, for movement up and down where only back support is really needed. The width of the back belt determines its relative comfort as will the spacing of the dee rings, to some degree. If the dee rings are too far forward, there may be stability problems with the belt. If the dee rings are too far back, they can dig into your hips and cause considerable discomfort. One disadvantage with the back belts is that they can torque, or twist around, on your body.

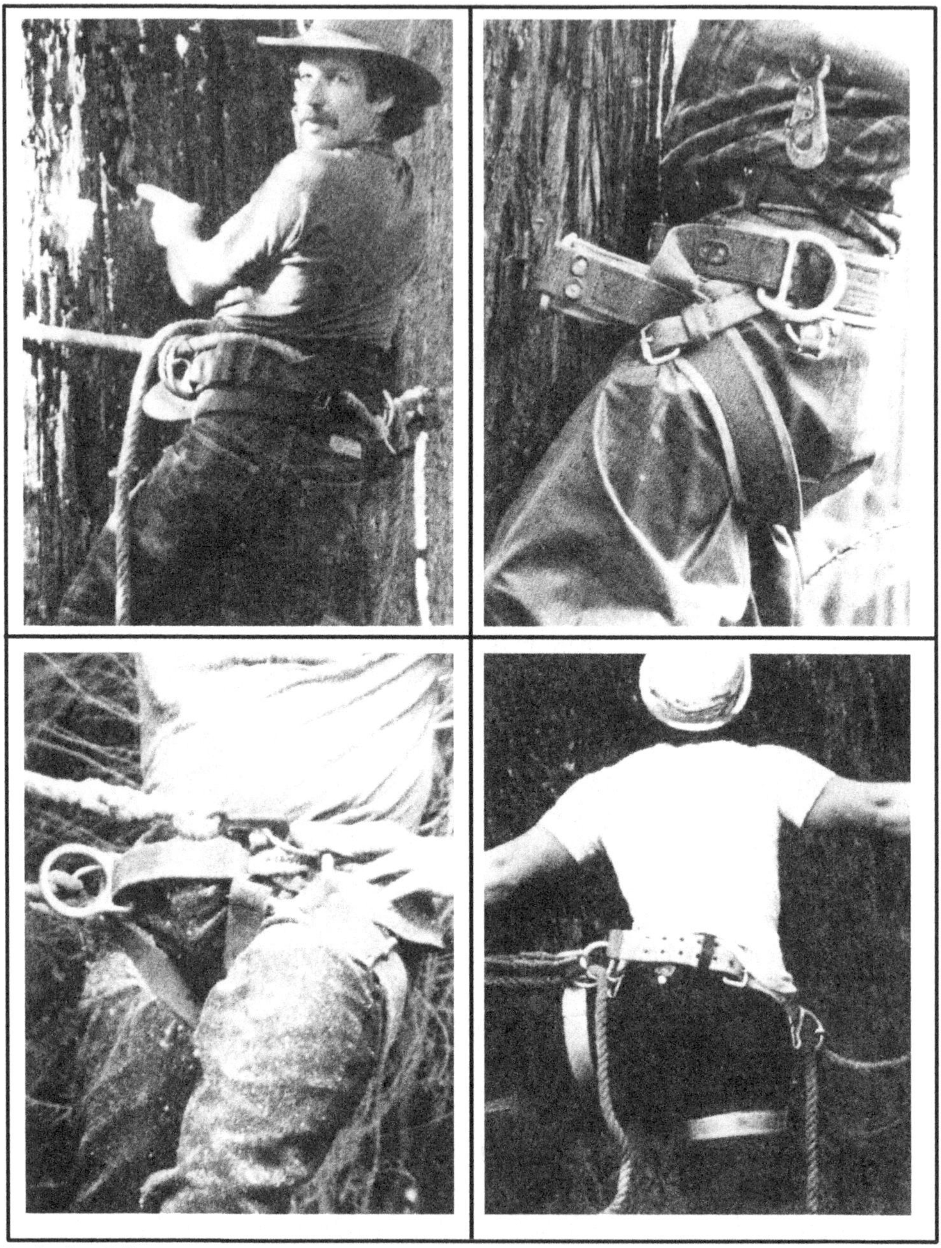

Production Belts

This can alter the utility and fit of the belt; it can put the dee rings and snaps at awkward reaches, like behind you. Suspenders used to hold these belts up may be needed if you're tethering a power saw, toting a heavy line or carrying a lot of tools. Otherwise, these belts may slip over the hips when they're loaded down.

Back belts have been used to rappel, or descend, out of the tree by slipping them under the hips and fixing a climb line through the dee rings. This works satisfactory for descents only. In effect, it's used much like a "Bosun's chair." But you shouldn't attempt to work from a back belt that is fitted as such. It's unstable, and it would be too easy to slip out of the belt if you lost your hold on the climb line.

THE BUTT BELTS

These belts support the climber at the waist and fanny. The added support in your thighs helps distribute the pressure of the belt more evenly between your back and butt, making them a lot more comfortable when working for prolonged periods in the safety and spurs. Butt belts are much better suited for tree work than back belts.

You can work with the climb line in a butt belt quite satisfactorily. The climb line is traditionally fastened to the dee rings by a "spreader" snap, although some custom butt belts will have a center, or slider, ring between the dees for the climb-line attachment. Without the spreader snap these belts tend to squeeze on your hips, which can considerably restrict your leg movements. This is a particular disadvantage with most of the butt belts when working out of the climb line. However, many climbers are quite adept at dealing with this disadvantage and can get around in a tree quite well in spite of it.

A variation of the butt belt will have the dees much extended out from their usual location by the hips. This feature has a good and a bad side. On the good side, it lessens the pressure on the hips and thighs when working out of the climb line. On the bad side, it often puts your safety and climb-line tails at a reach when you're working in awkward positions. It can also cause some stability problems when working from the safety. This will be noticeable in particular when you are safetied into small parts of the tree as the dees are extended from the belt and won't allow you to get as close to the tree as you would like. So the belt puts you at a reach to your work sometimes. The location of the dees, ideally, should be just in front of your hips. Although this may not be as comfortable when working out of the climb line, it won't put you at a reach to your lines and work. Butt belts with a slider ring between the dees are the better choice for climb-line work.

THE SEAT SADDLES

These belts are very common. In fact, it seems that most of the belts used in the industry now are of this type. In the seat saddle, there is a combination of two supports which work independently of each other. One of them is for back support when working out of the safety and the other is for hip support when working out of the climb line. Each support has its own set of dee rings—the distinguishing feature of the seat saddles.

When working out of the safety line, the portion of the belt used for back support is all the climber will utilize. The lower part of the belt hangs loose and often gets in the way. The back support on these belts is usually not adequately padded or meant for prolonged periods of working from the safety as the regular back belt is made to. The lower portion, or seat, fits around the climber's hips a little lower than that of the butt belts. When supported by the climb line, the seat saddle causes the climber's legs to be squeezed together even more than the butt belts are prone to. The use of a spreader snap is a must with these belts.

Since these belts are made with two distinct separate support systems, you can expect to get in many odd binds when working in the climb line and using the safety feature at the same time. When at side angles to your work and climb-line support, the climb line will pull on the lower part of the belt while the safety will pull on the upper part. The two forces are distinctly separate and tend to cock the climber around because they do not share a common focus. This often causes the belt to become twisted around on your waist and be of little actual utility. It can also keep you from facing the work, greatly limiting your options for a good working position.

When supported by the climb line and using the safety at the same time, it helps to snap the safety to the climb-line dees to neutralize the bind and torque. You are not meant to get into inverted or upside down positions in seat saddles. When working out of the climb line in these belts you must make sure that the leg straps on the lower half of the belt are fastened securely. Many climbers do not use the leg straps on these belts and more than a few times I have seen them with the belt up to their armpits or under their knees. This is one of the inherent tendencies of the belt. The selling feature of the seat saddles is probably how it suspends you from the climb line. It's much like sitting in a swing and not totally uncomfortable for moderate periods of time when the spreader snap is used.

THE LEG SADDLES

The final category of climbing belts to be discussed are the leg saddles. Their origin is obscure and probably goes back a long way. The old climbers that used to make their own belts usually made leg saddles from a hank of rope and an old back belt. There have been many variations in the construction of these belts. But no matter what type of construction is used, they basically support the climber in the same way. Unlike the rest of the belts discussed, the leg saddles are well suited for all aspects of tree climbing. Working from inverted positions is no worry to the climber who works in a leg saddle. Side-angle positions that are difficult to work in other belts will be much easier in the leg saddle also. The discomfort of pressure pushing the legs together in the other belts is not present in a leg belt; the climber has total freedom in their leg movements. In fact, the leg belt will increase the security of your footing in situations where the other belts would lessen it. This is a big plus for your safety while climbing and doing tree work. The suspension characteristics of the belt are what makes all of this possible. In a nutshell, the leg saddle suspends the climber at their axis, or very close to their center of gravity. In a leg saddle that fits well, a climber can assume practically any position and regain their upright position simply by shifting their weight. The climber does not always have to use their hands to hold, steady, or pull themselves in or out of these positions either. You can roll or turn to either side simply by shifting your weight in the belt. In some of the other kinds of belts, trying to roll or turn without holding on to the climb line will throw you over in the belt and make it difficult, at best, to return to a stable position. Observing how these belts function will enable you to understand why they are so well suited for tree work.

There is only one set of dee rings on these belts, placed at the hips where a climber will need them for safety work They can be used in conjunction with the climb line without the problems you would experience in the other belts. The climb-line attachment on these belts is often a sliding or pivoting ring that is located between the dees. This ring is located in the frontal pelvic region of the climber, the closest point to their center of gravity, and the reason why changing and returning to different positions is so easy. The portion of the belt that holds the legs is attached between the dees and the center ring. Since the supports are separate for each leg, they keep the entire belt from torquing or twisting around on your body when at hard side-angle work, a condition so common in the other belts. This feature is exclusive to leg saddles and keeps the belt positive on a climber's body with the dees always located where they are supposed to be. Many climbers don't like leg saddles because the leg supports can pinch the groin area or cut off circulation. The fit of the belt has all to do with that.

BELT CONSTRUCTION

If you shop around, you can find the four groups of belts and saddles that have been discussed. But the suspension and support a particular belt may afford the climber will not do them any good if the construction of the belt is poor. Current laws regulating construction have been a major setback in spite of their honorable intentions. Most of the people that make the rules that regulate belt construction are not climbers themselves; this can be seen by the design of many belts. While these laws are meant to protect the climber who buys a production belt, they were also formed to protect the manufacturer. These two-sided laws have resulted in construction designs that protect the manufacturer from liability rather than promoting true utility. As a result, some belts are strong enough and rigid enough to tow a truck with. This is not a bad feature, but after climbing in some of these belts you would think that's what they were primarily designed for. Not all of the designs are truly safe either in spite of the strength tests they pass. Some production belts have dee ring and hardware arrangements that can cause safety and climb-line snaps to become tripped, roll out, or disengaged from binds and clash. Most production belts are also outfitted with cheap accessory rings and snaps that usually break or rip off the belt within the first year of use. While the dee rings and buckles are amply strong in all production belts, the way they are fitted or fastened into a particular design may lead to their early failure. The riveting and stitching may pass the stress test but it often does not pass the test of time and regular use. Many production belts wear out at their stress points long before the rest of the belt wears out. Significantly, most climbers who use production belts have made some modifications to them. The most frequent modification you'll see is the adding of cushioning or padding to the parts of the belt that wear on them.

THE FIT OF THE BELT

No matter what type of belt you have or how it is constructed, if it doesn't fit you properly then it won't be of any benefit to you. If you buy a production belt, make sure you get one that fits well. A belt that is too loose will frequently torque around on a person. A loose fitting belt is also subject to slipping up or down on the body and can put a climber in a tough situation. A tight fitting belt is not subject to torquing but it can cut off your circulation and put you out of service quickly. Tight belts can also create terrible sores where a hard spot in the belt, like a buckle or dee ring, bites into your body.

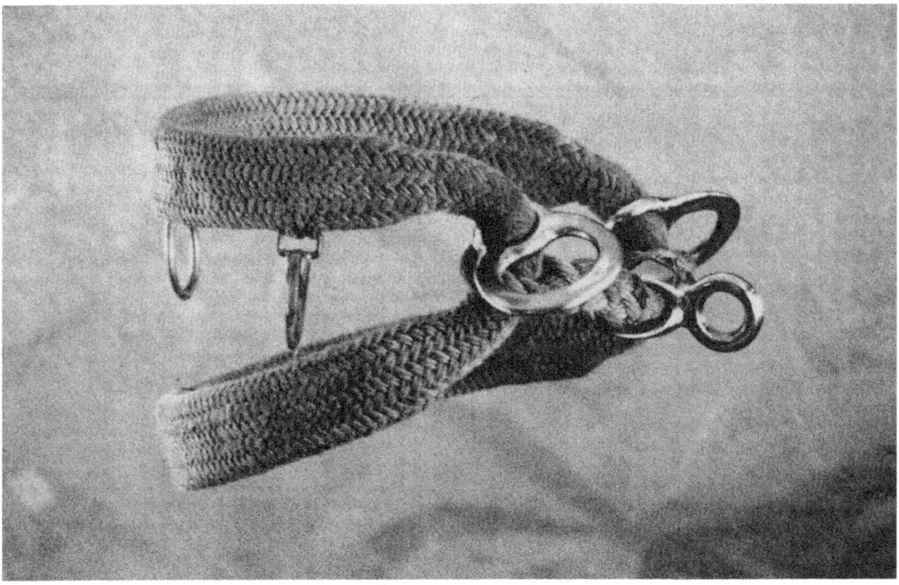

Author's Custom-made Belt

CUSTOM-MADE BELTS

Since tree climbing and the work associated with it is so specialized, I have always advocated the use of custom-made belts. The fit is so much better on a custom belt and they often lack the buckles and adjustments that create the hard spots you find in the production belts. You can also outfit them with quality accessory snaps and rings, and arrange the belt to your liking.

The material best suited for any good climbing belt is rope. It's affordable, easily obtainable, and can be knotted, woven, or braided together in countless different fashions. Rope construction does not necessarily require any stress point riveting or stitching common in nylon web construction. Thus, the stress points in rope construction don't pull apart or wear out before the actual material does. Rope is also extremely long lasting; a climber can expect decades of use from a custom rope saddle. (As long as they don't grow out of it.) There are so many different ways you can build a rope saddle it would be impractical to try and describe them all here. All it takes to make a custom-made belt is the basic hardware and accessories and a little rope. The rest requires a little imagination and desire for something of quality. The type of hardware I use is of my own forged and welded construction.

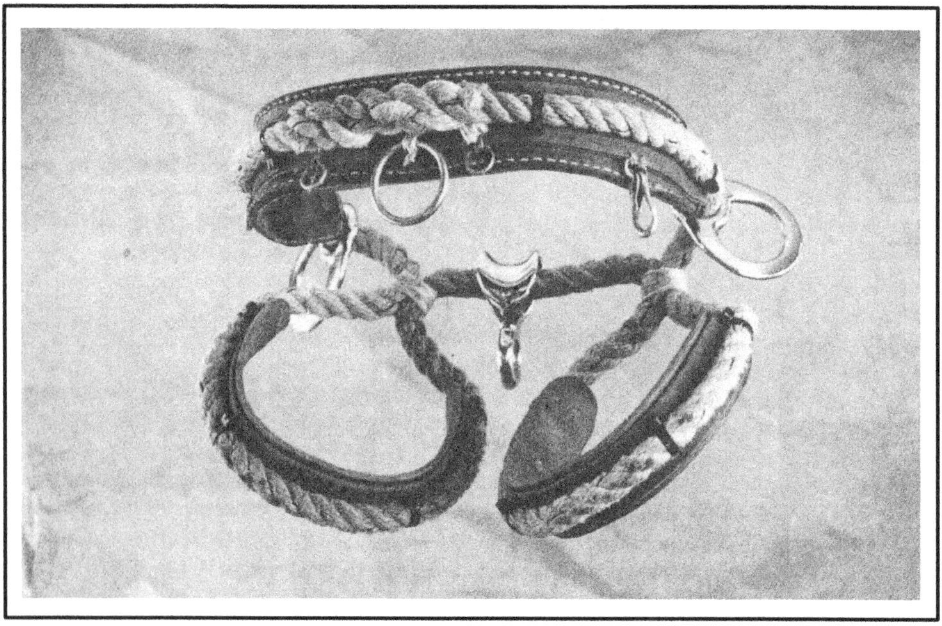

Author's Custom-made Belt

Chapter 8

The Tree Climber's Spurs

Climbing spurs are another personal tool of the tree climber. They have many names: climbing irons, leg irons, gaffs, hooks, points, and, of course, climbers. This is the one tool many people associate with tree climbing and it is kind of the tree-man's trademark. In many places the use of climbing spurs is highly controversial and not allowed except in the removal of trees. This will be elaborated on later in the chapter after some primary education on climbing spurs.

GAFF LENGTH

When choosing a climber spur or gaff, you should first know what kind of trees you'll be climbing. The great variety of trees may warrant you to have more than one set of climbers. Most tree workers do, based on the length of the points. Long points, those being three or more inches, are a favorite of climbers working in trees with thick bark The longer length of the point penetrates deeper into rough or loose bark and gives you a more secure footing. The extra length also reaches into sound wood between high bark ridges. Shorter points, on the other hand, are more comfortable and safer to use in trees with thin bark. This is most true when working in the small structure of skinny tops or the branching of limbs, where beginner and veteran climbers alike can stick themselves with longer points if they misjudge their footing. Under these conditions, short points are superior because they afford you the advantage of using your heel or toe to steady yourself. There are times when just the contact of a heel or toe against the tree can keep your balance under control. Short points, on the other hand, are a disadvantage in rough bark conditions; they can keep you spinning your spurs, gaining little but scraped knuckles. That said, quite a few tree climbers are well adapted to using long- or short-pointed spurs in

conditions where they would be a disadvantage to others. Though I don't recommend doing either, there will be times when you won't have any other options, unless you have more than one set of spurs. I strongly advise any climber to carry more than one set of spurs.

KICK-OUT

Kick-out occurs when the spur point loses its ability to hold the weight of the person it's supporting. It's the number one inherent danger using the spurs. If you're not tied or safetied to the tree when kick-out occurs, your handhold will be the only thing that prevents you from falling. In the lineman's trade, the term is referred to as "cutting out." In rough-bark trees, even long points may not reach into sound wood, or into bark firm enough to hold a climber and kicking-out can be frequent. The bark of some trees will often get caught in the gap of the spur, between the point and the frame. The bark caught in the gap will prevent the resetting of your points until it is removed. This is called "barking up"; it can be a difficult condition to remedy when both spurs are barked up. Kicking-out can also occur when the point of the spur strikes and glances off knots in the tree. Knots in themselves do not make for good footing due to their tendency to shatter or break when the weight of the climber is transferred to the spur point. Dead trees whose bark is slipping, or rotten, are another major cause of kicking-out. In such conditions, kicking-out can be a common occurrence and not always unexpected, or unable to be controlled by the experienced climber. Most experienced climbers can recover from kick-outs without a second thought, continuing their climb as if it never happened. However, for the beginner, kicking-out is usually not as easily forgotten.

Besides bark conditions, dull or unsharpened points can also be the cause of many kick-outs. Hard poles without bark, like some dead trees, can be so hard that the point of the spur may only penetrate a quarter of an inch. In conditions like this, short spurs with a very keen and sharp point will keep you from kicking-out. However, a sharp point is not really necessary in trees with thick, rough bark where penetration is easily accomplished.

Another major cause of kick-outs is when the angle of the spur point is positioned incorrectly in relation to the contour of the trunk. You must make a conscious effort to maintain the correct angle; aim the point of the spur into the tree and not down the side of the trunk where the spur can "run out." The so-called correct angle is frequently lost when a climber's knees come close to the trunk, a too common habit of new climbers.

Certain contours of a tree's form demand you to angle your spur points accordingly to keep from kicking-out. When maneuvering around large crotches and other irregular forms in a tree, you must position the points in such a way that they will hold in place while your body goes through various changes in position. When you know that the position you need to assume to make a maneuver carries the risk of kick-out, you must deliberately punch and drive the point deep into the tree. In regular climbing, deep penetration is not always necessary unless you're overcoming a difficult obstacle. Most experienced climbers know the conditions that cause kick-out and can regularly anticipate where and when it is most likely to occur. When kick-out is anticipated, it is not always an uncontrolled event, in spite of how it may appear. However, even an experienced climber can lose control of a situation if they're caught by surprise. Probably the worst time for kick-out to occur would be while running a power saw.

FITTING THE CLIMBING IRONS

The proper fit of the climbing spurs is an important consideration, which the new climber soon finds out. Climbing spurs have been called shin and arch busters for good reason; of the aches and pains new climbers cry about, those resulting from the spurs are the ones you will most likely hear. The pain can be grueling, to the point where you must stop climbing and let your shins or arches take a break. The best way to prevent pain in the arches is to wear a boot with a good reinforced arch. It doesn't have to be a heavyweight boot, just one with a good strong arch in it. But your boot should have a heel that is at least long enough to prevent the stirrup from slipping over it. Currently available through mail order catalogs is a foot plate, which attaches to the stirrup on the climber frame. The foot plate is supposed to lessen the pressure on the arches by distributing it over a broader area on the sole.

Tall boots or high climbers are not really necessary to relieve shin pain, providing your frame height is correctly adjusted and your shin pad is adequate. The height of the frame in most climbing irons is adjustable to size up with your shin. The frame should not be adjusted so high as to put pressure on the knee, yet it should be close to it. Too short of a frame puts increased pressure on the shin. This pressure from the frame comes from your weight exerting leverage through the stirrup. Longer frames lessen the pressure. So you're better off to adjust your frames high.

SHIN PADS

The shin pad is probably the single most important item for alleviating shin pain. Ideally, the pad should distribute the pressure of the frame over the shin as well as to maintain the frame's proper position. But not all pads can satisfactorily do either. The frame on the climbing irons exerts pressure on the shin from two different angles, a frontal angle and a lateral angle. Your particular shin bone, the adjustment of the frame, and the type of pad you're using will determine the way the frontal and lateral pressures are exerted on your shin. As a rule, the lateral pressure is more pronounced and it can leave the new climber with terrible sores on their shins after just a couple of hours of climbing. This is due to the fact that new climbers haven't developed the hardened skin tissue that years of climbing give.

The L pads are the most common shin pads you will see. They are usually made of leather and are somewhat firm when new. Their firmness helps maintain the frame's position and somewhat evens out the pressure that the frame puts on the shin. In time, these L pads become soft and lose their body. This can cause the frame to slip back, creating a condition called climber kickback, which can be very uncomfortable and lead to bad footing. The T pads are more forgiving in this respect; they keep their body a little longer and maintain the position of the frame much better than the L pads. T pads that secure with Velcro fastenings are now available. If they function the way the manufacturer claims they do, they may be the best choice of the soft pads.

RIGID PADS

The other kind of pad you may find yourself using is the rigid pad. The rigid pad cannot be excelled in its ability to maintain the position of the climber frame and prevent climber kickback. However, the fact that they are rigid to the frame is a big mark against them. The older style rigid pads fasten to the frame at a hard ninety-degree-angle. No matter how you look at it, a person's shin will not conform to it, either frontally or laterally. The sole contact point from the old-style rigid pads to the shin is at the very top of the pad. It can create the most wicked sores even on an experienced climber's shin. One manufacturer recognized this and changed the design of their rigid pad to conform to the front of the

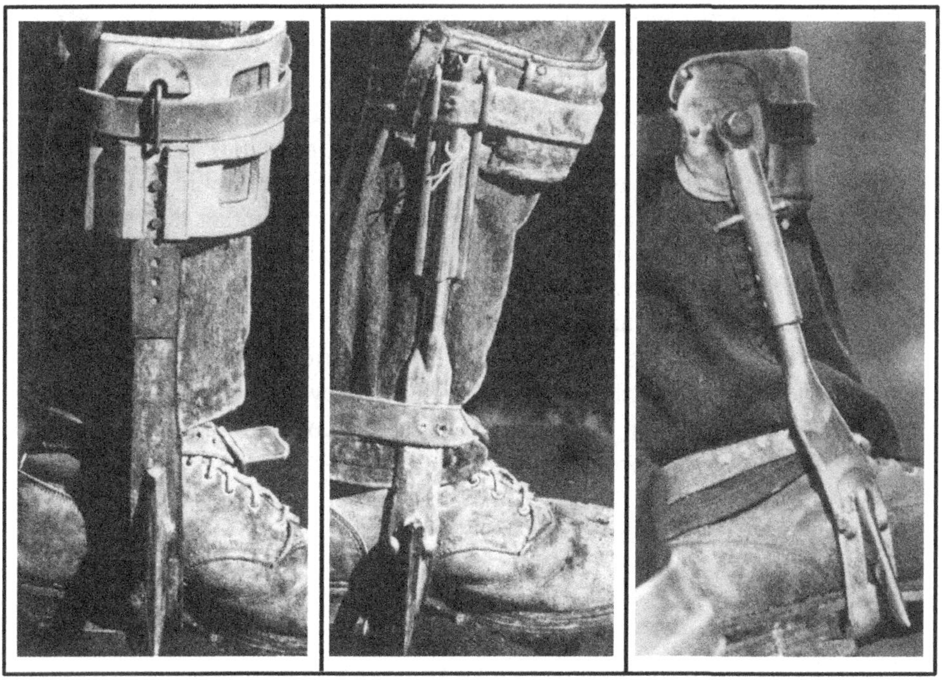

shin. This change helped a great deal but the lateral pressure was not remedied. I modified an old set of my pads many years earlier in much the same way the manufacturer changed theirs. I improved on it again years later and took care of the lateral pressure problem by making the whole rigid pad float on the top of the frame. Done by placing a ball joint at the top of the frame and fastening it to the middle of the pad on the lateral side. At last, a pad with the advantages of evenly distributing the frame pressure on the shin and also maintaining the frame's proper position.

THE STRAPS

The straps that secure the spurs to the leg are another important part of a good fit. Leather straps stretch and get soft with use. If you buckle up loosely with leather straps you'll usually have to stop at some point in the tree to tighten them another notch. In the lower strap, stretching can cause the stirrup to slip over the heel of the boot. Stretch in the top strap will promote climber kickback from excess looseness in the fit of the soft pads. So, with leather straps you'll find that a snug buckling up at first will eventually even out to a comfortable fit.

The rubber-impregnated nylon straps are long lasting and do not suffer from the effects of stretch and fungal deterioration. Since they don't stretch, their fit on the climber remains relatively constant and the adjustment notch you use in these straps will usually remain the same for the life of the strap. However, if you change boots, you'll probably find that you need to use a different notch. Changing boots sometimes makes it necessary to punch a new hole between the others to get the fit just right, but be careful not to make it too tight. Some climbers run the lower strap around their ankle rather than around the frame. This seems more a matter of personal preference; one way doesn't seem to have an advantage over the other.

The straps on many climbing irons are not permanently attached to the frames or stirrups. Therefore, it's important to buckle them up after use so they don't get lost. Loss of a strap can prevent a job from getting under way; it is prudent for a climber to carry a couple of extra straps in their bag for just such occasions.

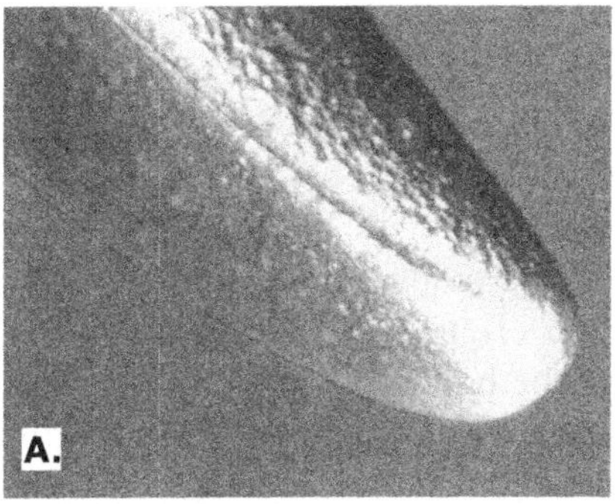

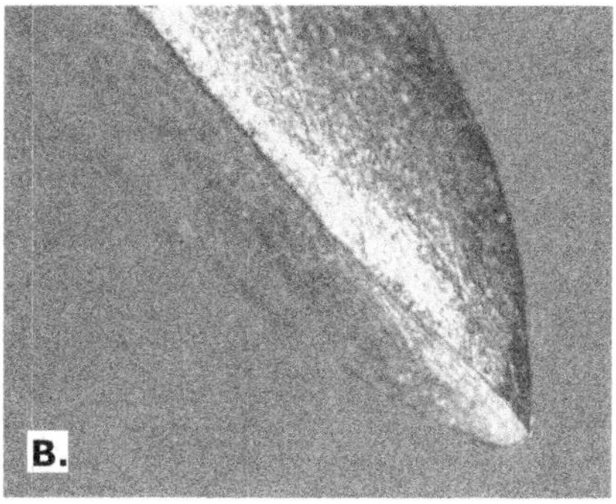

A. EXTREMELY DULL POINT.

B. INCORRECTLY NOSED OVER POINT.

C. CORRECTLY SHARPENED POINT.

SHARPENING

Periodically, it is necessary to sharpen the spur points. The point of the spur lasts a fairly long time between sharpening unless the points get ground into rocks or pavement. There are some telltale signs indicating that the points should be sharpened, such as peeling and kicking-out. You will find yourself having to drive your points into the tree with undue force to keep from kicking or peeling out. Peeling out entails one spur point slipping when your weight is first applied to it. A long strip of bark is removed from the side of the tree. How sharp the point needs to be to prevent peeling out varies widely from tree to tree.

Trees with thin bark and hard sap wood require a sharper point than trees with softer wood. I like to maintain my short gaffs with keen points that stick into hardwood without having to drive them into it. By comparison, my longer points remain on the dull side. In spite of being duller, though, the long points still penetrate into the thick bark of the big pines, firs, and redwoods. Often, this is all you need to hold you anyway. As a general rule though, it's best to maintain a minimum sharpness on your points.

Most of the sharpening takes place on the bottom of the gaff. A little on the sides can slow the taper of the point if desired. The top of the gaff, sometimes called the ridge or the spine, should never be touched with the file. Mount the spurs in a vise so both hands can work the file. On the bottom flat of the gaff, the stroke of the file can run diagonally across in either direction, starting from the point to the shank. But the stroke must be kept flat, and true to the original grind. The corner, or edge, must be sharp, particularly where the bottom and sides of the gaff come together at the tip. This severs the wood fibers and allows the point to penetrate effectively. You'll find many people underscore the flat side just under the tip at a little steeper angle for about a quarter of an inch. This helps direct the tip inward and affords better support with shallow penetration.

The tip itself requires just a few, very careful, light strokes with the file. Examine the tip to make sure that the profile of the gaff runs true to the point. Overworking the tip can blunt it, requiring a substantial amount of work to restore its proper taper and, ultimately, shortening the length and life of the point.

Grinders should never be used to sharpen the gaff. They tend to gouge out the metal unevenly and distort the profile and contour of the point. Many linemen maintain their points by using a hone after an initial sharpening with a file.

While sharpening the gaff, take care not to cut yourself or be poked by the point. You'll find that even wearing gloves may not prevent injury if the file slips and you run your finger or hand into the point. Be careful!

GAFF PROFILES

The profile of the point, its taper or fatness, has a pronounced effect on the performance of the gaff. Taking down the sides of the gaff too much will slow the taper of the points, the opposite of blunting. This causes the taper to become too sharp over all and results in a skinny point that is a nuisance in soft wood because of its super penetration. Kicking out won't be a problem here; getting one gaff out of the tree without setting the other one in deeper will be the problem. A too-narrow point is also susceptible to bending and even breaking off in extreme cases.

Filing gauges are available which measure the profile of the overall gaff through slots the point is inserted into. But the use of these gauges can lead you astray because the profile on a set of short points, such as pole points that linemen use, is much faster than the profile of a long point tree climbers use.

In many climbing irons the points are replaceable. Thus, when they become too short or ruined, it's a simple matter of buying and installing a new set.

MECHANICAL FAILURE

Some climbing irons have many mechanical fastenings that keep all of their parts together. Over the years, I have seen many a climber, including myself, get caught up in a tree because of some mechanical failure in the climbing spurs. Simple screws, tapered pins, cotter pins and rivets cause mechanical failure. They do wear out over time, which makes periodic inspection of the climbing irons mandatory. If you see parts of the fasteners becoming worn or loosening, fix them right away or you too will become caught up in a tree with one spur hanging in two parts. If finding replacement parts for your spurs is a problem, contact Wesspur Tree Equipment Inc., www.wesspur.com. They will probably have what you need.

THE USE OF THE SPURS

As mentioned earlier, the use of points for climbing is carefully regulated in some cities and districts. In rural areas, their use has not garnered the controversy that it has in the cities, and many climbers use them regularly for routine trimming. The controversy over climbing spurs is due to the visual and physical damages inflicted upon trees by them.

VISUAL DAMAGE

This can be a distraction but may not result in physical damage to the tree. Smooth-barked trees show the wounds left by spurs more pronouncedly, and some of them will show the marks for years after they have been climbed. However, there are many trees that do not show the marks where the points pierced their bark. These trees may be climbed with spurs a number of times before there are any obvious indications that points were used to climb them at all.

PHYSICAL DAMAGE

Physical damage from the use of spur points varies widely from tree to tree. Overall though, trees do not do well by the use of spurs, which is what the controversy is all about. Besides the visual distraction, wounds from spurs can cause major physical damage where the points penetrate the bark, cambium, and enter the sapwood. Wounds can play host to a long list of insects who will use them for cover almost immediately. Wounds are also the entry points for wood-rotting organisms; transfer of disease by the penetration of the point into the cambium has been recognized.

The degree of the puncture and the number of punctures in a given area tends to determine the harm done to a tree. Each puncture produces a certain amount of dieback immediately around it, varying widely from tree to tree. Most isolated wounds will heal satisfactorily. Groupings of wounds in areas where a climber works have the most serious effect on a tree. In these cases, the whole area may die back and have little chance to heal before a major infestation or infection becomes well established. When trimming trees for the power company, I saw different degrees of spur damage in trees we climbed every five or so years. Some of these trees had been climbed with spurs as many as ten times over a forty or fifty year period.

ISOLATED SPUR WOUND

RADIAL SECTION, DOUGLAS FIR, FOUR YEARS AFTER SPUR POINT ENTRY.
POST INFECTION IS INDICATED BY DISCOLORED WOOD AND DARK STAIN LINE.
A YOUNG AND VIGOROUS TREE WHICH SEALED OFF THE WOUND AND ARRESTED THE INFECTION WITHIN THE SEASON THE INJURY OCCURRED.
NOTE THE CHARACTERISTIC FLAP PUSHED OUT BY THE SPUR POINT.
THE WOUND OPENING WAS INITIALLY SEALED BY THE CORK CAMBIUM, FOLLOWED BY THE CALLUS AND SUBSEQUENT SEASON'S GROWTH.

SUBSEQUENT WOUNDS

RADIAL SECTION, TAN OAK.
FAR LEFT WOUND OCCURRED APP. 1964, SECOND, INDICATED BY THE STAIN LINE, APP. 1974. TREE WAS TAKEN DOWN IN JUNE 1984. THE WOUNDS, THOUGH SUBSEQUENT, CAN BE CONSIDERED ISOLATED AND SUCCESSFULLY SEALED.

MULTIPLE WOUNDS

CROSS SECTIONAL VIEW, REDWOOD FOUR YEARS AFTER INJURY.
PRIME EXAMPLE OF MULTIPLE AND DEEP WOUNDING IN A LOCALIZED AREA, THAT BEING THE YOUNG AND TENDER TOP. APP. 5 INCH DIA. AND 10 YEARS AGE AT TIME OF INJURY.

It's not difficult to climb trees without spurs. It just takes a little more rope, arm, and leg work. But some trees will prove difficult to climb without spurs; if it comes down to your safety, it may prove wise to use them. If the tree is exceptionally outstanding, it would behoove you not to use spurs if their use will cause harm. These are all things you must weigh out and discuss with the owner of the tree.

Even climbing without spurs can inflict some damage to a tree, particularly in young parts where the bark is thin. Damage is commonly found on the top side of young limbs where a climber turns a boot, which can break off bark in large patches, notably in the spring when the bark slips. Footholds in forks or crotches may result in similar damage. Small branches may break when a climber tries to use them as hand or footholds. In the course of shimmying up a tree, a climber can strip off many young leads, buds and laterals. Climb lines can cut through bark and cause girdling wounds around trunks and limbs. The safety line will strip off leads when it slips down the trunk or a limb. All this damage can be inflicted to a tree in the course of a single climb. In some instances the use of climbing spurs may prove to be less injurious, although I know many people would never agree with this. For reasons of safety and aerial rescue, no job or climb should ever be undertaken without a set of spurs on site. And every climber should be qualified in their use.

WEARING THE SPURS ON THE GROUND

This has always been a no-no with the larger companies. In fact, a lot of people will point out this infraction more quickly than if you use spurs in a tree that didn't need it. In the past, larger companies allowed wearing climbing spurs on the ground if you were going directly to another tree or to the truck to put them away. But now they have stopped that and wearing them on the ground is totally forbidden. I have seen some climbers go on about doing ground work with the spurs on. That's asking for a poke in the ankle. But I've also seen climbers get threatened with a safety infraction just for stepping away from the tree with them on. Now that's a little ridiculous. Sometimes it's not easy to bend over and remove the spurs where you come out of the tree, so you have to move to a better location to take them off. Remove the spurs if you're done using them. If for some reason you choose not to, make sure you decide wisely.

Chapter 9

Special Climbing Tools

In most climbers' bags of tricks you'll find an assortment of devices and aids for use in special climbing situations. When climbing trees, there is always room for improvement in techniques and tools. With these changes have come many new ideas and gadgets that make tree climbing safer and easier to learn and do.

ASCENDERS

The line ascenders that are commonly used in rock climbing are a godsend for the tree climber. These one-way, cam-lock devices are lightweight, strong, and indispensable for vertical ascents up a single run of rope. They can take the work and worry out of footlock climbs that are excessively high and risky. You can make vertical ascents as high as your line is fixed in the tree, and kick back to rest anytime without having to hold on to the line. Ascenders are also useful in some rigging applications. Of the different kinds of ascenders available, the "Gibbs" is more suitable for use in tree work. The design is simple and pretty foolproof.

DESCENDERS

Line descenders, also a rock climbing tool, can be used in place of the tautline hitch for rappels, using just about any variety of line. But pay attention, the drawback of these devices is that you must tether the line at all times. If you don't, or somehow lose your grasp on it, you'll go into a near free fall. A standard technique to avoid this hazard is to take a wrap on the feeding end of the line under your butt or around your leg and foot, which creates drag on the line. This is called abseiling and it greatly reduces your dependency on tethering the line by hand.

The Gibbs Ascender

Figure Eight Descender

The descenders are most useful in single-line descents where a regular tautline hitch, or prusik knot, would bind or seize on the line. The figure-eight descender is probably the most common type in use, but quite a few different kinds of descenders are available. Each has its own tricks you must learn in order to use them safely. Some are highly mechanical, such as the rack, and have many individual working parts; these I don't recommend. The figure-eight descender is the simplest to learn how to use, has no working parts, and even has the ability to let some knots pass through it. They're also useful as a brake for lowering limbs and wood. They can even be connected in series. As handy as these devices are for rappelling in single-line technique, you should never attempt to use them to work out of.

QUICK LINKS AND CARABINERS

These are lightweight alternative fasteners you may choose in place of heavier or bulkier kinds. The quick links are inexpensive, strong, lightweight, and easily obtainable from most hardware stores. They fasten and secure by a screw thread that, when snugged down by hand, is not as likely to fail as a snap would. But they are still a mechanical device you should keep an eye on. You can forget to screw them shut. The small sizes are ideal for fastening tools to your belt's accessory rings; you'll never twist off another cheap accessory snap. The three-eighths-inch size is more than adequate for lifeline fasteners; larger sizes can be used in some rigging applications. In effect, quick links are used much like a carabiner, although they are more heavy-duty and better suited for tree work. If you use carabiners, use only the heavy-duty locking types. I have seen the gates get twisted open on the light-duty carabiners from hardware clash on the belt and from line entanglements.

JAM KNOT AND THROWING HOOK

Traversing aids such as the jam knot and throwing hook are necessary for many aspects of tree climbing. The jam knot is nothing more than a wad of rope used expressly for jamming, or anchoring, the end of a line afar into a tight crotch. It's used primarily during long traverses where you're already supported by a climb line. About twelve to fifteen feet of half-inch rope doubled over, coiled, wrapped, and tucked into itself makes for a nice jam knot. A jam knot set properly in a tight crotch can provide a secure anchor. However, you must be able to distinguish one that is properly set from one that is not, and that takes

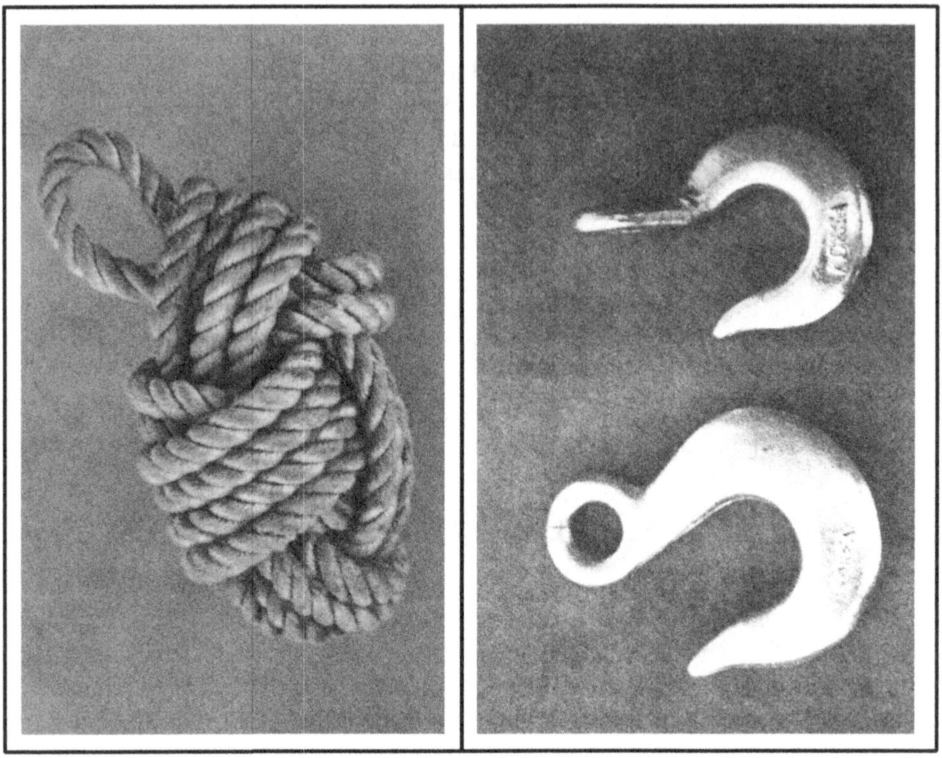

Jam Knot and Throwing Hook

experience. Don't rely on a jam knot for your sole support until you know the difference between the two.

The throwing hook can be used in place of the jam knot in certain situations. It can be set over limbs or smooth, open crotches and manipulated to catch its own line, providing a secure anchor wherever it can be fixed. After throwing the hook over a limb, you can change its orientation by twisting the line and then throwing a short shock wave down the line by snapping it. In this way, the hook can be turned around while maintaining its current elevation. Throw an underhand rolling loop to catch the line in the hook. Snug on the line easily. After a little practice you'll figure it out. These hooks can also be used to rig parts of the tree you're working off. They are commonly called slip hooks and are used for runs of chain. They come in many sizes and are available in all hardware stores. I have found that the position of the eye on the hook affects the ease in which the hook snares the line when you snug it up. So, on some of my hooks I twisted the eye around by heating it. But you can purchase slip hooks with the eye positioned both ways.

THIMBLES

The thimble is many tools in one. As a climbing aid, it enables the climber to do work from the climb line when there is no limb or crotch suitable to tie into. In rigging it can be used as an axis point, similar to a block, to run and pull line through. There are a lot of ways you can rig a thimble and a lot of things that can be used like a thimble. The important thing to remember is that any thimble should have enough surface area to brake some of the load in the line without creating a hard bite. This greatly reduces line wear and makes line control much easier. Throughout the book you'll see frequent references to the use of thimbles as climbing and rigging aids.

TELESCOPIC RODS

These are usefill to help you rig and retrieve lines in out-of-reach places. You can make a small telescopic rod out of the backpack fishing rods that collapse into sections. With the line guides removed, these rods can collapse down even shorter. A small tubular carrier can be fastened to an attachment ring on your belt to carry these rods. Cut a few inches off the tips to stiffen it up. Glue a small piece (about two inches) of solid number six copper wire, or the equivalent, with epoxy, into the tip. This wire tip can be bent into shape to snare the lines. Telescopic rods are rather light and break easily if you try to land something big with them. Keep the strain straight and they will pull more weight without breaking. Heavy-duty telescopic rods and poles are available in paint and hardware stores. Although they are heavier and bulkier, they are more practical when you need more strength.

BACKPACKS

For long or extended climbs, it's not a bad idea to sport a lightweight day pack in which to carry provisions. Food and drink are sometimes necessary for endurance climbs, along with the little things that make the work and climb easier. In my pack you'll always find a sharp knife, black tape, extra throw line and weights, and sometimes ascenders, descenders, fasteners, and the like. A pack can accommodate all these things and make it much safer to keep them together without damage or loss. When I get to a work area, or rest area, I'll hang the pack on a limb. If you're working or climbing at heights of over 200 feet for long periods of time, it's not a bad idea to tote a small fishing reel in your pack with enough line in it to reach the ground. Cold drinks, eats, and light lines can easily be retrieved with it. A good reel to use in tall timber is the Penn Senator 1/0, or an equivalent, primarily for it's free spool capabilities. But the light weight fly reels may prove the better choice in the smaller trees.

LINE GUNS

For setting lines beyond the range of human throwing ability, there are a number of different apparatuses available. A fishing rod and reel can cast a line as far as a person can be accurate, but it's only effective for horizontal casting. Overhead casting with a rod and reel is not impossible but it is somewhat difficult and takes a lot of practice to be accurate. For greater accuracy you can use a bow and arrow with a spinning reel attached. One thing about the bow is that it is infinitely adjustable in its power range depending on how hard you reef on it. A bow and arrow enables you to have a great deal of accuracy when setting lines in tight places.

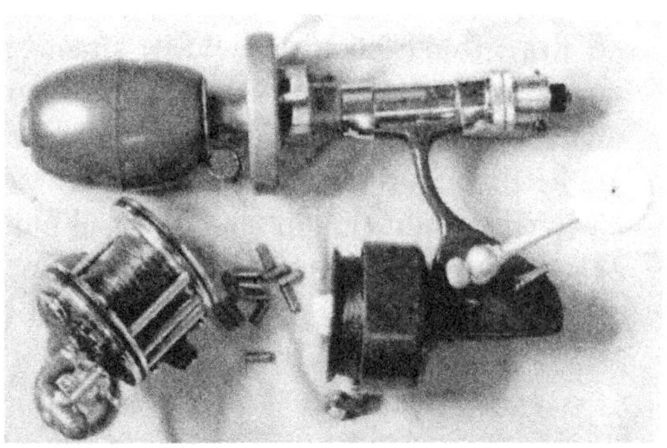

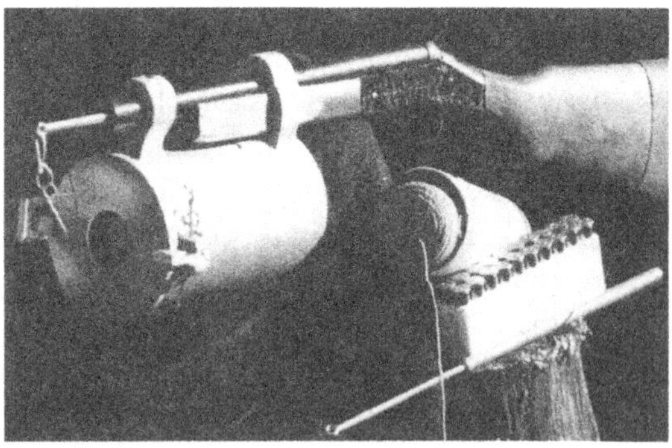

The twenty-two caliber line gun with spin reel combination can shoot at vertical heights straight up over 160 feet, pulling forty-pound monofilament line. This particular setup is made from the "Retriever Trainer" device that is used for training dogs to retrieve. The projectiles are plastic or canvas dummies. The addition of the spinning reel and seat is the only modification. The Penn 706 spin reel with manual bail is best suited to the gun because of the shock it inflicts. Automatic bails will trip from it and you will break a lot of line using them. The Retriever Trainer comes with light, medium, and heavy loads that make it possible to regulate the power and range of the shot to a certain degree. If you want to go all out, the 45-70-naval-arms line gun can shoot its projectile and line up to nine hundred feet. They're rather expensive and each shot runs up to twenty-five dollars—the cost of the line as well as the possible loss of the projectile. Line winders for the unit are available through the manufacturer but are rather expensive in themselves.

Chapter 10

Cutting Tools

The cutting tools used in tree work include a variety of hand saws, power saws, pole saws, pole pruners, loppers, shears, and even the ax. At different times, one or the other will prove more efficient and less tiring to use.

PULL SAWS

The draw cut or pull saws are the more commonly used hand saws. These saws range in size, length, tooth number, and tooth set. The one feature common to all is that they have a thin, curved blade with teeth set at a rake, in order to cut on the pull stroke. The tooth spacing of the larger of the pull saws is about four points to the inch. Those equipped with gullets, bull saws, and one-man crosscuts are meant for heavy-duty work and fast cutting. The gullets clean the sawdust from the cut and help considerably to keep the saw from binding. The efficiency of these saws is not to be underestimated; they can keep up with some of the small power saws used in tree work.

These saws don't break down and don't weigh much. They are much safer to use than power saws, they don't use gas or oil, they are dependable, and they keep you in good shape. Where you have to do a lot of heavy cutting, such as flush-cutting large stubs, the power saw may be a more practical choice over the hand saw. However, most climbers who have a lot of heavy cutting to do will use a hand saw in conjunction with the power saw when the latter proves to be unsafe in certain positions and when tripping dynamic cuts.

The smaller pull type saws are meant for light cutting. They make a fine, smooth cut in small leads where the larger pull saws rip and tatter them. Such fine cuts require a different stroking technique than the

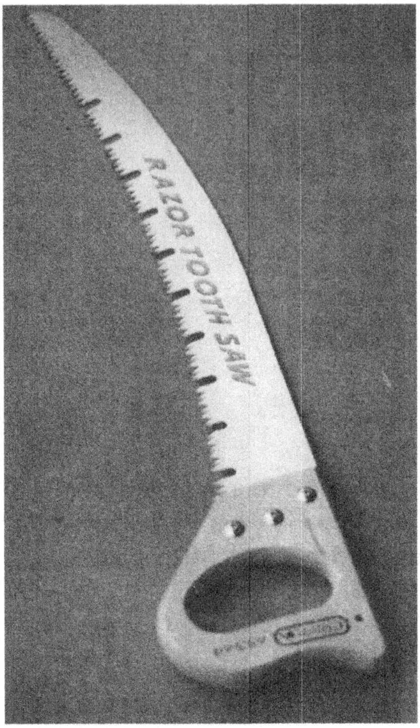

bigger saws. They usually entail quick or rapid strokes with a light touch, whereas you often get a two-handed grasp on the bigger saws and bear down with longer and slower strokes. In many small pull saws, the blade folds inside the handle. They're lightweight and you don't need a scabbard in which to carry them, so they're easy to pack on the belt's accessory snap. You will find, though, that a scabbard is essential to carry the larger pull saws. The rake of the teeth tends to grab and catch everything they touch. But scabbards are large and bulky to carry on the belt. And if they get turned over you may lose the saw anyway. For these reasons, many climbers don't use scabbards. Instead, they carry their saw on the belt snap by a loop of polypropylene rope fitted through the handle.

The new anti-friction style blades on some brands of pull saws have no set in their teeth, yet they cut extremely well without binding. This is possible because the teeth are the thickest part of the blade. The blade is made of hardened steel that doesn't bend without breaking. In spite of that, the unique grind in the teeth and the blade design makes these saws most efficient. They are extremely sharp; a slip or fumble can result in a cut to the bone.

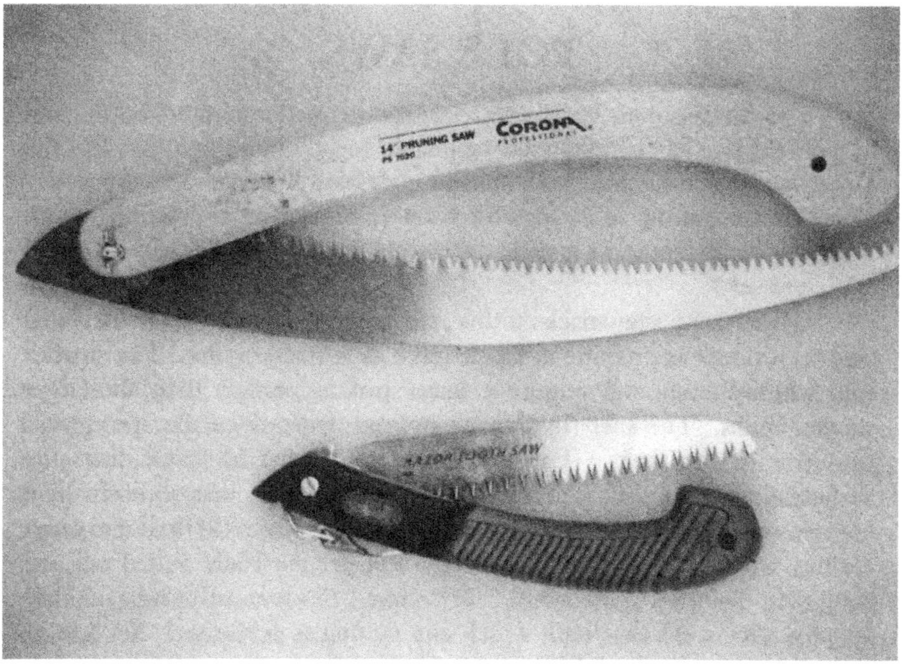

The rake of the teeth on pull saws can hold a branch from slipping off the blade allowing a climber to reach out and pull small branches to them. The larger pull saws can grasp and hold large limbs when the tip is driven into them. This is a practice that is useful in pulling out hangers that may be out-of-reach; it can also aid you in getting around in the tree when you're suspended by the climb line. The rake of the teeth on these saws is also useful for retrieving hand lines, climb lines, bull lines, and throw lines. Only one tooth need touch the line to catch and snare it. Be careful not to damage the lines.

PUSH SAWS

The push and push-pull hand saws are other types to choose from. The push type are meant for lighter cutting, have wide, straight blades, and finer tooth-spacing and set. The wide blade helps to prevent buckling on the push stroke, but it still happens. Force is not needed to cut with the push saws as much as a smooth and steady rhythm is. They are more efficient where you have to reach out and cut small whippy leads one-handed. The way things are going right now, it looks as if the push saw is headed for extinction.

POLE SAWS

Pole saws consist of a small pull-type blade mounted on the end of a pole. Most can be extended as needed for various situations. But the longer you extend a pole saw, the more awkward it becomes, especially when under-cutting a limb from a horizontal reach. The blades on pole-saw heads come in a wide variety of lengths, tooth spacing, tooth rake, and set.

There are a few tricks to the pole saw if you have never used one before. It does not require as much force as it does rhythm. The smaller and whippy limbs will require a faster stroking action than the larger stouter limbs. The exact rhythm or stroking depends on the springiness and size of the limb. The stroking action must be faster than the frequency of the limb. It should be noted that small, whippy limbs have a higher frequency than bigger ones. Until you learn to find the exact rhythm it takes to use a pole saw, you will get the blade pulled out and bound in the cuts quite often. Of course, the type of blade you use directly affects the ease with which any cutting is performed. It's best to have at least a couple of different blades for both the large and small cuts. Some of the newer blades referred to earlier have found their place in this specialty cutting tool. One such blade is even equipped with a hook on its tip to prevent pulling through the cut. It also aids well in hanger removal.

There are various kinds of pole saws, poles, and pruner combinations. The telescopic poles are convenient because they can be extended to the desired length without having to pack extra sections. However, they lose some of their efficiency at their maximum extension because the pole tapers and becomes weak. Sectional poles are stronger but heavier to use. They can be extended to greater lengths without losing as much transmitted force. The fiber-glass sectional poles are superior to any of the wood and aluminum types you can obtain. Some people may disagree on this. These fiberglass sectional poles are expensive but worth the extra cost for their lightness, durability, and dielectric properties. Aluminum poles are not safe to use in trees in the vicinity of power lines. You can electrocute yourself with just one goof-up. Even fiberglass and wood poles will conduct electrical current when they are dirty and damp. Pole saws with a pruner-head combination can be more trouble than they're worth. If you need a pole pruner, it's best that it be a separate unit. The added weight of the pruner head plus the rope will greatly diminish the efficiency of the saw in cramped conditions. Most pole-saw heads have a hook that can be

used to hang the saw on a limb or to grasp and pull out hangers with. Although the hook may be a hindrance at times, in the long run it will help more than hinder the climber.

POLE PRUNERS

Pole pruners are the climber's other choice for cutting small leads at extended reaches. The pole pruners are meant for lighter cutting than the pole saw, but some models can cut up to one-and-three-quarter- inch limbs. The average-sized pruner head will cut a one-inch limb. Pole pruners can make clean cuts in the fringe of small leads without the ripping, tearing, and frustration associated with pole saws in the same. You can jam the hook on the larger-sized limbs that won't quite fit inside it. Another way to cut these limbs is to hold the pruner head on the limb with a steady and firm pressure and work the blade into the limb. The blade will nip the limb and make an opening that will allow the hook to slip over it and complete the cut. This technique may have to be repeated before the hook can be secured and a clean cut obtained. Cutting oversized limbs too large for the pruner head can leave some ragged-looking cuts in the tree, especially if the limb rips off before the hook can be secured. Such methods have their place if the limb in question is merely part of a larger limb to be removed and, as such, will not be part of the finished product. In cases like this, many larger limbs that the pruner head cannot cut cleanly can be nipped by the blade and then broken off by reaching farther out on the limb and pulling on it with the hook. The blade of the pruner fractures a part of the limb so that it will break off there when it's pulled on.

The angles at which the pruner head makes the cuts directly affects the ease with which they can be made. Larger limbs within the capacity of the pruner head will always cut easier when the blade cuts them from the side and top. This way, the hook will be around the bottom of the limb to keep it from ripping and gravity will assist you by pulling the limb down. When cutting from below, the weight of the limb will rest on the blade and can actually prevent finishing the cut. It can even jam the blade. This can happen even with limbs within the normal capacity of the pruner head. So pay careful attention to your angle of attack. To unjam a stuck blade, the pole should be worked back and forth in the same direction that the blade pivots and in no other way. Working the pole to the side will spring the mechanism and cause the blade to mismatch with the hook, creating a condition called a tweaked pruner head. A tweaked pruner head cannot make clean cuts and leaves many limbs with rips and tears. When the cuts are made from underneath, ripping and tearing is not as prevalent, even with a tweaked head. The blade enters from the bottom first, undercutting the limb and then finishing through the top. Such cuts with a good pruner head will generally pop the limb off the cut cleanly. When cut from the side or top, the limb will always hinge. Knowing this will give you the chance to direct the hinging of most of the work. When I was doing line-clearance work this was a trick of the trade because you can control the direction of hinging and keep the limb out of the power lines. The limb will always move opposite the entry of the blade. You can even vary it to a degree by getting the work to sway a certain way before you cut it. You can do this with small tops and the ends of limber limbs. The idea is to time the cut with the sway of the limb or top. Besides keeping the work out of the power lines, this technique can also have some outstanding benefits such as getting your brush to fall out of the tree instead of down in it.

The pole pruners have the unique feature of being able to grasp and hold on to things. It's much like a third hand at times. Whatever fits inside the hook can be held from falling out by the blade being bit part way into it. This is useful for pulling out hangers and retrieving ends of rope that are out-of-reach. It can even allow the climber the chance to rig the rope into a top or the outer reaches of a limb. Although the practice of grasping a rope with the pole pruners is not recommended because of the damage it can do to the rope, it is acceptable to grasp the ends.

When tying the pole pruner on a line, be sure to tie the line on the pole itself or the actuation lever. The line should never be tied on or inside the hook for obvious reasons. This goes for carrying the pruners by hand also. You should never carry them with a finger inside the hook. All it will take to cut a finger off is for the pull rope to get caught. Most climbers place a series of knots or loops on the pull rope to aid their grasp on it. Without them it can be difficult to complete large cuts where you have to pull hard on the line. When making large cuts, a climber will often position themselves so they can grasp the rope with both hands and anchor the butt of the pole against their hip, thigh or leg.

LOPPERS AND SHEARS

Other cutting tools that may come in handy are the loppers and hand shears commonly used in gardening and pruning work They are well suited for tree work where you have detailed cutting to do. Loppers and shears range in size and design. They can effectively take the place of the pole pruners where you need clean cuts but not the reach. They can also cut in tighter places where the pole pruner's lever arm gets in the way of some limbs. The length of the handles, though, may prove to be a hindrance in themselves. Heavy-duty ratcheting loppers can cut up to three inches, but their use in the tree is questionable. The chief advantage of these tools is that they make clean and precise cuts. The hand shears are designed to cut shoots about as big as your finger, but you can cut larger ones if you bend or pull the work away from the blade as it enters the wood. A good source for loppers and shears is Wolf Garten USA, 5017 Boone Avenue, Suite 200, Minneapolis, MN, 55428, www.wolfgarten.us. Their anvil loppers are fantastic quality tools.

About the only care that the loppers and shears need is to be kept sharp and lubed. There is one thing that neither of these tools need and that is tweaking of the blade and hook. These tools are very similar to the pole-pruner hook and blade. They are not cheap; an inexperienced person must remember to work them like the pole pruner in the event they get stuck in a cut. They will get stuck at times and, in order to free them, the blade and hook must be moved only in the direction that they pivot. Sharpening of the pole-pruner loppers and shears is essentially the same. The only difference is if the blade has a full profile or hollow grind to it. Blades with a full profile take the most work to sharpen. When they become dull, the profile has to be brought down before the edge of the blade itself is sharpened. To sharpen the edge without bringing down the profile will result in a temporarily sharp but increasingly blunter blade—a blade that requires a lot of force to cut with. Blades with a hollow grind to their profile need only the edge itself sharpened. On either type of blade, when you sharpen the edge, just take off enough metal to get it sharp and no more. To sharpen the exact edge takes but a few keen strokes at a slightly steeper angle than the profile. The file should attack the blade from the edge towards the profile. The strokes should be even from one end of the blade to the other. This way, maximum blade life can be expected and, of course, the most efficient cutting. Many professionals use wet and diamond stones to sharpen their blades with. The blade needs to be replaced when it no longer matches up to the hook when fully closed. The hook on these tools needs minor sharpening too. It doesn't take much to sharpen the hook, and a sharpening will last a long time. Use a round file and run the strokes evenly from the low, inside portion to the upper outside. Don't overdo it or the life of the entire unit can be drastically reduced.

THE AX

The quality of trimming with an ax is questionable. But the ax can't be beat for busting out the deadwood in trees. The head of the ax is mostly used, but sometimes the blade side is needed to start a fracture on the tougher limbs. Extra care must be practiced when chopping with the blade; a miss can result in cutting yourself or your lines. An ax of three to four pounds is easy to work with in the tree. The length of the handle is not so important but the longer ones afford extra reach. The ax can be carried on a hook that is fastened to the belt, and a tether line can be fastened to the end of the handle. The line need only be long enough not to shorten your reach.

Sharpening the ax is much like sharpening the blade on the pruners and loppers. With the ax, two sides form the profile and the cutting edge runs between. Grinders really shouldn't be used unless the person using one is exceptionally light on the touch and has a keen sense of what the grinder is taking off. Most of the sharpening of an ax takes place on the profile of the blade. What the ax is used for determines the profile needed. An ax used for splitting wood will need a blunt profile in comparison to an ax used for chopping wood or cutting limbs. The edge

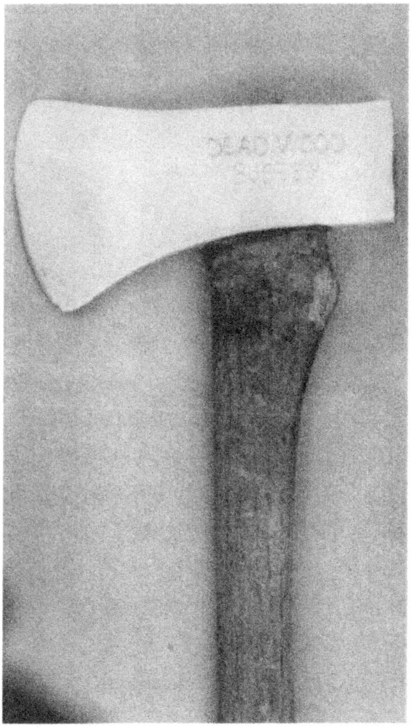

itself takes but a few keen strokes of the file to sharpen it. The strokes on the cutting edge should be at a little steeper angle than the profile. They should run smoothly from one side of the blade to the other without any flat spots between.

CHAINSAWS

Throughout the chapters on cutting the tree, emphasis is put on the safe use of the power saw. Ground experience is prerequisite to aerial handling of a chainsaw. You'll gain confidence and feel of the tool, and thus be better qualified at using it in a tree for the first time. The beginner and novice alike should also have experience and be adept with climbing techniques before using a power saw in a tree, in order to know how to set and maintain a stable working position. There are more requisites, including knowledge of knots, rigging theory, and execution of dynamic cuts. You risk an accident being up a tree with a power saw if you lack this knowledge.

When using a power saw in a tree, it should run well and be sharp. A poorly running, dull saw up in a tree is an omen for disaster. It is

Chainsaws and saw handling in vertical work.

frustrating and tiring to have a saw that is hard to start and runs poorly, let alone dull. The saw should be capable of idling down so the chain does not run. A climbing saw should have a workable kill switch that can be reached without any hesitation or fumbling. Ideally, the kill switch should be located near enough to the throttle so it can be reached with the same finger or thumb. There are times when certain dynamic cuts have to be triggered off under the full power of the saw and the saw shut down the instant the cut separates (See **Chapter 16— Catapulting Action**). The saw should also have an antithrottling lock in the handle to prevent accidental throttling when sticks or twigs get caught in the pistol grip. It happens. The saw should have a chain brake for kickback prevention. Some climbers don't like chain breaks because they can be activated by other things besides kickback. The chain is an influential factor in kickback. Ideally, you should use a full compliment 1/4-.325-round chain on the small saws. It has the best reputation for not kicking back. The saw should be well-balanced. A well-balanced, small saw is much safer to operate with one hand. Most climbers carry small power saws on a snap and ring connected to their belt. They should always, of course, be shut off when carrying them that way. The larger power saws are usually tethered on a rope connected to the belt ring by a snap or similar fastener. The snaps should be of the locking type and distinguishable from your regular climb line and safety snaps. A climber's saw should have a bar's length that will reach through a cut without having to double back around to finish it. This allows you to make the majority of your cuts from one side. This is one of the most important factors affecting the precision and performance of your cuts.

Chapter 11

Chain Filing and the Chain Grinder

In order to critique your ability to handle the power saw, you must first have a saw that can cut clean, fast, straight, and true. A poor cutting saw is of no advantage to anyone, particularly for the beginner who can't distinguish the difference between a saw that cuts so-so and one that cuts well. The beginner needs everything in their favor while learning how to handle the saw. To facilitate this, the beginner should learn how to sharpen their chains properly.

PITCH, GAUGE, AND COMPLIMENT

PITCH

Because there are small and large saws alike, you'll find different sizes or pitches of chain to match. Whenever you buy new chain, sprockets, and bar tips, the pitch of all the components must match. The pitch of a chain is measured by dividing the distance between three consecutive rivets in half. Chain pitch for small saws range from 1/4- to .325- to 3/8-inch. On the larger saws, the pitch ranges from .404- to 1/2- to 3/4-inch.

GAUGE

Chain gauge is measured in thousandths of an inch. This is the thickness of the drive link and the width of the slot it runs through between the rails of the bar. Chain gauge ranges from .050-, .058-,

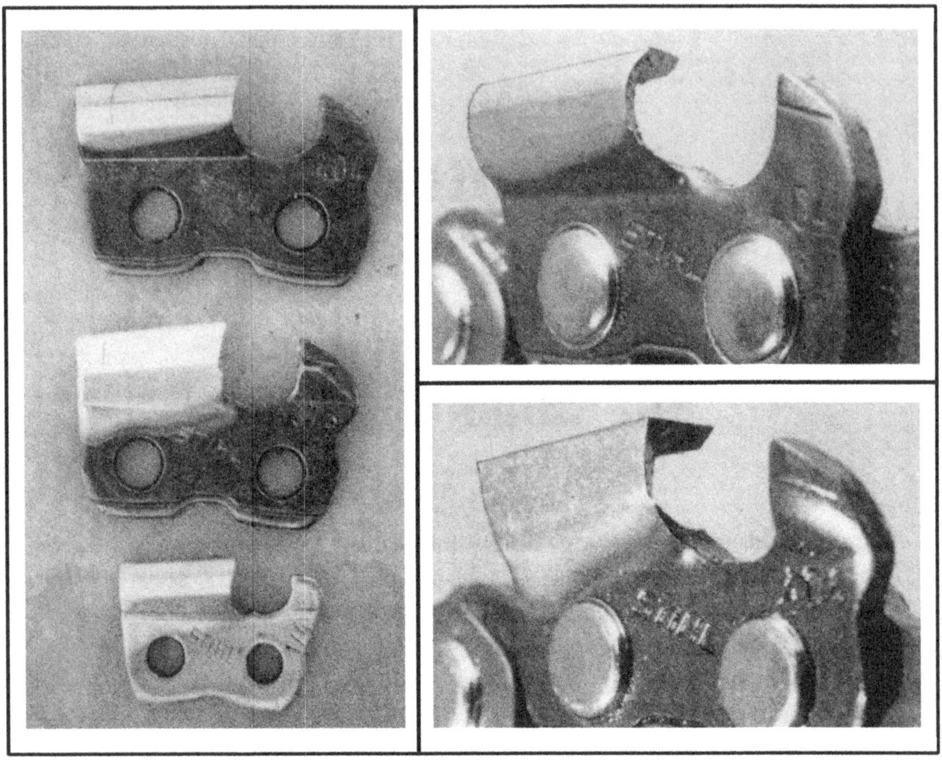

.063-, up to .122- thousandths of an inch. When you buy chain, keep in mind its gauge as well as its pitch.

CHAIN COMPLIMENT

Chain compliment is the order of assembly of cutters on a chain. There are basically three types: full compliment, semi-skip, and full skip. A full complement chain has the most cutters arranged alternately throughout its length. Having more cutters makes a smoother cutting chain, which, in turn, makes it safer to use. Most saws you'll buy off the shelf are outfitted with the full compliment unless you specify otherwise. In clean cutting conditions you'll get a long service life out of a full-compliment chain because there are more cutters to share the work.

A semi-skip chain has pairs of cutters arranged along its length with an extra driver between each pair. This is an intermediate choice for the power-saw user. It's better suited for larger saws that pull long bars.

Full-skip chains are found primarily on the large production falling saws. It has roughly a third fewer cutters in any length compared to a full compliment. The reason for this is that it performs better in big cuts than the full compliment. A full-compliment chain will stall or drag in a long cut because it has more cutters, more resistance, and more chips to pull out. If you use a full-skip chain for brush cutting, though, you'll find that it cuts more roughly and is potentially hazardous.

SAW CHAIN MYTHS

Keeping all the cutters on a saw chain even with the shortest ones is a myth. If there are just one or two odd short cutters on the chain, bringing the rest down to match will be a waste of chain, time, and money. An odd short cutter on the chain won't hamper the overall performance of the chain. But most persons that file chain habitually sharpen one side shorter than the other. In this case, the longer side should be brought down to match the shorter. To minimize differences, the beginner is advised to improve the platform and stance they file from. This will be discussed later.

Top plate angle governs how well a chain cuts. This is another myth. Minor intolerances in cutter angles and profiles will not interfere drastically with cutter performance. There is a margin of error within which you can effectively work. Many other factors besides a specific top plate angle govern how well a chain cuts. Filing aids and guides in themselves can be responsible for wasting chain because most beginners keep filing a cutter long after it may be sharp, just to match the angle on a guide. One filing aid that I recommend for the beginner is the Granberg File-N-Guide. This guide clamps on the bar and rigidly holds the file and cutters in position. It's precisely calibrated—a beginner can get a factory-perfect sharpness using it on their round chains. After using the guide for a while, the beginner will be able to wean themselves from it and begin to sharpen freehand.

CUTTER PROFILES

There are two basic types of saw chain in use today: the round chain and the square chain. Close examination of the two reveals the main difference to be found in the outside leading corner and side plate of the cutter. From a frontal view, the round chain best resembles a gouge. In effect, it performs similarly. Nearly all small power saws are outfitted with round chain. It's the easiest to sharpen and the safest to use. The square chain, in contrast, is found primarily on the larger professional falling saws used in the woods. From a frontal view, it resembles a chisel more than a gouge; the term chisel is a synonym for

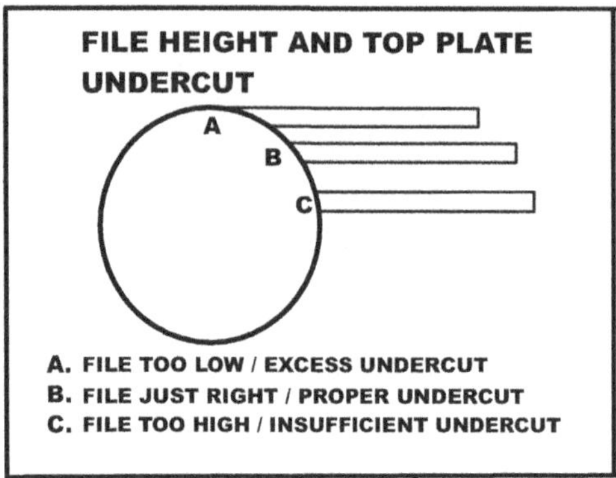

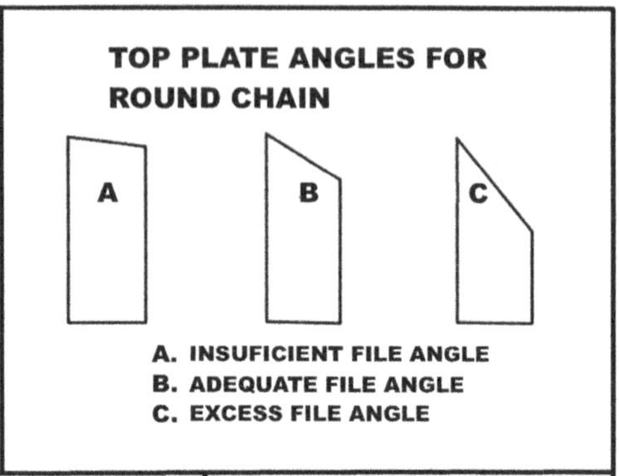

the square chain. This difference produces a much smoother and cleaner cut than that of the round chain.

ROUND CHAIN

When sharpening a round chain, use a round file. For the different sizes of round chain, specific sizes of round files are needed to produce the proper profile in the cutter. Even in one size of round chain, a larger file is used to sharpen the first half and, as the cutter is shortened by many sharpenings, a smaller file is used to sharpen the latter half. This is because the cutter gets progressively smaller towards the back. All cutters are designed this way. It enables the larger leading portion to do the cutting without the back portion of the cutter dragging behind.

When sharpening round chain, the file attacks the cutter from behind. When the proper-size file is positioned correctly to the cutter, a number of things are accomplished in a single sharpening operation. First and most obvious, the top plate angle is maintained. For round chain it's thirty-five degrees. Less noticeable is that the side plate, its profile, and the undercut of both the top and side are also maintained. The portion in the craw of the cutter called the gullet is kept clean, too.

In order for all of this to fall into place, another prerequisite for the position of the file, besides its thirty-five-degree angle, is the height of the file above the top of the cutter. It is recommended that one-fifth to one-tenth of the file's diameter protrude over the top of the cutter. This governs the amount of undercut in the top plate and so-called outside corner of the cutter. The height of the file can be considered just as, if not more, important than the thirty-five-degree top plate angle. The degree of undercut on the side of the cutter is governed by the angle to which the top plate is filed. If the top plate is indeed filed to thirty-five degrees, then the amount of undercut in the side of the cutter will also be thirty-five degrees. It just so happens that the file height above the top plate produces the needed undercut of approximately thirty-five degrees, more or less, in that part of the cutter. The lower the file the more undercut there will be, but too low of a file will produce a hook in the side profile of the cutter, which makes for a grabby chain.

SQUARE CHAIN (CHISEL CHAIN)

Examination of a square chain's frontal profile will reveal that it actually squares with the corner. This frontal corner is the critical portion of the chain that performs the majority of the cutting. If it is not properly maintained, the square chain will not cut very well at all.

There are several types of files available to sharpen chisel chain. The three-corner and double-bevel files are designed specifically for it. But you can get satisfactory results even using a small flat-mill bastard file. These files attack the cutter from the front. The corners of these files are aligned to the corner of the cutter. Once the position of the file is correct, the corner will be maintained, plus the top plate angle, and the undercut of the top and side plate. The correct position of the file is where it yields factory profiles. It sounds simple enough, but there is a catch. The top plate angle, its undercut, and the side plate can all be significantly altered by minute shifts in the angle of the file, even without the file's corner leaving the corner of the cutter. Unlike the round file, the chisel files have flat sides, or planes, and that crazy corner. There are more relative angles to assume than with a round file. This is the reason for the difficulty that beginners encounter in hand-sharpening chisel chain. It takes some practice.

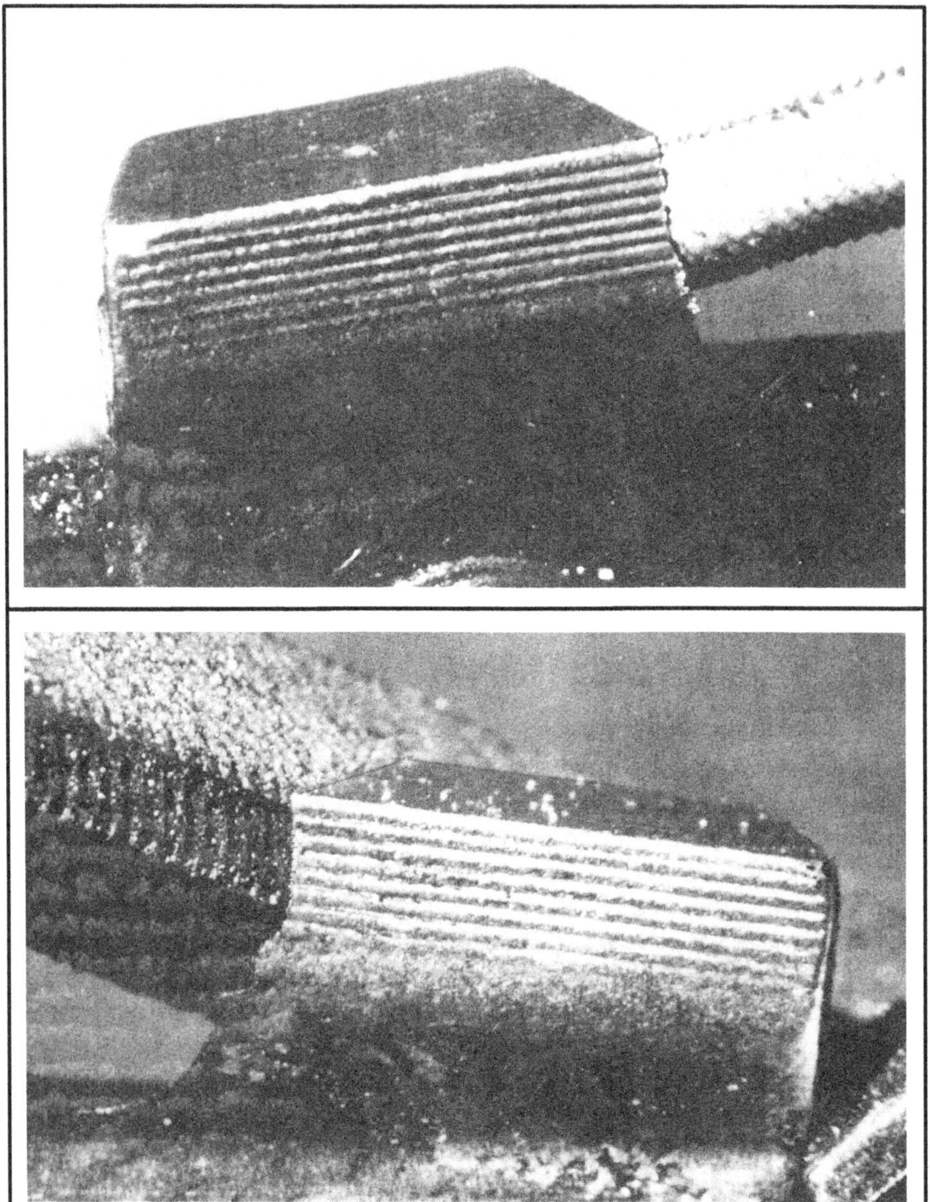

The “double bevel" and “three corner” files used for sharpening square (chisel) chain.

THE TANGLED CHAIN

No matter how tangled and confusing a chain gets, there are only two kinds of tangles; I’ll call them “A” and “B” tangles. Taken individually, each is quite simple to straighten, but in a long chain they can be combined in a multitude of ways and give even the most experienced sawyer a good lesson in patience and self control. The "A" tangle occurs whenever a span in the loop crosses. It seems to turn a loop of chain inside out. The "B" tangle occurs whenever the chain crosses over itself. In either tangle, two crossovers, or kinks, can be observed. How you straighten them is peculiar to each kind. In the "A" you pull the observed tangles apart and let the crossover pull, or drop out of the chain. In the "B" you merge the tangles together, so they will cancel each other out and the chain will straighten. Actually this is very easy when done one at a time, and that's what you must do, no matter how many there are, you take them out one at a time. Develop an eye to distinguish "A" from "B" tangles to know what you're dealing with. For the beginner, it helps to lay the chain on a flat surface while straightening it.

Enter the "C" tangle. This is a rare occurrence I've witnessed only once in 27 years. In this tangle the chain has also turned inside out so that the cutters are on the inside and the drivers are on the outside! As the chain will not cut very well this way it must be re-turned. To straighten a "C" tangle requires twisting the chain. Start by getting all the "A" and "B" tangles cleared out, then hold the chain with about one third between your hands (use gloves or rags) and trap the bottom of the large loop on the ground with your foot. Bring your hands close so the small loop droops down, with your hands pointed down, and rotate the small loop away from your knees and towards your face until it is vertical. Now remove your foot from the big loop, spread your hands a little and the bottom part of the big loop, which is still inside out, will invert itself towards your shins, stick straight up and fall back down leaving the chain re-turned. If the chain is too short (or too stiff) for this to work you may have to break and resplice the chain.

THE FILING PLATFORM

The position you file from and the rigidity of the filing platform greatly determines the ease of chain filing. Serious filing requires a comfortable approach. If your approach is uncomfortable, it'll show in the filing. The platform that you steady the saw on could be a stump, log, ground, bench, tailgate, or vise. Whatever it is, it should be rigid enough to support the saw and keep the bar and chain from rocking when you lay on the strokes with the file. This applies especially when using both hands on the file to bear down on a badly worn chain. The pressure you apply to make the file cut can tip a saw over if it's not supported properly. In a lightly worn chain such bearing down is not necessary. One hand can be used to steady the bar and chain on a marginally steady platform.

Your position to the filing platform is also important. If you cannot get in a good position to file, the platform will not be of any significance. Trying to find both at the job site can be difficult; you'll have to make some sacrifices and settle on a sturdy platform or a comfortable position. A good tool in such a situation is the common stump vise. This lightweight bar vise can be set firmly in any sound wood, allowing you the benefit of a good platform and a good position where otherwise you may get neither.

Once you are set and begin filing, make sure the chain doesn't wobble in the bar. You can adjust the slack in the chain to prevent wobble but bear in mind that a chain that is too tight is difficult to pull around the bar and will cut your fingers if you slip. Keep the chain loose enough to pull it around with two fingers. Then insert a stick, wedge, or other suitable device between the chain and lower bar rails to take up any excess wobble. When you pull the chain around the bar, pull it only in the direction that it naturally travels. Never pull a chain back in the other direction because it results in bad finger cuts.

DEVELOPING AN EYE FOR SHARPENING

The amount of sharpening needed in any chain will vary widely according to the degree of dullness or damage to the cutter. During any sharpening procedure, the person should have a developed eye for gauging how much sharpening is really necessary.

NORMAL WEAR

In a lightly dulled chain, the cutter's edge will shine. The dulled edge itself may only be a few thousandths-of-an-inch wide. Such a degree of dullness occurs during the course of normal wood cutting. Usually a light stroke, two or three with the file, will bring a cutter like this back up to a keen sharpness. As you work the file, take a close look to observe how much metal it's removing. In good light, the process of the file cutting a new edge on the cutter tooth can be observed with the naked eye. As soon as the shine on the cutting edge disappears, it's sharpened. The dulled edge can be observed better from different angles. When it is removed, the edge on the cutter will not reflect any light. After you develop an eye for it, you'll get much more service life out of your chain.

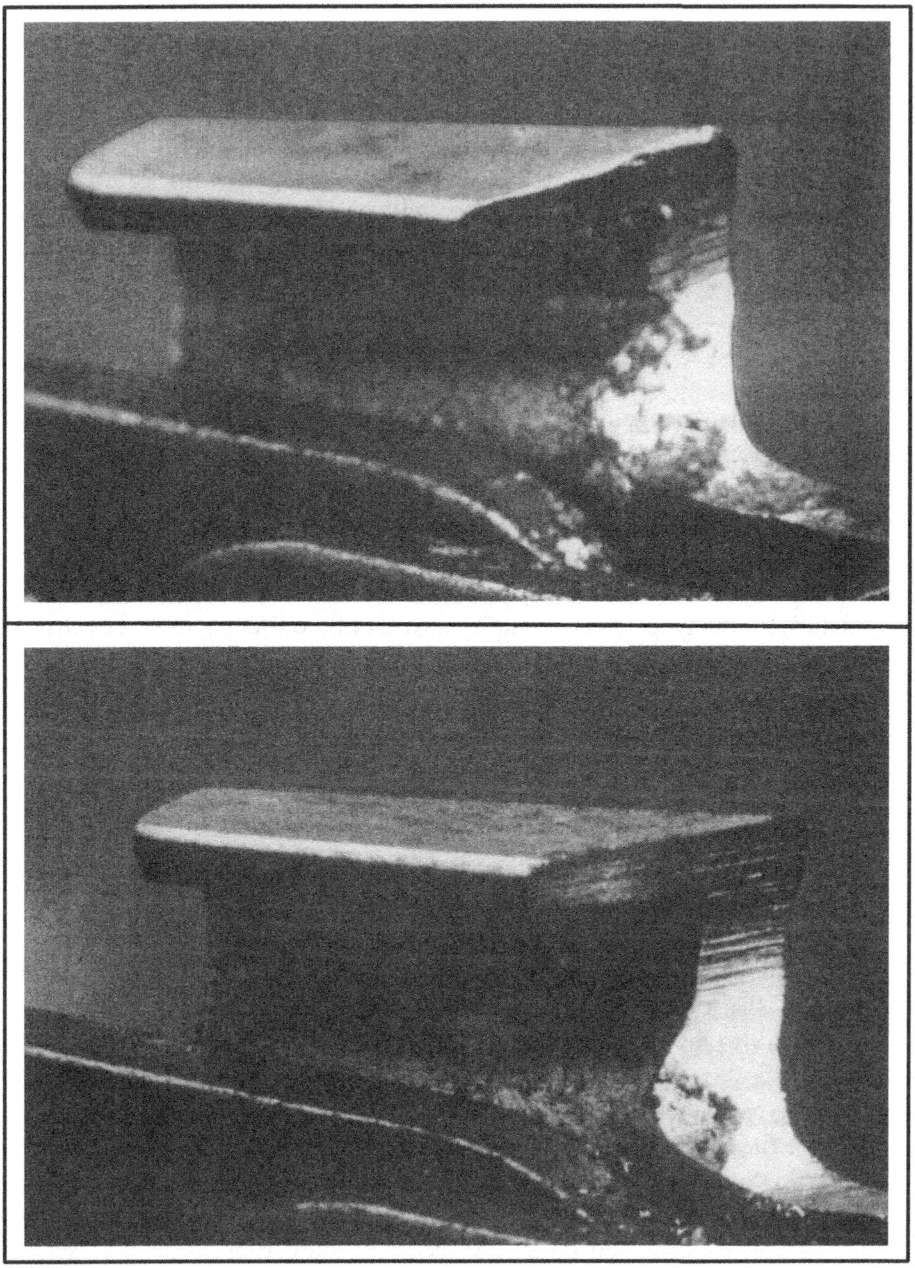

Normal Wear: Top, Shine on Cutter Edge-Bottom, Properly Sharpened

SILT

Silt damage varies according to how long you cut in it, but it doesn't have to do much to the chain before you realize it needs sharpening. Silt damage is more extensive than regular wear; this is obvious by the amount of shine on the edge of the cutter. Here again, you need not take off any more metal than necessary to remove the shine. The shine, in this case, can be up to five- or ten-thousandths-of-an-inch wide and require as many as a half dozen strokes of the file to remove. Sometimes the corner of the cutter will be worn back farther than the edge. If so, take the edge back as far as necessary to get a sharp corner. This is very important in chisel chain.

ROCK AND SAND

This damage is easy to see even without being in the right light to view it. In fact, such damage doesn't shine so much as the edge of the cutter is just scraped and worn back. There'll be scratches and gouges in the cutter with the chrome worn off, exposing the raw metal under it. Hand-filing a rocked chain can mean an hour or more of grueling work to restore. Hand cramps from pressing the file are associated with rocked chains. As many as twenty or thirty strokes of the file may be necessary to restore each cutter. This kind of filing can generate a lot of heat, making the cutter hot to the touch. A badly rocked chain is only worth restoring if it's fairly new. Otherwise, it should be replaced.

METAL DAMAGE

Metal damage consists of bent, broken, and deformed cutters that are often between cutters that never got damaged. Most of the time, metal-damaged chains are worth restoring, although they may never be quite the same again. The damaged cutters should be filed down until they're sharp and then the rest of the chain evaluated. It's not always necessary to take all the cutters down to the length of the shorter ones if they're few or oddly scattered between the good cutters. If the damage is extensive, it's best to replace the chain. Some bent cutters are difficult to start a file on because their profile can become altered and won't accept the file. Some of the cutters may also become hardened from the instant heat generated by striking the wire or nails in the wood. Such hardening of the cutters can roll back the teeth on numerous files. The actual hardness on the cutter may only be a few-thousandths-of-an-inch thick but it will destroy a file before it's taken off. If you have a chain with hardened cutters on it, you'll know right away. If there's some life left in the chain, a chain grinder will sharpen it and remove the hardened edge.

TIE STRAP DAMAGE

This can occur from the straps being nicked by the file or grinder. There's not too much you can do about it. Nicked tie straps can break and cause premature chain failure. Broken straps are easily fixed by resplicing the chain. At times you'll find broken straps between cutters that weren't even nicked. Most often, such broken straps will be where the chain was spliced together. This could happen because of the tension of the splice or how firmly the rivets are formed to hold the splice together. Most tie-strap breakage will occur when the chain is stuck in a cut and the operator tries to free it by pulling and prying with the bar.

DRIVER DAMAGE

Driver damage will occur when the chain is thrown off the bar and the sprocket or rim clashes with the drive links. In the large professional saws, driver damage can totally ruin a good portion of a chain. This is especially true of the sprocket-drive saws; the drivers themselves can be torn right off. Rim-drive saws are much more forgiving in this respect. The most damage they will inflict on the driver is an annoying burr that has to be hand-filed to remove. No matter how much hand-filing you do to remove all the nicks and burrs, the drivers will still fit tightly in the bar groove. The drivers will loosen up back to normal after a tank or two of gas is run through the saw. It's common practice to do this. It's difficult, though, to know the extent of the damage inflicted on the bar in some cases. Badly tattered drivers can produce a significant amount of wear on a bar.

KINKS IN THE CHAIN

Kinks in the chain will have the same effect on the bar as damaged drivers. A kink can wear on the bar for a much longer period of time and is not likely to straighten itself out. As long as there's a kink in the chain, you'll also be wearing the bar. Some kinks can be taken out of the chain by bending or hammering them out. If this is not possible, splice in a new section of chain where the kinks occur.

BREAKING AND SPLICING CHAIN

Breaking chain is not difficult as long as you have the right tools. Out in the field you can get by adequately with a vise grip chain breaker or a simple hand punch and anvil. Production anvils are slotted to

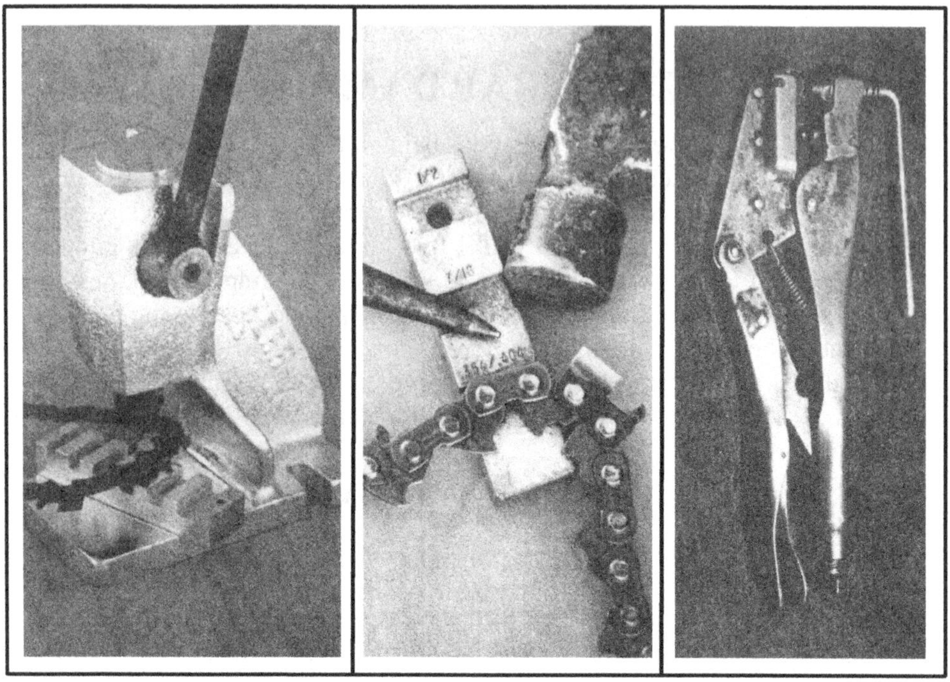

Chain Breakers

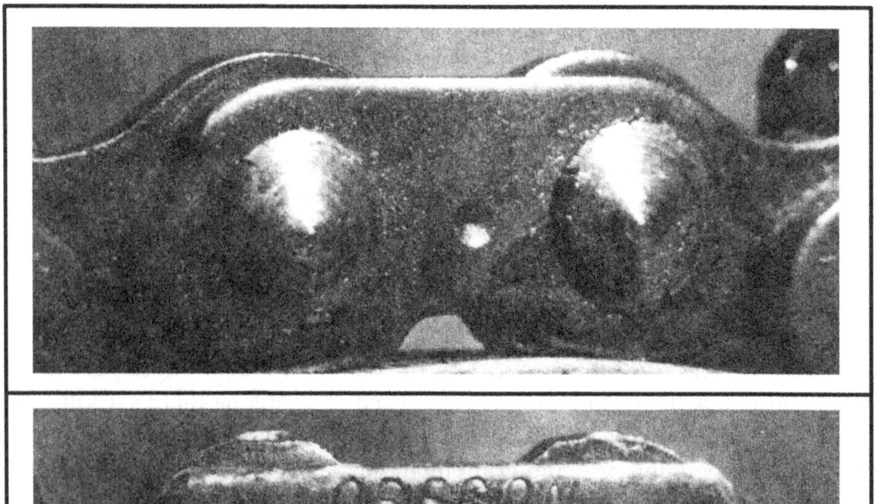

Spun Rivet "Top", Peened "Bottom"

accommodate different sizes of chain. The slots are inscribed with the pitch number. If you're not sure what pitch chain you have, lay the chain in each slot until the tie straps seat themselves in the proper one and the drivers straddle it. Before attempting to punch out the rivet, you can file the head of it down first. It greatly simplifies the hand-breaking operation. Without filing the head of the rivet down, you'll have to hit the punch hard to break the chain, which often results in smashed fingers and flung punches. Out in the field, if you have neither punch nor anvil, you can get by using a crescent wrench as the anvil and a nail for the punch. It's crude but effective.

The bench model chain breakers are the way to go if you do a lot of breaking and splicing. With them, you don't need to file the head off the rivets, unless your anvil is worn out. The shoulders of the slots are chipped away on a worn-out anvil. This causes the top shoulder of the drivers to jam inside the slot when the pressure of the breaker is exerted on the rivet, resulting in kinks and tattered nerves. When breaking chain at a cutter tooth, make sure that the chain is set properly in the slot and the cutter tooth is on top. Breaking chain with the cutter tooth any other way can grossly distort and kink the cutter, tie straps, and drivers.

The splicing operations requires the necessary tie straps, occasional driver or cutter tooth, and a small ball peen hammer. Install the tie strap properly, taking care not to install it upside down. Next, set the chain on a steady, hard surface like the anvil. Smack the rivet squarely a couple of times to swell the head. Then, neatly peen the head of the rivet over with the ball end of the hammer. Avoid just smashing the rivet because the tie strap will not be drawn together properly. When the rivet head is peened properly, the tie strap will be drawn together snugly to the driver. It takes but a few minutes.

If you break and splice a lot of chain, you will prefer to use the bench model rivet spinner. It takes very little time to do both rivets, and the finish is much the same as the factory's. If you use a spinner, take a second to place a drop of oil on the rivet head before spinning it. Otherwise, the anvil in the spinner will chew up the rivet head and produce a crummy finish. When using the spinner, you can draw the strap snugly to the driver. If you go too far, it can create a stiff spot in the chain at that point. But not to worry, it will loosen up after running a little while.

THE GULLETS

In chisel chain, the gullets need periodic cleaning out to keep the chain cutting efficiently. The gullets only need be taken out as far as the corner of the cutter. Taking them out beyond that point will put a hook in the side profile of the cutter and may cause breakage of the tooth. A hook in the profile will also make for a grabby chain when cutting brush and such. When a person takes out the gullet, it should be scarfed at least at the same angle as the top plate angle. The reasoning behind this is that this portion of the cutter, although not involved in any major cutting by design, can help keep the sides of the cut clean if it has an undercut to it. This holds true especially if you do not get a full cut on the side plate in your regular sharpening. In this case, the act of cleaning out the gullet makes for a sharper side plate on the cutter. Double-beveled files do not cut deep enough through the width of the side plate. Thus, they produce a major protruding gullet in the craw of the cutter. Round files are used to clean out the gullets.

THE RAKERS

The rakers, or depth gauges, in either round or chisel chain, govern the amount of bite the cutter takes. As a cutter gets shorter from periodic sharpening, the rakers have to be brought down to keep the chain cutting properly. If you do not file your rakers down, the chain will cut less and less well. There are gauges available for adjusting the raker height. Use a gauge; an even raker height is essential to a finely tuned chain. If you do not have a raker gauge, you can take the rakers down freehand. If you do it this way, you'll have to count the number of strokes and carefully monitor the feel of the cut through the file. Don't take off too much. If you don't have a gauge for your rakers and you're curious about their height, rest a straightedge over a couple of cutter's top plates and insert a feeler gauge between it and the raker.

If you take too much off the rakers, the chance of kickback will increase, especially when attempting bore cuts. The saw will perform poorly when it's dogged up in big cuts. The chain will bite and grab. For limbing, however, a low raker height can increase performance. Overall, having the rakers a little high is better than having them too low. The kind of wood you're cutting will determine where the rakers should be set. Soft wood will accommodate a lower raker height, somewhere between thirty-five- and forty-five-thousandths-of-an-inch. A slightly higher raker height—from twenty-five to thirty-thousandths-of-an- inch —is necessary for good performance in hardwood. File the raker down as you would when sharpening a round chain; that is, attack it from the rear. The file will squeal and chatter across the top of the raker if you do it the other direction. After the raker height is adjusted, you will need to reform its profile. This is done simply with a couple of strokes over its leading edge to round it over. If you use a raker gauge and have had it for

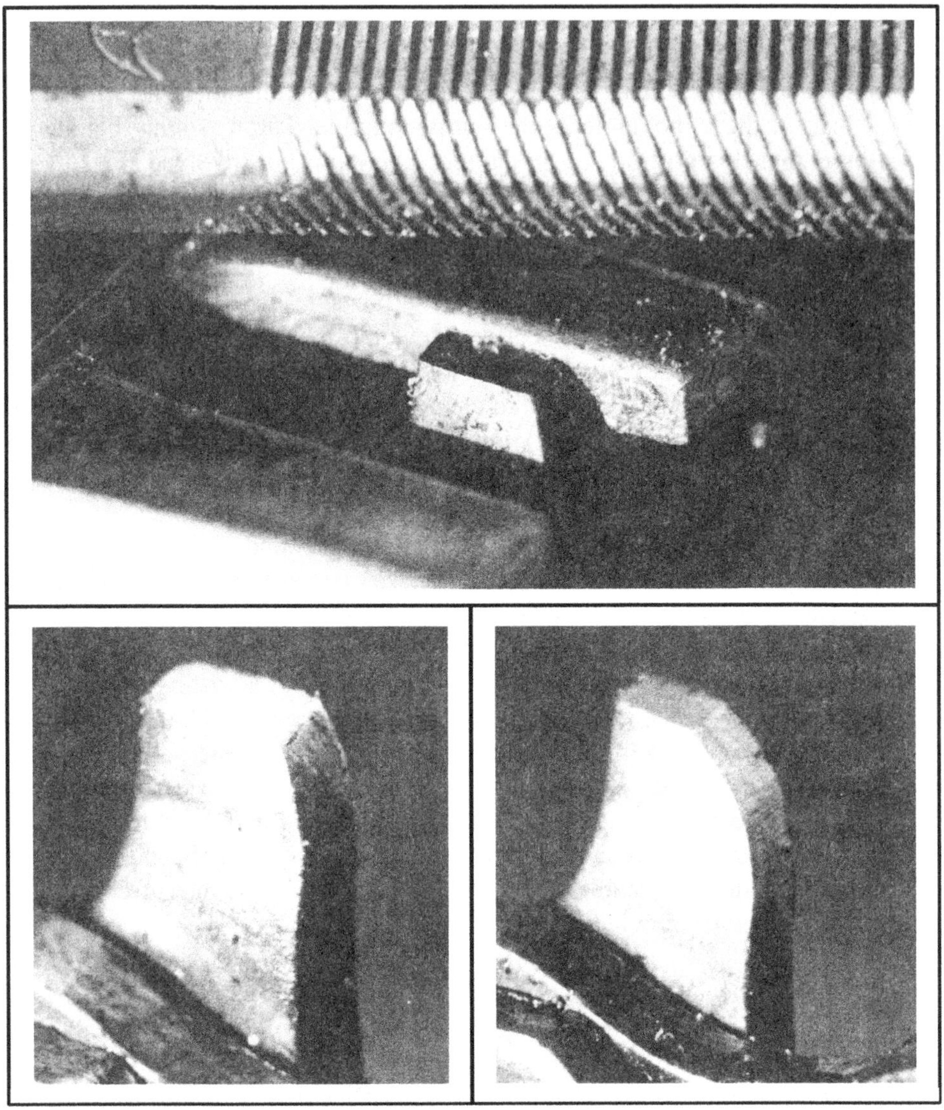

The Rakers

some time, take a careful look at it to see if it is becoming worn. The gauges themselves can become filed down, resulting in lower raker heights than indicated.

THE CHAIN GRINDER

If you get into professional timber falling, you may desire to sharpen your chains with a chain grinder. It makes sharpening saw chains much easier and faster.

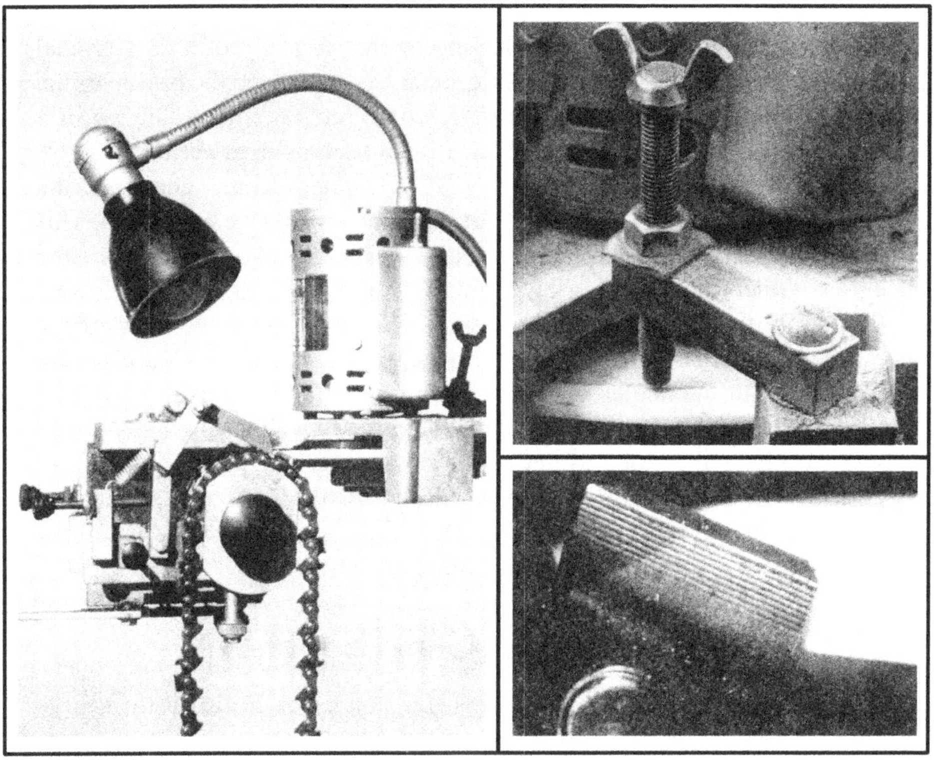

WHEEL PROFILES

Before you mount a grinding wheel, gently tap it with your fingernail or a small, hard object. This is to check for cracks in it. If there are no cracks in the wheel, it should ring clearly. If it clunks instead, there is a crack running through it somewhere. Do not use a cracked wheel. They will explode after they are mounted and the grinder is turned on.

After the wheel is mounted, you'll have to dress its profile. This is necessary upon the purchase of a new grinder or upon replacing an old wheel with a new one. Dressing the stone's profile on chisel grinders is done with the diamond-peg dressers mounted on the unit. There are two of them. One peg is for dressing the top of the stone, or for the top-plate angle. The other is for dressing the edge, or side-plate angle. The position of the pegs is adjustable and not preset at the factory. The purchaser of a new grinder must dial in the dressers to obtain the angles needed in the stone. Be gentle when dressing the wheel. Shape the stone in slow, light passes with the diamond-peg dressers. They'll last considerably longer this way. The preliminary setting of the diamond-peg dressers and the shaping of the stone's profile is a crucial part of learning how to use a chain grinder. As you shape the profile of the wheel, observe carefully how it affects the outcome of the angles in a cutter tooth. With my Silvey grinder, I finally set the pegs permanently to dress the stone with approximately a twenty-degree cut from the horizontal off the top of it, and about the same on the side or vertical. This produces nearly identical factory angles in the top plate and side of the cutter. Other models of grinders will require you to dress the stone differently to achieve the same angles. The stone angle, position of the rails, and cutter approach govern the grinding angles. Once you're satisfied with the angles you have, lock down the dressers and don't let anybody change them. One of the nice things about a chisel grinder is that you can dress the stone to get a full cut on the side plate of the chisel cutter. This is not possible with the design of the files used to sharpen chisel chain. All they can do is cut part of the side plate. This is a main advantage of the grinder over hand-filing chisel chain.

SHARPENING THE CHAIN

While learning how to dress the stone, you'll also learn a little about how the rails and stops work to position the cutter for sharpening. Experiment with them by adjusting, grinding, and observing. Adjust the stops and actuate the sweep lever to engage the cutter to the stone very slowly and carefully. There are two stop knobs to play with. One stop knob governs the range of movement in the swing arm, or sweep lever. It positions the rails that hold the chain to the tangent of the stone. The tangent can be confusing. As a grinding wheel gets smaller from use, the tangent can change. The position of the swing arm can also change it. The tangent has a direct effect on the angles to which the cutter is ground. Silvey grinders have calibrations to follow for setting the tangent adjustment. However, after you become familiar with the model of grinder you have, you may find a different tangent more to your liking. There is another stop knob which holds the cutter's position on the rail and controls its inward approach to the stone's profile. Each stop knob has an effect on the cutter's exact position. With chisel chain, the exact position you need is governed by the corner of the cutter tooth and the corner of the stone's profile. Bring the corner of the stone's profile and the corner of the cutter together. You can ruin many of the cutters on a chain if you are hasty. Even if you do it slowly and carefully, you'll probably ruin a loop of chain before you get the hang of it. This is one of the more difficult aspects of learning how to use the unit. You need good

A.

B.

C.

GRINDER / CUTTER PROFILES

A. CORNER TOO HIGH

B. CORNER TOO LOW

C. CORRECT CORNER AND CUTTER PROFILE

vision and a light touch on the controls. Trying to see the corner on the stone's profile can be hard in bad light. The gray stones are a little easier to use than the white in this respect.

Once you have the stops set just right, engage the cutter to the stone with the sweep lever or the cutter stop knob. In the past, I used the sweep lever to do it, until I found out that I could control the operation more precisely by presetting the sweep stop and using the cutter stop to engage the cutter to the stone. The amount of engagement of the cutter to the stone is often within one-eighth of a turn on the cutter stop knob. On some models of grinders you have to use one hand to hold tension on the chain so the cutter is held firmly in the rails and against the stop. The more expensive grinders hold the cutter automatically, so the cutter does not wiggle in the rails during the sharpening procedure.

If you are too hasty with the grinder, you will grind away a lot of chain and burn a lot of it up. Be gentle with it and your chains will last a lot longer. There is no reason why a person can't get as much life out of a chain by grinding as by hand-filing, though you may not believe it at first.

CONTAMINATION IN THE STONE

The profile of the stone will accumulate pitch, oil, and organic residues from the chain. These residues will build up and glaze the surface of the stone, having a number of negative effects on the chain. For example, overheating and burning of the cutter tooth; distortion of the cutter profile; and failure to cut the chrome. When you recognize the symptoms of stone contamination, redress it to a clean and fresh profile.

After a chain is ground, it may be necessary to take out the gullets and adjust the raker height. These two operations still demand some hand filing on the chain. If you have gullets to take out, you may want to do it before sharpening the chain, because cleaning the gullets often results in the round file hopping or slipping and catching the cutter profile and corner. After you have cleaned the gullets, ground the chain, and adjusted the raker height, you may want to clean the chain in solvent or saw mix; it gets heavily coated with grinding dust and filing particles in the process of sharpening it.

SNAPPING ON A CHAIN

This is a simple technique that eliminates the tedium of backing down the bar assembly to refit a thrown chain. However, it is only applicable to the bigger saws. Stand the saw on the end of the pistol grip, preferably against something. On rim drive saws, ensure that the chain drivers are properly engaged. Depending upon the size of the saw, place your knee or your foot against the lower side case, or bar. Apply pressure to brace the saw in place and then bow back the bar by pulling on the tip with your middle fingers. By bowing the bar in this manner it shortens it enough for you to use your thumb and index fingers to slip the chain back on the bar tip. Once the chain is fitted let the bar straighten. Then snap the drivers back into the rails. This procedure only takes seconds to do. As simple and convenient as the procedure is, take care to ensure no cut fingers by making sure that the saw won't slip or kick out of position as it is inclined to do on a hard surface. Brace it against something to prevent slippage. On grass or soft ground the pistol grip will dig in and secure the saw. You are also advised to use gloves.

Chapter 12

Entering The Tree

Entering the tree can be done in many different ways, but the beginner should start by learning how to use the fixed line. It is undoubtedly the safest method anyone can use and is relied upon for most trimming. The climb line can be fixed in the tree using the throw line. But the climb line itself can be thrown into the tree over short distances by heaving coils or using the throwing knot. If you have the line in a crotch or over a limb and the end isn't within your reach, you can get it down by throwing a rolling loop. A rolling loop is formed by drawing back on the line with your forearm raised and then propelling the slack you've drawn up the line with a smart forward thrust. This will get many a line to work through crotches and over limbs down to where you can reach it. It works on the exact same principle as the roll cast used in fly fishing. There are many styles of the rolling loop that you can learn, such as the overhand, the underhand, and the sidearm. Practice it, it's often used for setting and fixing lines in out-of-reach places during climbing and working.

If you use a throw line to fix the climb line, take note of the limb or crotch it is in, or over, and fasten the climb line to suit it. Direct knotting of the two lines will only enable the lines to pass through smooth or well-formed crotches and limbs. By hitching, tucking, or splicing the lines together, you're sure to pull them through crotches that most knots won't pass through. If the line is fixed over a limb, make sure that it's a strong limb with a positive or even angle to it. This will prevent the line from sliding or working its way out the limb. Avoid fixing the line over any stubs, dead limbs, or tight crotches.

How high the line is and where it is fixed in the tree determines the best method to enter it. Over short distances, the double-line techniques are preferred and, ultimately, safer. For long hauls, the single-line techniques are best and less fatiguing on a person.

DOUBLE-LINE TECHNIQUES

These vary considerably, but in most of them you rely on the taut line hitch to hold your position. The end of the climb line attached to your belt is considered the static side of the line, and the part that hangs below you is the running side. The tautline hitch can be fashioned from the tail end of the static side to the running part of the climb line within a comfortable reach, within a range of about twelve to eighteen inches. This distance can be referred to as the span. You don't want the span so long that the hitch is out of reach, but you don't want it too short, either. Your particular climbing belt will play a large role in determining the length. By pulling smartly on the running part of the line and simultaneously thrusting your body upward, you can make your way up the tree. For each bit of distance you gain, you slide the tautline hitch up the running part of the line to hold your position. This is called body thrusting, or cinching. It's a common technique in tree climbing, used to cover short distances and to shorten the length of your lines for working positions. While cinching, you'll find out how important the length of the span is. If it's too short, you gain very little for your efforts because you just can't pull very much running line. If it's too long, you'll have difficulty reaching to set your hitch each time and you can waste some of your effort. It won't take long to figure out the length you need to be comfortable.

You will require much less effort from the upper torso if you can gain footholds while cinching. Careful placement of the climb line affording a path up the tree with footholds will save you a lot of energy and work. Straight-up vertical cinching where you have no footholds is most tiring and tends to be done only over very short distances. However, looping the running part of the line around one foot and bearing down on the line makes it easier. Your legs will do most of the hauling on the line this way, and it will be less fatiguing on your upper torso. If you have a considerable distance to climb straight up, then the use of an ascender on one foot is highly recommended. It makes the work much easier by eliminating the loop procedure.

Sometimes there is someone on the ground to help pull on the running part of the line. If you want to take advantage of it, a spring-loaded ascender can be used in lieu of the tautline hitch to hold your position in case your partner loses their hold on the line. It's much faster than working the knot up the line and, ultimately, it's safer too. Just remember that being hoisted up doubles the load in the line as well as the limb or crotch it's fixed in.

RAPPELLING (DOUBLE-LINE)

Before a beginner gets too high off the ground, they should get used to the feel of descending. Pulling down on the tautline hitch will slacken the span and ease the bite the knot has on the line. Thus, the running part of the line will feed through the knot and you'll descend to the ground. You can control the rate of descent by how you pull and work the knot. If you ease up on the knot and let the running part pull the span tight again, you'll stop your descent. This is the unique feature of the tautline hitch. How well it works depends on the snugness of the knot and the kind of rope you're using. If the knot isn't snugged enough, there's a likelihood of it slipping to some degree. If it is snugged up too hard, it can seize on the line and make descents difficult. Stopping abruptly can tighten the tautline hitch and promote seizing. Too rapid a descent, referred to as burning out, can fuse or melt synthetic rope. Avoid burning out. To sum up, before any beginner gets too high up the tree using the double-line techniques, they should practice everything discussed so far and get the feel of rappelling and working the tautline hitch.

SINGLE-LINE TECHNIQUES

For achieving great heights, the single-line techniques are the most practical. In this situation, a static line is preferred. You can set the line using the throw line, bow and arrow, or line gun. The line is generally knotted to a limb with a single or running bowline, and dangles straight to the ground. It's best to set it on an open or clean side of the tree so you don't have to climb up the line through a lot of limbs or brush. Beginners often find comfort in limbs and brush though, because it offers a sense of security, whereas out in the clear, beginners are more aware of the height to which they are climbing.

Line ascenders are more commonly used in the single-line technique, but the prusik knot, like the tautline hitch, was used prior to their development, to the same effect. One system of using the ascenders, called the frog, uses two and sometimes three ascenders. If there are knots to pass over on the line, then three ascenders will be needed. One ascender is rigged to the feet using either straps, rope, or stirrups. Another ascender is set about head high on the line and fastened to the belt with a short length of line, approximately twenty inches. Once set up, push off with your feet on the lower ascender and then thrust the top ascender up to hold your position. You can raise your feet and push off again. It's actually quite simple. If there are knots to pass over, a third ascender attached directly to the belt's center ring is needed to hold you so you can break down the top ascender and pass it over the knot.

ROPE WALKING

This system is more energy efficient. It has been reported that heights over one hundred feet have been attained in an average of about thirty seconds using this system. It's more complicated to set up though. An ascender is fastened directly to one of your boots using straps or buckles. Another ascender is set on the line over that one and is tethered to the other foot by a line or strap about twenty inches long. A bungee cord is attached to the second ascender, and it is stretched out to fix to a top ascender rigged the same way as in the frog setup. The ascender on the tether is pulled up the line by the bungee cord as the top ascender is thrust upward. This system allows a climber to use each leg independendy in a manner quite natural and comfortable. There are a few variations in the way the top ascender can be rigged and the bungee attached. In one, a chest harness holds you up to the line where it rides through a roller. It's not terribly practical for tree climbing, though.

In either system, if the ascender you use on the bottom is spring actuated, you may need a person on the ground to hold the line tight during the beginning of the climb. This is because the spring pushes the cam against the rope and can cause enough drag to not allow the line to feed through the ascender. However, the line will begin feeding freely through the ascender by itself once there is enough of it hanging below to override the tension the spring exerts on the cam. You can get going by yourself by pulling the rope through as you begin climbing. It's a bit of an awkward maneuver, as the beginner will find out. In single-line technique, the figure-eight descender and other friction devices are used for rappelling. Beginners are advised to practice all single-line techniques at ground level. In particular, practice switching over to rappelling while on line. This requires that you break down the ascenders to gain the descender support. This isn't a procedure to practice very high off the ground.

HAND-OVER-HAND TECHNIQUE (DOUBLE- AND SINGLE-LINE)

This technique is widely used in climbing and working. In short jaunts it's much faster than cinching your way up to a limb or crotch. Quite literally you pull yourself up the line while using what footholds you can. Remember, if you're tired or somehow lose your grip on the line, you could take a short fall into the slack you've gained. So, if you're going to pull yourself up to a limb or crotch like this, make sure you're not fatigued, and have a strong grip and good footing. It's the footing that usually slips in this style of climbing; this makes a strong grip mandatory. Climbing hand over hand is a good conditioning exercise.

Pay attention to the spread between the runs of line in double-line hand-over-hand technique. In particular, this applies to what the line is around and how close you are to it. If the line is around a large limb you're pulling yourself up to, the spread in the rope will become greater the closer you get to the limb. You may not be able to grasp both strands of the line for the spread between them as you approach the limb. If you cannot reach both strands, you will have to finish the last part of your ascent by cinching.

FOOT LOCKING (DOUBLE- AND SINGLE-LINE)

Foot locking has been used for years in climbing to gain entrance into the tree. Unlike other methods, traditional foot lock climbing uses no safety feature to secure climbers in the event they become fatigued or somehow lose their hold on the line. It's an old style of rope climbing that some people regard as essential to know, but you should secure yourself by some alternative means whenever you do it. While holding yourself to the line, raise your feet and pull a loop of line with one foot. Bring that foot up and over the other. Bind the line by locking your feet together, then push off using your legs and get another handhold. It takes a little practice.

FREE CLIMBING

This type of climbing is sometimes referred to as three-point climbing, in that either two hands and one foot have a hold, or two feet and one hand have a hold. Free climbing is a practical means of movement through small trees and even parts of larger trees, where you have adequate hand and footholds. "Free" meaning not using any lines to aid the movement. With the aid of climbing spurs, you can expand the limits of free climbing greatly. This does not imply that you are without a means of safety in these situations; it simply means that you aren't relying on any lines for support during the movement.

THREE POINT CLIMBING AND USING LIMBS FOR SUPPORT

Some trees, or portions of them, have limb arrangements that make it easy to climb through them. But you must know for sure that the limb or limbs you rely on for support are sturdy enough to hold you, especially if you slip. The species of tree has much to do with it. While climbing through the limbs of a tree keep your hand and footholds close to the trunk. This is most important as a marginal limb could easily break if you bear weight on it farther out. It's a common practice to stub off the

Three Point Climbing and Using Limbs for Support

small limbs that you use to secure a line to, or use for a hand or foothold. If you're intentionally breaking smaller limbs out of your way during a climb, turn your head away when you do it. The reason for this is to avoid being struck in the eye by the splinters that are propelled from the tension side of the break. For this reason, and many more, eye protection is important while climbing and working in trees. The dead limbs and stubs of some trees can be trusted at times for support. You have no choice about trusting them, of course, if you're in a dead tree to begin with. You can check the suitability of a dead limb or stub by sounding it. Sounding is done by striking the limb with anything you have handy. If it's a good limb or stub it will ring, or vibrate, and if it's of sufficient size it can be relied on. However, if the dead limb or stub makes a short crack when you strike it, don't rely on it at all.

SPUR AND SAFETY CLIMBING

The simplified idea of climbing a pole with the safety and spurs is what many people envision as tree climbing. In forest trees, it's a lot like that sometimes. But there is much more to spur and safety climbing.

Trees have limbs, divisions, sweeps, and obtuse contours to climb past. Any one of these things can stop a climber cold in their tracks, trying to figure a way around them using the safety and spurs.

The beginner should start out by climbing up a straight vertical trunk of a tree or pole using safety and spurs. If a tree is chosen, it should be one that is destined to be removed because of all the spur marks it will acquire while you're learning. If it is a pole, shave the splinters off periodically. And whenever climbing poles, use a set of short, sharp pole points. On either tree or pole, clean and smooth off any stubs or knots and remove any nails, hardware, or other fasteners that can cause kick-out or injury. It's not a bad idea for a beginner to wear gloves. The diameter of the tree or pole you learn on is important; it should be at least twenty-four inches. Smaller diameters than that are more easily the cause of falls by the beginner. Larger diameters are preferable to learn on since kick-outs rarely result in extended falls; there is more surface area for the safety to get a bite on to stop it. If kick-out occurs, you must clinch the safety tight to the trunk immediately to prevent the fall and reset your points at the same time. It's a reflex that is vital. The beginner should practice it at ground level by clinching the safety for a hold on the tree and pulling out the spurs, then resetting the points.

Practice it until it's easy and you feel comfortable with it. This way your reflex time can be narrowed down and you'll be more capable of dealing with kick-out when you're higher up in the tree. There's no need to go very high to get used to using the safety and spurs. There are lots of exercises you can do at ground level to get familiar with the gear. One of them is circling around the trunk, or pole. This is done by sidestepping in the spurs around the trunk and scooching the safety. There should be some slack between the dee rings and where the safety is grasped. This amount of slack is necessary for working the safety during most movement. It's a common bad habit for beginners to choke up on the safety and not give themselves enough slack to work it properly.

ADJUSTING THE SAFETY

While at ground level, a beginner should also practice lengthening and shortening the safety setup they're using. Get used to making the adjustments solely with your hands and not necessarily by having to hold yourself to the tree to do it. However, in small spindly trees and awkward positions, it's sometimes necessary to hold yourself to the tree. Taking up excess slack can be especially difficult when there's more than you can pull at one time. It can make a climber resort to holding

Adjusting the Safety

themselves to the tree by holding on to the safety with their teeth. This seems to be the only alternative sometimes; the mouth acts as a third hand to hold the line while the other two make the needed adjustment to take out the slack. If you climb trees for very long, you'll probably find the need to do it some time.

SLINGING THE SAFETY

Slinging a safety is another ground-level exercise the beginner should practice. It's a technique used to get the snap end of a safety line, or even the climb line, around a trunk, spar, or limb you cannot reach or reach around. Draw up slack on the safety you're using so you're close to the trunk. Sling another safety around and catch it. To be able to sling a safety in any situation requires the room to do it. The presence of limbs and brush can prevent you from slinging. But in most climbing, there is ample opportunity to sling. The safety you sling must be lengthened out enough to reach around the trunk In the process of slinging, the snap end can come around fast. Thus, it is often allowed to slap the trunk first and then be grabbed. It's wise to use a stick or even the hand saw to

snare the line.

On large diameter trees, it's not as easy as just throwing the safety around and catching it. In fact you'll have to begin with a back swing on the safety and then finish with the projected forward sling to get it around the trunk. Progressive lengthening with a number of back throws and forward slings is necessary on larger trunks, which is when the snap can come around very fast. Such techniques can be repeated as many times as necessary. The limits of slinging a safety end somewhere in trunks over six feet in diameter. But even in larger trunks or on spars just beyond your ability, you can extend the limits of slinging by using available limbs, crotches, and sticks to catch or secure the snap end so it can be reached and retrieved on the far side.

Slinging a safety around a limb is generally easier than around a tree and you often have the choice of going under or over the limb. The safety will wrap itself around small limbs if it is slung too hard. But it is often necessary for it to wrap around the limb as it acts as a bite, holding its position after the snap is fixed. This is a valuable trick to know; in many working positions you haven't a crotch or stub to keep the safety secure from slipping where you set it.

SAFETY POSITION

The position of the safety is very important in climbing and working. The way it supports you has a direct bearing on its utility and your safety. The safety has three basic positions: positive, even, and negative. There are more ways of using the safety that will be discussed later.

Any time the safety is angled upward, it is considered to be in the positive position. It can serve some support so you can ease your weight out of the spurs. This can be a relief to a climber that gets shin sore from the spurs. How much support you gain depends primarily on the type of climbing belt you use. The leg and butt saddles offering the most benefit of support from a positive angled safety. Small structure and smooth bark does not hold a safety well in the positive position; the safety will be inclined to slip unless there is something for it to catch on like a limb or stub. Large diameter trunks do not cause the safety to slip down as much, especially if the bark has a rough texture, which makes the rope stick better. Whenever a safety slips, it can upset your footing and cause you to fall. It would be especially hazardous to have happen during the course of cutting with a power saw. Remember, the positive angle has lots of advantages in the way it supports a climber, but only as long as it is secured by a good bite around the trunk or held by a limb or stub. The positive position is also a prelude to your first steps up a tree.

The even position is where the safety should be set whenever you rest or work in small vertical structure. At this angle, the safety is not inclined to slip when you rest back in it. The even position is also where most adjustments are made in the safety, and it is the angle the safety will be in during a lot of work in vertical structure.

The negative position, or downward angle of the safety, as obtuse as it may seem, is used in a lot of work and climbing. In climbing, this position of the safety allows a climber to extend their reach so another line or safety can be set higher. This position is also necessary in certain kinds of tree work in order to keep the safety clear of a cutting area. It's a tough position to work from, as all of your weight is in the spurs. There is absolutely no support other than the bind that holds a climber with the safety at this angle. Having the safety in the negative position can drive the points of the spurs deeply into the tree. As rough as it can be, it is still necessary to use this position; a lot of tree climbing and work cannot be done safely without it.

The beginner should practice all the exercises discussed so far: circling around the trunk, making adjustments in the safety, slinging the safety, and positioning the safety. When you're comfortable with these exercises, you're ready to begin upward climbing.

Upward and downward climbing is more or less a free-style affair for anyone that climbs trees with a safety line and climbing spurs. The actual sequence between steps and between raising or lowering the safety is highly variable and peculiar to each person's style. The size of the trunk, its type of bark, the footholds, and any lean that may be present in it will greatly influence the way in which you climb it. Remember, in small structure and most little trees, you usually have to abandon the strict style of safety climbing and resort to the free climb or three-point style.

Climbing a fair vertical trunk is another matter. Between fifteen to twenty inches diameter, raise your safety to the positive angle. You'll need some slack in the safety to do it. Then clinch the safety for a hold. With a good hold, or bite, you can then ease your weight off one spur and reset it higher up. With that spur firmly set, transfer your weight out of the lower spur, pull yourself up and then reset it. In a fifty foot ascent, an experienced climber will need about twenty to twenty-five repetitions of this procedure. In a variation of this procedure, you'll raise the safety for every step taken. In most situations you'll probably alternate between the two. Beginners should practice close to the ground. In vertical climbing, practice a smooth style that eliminates all unnecessary expenditures of energy.

FLIPLINING

This is the technique used to work a safety up and around large diameter trees. Knowing how to flip a line can greatly aid your everyday climbing. In fliplining, the main idea is to draw back sufficient slack in the safety and throw it hard enough to form a loop of slack that will travel around the trunk. It's a sidearm rolling loop with accent to the ascent. This is easier said than done and takes a lot of practice to perfect. It's most tiring on the upper torso and forearms. How hard you throw that slack and the angle at which it is thrown determines how well the loop forms and travels. Most beginners choke themselves too tightly to the tree and don't give themselves enough slack to throw a decent loop. The slack must be thrown from the even, or just negative, position if you're climbing upward. It must be assumed that the slack you throw from one side will have to be caught on the other side. Thus, if the loop is formed and thrown from the right side, the left arm will have to receive the slack. Large trees can require you to alternate throwing the loop. This helps to avoid getting the line caught in the imperfections of loose

bark, which can happen often if you throw the loop from one side only.

Double flipline setups make it easier to scale the trunks of trees in excess of ten feet in diameter. One of the lines is used to hold your position steady while the other is lengthened and worked up the trunk. For this size of trunk and the amount of rope you'll use, it is best to have an adjustable tail on each side of the setup. As you bring the lower safety up to take the place of the upper safety, the two will wrap together at the dee rings, requiring you periodically to unfasten one in order to unwrap them.

Up the tree you will begin to encounter stubs, limbs, and other obstacles you'll need to get around to continue the climb. A strong flip of the safety will form a good loop that can clear many stubs, but you can also elect to cut the stubs off. Passing the line over can suffice to get by many. Quite often it has to be done this way and entails no more than pulling the line out from under the stub and passing it over to clear it. This is quite simple to do but you need some amount of slack in the safety to manage it.

PASSING THE SNAP

If a stub is too long to pass the line over, or in the case of a limb, you can pass the snap over it if you can reach over the limb and grab the safety. If the limb is on your left side, the snap should be also. You'll have to position yourself accordingly and lengthen the safety to make these moves. Reach over the limb with the left hand and grab the safety line. Pull it up and transfer the hold on the safety to the right hand. The snap will, or should, slack off. A little adjustment, if necessary, will slack it. Next, use the left hand to disengage the snap and pass it over the limb. Then snap it back to the dee. Be sure your points are secure and that you have enough slack in the safety to complete these moves. Once you have a good grasp on the line with your right hand, the rest of the moves only takes seconds. It's not a difficult maneuver, but you should practice it at or near ground level until you get it perfected. This technique is regularly used in many situations where you're already supported by the climb line or another safety. Whenever possible, you should pass the snap as described rather than unbuckling the safety around the tree altogether and then having to sling it around to reset it. If the limb you're trying to get by is too large to reach over to make the required moves, you'll need to use a second safety to continue the climb past it.

DOUBLE CROTCHING

The use of two safeties, or a climb line and safety, is often the only practical and safe way to overcome many obstacles in tree climbing. It is sometimes called the double-safety technique. You're never in danger during the snapping or fixing of another line because there's always one line holding you while you're fixing the other. Whenever you can, fix the second safety as high as is practical to lessen the number of times it needs to be done. For instance, instead of fixing the safety over one or two limbs, you would do better to fix it over a few more if possible. Certain groups of limbs will allow this if you grunt a little and put a negative angle in the lower safety. This way you can reach higher to place the second one. The double safety can be used to overcome divisions where the trunk doubles or branches off and where large growths such as conks or burls swell the trunk.

One school of thought in tree climbing is to make as few moves as necessary to get where you're going. But sometimes it's better to set your line in a closer crotch if it'll take too long to secure the line in the farther

one. You must weigh these things out as you look ahead to where you're going.

SAFETY ON A TAG

This method of using the safety capitalizes on its extended length on a single run. Essentially, you can get a safety hold twice as far as when it's doubled back. The safety is snapped into itself where it is fixed. This is used mostly as a positioning aid while working and not so much in regular climbing, because, in order to release it, you have to make it back to where it is fixed.

SAFETY WITH A BITE

This is fixed the same as on a tag, but the snap is drawn around to make the arrangement bite into the trunk, or limb, on a particular side. The bite can keep the tag setup from slipping down a trunk or from slipping around a limb.

SAFETY WITH A WRAP

When climbing slender trees that have no limbs, a safety set in the regular fashion might fail to stop a fall. But with the wrap, the safety will catch you and stop the fall. The safety with a wrap is also used in the outer reaches of limbs to hold your position. In many small trees you can still climb with the wrap if you loosen it up and carry it.

SAFETY SET ADVERSELY

This obtuse arrangement of setting the safety pulls downward, or aft, on the climber. Used primarily in securing a working position. Remember to look behind and below your working position for a place to set a safety adversely.

OBSTACLES IN TREE CLIMBING

While climbing and working in trees, you'll encounter obstacles. Most, if not all, obstacles can be overcome by setting a fixed line in the tree beyond them. But it is not always possible to do this, for a number of reasons. Unavailability of the necessary tools and equipment for setting fixed lines is one of them; practicality is another reason. There may be only one practical way to get up the tree, which often requires the use of the safety and spurs. The main focus of the up-coming chapters is on cutting the tree down or wrecking it out, so the use of climbing spurs is frequently discussed and shown as a means to overcoming various obstacles.

LEAN

One of the more common difficulties encountered while climbing and working is lean. Use the three-point method in small trees that lean, but still use a safety and keep it loose so your movement isn't cramped. If the safety is too short, it can cramp your style and make you susceptible to losing your balance. As somewhat of a good rule, never rest back in your safety set in a positive position on a leaning tree unless there is a limb or stub to hold it. The negative slope on the underside of a leaner will too easily cause the safety to slip.

To help maintain your balance while working on a leaner, you can practice the knee rest. Set one spur firmly in the tree and lock that leg straight. Bring the other leg or knee up and rest it against the trunk. Put the safety in a negative position and remove all the slack to make your position rigid. This can make your position on a leaning tree much more stable, and by it make your work much safer.

When climbing large leaning trees, you may have to use the strict style of safety climbing if you have far to go. If there are limbs near the ground, it may be safe to three-point climb up to them. Working a safety around a big leaner can cause a lot of back strain. It can be complicated even more by the presence of imperfections or stubs on the low side of the tree, which can force you to lie against the trunk, or on your belly, to work the safety over them. Slinging a safety around the trunk of a big leaner can be a difficult task. You may have to resort to lying on your belly to do it. On smaller trees that a person can reach around, these moves are generally not that difficult. Tree workers will seldom climb or work from the low side of a leaner. However, it happens on occasion when a tree is in a slight lean and all the work is on the side. Keep in mind that the spurs lose their ability to secure your footing on the low side; a climber can be left hanging and unable to recover a position back on the high side.

SWEEP

Sweep refers to a progressive curve in the trunk of a tree that usually begins at a hard angle and may eventually straighten out to the vertical. The hard angle encountered at the beginning of some sweeps can force a climber to walk, crawl or crotch-hop across it. When approaching the more ascending part of a sweep, adjust your lines and climb the rest as you would a lean.

THE DOGLEG

The dogleg has been the nemesis of many a climber. Essentially, it is a sweep, but higher up in the tree and approached from a hard vertical angle. Kicking-out occurs frequently when trying to overcome a dogleg so having a safety set in some manner is a must. Climbers will have to bearhug and shimmy up the trunk to get onto the sweep. This can be most awkward. It can be avoided if you fix a line past the dogleg to aid you in getting up on the sweep. In some cases, you can set a second safety, with a bite, on the side of the dogleg, with a loop for a foothold. With a bite, the foot loop will stay wherever you put it. Remember, many kick-out and stability problems are associated with the dogleg so you must have a climb line or safety set before dealing with it.

TWISTS AND TURNS

In overcoming these obstacles a climber will learn a good exercise in balance control. Here, it's best to use the three-point method; it's the smoothest and most natural way to get over most twists and turns. Always use a safety but keep it loose so it won't interfere with your moves. In climbing up or down twists or turns, keep your footholds, or the point of the spur, on the high, or positive-angled, portions of the trunk. This will prevent many kick-outs. In horizontal movement over twists and turns, you'll have to get by a lot of them on your hands and knees. In large trees, you will often have to resort to shimmying and straddling to get over many.

GETTING ON TOP OF A LIMB

This seemingly simple task can actually be one of the more difficult you will encounter when climbing many a tree. The presence of other limbs in the vicinity is always a great help. Sometimes a good look above the limb in question will reveal a place to fix a line to assist your ascent. This is really the best way to get on top of another limb. If you cannot fix a line, the down and dirty way of shimmying, leg locking, and hoisting yourself up will be necessary. On large limbs you can set a loop on their side to help you up on them. Set a safety with a bite on the side of the limb and then fashion a loop that you can use for a foothold. A loose tail at the top of the limb comes in handy as a handhold. When fashioned and set properly it will be much the same as saddling up on a horse.

THE DOUBLE

The double is where the trunk of the tree splits off into multiple trunks, be it two, three, or more. Overcoming the double with safety and spurs can be specially hard in large trees. As you ascend up the trunk of a large double it will generally widen out, which means you'll have to lengthen the safety as you go up. The concern here is, if you kick-out, the safety will not always bite the trunk; instead, it will drop for lack of any taper in the trunk to hold it. In most climbing, the taper of the trunk widens out below the climber and a slip will often result in the safety catching the taper and stopping the fall. In the double this is not always the case. But not all doubles will taper as such or be representative of this particular hazard. The smaller ones are much easier to overcome, generally. The exact taper or abruptness of the double, besides its size, will also determine the difficulty rating. A finely tapered double will split off gradually and you may have to climb some ways past the union before a safety can be fixed around one of the single trunks. If you can reach between the trunks and grasp the safety, you may be able to achieve your

goal without need of a second safety. Much similar to passing a snap over a limb, but here you're usually in a much more awkward position and more likely to loose your footing or grasp on the line. So this maneuver has a certain element of risk. Play it safe. If it doesn't feel right don't do it. It is best to rig overhead lines if possible and/or use two safeties.

SAFETY FROM SPAR-TO-SPAR

In trees or spars that are close to one another, a climber will often use the double safety to assist in horizontal movement between them. Many a climber has done so without the second safety and taken a bad fall because of it. Don't take a chance, use that double safety. If the tree is slick or skinny, set one safety with a wrap to prevent it slipping while you make the move over. In this situation you can often fix the second safety by slinging and catching it with a stick or the hand saw.

THE SHORT TRAVERSE

The short traverse is usually accomplished by fixing the climb line afar and slacking the safety. The climb line can be fixed at far reaches with a throw line, using the boomerang shot. If you have a long stick or telescopic rod on hand, you can reach out and retrieve the end of the climb line from a moderate distance. Even extending your safety will allow you to reach and snare the climb line with the tip of your hand saw. Once the climb line is fixed, slack the safety off and you'll swing over to your objective. This procedure is often performed in the reverse order.

THE LONG TRAVERSE

The long traverse is accomplished only by attaining a suitable overhead tie-in that will allow enough scope in the line for you to make the jump from your tree to the objective tree. With a good overhead tie-in you can cover considerable horizontal distances. One way to start is by kicking off the tree you're tied into. With sixty feet of tie-in, you can kick off ten to fifteen feet. With one hundred feet of tie-in, you can kick off up to twenty feet or more, depending on the situation. By using the jam knot, or another suitable snaring device, you can regularly set a line afar and traverse over greater distances. If you're pulling on limbs to get to the next tree, beware if they're bending from the angle you're pulling on them: they could break. When you can, pick a limb that angles towards you to pull on. From this angle, even a small limb can bear a hard pull.

The following is an example of a long traverse. Climb to the top of the first tree and tie in. Descend down to the traverse level. Brace your feet against the tree and then kick off. Grab a limb on the objective tree and pull yourself to the trunk. Safety in there. You now have the option to pull out the climb line from the other tree. Remember, the tie-in is the most important factor; it can make a long traverse relatively easy or difficult. In any traverse, the risk of crashing backwards is a reality. Be sure you make accommodations by removing any stubs in the crash area that could hurt you if you slipped.

BRUSH AND VINE CONDITIONS

Trees that are full of brush, deadwood, and vines can do more to slow down a climber's progress than anything else. Such conditions can make access into the tree extremely difficult. To make things worse, vine-covered trees are frequently dirty and infested. Whenever possible, try to fix a line in the tree for a vertical ascent to the work area; this will allow you to avoid the vine condition. Entering the tree can also be done by traversing. Both climbing and working in these conditions can be extra dangerous because snap failure from disengagement is all too common. If you are ever working in a vine-infested tree and hear a snap click, immediately secure your position with a four-point stance and check your snaps before making any other moves. Vines can also cause parts of the tree you cut to hang up or be steered in the wrong direction. Overhead work can fall down on you instead of over you. Dead trees that have vines engulfing them can also be hazardous to climb or work in because the exact soundness of the tree is difficult to ascertain.

BARK

The bark of many trees can also be an obstacle, particularly in older trees. It's a good idea to wear gloves in trees with rough bark where kicking-out is likely... gloves will save on tattered knuckles! Some bark has flaps and cracks in it that the safety can become stuck under or in. Such bark conditions in large trees can seize a safety so tightly that you'll be stuck and unable to get around to free it. If it happens to you, try knotting the ends of the safety together and tying yourself to the safety with a loop, slip knot, snap or thimble. This can make it possible for you to get to the back side of the tree to free the line. For the beginner it's a technique that should be practiced near the ground.

Trees with high bark ridges may not allow penetration into sound wood even with long points. In this type of bark, you must be careful where you set your points since only the bark is supporting you. It's best to set the points in the widest or sturdiest ridges of bark. The thin or narrow ridges frequently break off and become stuck to the point.

Smooth bark, such as that found on the eucalyptus, can present risk and difficulty. Many climbers express a certain dislike for eucalyptus. Getting the safety line stuck is not a problem, getting it to stick is. I found that a safety coated with rubber cement, or similar gum rubber compounds, makes climbing the eucalyptus tree much safer. In small trees like this, you can try climbing with your safety set with a wrap around the trunk. It will arrest the fall if you slip or kick-out.

TRUNK CONTOUR

Depressions and bulges in the trunk can be obstacles in themselves. Proficient use of the double safety and flipline techniques can easily remedy this. Watch your footing when stepping over any obtuse bulges in a tree. Keep your points set on the top, or high side of them. Use them as foot rests whenever you can. When working in a tree that has prominent contour, bulges and stubs, make sure your safety line does not catch on any one, putting it in the path of a cut. It does happen in these conditions. So you must mind your lines.

LARGE AND SMALL

Some climbers will find the size of a tree an obstacle. With big trees, you can practice using the flipline to scale their trunk. Setting a fixed line to enter them, or a traverse into them from a smaller tree are widely used techniques. With small trees that you're afraid will bow or break when you're near their tops, you can set guy lines to strengthen them. Tying such trees off to a neighboring one will also suffice, and it doesn't take as much line as setting guys.

AERIAL RESCUE

No book on climbing would be complete without a discussion on aerial rescue. Accidents happen. Unfortunately, the circumstances accompanying them are too many to elaborate on. Case scenarios can involve: major arterial bleeding, trauma, electrocution, and unconsciousness, to name but a few, so what to do exactly is up to the situation and anybody's guess. What "I" can say about it, is for the beginner and professional alike to practice mock situations. This can eliminate trial and error during a real event. Ideally, there should be a qualified climber and tools on site that has other climbers working. And everyone on the crew should be trained in first aid and cardiopulmonary resuscitation (CPR). This is essential for a speedy, qualified and safe rescue. Unqualified persons attempting rescue in a tree can become a victim themselves or compound the injuries of the person they're trying to save. Hence the need for training.

To become qualified requires thorough training in climbing, knots, rigging theory and first aid. I believe this book covers the first three adequately enough for a person to become qualified in those respects. As for the first aid and CPR, certificates of training can be obtained through most community health services programs.

One thing I'll add that helps speed a rescue; always have enough rope on hand to get the injured person to the ground. Using double-line techniques, especially in tall trees, can run you short of line. Therefore, single-line techniques should also be included in any mock exercises, in particular the technique of "belaying." This can save the time, need and complications of having to recrotch a line to lower a victim. Review **Chapter 9— Special Climbing Tools**. Ascenders, descenders, thimbles and the like described in that chapter should be part of a first aid/rescue package carried on every crew.

Chapter 13

Cutting the Tree

Cutting down a tree in sections is sometimes referred to as tree wrecking. Most trees that need wrecking are usually between homes, roadways, and power lines. These obstacles can prevent the removal of the tree by simply falling it. The trees and situations vary so greatly that it's impossible to say just how they might all be taken down, but most trees that need wrecking can be handled with the practices discussed in these chapters about it. A close evaluation of the job is in order before any work begins.

SCOPE OF THE JOB

How a tree must be cut depends upon its structure and condition, its proximity to various obstacles, and the amount of room that can be made to drop or lower the pieces. The interrelationship of these three factors creates the scope of the job. There may be more than one way to wreck the tree out. The best plan though, is based on the safest, sanest way to do the work, which is not always the fastest. Never sacrifice safety in lieu of getting a job done sooner. Shortcuts are the main cause of accidents in this kind of work. Always work within the scope of the job.

HANDLING THE POWER SAW IN THE TREE

When cutting with the bottom of the bar the chain will pull on the saw and it will expel the chips toward the power head and out of the side case. In this conventional manner you'll do most of your heavy cutting with a power saw. When cutting with the top of the bar, called backchaining, the chain will push on the saw and expel the chips out the other side of the cut away from the saw. This method is used a lot in the smaller cuts. The push and pull tendencies of the saw are most noticeable when you're hanging free in your lines. The saw can virtually push you away or pull you to the work. As a rule, you shouldn't do any cutting when suspended freely by your lines. It can cause you to lose control of the saw, especially while backchaining. To keep control of the push and pull tendencies of the saw, you need to anchor your position with your lines and fix a firm stance with your foot and legholds. If you cannot do either, it may not be safe to proceed using the power saw.

LATERAL POSITIONS

As human beings, we have bilateral symmetry. This gives us a right and left side. Chain saws have a right and left side too. But they do not have bilateral symmetry. They are primarily designed for right-handed operation. You'll even find that the tree has a relative right and left side to it. What this all adds up to, in tree work, is what's called left and right lateral positions. This may be a little confusing right now, but soon you will see how it affects your ability to make certain cuts from a right or left stance. It governs your saw-handling capabilities quite a bit. For instance, you may be naturally more proficient when cutting from a right

Chainsaw handling in leaning and horizontal positions.

lateral position. Change to a left lateral position and your ability may fall off and your cuts fail more frequently. A left lateral stance often requires you to change your grip on the saw. If you are right-handed, it can cramp your style and thus your handling and precision are affected. Remember the things that affect your saw handling and you'll know better what position to get in to make a desired cut. You'll hear references to left and right lateral positions throughout the chapters where cutting the tree is discussed.

USE THE PROPER GRIP

Always keep a two-handed grip on the power saw, because this way you can exert the most control on it. The reasons given for operating a power saw with one hand stem from several factors. "Stability" - especially when reaching outward to cut with a power saw. Such a shift in position when using a two handed grip can throw a climber completely over in their belt if they lack adequate footholds, so climbers will often hold on to a line, or the tree, with one hand while reaching out and cutting with the other.

"Managing the work" - this is using one hand to hold or push on the work while cutting with the other. "Keeping clear" - at times a climber needs to keep their distance, or cut from behind something, to keep clear of the work or the rigging. "Convenience" - many climbers find it convenient to cut with one hand, easy to do with small saws.

It may be a convenience or necessity to operate a saw one handed at times, but it should never be done out of negligence. Most of the time you have the option to change your position to enable you to use a proper two-handed grip. Use it!

PERFORMANCE OF A CUT

As a rule, make your cuts in wood absent of knots and defects. This makes for more consistent results in the performance of your cuts. Learn how to accurately judge the stress and balance of the work you're cutting. Stress and balance are very important factors that can influence the performance of your cuts. The soundness of the wood can affect the performance of the cut. Don't depend on dead or rotten wood to swing or hold a cut. Picking the right cut to use is a determining factor in its performance; learn the different kinds of cuts. Improper execution affects the performance of your cuts. Set your lines and stance to give you the best position to do the work. This is one of the biggest factors affecting the performance of your cuts, as well as being a requirement for doing work correctly and safely.

THE BASIC CUTS

These are the crosscut, the diagonal cut, the rip cut, the bore cut, and the nip cut. The basic cuts are simple and don't take long to learn, but knowing how to combine them to achieve a specific effect does. All of the cuts you'll use have a mechanical feature to them. Getting the proper amount of a basic cut in combination with another cut has a great deal to do with the success of the cut. It pays to experiment with the cuts you're unfamiliar with. This will eliminate the trial and error in jobs that can't afford it.

THE CROSSCUT

In its truest form, the crosscut is a single cut made through the tree at a ninety-degree angle to its grain. At this angle, a sharp chain will cut the wood at its peak efficiency. The crosscut is often the basis for most combinations and variations of cuts. A partial crosscut may be the beginning of an undercut, face cut, or the finish of a back cut. A full crosscut is used mostly for bucking lengths of wood from limbs, spars, and trunks of the tree. It's also used as a flush cut whenever called for.

Although it's usually a simple cut to make, in certain situations it requires a good eye and expert handling of the saw.

THE RIP CUT

In its true form it will run parallel to the grain in the wood, as in making lumber. The rip cut is mostly used by a climber to split trunks of large trees apart. Multiple trees whose trunks and spars grow tightly together often have to be ripped apart. Even singular trunks that are too large to manage may have to be halved or quartered by ripping. The rip cut is sometimes used in conjunction with other cuts for special purposes.

THE DIAGONAL CUT

This is a sloping cut. Most commonly, it runs at angles between twenty and forty-five degrees. But you may see a reason for steeper or narrower angles than that at times. The diagonal cut is mostly used to open the face in a falling cut; it entails only a partial diagonal to accomplish. Full diagonal cuts are frequently used as large flush cuts, since most crotches and limb conjunctions run at angles anyway. The diagonal cut is used exclusively when keeping the cuts level with gravity in the leaning parts of the tree. The diagonal cut is sometimes called the salami cut when used for the purpose of getting cuts to slide apart.

THE BORE CUT

This is a special kind of cut, in existence since the advent of the chainsaw. With the ability to bore into the wood, a multitude of new functions have come into being that were not possible before. Probably the best use of this cut is for the prevention of splitting and wood pull in large or heavy cuts. You'll often hear references to the bore cut in that kind of cutting. Do not start a bore cut straight in. The bore cut should be started with the bottom quarter of the tip. Once the tip is started, straighten it out and then plunge the bar into the tree. It is less prone to kicking back this way. Kickback is prevalent when starting bore cuts—without exception, use a firm proper grip and consider carefully how you position yourself and set your lines. When making long bore cuts up in a big tree, it's best to start them with a small saw and then insert the big saw to finish. The chain is influential when starting a bore cut. Full compliment is the safest and the rakers shouldn't be taken down too far.

THE NIP CUT

Nip cuts are mostly executed using the lower quarter of the bar tip. But at times it's necessary to nip using the upper quarter. This type of cutting is regularly used to open or clean out small portions of a cut, promote a cut to break, and as a prevention or avoidance of getting a saw stuck in certain cuts. Always use a proper grip when nipping.

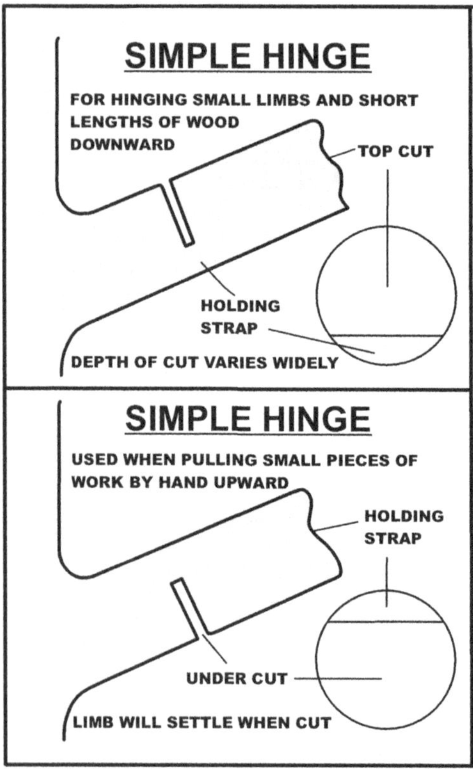

SIMPLE HINGE CUT

This is a widely used cut in trimming and removals. The idea is to partially cut through a particular side of the work so it will break or hinge over to a desired direction. Simple hinge cuts tend to leave unsightly rips, tears, and stubs; use it discreetly when trimming a tree. The simple hinge cut should also be reserved for the SMALL limbs and cuts. Large limbs don't simply hinge very well using this cut; instead they often break violently, splitting pronouncedly up or down the stem. Some limbs will break off completely and quickly without any hope or indication of hinging. So, it's important that the cut is used wisely! On small tops you're pulling or breaking over by hand, keep the cut a true crosscut and make it two-thirds or more of the way in. This type of hinge, or strap, on a small top, gives a certain amount of flexibility so that the top can be managed to one side or the other while pulling it over. Not so in a regular face-type hinge cut. Make sure that it's cut deep enough to keep splitting to a minimum.

DROP CUT

This is a simple crosscut that requires a fair degree of care and skill. The drop cut is used mostly on SMALL limbs, but SMALL spars and pieces of wood can be dropped with it too. The essence of the cut is speed. The goal is to get what you're cutting to drop off the cut with little or no hinging at all. You need a good cutting saw and proper position to execute this cut. A failed drop cut usually results in the work hinging or twisting over. A person should learn the drop cut by starting with smaller cuts and working up to larger ones. On the larger limbs, you have more of a margin to complete the cut if it is started on the side

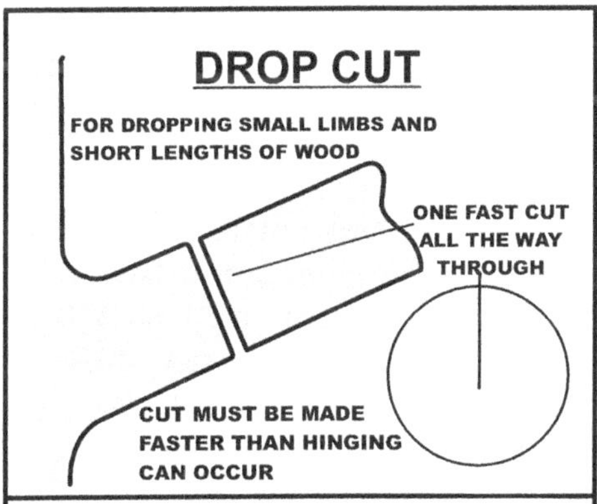

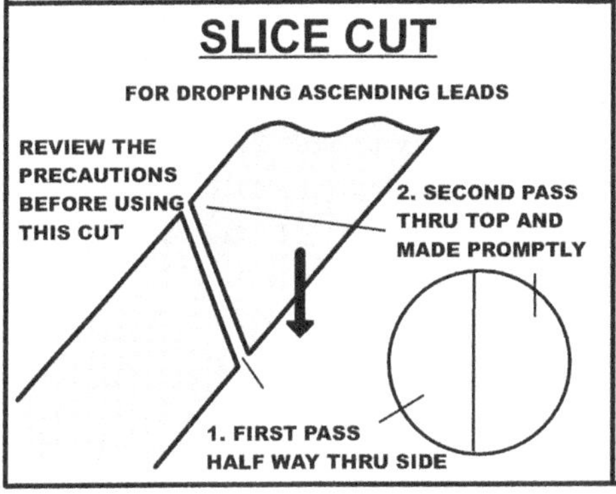

of the limb and finished by coming through the top. The drop cut is usually made under the full speed and power of the saw, so you should make doubly sure that your lines and body are out of the path of the saw's follow-through of the cut. This is a proper-grip situation.

SLICE CUT

This cut is executed in much the same way as the drop. However, it is better suited for the more upright portions of the tree, such as small spars and leaning tops. Since these portions of the tree are ascending in nature, the cut should be made at a diagonal so the butt will slide or drop off the cut. It allows you to drop this kind of work in a more confined area. This cut should never be used on any overhead top, spar or trunk that has the potential to drop straight down. Observe your surroundings. Obstructions within the tree, or from neighboring trees, will hold some work from tipping away. This can cause the butt of the work to slip off the cut, lead in the fall, and everything will come crashing down on you, a hazard associated with the slice cut when used negligently. For that reason, this cut has a bad reputation and is not recognized by safety institutions. Sometimes there are just reasons for using the slice cut in tree work, but your savvy is very important in deciding when and how to use it.

JUMP CUT

This cut is more effective in dropping the larger limbs and spars that the drop or slice cut can't. First, an undercut is made and then a matching top cut finishes it. When properly executed, the limb will leave its stub cleanly with a pop. Deep undercuts are possible after a limb begins to settle down. Use a firm proper grip, right lateral stance preferred, re-insert the saw into the undercut, throttle the saw up and backchain while quickly and simultaneously pulling the saw out. Repeat as necessary to get a sufficient undercut, but the chance of getting the saw stuck increases each time you do. Finish with a prompt and matching top cut. Limbs that are especially heavy can start breaking over before the top cut is completed. This will occur more frequently if the top cut is made too slowly. It's also caused by an undercut that's too shallow, even though it may have been deep enough to pinch the saw in it.

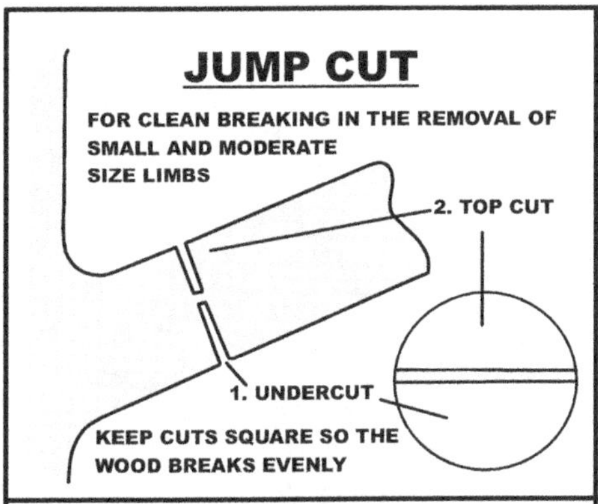

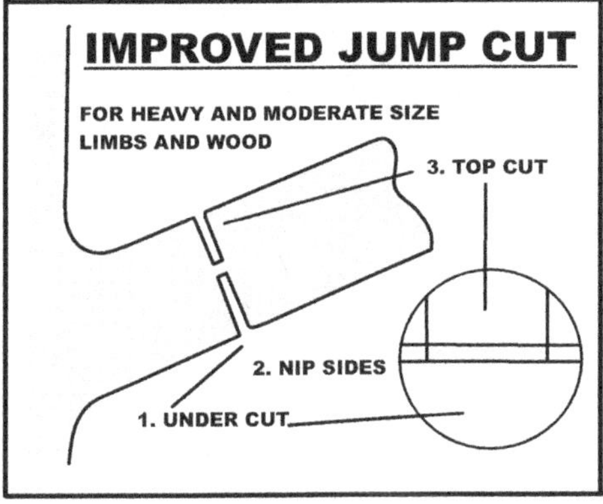

IMPROVED JUMP CUT

Basically the same as the jump cut, but before the top cut is executed, a nip or small cut is made on each side of the limb to sever more of the breaking wood. These cuts are often referred to as sap cuts. Remember the idea behind the jump cut and behind the improved version is to first sever as much wood as you can without the limb breaking over until you're ready to trigger it with the top cut. But there are limits to even the improved jump cut.

THE TWISTER

This is a variation of the simple hinge and used much for the same effect. The cut is started on the side of the limb at a diagonal angle and continued until a break or split occurs. Sometimes a little nip on the top of the holding wood is executed to prompt it. This cut has better results hinging some limbs than the simple hinge cut. The action is to twist over more than hinge over. So check the natural tendencies of each limb

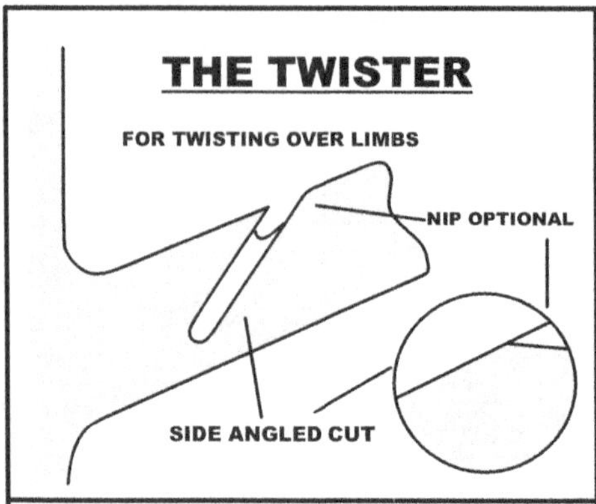

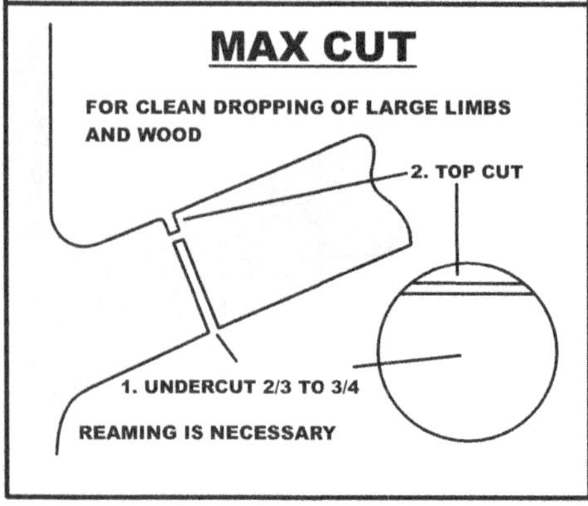

before using this cut, because many limbs have the natural tendency to twist over by some offset weight on them and this cut can promote it.

MAX CUT

The name of this cut is derived from the size of its undercut. The undercut comprises up to seventy-five percent or more of the cut itself. The idea behind the cut is to get what you're cutting to drop off the cut with little or no hinging, the same as the drop or the jump. This cut though, has better success than they do in LARGE wood. The reason for this is the size of the undercut. It leaves very little top wood to cut in order to trigger the action. To get an undercut this deep without getting the saw pinched in it, you have to understand what reaming is: it is the act of keeping the current part of a cut open while allowing the beginning of it to close. It involves some boring at times. There is a thorough discussion about reaming in the chapter on bucking the tree (See **Chapter 34**). After learning how to ream you'll have a much higher degree of success in all of your cutting.

FACE CUTS

These are highly functional directional cuts. They are the same kind of cuts used in falling trees and the same principles apply when they're used up in the tree. There are many variations of these face cuts. Even though they closely resemble one another, subtle changes can have pronounced effects in their performance.

All of these cuts are designed to hold the work on the cut long enough until it's guided over by the hinge wood. There is not, or shouldn't be, any splitting or ripping associated with these cuts unless they're improperly made or used. I strongly advise the beginner to read the chapters on tree falling to gain a fuller understanding of the theories and applications of face cuts. They will not be elaborated on any further here.

THE BENDER

This is one of the more unusual cuts to hinge over a limb. Unlike the movements caused by the other cuts discussed so far, the movement

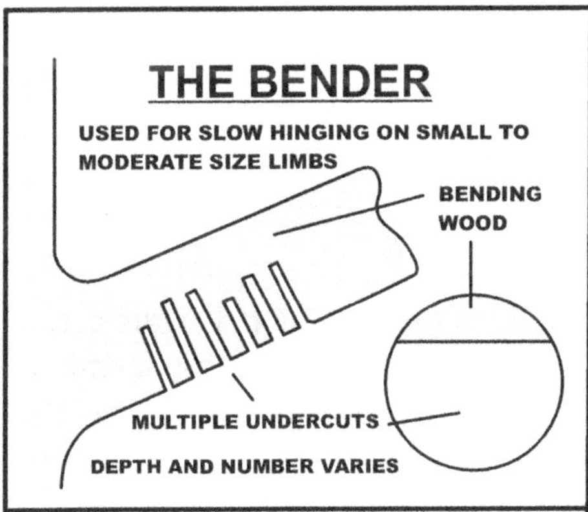

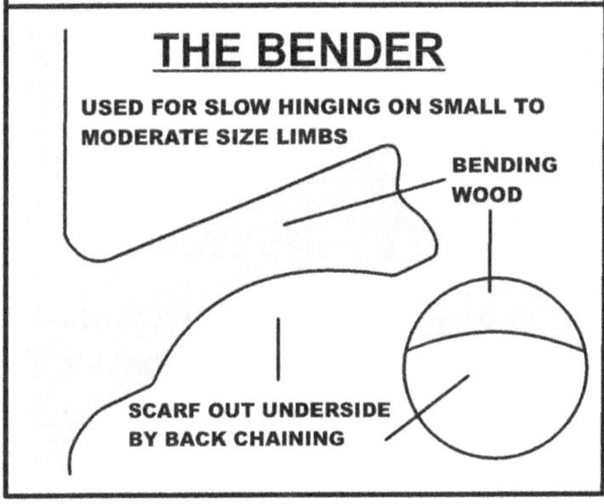

of the limb from this cut is very slow and gentle. In fact, most limbs hinged over using the bender will never leave their stubs. You should understand by now that an undercut made deep enough into the underside of a limb will cause the limb to settle. Make a series of undercuts to get the limb to settle some more. This is the principal of the bender.

Be sure to pull the bar out smartly while executing the cuts or you'll chance getting the saw stuck. Take note that the bender is best performed from a right lateral position to the limb, as most people can control the saw better from the right. Top cuts can prompt further hinging after the multiple undercuts have collapsed the limb. But they have been known to cause breakage if they're placed in the more heavily stressed portions of the bend.

It can take a lot of individual cuts to hinge the limb over. Observe the limb carefully while you do it. If you notice it bending more in one spot than another, don't undercut any more wood from that area. You want to distribute the bending over a given area and not all in one spot, or the limb can break instead of bend. This is a good cut to experiment with in different kinds of trees because the wood varies from tree to tree. Some trees will exhibit a better tendency to bend without breaking than others will. Once you learn how to use this cut you'll be able to ease limbs down on the eves of roofs and on fences without smashing them. In a variation of the bender the entire underside of the limb is scarfed out by backchaining.

THE LEVEL CUT

The level cut is used by a climber to manage short lengths cut from the trunk of a tree that leans over an obstacle. The cut is started, made, and finished on the level. Each piece of wood that is cut must have a low center of gravity. That is, it must not be top heavy from its lean. The level cut is a full diagonal cut made through the trunk of the tree. The harder the trunk leans the more extreme this diagonal becomes. Along with that, the harder the tree leans the shorter the pieces will have to be cut.

THE SALAMI CUT

A sloping cut used to prompt a cut to slide apart. In large trees with vertical structure, it's useful to slide the cuts off that are too large for a climber to manage any other way. The face of the slope indicates where

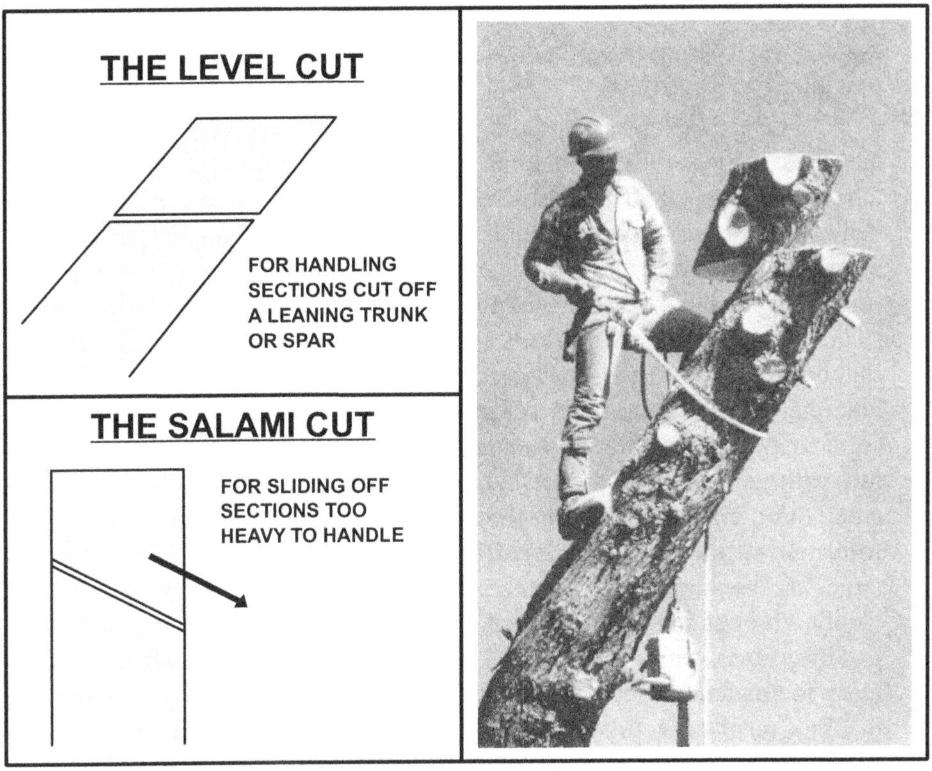

the work will slide off to. The salami cut is somewhat wasteful of wood due to the shapes that result from it. Because it's a long, sloping cut down the trunk, the climber must make doubly sure that their safety lines are not in the path of the cut. Keep the cuts short. As a rule not over twice its diameter.

THE FLUSH CUT

This is the last cut used when removing any limbs, tops, spars, and the tree itself. It has no real mechanical functions to elaborate on, but a lot of opinion about the flush cut is expressed. In tree removal and wrecking, it serves to keep the tree free of any stubs that will catch and snag a climber's lines and rigging. When limbs and wood are being lowered on rigging, it's essential that there be no stubs in the way. If the work hangs up on a stub you may have to rappel down to unsnag it. It's also much safer to work in a tree that is absent of any stubs. Besides short falls or kick-outs, even your own regular movements can result in an injury if you should hit one unwittingly. So, unless there is a specific purpose for leaving a stub, remove them with a good flush cut before moving on to other work.

In trimming and pruning, the flush cut serves two major purposes. It preserves the natural or trained beauty of the tree by not having the distraction of a mass of unsightly stubs. A tree full of stubs demonstrates that the person who did the work was ignorant of good trimming practices. On the other hand, a person that follows good trimming practices can enhance the beauty of a tree by removing any stubs they create. It also reflects their pride in the work and their care for the tree. The flush cut also promotes rapid healing by the callus. Painting of the cuts has been recognized to not prevent or slow down the entrance of wood rotting organisms. However, for cosmetic purposes, a tree with its cuts painted does look better than one without. If you use paints, don't apply them thickly - they can present a barrier to the formation of the callus. It would be best to thin it down. If the cut is large, it should be sealed and covered with a good grade of thin aluminum or stainless sheet metal. Use the stub that was cut off as the pattern to make this cover. You'll need to remove the bark off of it to make the pattern correct. Trim to fit close to the cambium, but not over it! Tack in place with small stainless nails. When fitted properly, the callus will form over and seal the edge of the sheet metal within the first growing season.

MAKING LARGE FLUSH CUTS

It takes a certain knack to line up the saw correctly so that the cut will be straight, smooth, and even. Ideally, any large flush cut should be made with a saw that can complete the cut in a single pass without having to double back. Most large flush cuts should be executed from a left lateral stance, the saw aligned from the side of the work, not the top. From this side, the main case of the saw will not butt into the trunk. The tip of the bar should be orientated toward the top of the union and the gut of the bar lined up with the side of the trunk This will keep the cut even to the contour of the trunk, thus avoiding the possibility of a sloping cut that could track into the tree itself. On many large flush cuts it may be necessary to use an undercut.

FLUSH CUTTING TIGHT CROTCHES

Flush cutting a tight crotch may present some difficulty for the beginner in determining where the cut should be made. The reason for this is that the union where the wood actually joins is usually below where the bark comes together. Because of this, most flush cuts of this type are regularly made too high. Although the cut may appear correct in some cases, in essence it will actually be a stub. But when properly made, the cut will begin its slope from the point where the wood of the two spars join. This is usually easy to tell because the sapwood of the spar being removed joins into the other spar without any bark in between.

Quite often the crotch may be so tight that to start the cut the tip of the saw will have to be bored in between the two spars. Even after the cut is made, the stub may have to be kicked or pried off because the bark between the two spars is sometimes compressed tightly and holding the two together. Stubs that are sunk into the side of the tree, referred to as "included" can be effectively bored out if there is room to plunge the tip of the bar in without nicking the trunk.

FLUSH-CUT AWARENESS

It has been recognized that flush cuts made so close to the trunk that they remove the collar or bulge around the limb do more harm to the tree than good. The collar is the wrinkled mass protruding from the trunk and bulging around the base of the limb where the two join. When seen in a cross section, the bulge is tissue from the trunk rather than the limb. In the course of trimming a tree and implementing a flush cut, it is now believed not to be good for the tree to cut into this collar. It hastens cavity development in the trunk. This holds more true in older trees because younger ones can heal their cuts much faster. Not all trees and crotch unions will have prominent collars as such, and in a good many of them the flush cut can be carried out in the traditional fashion as it always has been. But don't take my word as the gospel. Nothing in this business is written in stone. There are publications available through local ISA (International Society of Arboriculture) chapters that specifically cover the theory and application of flush cuts. From this discussion and what you can read further about it, you can develop your own opinion about what's proper.

Chapter 14

Brushing Out the Tree

In this discussion about brushing out the tree, the examples given apply to when you have room under the tree to let all the limbs drop. The room needed to take down a tree in this manner, excluding working on a slope, is never more than what its canopy covers.

GENERAL TIPS ON BRUSHING OUT FOREST TREES

For forest trees, including spruce, pine, redwood, and fir, the limbing should start at the bottom and progress to the top. Starting from the bottom opens all the room necessary to cut and drop everything above. This way, everything you're cutting has a straight, clear path to fall to the ground without hanging or tangling in other limbs. You'll have the choice of how to cut each limb and how to have it land. Starting from the bottom also allows most trees to be completely limbed to their top in one ascent. However, in groups, each tree may have to be taken on individually. Generally, it's best to start with the smallest and work up to the largest in the group. If they're close together you may be able to work two or three at a time.

Most of the work in these trees can be adequately performed out of the safety line and spurs. This means climbing up the trunk and cutting off the limbs as you go. In spite of not needing a climb line in a lot of the trees, you'll still see many climbers pack one up with them. You won't see this as much in the small trees as in the larger ones. It's just a good safety measure to pack a climb line if you're going up over forty feet. It's better to pack it up with you than to leave the coils lying on the ground and have the limbs land on them. It'll tangle the coils and there's the possibility of it catching your line and giving you a heck of a jerk. In the

larger forest trees, because of their sheer size, it may be the best thing to climb to the top and set a climb line to work out of. This entails two ascents up the tree. Having the climb line set does not mean that you'll be working out of it alone; you should still have a safety around the tree or fixed on a limb somewhere. This is just good safety practice.

As simple as the procedures may seem in these trees, the work can still be quite hard. You're in the spurs much of the time and working out of a safety for hours on end at heights of up to two hundred feet or more. If the tree leans, it can be especially difficult to climb and wreck out. In this case, you may be restricted to working off the high side and having to reach around to cut the low side. This is not an easy task. Ideally, you should fix a climb line in an adjacent tree to help support you while working in a leaning one. This will make working in a leaner a whole lot easier. Often there are no neighboring trees to tie into. You may be able to set a second safety over a limb on the high side of the trunk to help support you while reaching around to the low side. Use the double-safety techniques for most of this work.

The small forest trees are pretty simple and safe. Their limbs are generally ascending in nature and not very heavy. The wood in the limbs is also resilient and you'll find that most of the cuts you try to use will work out the way they are supposed to. A chainsaw is not necessary to brush out these small trees and you can get by adequately using the hand saw. In the moderately aged forest trees you will find a combination of an older tree and younger tree. The lower part contains older and heavier limbs while the top retains juvenile characteristics. It's best to work out of a double safety in the older parts, and it's best to set your position to cut these limbs from a good side stance or higher. You'll find that the heavier limbs command special attention and respect. They can split out if you treat them casually. However, one virtue of most forest trees is that their limbs will generally not run a split into the trunk.

GENERAL TIPS ON BRUSHING OUT BROAD TREES

The limbing procedure in broad trees (oaks, maples, walnuts, etc.), often has to be done in sections. This results in about half of the tree getting brushed out before any other part is started. Each section or spar of the tree will usually need its limbs or brush removed from the bottom first. In broad trees, the limbing procedure requires a lot more double-safety and climb-line technique. However, you'll generally have more options for setting your lines in these trees than you do in forest trees. The developing spars in a broad tree are made up of a number of limbs that branch off a main stem. In the small trees, the spars are usually ascending in nature. In a typical small, broad tree, there can be several spars branching off a main trunk and you may have the option to drop each spar entirely or else you can position yourself to cut it down in its individual parts. As a rule, the spar will take up more room to fall and land in a given area if dropped in its entirety. By careful cutting and hinging you can drop the individual limbs and main stem of the same spar in a smaller area.

The sequence in which you cut the limbs and spars out of these trees entails a different kind of movement through them in comparison to the forest tree. Instead of the limbs being right in front of you on the main trunk, they'll branch off to one side or another. Your relative right and left lateral positions and stances will be more clearly defined. This is true in forest trees too, but in them you usually have more of an option to pick your position unless the tree is in a lean. You'll seldom work very high in broad trees. In most of them you can do your work using a short climb line and safety. Some of the big oaks, though, can reach nearly one hundred feet high. Fixing a climb line is generally the first thing you do in large, broad trees. It would behoove you to set several lines when you get to the top of the tree and throw them out over each main spar in the tree. This can save a considerable amount of climbing in some trees. Since you frequently rely on the climb line for support in broad trees, you don't have to depend on the spurs as much. This is true for most broad trees; in fact, you'll have a lot of opportunity to stand or sit on the spars so you seldom get shin sores from the spurs. Not so in the forest trees where you can spend the whole climb in the spurs. However, due to the shapes that some of these broad trees grow into, not all of them will offer that advantage. Some broad trees will not have a suitable lead to tie into for support while working in them. In the big trees, you will often have to crotch-hop out to where you'll do the cutting or lie on your belly for some of it. You can still stabilize your position by the frequent use of tagging, biting, and adversely setting your safety lines.

Improperly executed cuts in broad trees can prompt splits to run up or down the stem, past crotch unions, and into the trunk. Never safety around any large limbs you're cutting off, especially if you cannot get in a position to properly execute the cut. Remember, if you can't properly execute the cut, it may not be safe to proceed with the work. Never attempt to cut an entire spar off a large, broad tree unless you know exactly what you're doing. The best thing to do is play it safe and climb out on it and take it down in pieces. This way, you will not be working with such extreme leverage forces.

TO HINGE OR NOT TO HINGE?

In brushing out a tree, the amount of hinging you impart to a limb dictates how it will leave the tree, fall, and land in the hole. The hole is the area that you cut the limbs to fall into. In most situations, you want the limbs to land flat on the ground because any limb that lands flat will stay put and not be inclined to take a so-called bad bounce. A limb that lands on its brush or butt end is inclined to spring, bounce, or land farther away from the tree. It is all in your control depending on how you impart the limb to hinge and drop. A number of factors determine the degree of hinging necessary in the removal of a particular limb. These factors are the height the limb is above the ground, its attitude, its aerodynamics, and its size. All of these factors have a strong effect on each other; when you consider one, you must consider them all.

THE HEIGHT OF THE LIMB

Close to the ground, a limb has very little time to fall. The higher you go up the tree, the more time the limb will have to fall before it reaches the ground. This has a strong effect on how a limb will land in the hole, considering the other factors.

THE ATTITUDE OF THE LIMB

This refers to the angle of the limb off the side of the tree. For example, with an ascending limb close to the ground you may desire that it hinge to a minor degree before it begins to free fall. Being close to the ground does not give it much time to fall, and with a minor degree of hinging it should land flat as a pancake. Higher up, the same limb cut the same way, will land much differently. It has more time to fall, and the butt end will have time to take the lead during the fall. It will land farther away from the tree on its butt end and then lay out. In this case you should hinge the limb moderately before it leaves the tree. Higher up yet, you will need even more hinging in the ascending limb to correct its approach by the time it hits the ground.

Pendent, or drooping limbs that are low lying to the ground are notorious for hitting on their brushy end first, with their butt ends propping against the side of the trunk or springing beyond it. Always get above these limbs to trip them loose; a side stance puts you in a vulnerable position. You can remedy the tendency a lot by executing an improved jump cut some distance from the trunk. This helps higher up the tree too, because it can give the butt of the limb room to take the lead in the fall without coming into contact with the trunk of the tree.

AERODYNAMICS OF THE LIMBS

The wind resistance of the limb is another factor which can affect how a limb lands in the hole. Bushy limbs will catch a lot of wind and orient themselves butt first very quickly during a fall. The distribution of the foliage on the limb has a lot to do with how it will land. Limbs that have all their foliage on the terminal end will react quickly to the wind. Limbs that are uniformly covered with foliage from the butt to the end will react more slowly.

THE SIZE OF THE LIMBS

From high up the tree there is a greater degree of success landing the larger limbs correctly than the smaller ones. Compared to large limbs, small limbs have a greater distance to fall and can more easily be blown by the wind. The slightest breeze can carry small limbs far away from where you need them to land. You may not be able to free-fall the smaller limbs from very high up if the wind is blowing.

After you look at a limb and weigh out the above factors, your next step is to cut the limb. Do you want the limb to leave the cut quickly without any hinging, or do you want a certain degree of hinging to occur before it leaves the tree? You have a high degree of control over the limb's fall depending on how you cut the limb. Beginners may have a rough time trying to keep control of it at first. But after doing it for a while, a person will begin to better understand how all the factors play off of one another.

SLINGING A LIMB

This is the technique of using the momentum that a limb gains, or section of wood, as it hinges, to propel it back, or to one side. There are many applications to this. For it to be successful the work must not fall free of the cut until it fully hinges over, and it must be at that time precisely for the momentum to carry it where you need it. If the work falls loose before that, or on a back swing, it will land short of your goal or where you didn't want it to; eaves of a roof, fence, road, power lines. There is an element of risk in tight quarters for those reasons. In spite of it, it is a widely used and understood technique in this business. It takes a lot of understanding and good judgment to know where and how it can be used effectively. Simple hinge cuts and face cuts both can be used to sling the work, but each cut must be tailored to fit the situation and the execution must be performed properly. It takes practice.

CULPRIT LIMBS

When you go about limbing or brushing out any tree, you should be aware of the so-called culprit limbs. These are limbs that can cause physical harm or property damage. The tricky thing about them is that they don't look dangerous.

THE STRAFER

This term was coined during World War II. It means to attack quickly and unmercifully. The strafing limb was referred to in the section on the attitude of limbs. Particularly those that are long, pendent, and close to the ground. The remedy for strafing limbs was also discussed. It is just mentioned here again because they are such culprits.

THE TANGLER

Not all trees grow free of tangles. It's in your best interest to observe each limb you cut for tangles with other limbs before you cut it loose. If you're cutting a limb that is tangled with another limb over your head, the overhead limb may break and hit you. If it's tangled on the end, it can prompt the butt to swing away from the tree, causing the entire limb to land well outside the perimeter of the tree's canopy. If tangled on its stem, the end can drop and the butt kick up! It can strike you. Observe the limbs carefully and pick and choose the order in which to cut them out. This might require you to do some scampering around in the tree.

THE DOUBLE-CROSSER

This limb will not noticeably be tangled with anything. But when it hinges or falls it can cross leads with another limb, thereby ruining your plan. Observe the area where the limb will hinge, or fall, and see if any leads are going to cross.

THE TWISTER

Twisters will foil your cut due to the heavy, offset imbalance in the limb. I've seen it foil many a jump cut and turn it into a twist-over hinge. If you're going for a jump cut to begin with, this twisting action may really ruin your plan. The only remedy may be to climb out on the limb and remove the leads creating the offset imbalance. Or change your plan.

THE CRACKER

Cracked or broken limbs are another problem the climber has to contend with. Generally speaking, it's an easy defect to spy in the limbs you're cutting, so you can usually account for it. As a rule, cracked or broken limbs are not dependable enough to predict how they will hinge or leave a cut. It pays not to take any chances with them if you're counting on controlling them. Limbs that you can't tell are cracked and broken present certain risk. Your work can prompt an unknowing cracked limb to break over or beside you. Be observant!

THE GRAFTER

Grafted limbs are also tricky. As a rule, whenever you cut a grafted limb, you are relieving some kind of bind or pressure. They are not always noticeable and can catch you by surprise. In some cases, a grafted limb can hold certain parts of the tree together, after it's cut the parts can come apart. For example, take the case of a graft holding a double tree from splitting apart. In my experience, I've seen it happen once. But I've seen many other similar cases where it was decided not to cut the graft loose for this reason. It's not possible to accurately predict the outcome when you cut a pair or more of grafted and crossed limbs. Keep your eyes open for them.

HEAVY LIMBS

The real problem with heavy limbs is usually the sawyer. A beginner may have a hard time determining exactly what is a heavy limb. Heavy limbs are under a lot of tension and pressure. They can break just as a result of placing an undercut or sap cut. Attempting to cut them off cleanly is often in vain and generally results in major splitting, wood pull and loss of control. Your only option may be to climb out on the limb and take some of the weight off it. By doing so you will ease the tension and pressure on the limb and make it safe to cut the rest. The techniques for setting lines and getting out on a limb to cut it in pieces are described in **Chapter 15— Overhanging Limbs**.

PROTECTING LIMBS

At times, in either forest trees or broad trees, you may leave a particular limb below onto which to drop others. That limb may be directly over a fence or eve of a house. In essence, it protects the fence or eve by breaking the fall of the limbs you're dropping from above. In such a case, you can often use that limb to protect the property but also get the others you're cutting to roll off of it to one side or the other. This is a fairly common practice, but there are some catches to it. Any limbs you drop on the one below should be cut into small pieces that won't crash against the protecting limb too hard. Also, if you plan to load the protecting limb with others, the limb may break from the load. This is especially true if the ground worker is pulling the brush off of it. The protecting limb frequently cracks or breaks from the added stress of bearing it down when pulling off the limbs.

CLEAN-UP CONSIDERATIONS

While a climber is in the tree brushing it out, clean-up operations can be in progress simultaneously. One way to do this is to have the climber cut out a number of limbs and then stop long enough for the ground worker to enter the hole and pull them out. Alternating in this fashion works well. However, the climber should always look below for acknowledgment that it is okay to cut more limbs. The climber should also give a verbal warning when limbs are about to come down. The ground worker must let the climber know when to stop cutting so they can enter the hole to pull the brush out. Failure on either person's part to give warning will inevitably result in the ground worker being struck.

While the climber waits for the ground worker to clear out the hole, they can reset their lines and get into position to send another volley of brush down. In this way, no one is ever waiting on anyone else.

Depending on the situation, there may be more than one hole to drop brush into. A climber may be working on one side of a large tree while clean-up operations are in progress on the other side. But there must be some distance between the two operations in order to be safe. There must be no chance of a limb taking a bad bounce and clobbering a ground worker. If a chance exists, there is not enough room between the two operations, but when there is, it can make a job move right along. For example, the climber can knock out a volley of limbs on one side of the tree to get the ground operation going for half an hour or so. And while they are working, the climber can move to the other side of the tree and knock out a volley of limbs and brush there. This is what teamwork is all about. I've done this a number of times over the years in the large cypress hedge rows we have on the coast.

In large trees, a climber can create a lot of work for the ground crew in just a few cuts. A lot of times it doesn't pay to send down too much brush at once because it piles up on itself and can get very tangled. It can create more work to cut and pull out than if you sent the same amount down in two sets. If you're going to send down a volume of big limbs, it might be best to let the ground worker enter after every other limb so that they can cut each one up into manageable pieces before you send down more. This way, when the ground crew comes in to pull the brush out, it may be in a big pile, but it'll be all cut up. As a climber, you should recognize the things that may slow the ground operations.

Chapter 15

Overhanging Limbs

The removal and pulling of overhanging limbs constitutes a good part of a climber's work, especially in the line-clearing business. Though most overhangs can be considered routine, there are always those that present a challenge. The term overhanging means that there is something below the limb preventing its removal by simply cutting it off.

THE SMALL OVERHANGING LIMB

This limb can be cut with a hand saw and removed by hand without any lines or assistance. Wherever they are, you'll use the same

techniques for handling them. Their removal starts with setting your lines and putting yourself in the most advantageous position. That position may be under, over, or beside the limb in question. A small limb can be difficult to manage if you're not in the right position. Once you get in a position you feel is right, anchor yourself. If you're not anchored, you may pull yourself to a limb instead of pulling the limb to you.

Some limbs in this class may be hinged downward easily enough and then discarded into the hole. Use the simple hinge cut. Hold on to the butt while cutting it. Many a limb has unexpectedly broken free of the cut and fallen into roadways and power lines because a climber did not follow this advice.

It's not always necessary to put the hand saw away in order to discard the limb into the hole. They may be so small that one hand is all it takes. If you're in an awkward position, it may be best to put the hand saw away so both hands can be used. This is where a light line on the hand saw comes in handy because, frequently, you have to just let go of the hand saw to get both hands on the work.

When side-hinging a small limb, you can get in position to push or pull it. Whatever position you choose, make sure it's rigid and affords you the anchoring necessary to push or pull the limb. As previously mentioned, if you're not anchored properly you may not be able to use your power to budge the limb even if it is small. Be aware that all limbs have the desire to drop down during side-hinging. It's a good idea to have a hold of the butt and a grasp on the stem a little farther out to hold the weight while pushing or pulling it. This is very important to remember in line clearance work. Such limbs have snapped and dropped on the power lines because the climber did not handle them correctly. A partial crosscut on the side of the limb is all that is needed, but it must be on the opposite side of where the hinging is directed. Often it's best to nip the bottom of the limb just a whisker. Put the hand saw away, get the proper grasp on the limb, and put your power to it.

When a small limb must be raised to clear the obstacle, positioning yourself over the limb to pull it up is the best way to manage it. But since it's small, it may be convenient to raise the limb by pushing it up from below. Pulling the limb from above will give you the most control you'll ever get on it. Just make sure that there's room to do it without it tangling or interfering with other limbs. It may be necessary to trim or cut around the limb to get the working room you need. When pulling the limb upward, it must first be undercut. Position yourself to execute the cut. The cut is usually made deep enough when the limb pinches on the hand saw. After that re-position yourself above the limb to pull it.

If you have a problem pulling the limb, maybe you misjudged its size and weight. Or perhaps your position is not adequate to manage it. If you're not careful, you can lose a limb that is cut up and ready to break over. If the tree is in seed or fruit, the limbs, even if they are small, can be extremely heavy. In this case, you are on the threshold of tackling moderate-sized limbs, which require other safeguards and procedures to handle properly. Everyone does it sooner or later. To avoid it, just look at the situation carefully and be honest with yourself. If for any reason you don't think you can handle the limb, you're probably not dealing with a small limb. It may fall into the realm of moderate and heavy overhanging limbs.

MODERATE-SIZED OVERHANGING LIMBS

Removal of moderate-sized overhanging limbs is done by either climbing out on the limb and cutting it into manageable pieces that can be discarded into the hole (called "piecing out") or by rigging the limb with a line to pull, catch or lower it.

Most cutting on these limbs can be managed quite easily with a hand saw, but some parts, like butt-ends and stubs, are usually removed with a power saw.

PIECING OUT THE OVERHANG

When the limb is to be pieced out, fix a climb line in a suitable crotch above the limb so the line will support your weight while you're away from the trunk and out on the limb. The higher above the limb you tie in, the easier it'll be for you to work farther out on it. With limbs that angle upward, the natural tendency of the tie-in to swing you back toward the trunk will cause the limb to raise. This effect diminishes as the angle of the limb evens. On drooping or pendent limbs, the tendency for the climb line to pull you back will exert downward pressure, possibly enough to break them. You can reduce this effect considerably by getting the highest tie-in available over the parts of the limb you'll be working on. You'll also find that the upward-angled limbs are easier to cut and manage the pieces off because you're reaching up or even to yourself. On even limbs, you're reaching outward to cut and pull the pieces off. On drooping limbs, you're reaching below, or downward, to accomplish the same task. The peculiarities of the limb angle are essential to know.

Piecing out the overhang.

After you tie in, come down over any other limbs, or trim and remove the ones that you know will catch the run in the climb line. This will give you and your line a clear run out to the end of the limb you're going to piece out. If the limb is angling upward, you may have to take slack out of the line as you progress your way out on it. The preferred way to hold your position on the limb while pulling slack is with a leg lock, but you may safety to the limb if you can't get a leg lock on it. On even limbs, you have to pay out line as you work your way out on them. The same applies to drooping limbs when you're working your way down them. Paying out line only requires one hand; usually you will not have to stop your movement while doing it.

Keep your weight in your climb line as you climb out on a limb. Lean to the side of the limb also. It helps a lot and it also makes adjustments in your climb line easier. If you're in the habit of working your way out on top, you'll exert weight on the limb more often.

If there's any relative side pull from the climb line, to one side or another, you should face it while you work your way out. Also, it's not always necessary to fix a safety to get out on a limb, to fix lines, or even to cut and work it off. You can often use a leg lock to hold your position while you do the work and not have to rely on the safety all the time.

If the limb is being entirely removed, cut what branches and brush off of it you can while working your way out on it. This helps lighten and strengthen the limb. If you draw up tightly on your climb line, it'll tend to pull you to the high side of the limb and can even pull the limb up. When you let out line, your weight shifts and the limb lowers or even bears down. This is one way you can adjust your working position on the limb. When it becomes necessary to fix a safety, set it so it holds you securely. Unless there's a crotch or stub to hold the safety in place, you'll have to fix it to the limb with a wrap. This is ever so important when you work with a difficult or short tie-in. Such tie-ins can bear a hard back pull on you the whole time, and can cause a slip if the safety is not secure.

LATERAL POSITION CHANGES

To work both sides of a limb may require a lateral position change. This term can be better explained if you think about how a mirror reverses right or left lateral images. Quite often, you will have to reverse your position on a limb in the same way. On ascending limbs with a high overhead back pull from the climb line, this maneuver is easy. If you're on the relative right side of the limb with a right-foot leg lock and left-foot spur hold, make the following moves: adjust and safety to the limb; grasp the climb line over your head; hold yourself up by the climb line; tuck your upper torso under and around the line and at the same time change your footing to a left-foot leg lock and right-foot spur hold. On even or descending limbs this can be difficult to do for obvious reasons; the climb line is at a harder angle relative to your position on the limb. Climb-line angles will govern the difficulty of the change considerably, especially if there is a relative side pull in it. However, if the limb is strong enough to support your weight, it can nullify the difficulty. The beginner should know that lateral changes are performed frequently in the removal of many overhanging limbs. The main reason for this is that it gives you a better position to work either side of the limb.

In many situations, it is possible for a climber to work off other limbs within reach of the limb they're working on. The ends of some limbs are pretty flexible, enabling you to adjust your position and pull many other limbs within your reach with the rope, throw line, hand saw, or pole pruners. This is particularly advantageous while trimming and shaping trees as well as speeding along the removal of many a limb on the side of a tree. Most limbs that you're working on in this way will get lighter as you work your way back to the trunk. To compensate for the change in your position and the possibility of the limb rising, you will have to adjust your lines accordingly. Beware that cutting the weight off the end of a heavy limb can make it spring, shake or raise abruptly, i.e. a dynamic cut. It can roll you over if you're not expecting it. This is no time to be running a chainsaw. Secure your perch, get a grasp on the climb line with one hand to take up any slack when the limb raises, and trip the cut with a hand saw.

DISCARDING AND THROWING LIMBS

All kinds of limbing can be done with a good, sharp handsaw, and many climbers can handle limbs up to 50 lbs. in weight. Rule number one: don't cut more than you can manage! What should you do with a limb once you cut it? In line clearance, you will be working over and beside the power lines, over roadways and over a lot of structures, so you're often without much room to discard the limbs you cut. How to do it depends on the amount of room available and the size of the limb.

THE DROP (BRUSH FIRST)

For most limbs cut with a handsaw, you will be holding them by the butt end. Observe the taper and belly of the limb. The taper and belly have a direct bearing on how a limb will orient itself in a fall. As a rule, the belly, or bow, of a limb will indicate the direction the butt will naturally lay out when you drop it. So you have a lot of control on how a limb will lay out by how you orient the belly of it before you drop it. By putting impetus one way or the other you can change, or enhance, the natural tendency.

THE DROP (BUTT FIRST)

If you want to drop a limb through others with the hope of it reaching the ground then drop it butt first. As a rule, a limb that falls butt first will not lay out until it hits the ground. A limb dropped as such is also not likely to take a so-called bad bounce thereafter, quite unlike a limb that hits on its brush end first. However, a limb that lands butt first hits hard, and can stick in the ground or punch a hole in a roof.

THE WING

Limbs up to 10 pounds. Grasp these small limbs by the tip of their brushy end and use a flick of your wrist and forearm to wing them to a desired direction. This action is one of the better ways of dealing with small limbs.

THE THROW

Limbs up to 15-20 pounds. Grasp the limb by its mid-stem, or balance point, and throw it like you would a spear. It's best to throw limbs with the butt end leading. It's aerodynamically correct, it's accurate, and you stand a much better chance of getting a limb through tight or congested parts of the tree.

THE CHUCK

Limbs up to 40-50 pounds. Grasp the limb by its butt end with one hand, then pick it up by its stem with the other. With a hold like this you chuck the limb brush-first with impetus on the butt end to overtake and lead. With this size of limb and using the chuck, more horizontal distance can be gained in the discard over using any other method.

BUTT-TYING

Limbs that have enough room to hinge over an obstacle can be caught in a line and lowered to the hole by butt-tying them. Even if you could free fall certain limbs, some situations may make it more convenient to lower them this way.

If there's a lot of work to do, you should run the bull line through a block located over the limbs to be removed. If there's just a few limbs, you can crotch the line instead. Observe where in the tree you set the block or crotch the line. It can make a big difference on which side of the tree the limbs lower down. By using hitches or snap-on gear you can take more than one limb at a time. Snap-on gear is the best means, as hitches can come loose from one or more limbs if they hang up on something before reaching the ground.

PULLING LIMBS

Here, you may still have to climb out on the limb to secure the pull line, but you usually won't have to go out as far as it takes to piece the limb out. The line can also be set at farther reaches using the throw line, throw hook, stick, or pole pruners.

It's important to take note of the arrangement of the limbs to be removed. You may have to do some trimming or removal of other minor limbs that may block or crowd the work. If the tree is being removed, whenever possible, you should leave the risky parts for last. When pulling limbs that overhang power lines this is the number one rule. So, if you're wrecking out the tree and it has limbs that overhang power lines, your first moves should be to remove all the limbs over and around the risky ones.

If you have just a few limbs to pull, you can run the pull line through a crotch if it's smooth and suitably located. But, if you're going to do some heavy pulling then run the line through a block. The line must run from the block to the limb without any interference from other limbs.

Where the limb is rigged is very important and deserves careful consideration. As a rule, whenever pulling limbs, it is best to rig them so

they are butt-heavy. There are a number of very important reasons why. A tip heavy limb that's being held, or pulled, can fall over the wrong way when the butt is cut or broke loose; the end falling over can take out power lines or private structures; the butt end of a limb being held like this will kick upward. It can shoot back if the purchase in the line is

LIMB IMBALANCE

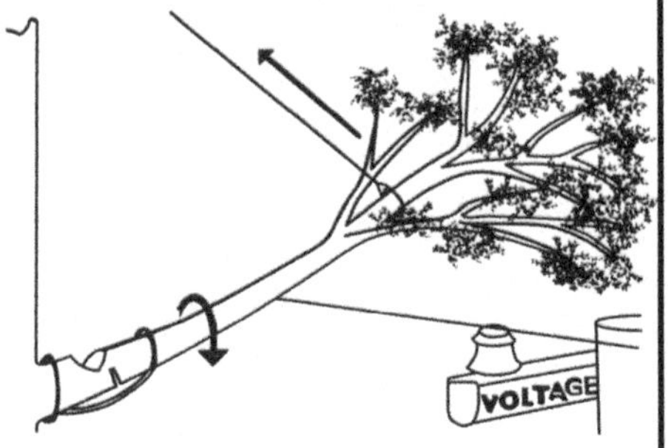

SWEEP AND OFF BEARING WEIGHT CAN CAUSE A LIMB TO TWIST OVER WHEN IT'S PULLED.

ACCOUNT FOR IT WHEN WORKING OVER POWER!

coming from that direction; a climber can be severely injured by it. It takes more power to pull a limb that isn't butt-heavy since the majority of the weight is then outside the rigging. Limbs that are butt-heavy and hanging in the line can be lowered down through other limbs much more easily.

Even rigging a limb so it's butt-heavy may not keep it in control if there are other imbalances. Many have the tendency to twist or turn over while they're being pulled. This is due to either a high center of gravity or a side-bearing load on the limb. So, before you pull some, it might be best to cut some of the weight off one side or the other. If you anticipate a limb twisting over when you pull it, you should butt-tie it to keep it from shooting back Frequently they will shoot back when they twist over, so butt-tying can be important.

As a climber doing your own pulling, you may want to use a hoist and hold block. This allows you to let go of the line while doing any cutting or other management to the limbs.

PENDENT LIMBS

Heavily drooping limbs cannot always be satisfactorily pulled upward. The force required to pull some may be greater than the strength of the wood to hold the butt in place. Better results can be had if the limb is pulled or swung to the side. In either case, you should butt-tie the limb to keep the butt in place. Drooping limbs are better off butt-tied and lowered to the hole. This is only possible where there is room below to manage it. When butt-tied, drooping limbs don't fall over as far as an ascending limb of equal length. This is important to know as it gives you an idea how much room there is under a limb to let it hinge and still clear an obstacle.

SWINGING LIMBS

At times it is necessary to swing limbs to clear an obstacle. A line is needed to hold the limb and another to pull the limb to the side. The holding line requires room to follow the course of the limb. The pull line need not be as strong as the support line unless it is going to be used to lower the limbs. Butt-ties are highly recommended. The best cut to use for swinging limbs in this manner is a wide face cut with a gap. These procedures can take a substantial amount of rigging and planning. For a more detailed description of this technique se**e Chapter 28— "Holding and Swinging Side Leaners."**

LARGE OVERHANGING LIMBS

Most large overhangs can be pieced out using methods discussed for small and moderate size limbs. Most large overhangs are removed in this manner anyway, because their size makes it impractical or unsafe to pull them in one shot. I pulled a eucalyptus limb that was 60 feet long in one shot once. It overhung the county road and high voltage lines. If you try something like that, make sure you have the room, the proper angles and the rigging to manage it safely. Follow the rules for pulling moderate size limbs, but be redundant in your plan. With this size of limb you will use capstans, come-alongs, winches or vehicles to do the pulling.

Chapter 16

Topping the Tree

GENERAL TREE-TOPPING PROVISIONS

The practices used in tree-topping are essentially the same as those used in tree falling. A person must have a fair degree of knowledge about falling trees to understand what is involved when topping them. A few differences should be noted. The potential hazards resulting from an error in tree-topping are higher than in any other phase of tree work. In any other work a climber is doing in the tree, they can almost always put themselves in a safe position above or to the side of their work. In tree topping, there is really no place for the climber to get above or out from under the top. This is really tree falling except that you're safetied to the stump. The climber is right at the crux of the action with no place to go. You can't afford to make any mistakes here.

I strongly advise the beginner to read the chapters on tree falling before they top any trees.

SHIFTING THE FAVOR OF THE TOP

Some tops can be deceptively well-balanced. When you encounter a top like this, trim some weight off one side to shift the balance to the side you want the top to fall toward. This is called shifting the balance. You can even go as far as taking the limbs you cut off of one side of the top and load them up in the limbs on the other side. This is referred to as loading a top. It's a good trick to get the balance of a top where you need it. If you fail to do either of these things and you've misjudged the balance of the top, it could set back.

TOP SETTING BACK

If you realize the top is going to set back, there are a number of things you can do. First, stop cutting and get a wedge in the back cut. If you don't have a wedge, leave the saw in the back cut. It can keep a top from setting back hard. Next, check the hinge wood. If there's sufficient hinge wood to hold the top, there may be no need for alarm. But if part of the hinge is cut through, any rocking, wind, or shaking of the tree may cause the top to break over the wrong way. If this is a concern, advise any persons below you to go to a safe position, as the top may fall in a road, over power lines, or on a house. **Your life may well be in serious danger!**

Most small tops don't require a lot of power to push them over; you can also reach up and pull them over. On tops beyond your ability to push or pull over, you can throw a line up in them and have a person on the ground pull them. If you have a pole saw or pruner with extensions, you may be able to use it to put the line in the top or to trim some of the weight off the back side. In larger tops, you should always carry a wedge. After an experience of having a top set back, you'll get better at determining their true favor. If there's any doubt, you'll know what preventive measures to take to ensure that it does go the right way.

CUTTING THE TOP ASTRAY

Another error a person can make when cutting a top that has deceptive balance is to cut it completely loose and have it go astray. Unfortunately, there is nothing you can do when it happens except take cover wherever you can. The cause of this kind of error is false expectations. You believe the favor of the top will carry it over to the face and you believe it will do this if you keep on cutting. This is a common error in tree falling too, but in topping you can see that it can be more dangerous.

HEAVY TOPS

Some of the worst stories you will ever hear about massive splitting in the tree, resulting in injury to the climber, come from cutting out heavy tops. Enter the top and cut out the weight that makes it so heavy, or cut the top out in several pieces. This is the most prudent way to cut out a heavy top. It's a commonly used safety precaution in tree topping. When coming down to cut the remainder of the top, you will often rappel down using the climb line. Some climbers have been known to cut out the very top they were tied into. This kind of thing happens when you get in a hurry and don't pay attention to what you're doing. So, always look up at the top before cutting it out; this way you'll spot your climb line if it's there.

BACKING UP A HEAVY TOP

If you decide to cut out a heavy top, you must understand what happens. As a firm rule, the back cut, once started in a heavy top, must be able to continue without any hesitation and must be made as quickly as possible with a minimum hinge before the face closes. You need a powerful and sharp saw to do it. If your progress is slow when making the back cut, a heavy top will start breaking an excessive amount of wood. This can induce a split to run in the top or the trunk of the tree. Binding the top and trunk with chain can prevent a split from running deep.

SECURING YOUR PERCH

When topping trees it's important you have a secure perch, but it can be difficult on a bare trunk. One way of bracing yourself could come by using the following procedure. First, set your safety with a wrap.

Then set one spur deep and bring the other leg up against the trunk. Push against the trunk with that knee, or shin, to keep the safety taut. This provides rigidness and improves your stability. When possible, utilize some limbs and/or crotches to assist securing a perch. Even with that you should brace yourself and be ready for the catapulting action that is so common in topping trees. Also, it's always a good idea to tie in with the climb line before topping out a tree. If something goes wrong and you get hurt: at least you're tied in with a means of getting to the ground.

CATAPULTING ACTION

On straight trees there is an initial push force exerted on the trunk by the top as it begins tipping over because the top is connected by the hinge and wants to rotate about its center of gravity. The trunk in turn pushes on the top accelerating it in the direction of the fall. About the time the top has laid over horizontal and is leaving the cut the trunk has stopped moving back and is still pushing on the top which is now accelerating from a centrifugal pull that reaches its maximum about the time the top leaves the cut. This pull on the trunk combined with the breaking of a beefy hinge can result in significant catapulting action. When cutting out heavy tops it's automatic.

This catapulting has been the highlight of many a tree-topping story. All trees do it. So you have to expect it and be ready for it. Secure your perch so you won't get thrown out of it, and shut the saw down the instant the hinge wood breaks. Remember, you can control the action by how much wood you leave in the hinge to break. Don't leave too much.

PULLING TOPS

The hazards and mishaps from pulling tops are many. As a rule, you should pull your tops. It's a good safety measure. But a lot of people have gotten hurt by this practice because they didn't follow the rules and concepts of the line angles necessary to pull certain tops. It's hard to get a good angle of pull on some tops because they may be so high up. The error that can occur is that the angle of pull is inadequate and fails to deliver the force needed to pull the top outward. Instead, it pulls downward. If this happens, you're likely to lose the top backwards. To remedy it, get the line angle pulling from an outward direction on the top. This generally means to get a long way from the tree and have a lot of line. You may improve the angle by pulling from uphill. Or even by getting someone to pull the top from up in another tree.

Another line-angle rule to adhere to is to keep the angle of pull in lead with the direction the top will be cut out of the tree. Pulling off to one side of it by slight degrees rarely results in any mishaps. But you should never exceed that angle by more than forty-five degrees or you will begin pulling more on the corner of the hinge than in the direction of the intended fall. Exceptions to this are elaborated on in the tree falling chapters.

Failing to set the pull line high enough over the hinge has been the cause of many lost tops. You always have more leverage to pull a top the higher up over the hinge you set the pull line. It's really as simple as that. But many people, over the years, get lazy and don't set the pull line high enough. As a rule of thumb set the line halfway up the top from where you cut it out. There are many exceptions to this. At times you can get by with less and at times you will need more. The interrelationship of the other two factors mentioned will have a lot to do with where you set the pull line.

Over- or under-tension of the pull line has been the cause of many a topping accident. The exact tension in a line needed to pull any top is dependent on many things besides the ones already covered, although those discussed do govern it a great deal. At times you'll need the line tensioned to pull the top only after it is cut up. Other times you will need the line tensioned to pick a top up first and hold it so the cut can be made. Then you can give the signal to pull it over. There is often a lot of miscommunication about these details. Probably the biggest confusion has been over-tensioning and pulling of the line. What's important is to understand the procedures and signals between the climber and the person doing the pulling. Don't get them confused. Since you may be the climber, you can't afford this kind of error to happen.

The exact procedures for pulling treetops are much the same as pulling trees (See **Chapter 31**). The difference between the climber and the faller is that the faller can walk away from a tree that is being pulled and a climber can't always. In some trees, though, it may be the safest thing for a climber to do. Descending out of a tree before pulling a top is a procedure that requires very careful planning. You need just enough holding wood to hold the top until you get down and out of the way. Leaving too much hinge wood may require another trip back up the tree to do more cutting. I advise a wide face cut because narrow ones in combination with a beefy hinge lead to a top tipping and not breaking free of the tree. A situation like that may not be correctable. Hence, do it right the first time! Working out of a climb line that's fixed in an adjacent or nearby tree can offer a climber a safer route to leave the tree they're topping. This involves knowledgeable use of the climb line and traverse procedures (See **Chapters 6** and **12**).

PULLING SIDE HEAVY TOPS

The resulting catapulting action while doing this can throw a climber completely off their perch. The action is not just back and forth, it's orbital. It is the direction of pull versus the direction of recovery when the tree loses its top. This is not a safe time to be running a chain saw. Tall or spindly trees that are in a lean are candidates for this. I recommend knowledgeable judgment and preparedness in this situation.

PULLING ON THE BUTT OF A TOP

This is a method used to prompt a treetop to land farther out or away from the tree. It works well to get a top to clear an obstacle that lies just under the tree. With a line fixed to the butt of the top pull smartly after the top tips over and breaks free of the cut. Make the face angle approximately 45 degrees and leave minimum hinge wood to break.

Good line angles are important here. Without a direct angle of pull from the desired direction the results can fall short of your expectations. The power, timing and pull speed in the line are other factors to consider. Using a stretched out bungee between anchor and line can significantly increase the range effect. Do not confuse this with the discussion on pulling tops. If a top actually needs to be pulled to get it over then the location of this line will not adequately do it.

OBSTACLES IN THE WAY OF THE TOP

This factor is probably the second biggest cause of accidents in tree topping. Obstacles can be hidden limbs, vines, wires, and other tops that can deflect the top you've cut off its course. If the top side swipes another tree's limbs while it is going over, it will cause the butt to roll off the side of the trunk. If this happens to be the side you're on it'll land in your lap. Should the top hit broadside against another tree, it will cause the butt to push hard against the trunk and make the tree bow back from the pressure. If or when it breaks loose, the butt of the top can shoot back and hit you. High back cuts can prevent this from happening. Should you cut a top completely loose and it's held by an unseen limb from another tree, it can cause the top to twist off the stump and fall straight down on you. If you're working in the vicinity of power lines and fail to notice them, electrocution is also possible. Tops need a clear path to tip and fall!

TOPPING TREES IN THE WIND

Don't top trees in the wind. The wind has been the reason of many a lost top and injury. The wind can exert a tremendous amount of leverage on a tree. It can cause a top to set back, go astray or split out.

TOPPING NEAR THE GROUND

Never cut the top out of a tree where your height above the ground is less than the distance from your position to the tree's top. There are exceptions to this rule. It may be safe to top: if the trees are small; if you're topping downhill; and if all is clear. However, if that criteria is not met it can be very unsafe indeed because it puts you in an area where you're faced with both ground and aerial related hazards.

SMALL TOPS

Most small treetops will bow over to whatever side you're on. And they'll bow more pronouncedly if you extend your safety and hang off to one side. You can use this to your advantage to get small tops to favor a particular side. If the top you're in is particularly limber and sways from your movement, you should safety close to it and brace yourself against the trunk with one or both knees. This will help you maintain your stability and keep a small top from swaying badly. In someone's backyard, you may be in a small tree twenty to thirty feet up doing this. But in forest trees you may regularly be working with trunk diameters of a few inches and at heights well over one hundred feet.

Tops have broken out before while a climber's been in them. This is generally caused by a structural defect in the top, which the climber didn't recognize. The defects you should watch for are tops that emerge from natural split crotches and sucker tops that grow from an old cut. The ability of a good, sound top to hold a climber's weight is governed by three factors. The first is the taper of the top: a stout taper makes for a steady top, while a fine taper makes a top limber and thus, prone to swaying. The second is the degree of lean, if any. Size for size, you can work higher in a straight top than a leaning one. And the third is, how far the climber extends their safety. Far-reaching extensions will draw a limber top over. When you're at the point where the top stops recovering from sway, you've gone too far. Unless, of course, you're tied into another tree.

IMPROVING YOUR STABILITY IN SMALL TOPS

Any time you can rig your climb line in a taller and sturdier tree next to the small one you'll be working in it should be done, because nothing else can offer greater stability in a small, spindly top. This is especially true if the support from the climb line holds you in a small leaner. However, the effect of the back pull from a climb line in itself can make you put weight on one side of a small tree you're in. Rigging a double tie-in to work in the top will neutralize the effect of the back pull from a single tie-in. You might be able to tie the tree you're in to a neighboring tree to help strengthen or steady it; this method works well. In broad trees, you may have to bind a number of small tops together in a single tree to get the same support. One last way you can sturdy up a small tree is by guying it.

SPURS IN SMALL TOPS

The methods used to sturdy up a small tree enable you to work in wood as small as two inches, at times. This doesn't give you much room to set your spurs. In fact, most beginners in this situation poke themselves in the calves and ankles by mis-setting their points. So, whenever you're in the far reaches of small tops and limbs, watch very carefully where and how you set your points.

PHYSICALLY MANAGING SMALL TOPS

A climber will often wrestle and manhandle small tops in order to discard them into a certain hole. The butt heave can be used to propel a small top out to an area it won't reach by itself. This is done by placing the palm of one or both hands under the butt of the top and giving it a heave right after it breaks the hinge and while it is still tipping over. The secret to success is the timing. You want the hinge to break at approximately thirty degrees and not later than that. It takes a little practice. Sometimes you can quite literally cut the top loose, pick it up,

and throw it out of the tree. In this respect, it can be compared with managing a limb. Once you have a hold of a small top, you can drop it to the ground, too. You can drop the top butt-first or top-first. Butt-first is the best way to drop a small top through other limbs and such.

SAW HANDLING IN SMALL TREETOPS

The hand saw is quite adequate to cut out small tops. When using one in a limber top, the stroking action can induce an oscillation in the tree itself. It can get a tree rocking quite a bit. For this particular reason, it may prove to be dangerous to do in a dead tree. In any tree, the effect can almost be eliminated by the rhythm of the strokes. Speeding or slowing down the action will do it. The hand saw is the safest means to cut small tops you're going to throw out of the tree. If you're going to perform a butt heave on a small top, you have to let go of the saw quickly to get your hands on the butt. Therefore, it's wise to tether the hand saw with a light line so you won't lose it.

Normally, using a chainsaw in these little tops is not recommended. You really don't need it anyway. However, you may have worked your way up the tree with one. If you're fixed securely, it would be safe to use the power saw to make the face cut, then use the hand saw for the back cut.

A lot of the cutting with a chainsaw while topping can be done by backchaining. The saw chips are discharged out the far side of the cut while backchaining. This makes facing up, or backing up, a small top easy and more precise. In small tops it's critical that you be able to monitor the progress of the cut when using a chainsaw. Backchaining can be performed with the main case of the saw either up or down relative to the cut or to your position. The progress and monitoring of the cut is most easily observable when the main case is down. The relative side and stance you cut from will govern whether the main case of the saw is up or down. You have the option if you can change which side you cut from.

MODERATE AND LARGE TOPS

Tops of this size can be as large as a small tree in itself. You'll be working with leverages and forces that can reach many thousands of pounds. Most of the tops in these trees fall into the realm of mortal danger if you misjudge and lose control of them.

LIMB CLASH

This is an important consideration when topping out large trees that have not had any of their limbs removed. Limb structure within the tree may not allow for the top to be cut out safely without first removing some of them. This is particularly important in the larger trees because their tops are heavy enough to bow over and break the limbs they're meant to fall over. In smaller trees this may not necessarily be so because their tops are light and their limbs usually limber enough to allow the top to roll onto, across, and over them without always breaking them. But the breaking of limbs by a big top that is falling over can have serious repercussions. For example, if the climber should be standing on or safetied to one. They can split, explode, and spring into your position. They can even cause the top to veer and roll to the side.

RELATIVE AND REAL MOTIONS IN TOPPING TREES

As a top tips over, the limbs on the falling side will swing down. And on the other side they will swing upward. What you have then, is the limbs on one side of the tree coming together and the limbs on the other side moving apart. This is the real and relative movement of the top and the limbs. Some situations require much cutting of undesirable limbs before the top can safely be cut. In tops with drooping limbs it is very important to do this properly, because such limbs on the back side of a top can drag over you when it goes. In most large broad trees it is totally unsafe, impractical, and unscrupulous to even attempt to get a large top through its lower limbs.

PREDICTING HOW A TOP WILL LAND

The size of the top and the height at which you cut it out of the tree are two big factors that govern how it'll land on the ground. Another big variable is how you cut it out of the tree. That has to do with how wide you make the face cut, and if you snipe the bottom or not. What the top comes in contact with before it hits the ground, and which end makes the contact, has a lot to do with how a top will land. Any top, given enough time to fall, will eventually land butt-first and plant itself. I've seen some large tops stick their butts five to six feet into the ground and look just like a tree growing there. Most of the time it doesn't matter how the top of a tree lands on the ground. But it will if you're putting it in a road, or if there are underground utility lines that may get damaged.

OLD TREETOPS

It doesn't take a keen eye to determine the balance of a large, old top. They're almost always decidedly one way or the other. Tops like these may have little vertical form, which can put a great deal of strain on the tree if they grow one-sided. A climber can find themselves inching their way to the extremities of a top like this on their belly or by crotch hopping. This may be the only way to get out on some to lighten them up. Old tops can develop extensive heart rot in the trunk, making it particularly dangerous to cut them out. Telltale signs of it are open knot holes, critters living in the top, fungus growing on the bark, and slime oozing out of a knothole. The binding of the trunk is a simple safety precaution used to prevent the chance of a split occurring.

USING EXPLOSIVES TO TOP TREES

Chances are, most climbers will never do this. However, most climbers have probably cut out some tops that should have been blown out. I looked at a job for the National Forest Service where they were topping 150-200 foot tall trees down to forty-foot stubs. This was for wildlife habitat. The climbers that got the contract were using explosives to blow out the bad tops. These were the rotten and big, heavy ones. The rest they were cutting out using the techniques described in this chapter and the tree falling chapters. Not all the bad tops were successfully blown out the first time, which required the climber to go up and set more charges. But this time the tree was fractured by the previous attempt. If you're going to blow out a top, you should do it right the first time. The tree has to be notched out first and the charge set in. The charge itself is held in place by the piecut. Now making a notch or opening in a suspected bad top is not always a safe thing in itself. It can cause a heavy or rotten top to collapse or split out. A safer alternative of placing the explosives could come by boring the top with either the saw or an auger. Bore cuts are less weakening to the top, plus the charge can be set deep inside and be more effective.

The use of explosives is necessary from time to time because some trees are too dangerous to cut or top out. However, the unskilled use of explosives make them more dangerous. If you decide to use them, get the help of a qualified explosives expert.

Chapter 17

Free-Falling the Wood

The cutting and free-falling of bare wood from a tree can be perfected to an art form. This is because the wood is absent the limbs and brush that add leverage and wind resistance, so the laws of mass, motion, and momentum apply well to it. Where any free-falling is permissible, there's generally a wide margin for error. If that's the case, you should practice some of the theories discussed here about free-falling wood. It's just good practice. The wood you cut from a tree will have different attitudes and will project at different angles from the tree.

TIPPING VERTICAL WOOD

The best place for a beginner to learn how to cut sections of wood is in a freestanding vertical trunk, absent of any lean or favor. It is the ultimate example of simplicity for demonstrating the principles of free-falling upright lengths. This attitude is typical of most forest trees once shed of their limbs and top.

Say you have a standing vertical spire of wood that is so straight and upright it may appear to be perfectly balanced. It may indeed be so well-balanced that it won't tip over without some kind of impetus. To free-fall lengths of wood like this, it has to be undercut past its center of gravity. If not, then it'll have to be wedged or pulled with a line. The idea here is to use the cut to make it tip over. The undercut has to be deep enough to undermine its balance, over halfway through. See also Chapter 26— " Rear Placement of the Hinge." The diagonal cut used to open the undercut need not be more than thirty degrees. This produces a narrow but deep opening, or face. Wider openings in the face are not needed in order to tip the wood over, they're just more work to make. However, wider-angled face cuts can have significant effects, which will be discussed later. There is essentially no tension or leverage

on these spires of wood. The only inclination they have to fall is produced by the depth of the undercut. So they will usually stand until they're cut almost all the way through in the back This means that the hinge must be cut up very fine.

The back cut should be started so it will match evenly with the kerf of the undercut. If it is above the undercut, as would be proper in regular practice, the section may not tip over even if the back cut is progressed beyond the undercut. In order for the section to tip with a high back cut, a minor split has to occur between it and the plane of the undercut. The resistance for the split to run between the two cuts can be more than the inclination for the wood to tip. When the back cut is made too high, it can progress past the undercut and into the face. If and when a split occurs, it will be when the saw is still in the progress of cutting into the face. When the wood goes, it'll take the saw with it and tear it right out of your hands. A climber can get hurt and it can break up a good power saw. If this occurs, your technique is flawed. Your saw will end up cutting a stray kerf in the section that is falling. It is possible for this error to occur in over ninety-nine percent of your cuts that utilize matching combinations. Keeping the back cut even to the kerf of the undercut will prevent this from happening by virtue of the grain in the wood not having to run a split. The section will be standing merely on a fine strap of hinge wood. When it's cut fine enough, it'll tip over to the face. In small cuts this is easy to do. Larger cuts involve more work and precision.

In a ten-by-two-foot-diameter vertical trunk, a proper undercut would be thirteen to fourteen inches deep. The section will tip when the back cut evens up to a hinge strap of about three-eighths of an inch. After the undercut is completed, align and begin the back cut. Draw the saw to the corner on your side and set the dogs. Then sweep the bar to even up the opposite corner. Throttle the saw lightly in short pulses as the back cut starts to even up on the off-corner. Observe the section of wood and the kerf of the back cut for indications that it's going to tip. The wood will start to lean to the face and the back cut will start to open. If those indicators don't appear, or if it looks like the section is going to set back, stop cutting and stick a wedge in the back cut or leave the saw in there to act as a wedge. Go to the off-corner and check it out. It's important to place the wedge because the rocking motion from you moving around can cause the wood, or even a top, to set back. If there is still too much wood, reset the dogs and cut a little more. The section of wood should tip over when the back cut evens up to about three-eighths inch all the way across. The only reason it won't is if you grossly misjudged the balance.

A deeper undercut will prompt such sections of wood to tip over sooner by virtue of undermining their balance more. In small wood it's best to position yourself to backchain the cuts with the main case down. It's not always necessary to dog the saw in small wood. You can observe the progress of the back cut by peering down the leading edge of the bar and drawing it toward the undercut. This is the best way to monitor and make precise cuts in these procedures.

If you fail to cut the hinge fine enough and have to force a section of wood over with a wedge, or by pushing on it, it can tip over, close the face, and just stay that way. In this case, there's too much hinge wood and not enough momentum to break it. This happens frequently when you're tipping short pieces of wood. The longer pieces tend to break the hinge because they have more momentum and will carry over better. But even they will stay put if there is too much hinge wood to break. Cutting a section that has tipped over but not left the cut can be a little tricky. If one corner of the hinge is cut through before the other, the section can veer off to the holding side. It's important to cut the hinge squarely so it breaks evenly. You can run the bottom quarter of the tip along the hinge,

or holding wood, in even passes. This is referred to as nipping the hinge wood. Watch the section to see if it starts to move to one side. If it does, nip the corner that is pulling the wood astray. If you use the gut of the bar to do this there is a chance of a little bit of wood pull catching the chain when the section leaves the cut.

As you can see, the precision of the cuts must be exact. If a person lacks the experience or expertise needed to make cuts this fine it would be a good idea to have a line to pull the sections over. But even that is no remedy for errors in your cutting. A word of caution if you're doing this in a wobbly tree: don't do it as long as the tree is wobbling. It can rock the section off the cut the wrong way. Also, in limber poles, you'll find that whatever side you're on may also be the side of favor of the pieces you're cutting off. This occurs frequently in the tops of tall or limber trees. The effect diminishes in bigger and sturdier wood but you can use it to your advantage in smaller trees. It's important to use a saw with a bar that's long enough to reach all the way through the cut. It's one of the key factors that makes precision results possible in this kind of work. Much time will be saved by knowing how to free-fall vertical lengths of wood. The climber can do it all by themselves just by the cuts they use.

RATIO FACTORS

One thing to notice about falling vertical lengths of wood off the top of a pole is that, when they tip off the cut, they don't stop turning. They will continue to tumble as long as they have the room to fall. There's not much you can do to prevent this from happening, so the best thing to do is to take advantage of it. The amount of turns a length of wood will take before it reaches the ground is directly associated with the ratio of its length and its height above the ground. The momentum the lengths acquire when they tip over causes them to keep turning. That momentum can be varied to some degree by the angle of the face cut. A narrow face will tend to make the section leave the cut in a more natural and predictable manner. A wider face will induce the section to turn over farther before it leaves the cut, which can speed up the tumbling. These variables can be controlled as long as you're consistent in your cuts. If you keep the face approximately twenty-five to thirty degrees and don't leave a beefy hinge to break, then these tumbling ratios will work for you.

RATIO OF .50

When the length of wood is one-half, or .50 of the height of the pole, it will take a nose dive, hit on its top first, and the butt end will fall back hard toward the trunk. This length is really not all that desirable to cut off a pole because the butt end can strike the trunk. If it's fallen downhill, it will not be so likely to kick back but it certainly will if it's fallen uphill. For that reason, shy away from cutting off half a pole's length.

RATIO OF .33

When falling any length from .33, or one-third, and longer, they'll always land on their top first and the butt will fall back to the trunk.

RATIO OF .31

At .31, a diminishing point occurs and the section's inclination is to land right on its top. I've seen these lengths stick into soft ground and have to be felled later. This length is the dividing line between them tipping fore or aft after they hit level ground. Lengths shorter than .31 are inclined to start hitting on their top and then fall away from the trunk.

RATIO OF .18

Finally, at a length of approximately .18, the sections will land flat on their back with the top facing the trunk. They will take a 270-degree turn and approach to the ground. In soft ground, they'll hit flat with no tendency to take a bad bounce. On hard ground they'll hit flat all right, but they can deflect if the ground is uneven or if there are other pieces to ricochet off. They will hit hard; the wood can severely fracture and split. If you're using the wood for lumber products, a longer ratio is better.

These ratios are fairly accurate and anyone can predict how the pieces will land if they use them. But keep in mind that these are figured for level ground. They will not necessarily hold true on steep ground. The grade will change the way the length lands depending on its relative angle of approach. You will have a fair degree of success if you imagine a level line extending off the bottom of the trunk. Then imagine the approach to the grade. Remember, the opening of the face cut and amount of hinge to break is a major variable. The wider face cuts tend to speed up the process and the narrow ones tend to slow it down as will breaking too beefy of a hinge. Although it's not always necessary, you can pack a tape measure and use a calculator to determine your lengths.

FALLING AND GUIDING WOOD THAT LEANS MODERATELY

A subtle lean will not exert much force on short lengths of wood, but it will in the longer lengths. Lean can give the sections you cut a distinct favor to fall in a particular direction. But you can quarter the work to either side of it the majority of the time. Quartering the lengths means to face the cut on one side or the other of the true lean, not more than forty-five degrees. If you stay within this margin your success rate will remain high, but if you try to exceed it, your rate will begin to fall. Quartering wood from its favor works best when the undercuts are made deeper than a third of the way in. As mentioned, short lengths will tip, but they cannot always break free of the cut if too much hinge wood is present. So, even in wood that leans moderately, you can get it half-cocked over and not free of the cut, and care in cutting it loose is important if you desire that it leave the cut squarely.

Undercuts are not always necessary when cutting short lengths off a leaning tree or spar. If the pieces you cut are about firewood size they will slide off the cut when it's completed.

FREE FALLING WOOD THAT LEANS MODERATELY TO HARD

Whenever you can, secure an overhead tie-in that allows you a working position off the side of the lean, or use a stub, step, or stand that serves the same purpose. This makes it much safer and also makes for a much higher degree of precision in your cuts. When working strictly from the high side, you cannot monitor or observe the cuts as well. You're blind to what's being cut underneath and cannot tell as accurately the depth and angles of the cuts. Many more errors and mismatched cuts are made. Remember to keep your cuts square to the trunk. It's easier to match up a cut that is square than one that is not.

Short lengths of leaning wood can be dropped smartly, adhering to the rules of the drop and slice cuts. Short meaning not more than three times the diameter. Watch how you use hinge cuts here. It can sling the wood back quite a ways before it rips the bark off. Sometimes it doesn't; sometimes a short piece of wood will rip off the cut on a backswing after hinging over. A strap of bark can promote this.

For dropping the longer and heavier lengths, kerf undercuts should be used as a safety measure to prevent splitting or wood pull from the cut. But with any kerf undercut, you won't be hinging the wood, you'll be dropping it off the cut, with much the same effect as the jump, drop, or slice cuts. In the bigger wood you have the chance to use the max undercut. If you recall from the description, this cut will get the wood to drop more precisely than the jump cut. This is because the finishing top cut amounts to so little and there is a minimum chance for error in matching the two cuts.

FREE-FALLING HEAVY WOOD

Much of what has been said about cutting leaning sections of wood applies well in the horizontal angle as well. You're advised not to use the simple hinge cut except on the short firewood lengths, and only in the smaller-diameter cuts. Wood at this angle tends to split more pronouncedly when the simple hinge cut is used. But you can still drop short lengths if you adhere to the rules of the drop and slice cuts. The max cut works best to drop big horizontal wood in tight holes. For example, places where you need it to drop straight down without any hinging or tipping.

Chapter 18

Managing the Wood

Here we will talk about how you might handle, discard or manage the wood you cut out of a tree.

The pieces you throw, drop, or push out of the tree will pick up considerable speed should they be discarded from very high up. If they're landing on a hard surface or hitting against each other, they can bounce or ricochet quite a distance. Steep ground is especially unforgiving. Quite often, the hole will have to be barricaded to contain and keep the pieces from bouncing outside it. The best thing to use for a barricade is all the pieces already taken down. As each piece is discarded into the hole, it may have to be removed and used to extend and reinforce the barricade. This is important if the hole is small. It's not desirable to have the pieces hit on one another and deflect outside of the hole. The use of

sand, dirt, or gravel can kill the impact of the fall and keep most pieces from bouncing, deflecting, or ricocheting outside of the hole.

Besides being accurate at landing the pieces, you must also watch carefully how they land. The size and shape of them greatly determines how flat they will land. Look at each piece and imagine what it'll do if it lands on a particular side.

SMALL VERTICAL WOOD

The easiest pieces to work with are those cut out of a small free-standing vertical trunk. The diameter of the trunk where you begin cutting may start at a few inches. That might be very high up a tree absent of its limbs and top. And trees, when absent of their limbs and tops, are wobblier to work in. Your movements in the tree can cause it to wobble so much that it becomes unsafe to do any cutting until the movement stops. And for this reason, you're advised to cut very short lengths—as for the beginner, no taller than twice the diameter.

A simple crosscut made most of the way through will suffice. Do not cut all the way through because the movement of the chain can propel these small sections off the bar when you complete the cut. The chain on the top side of the bar is moving away from the climber and on the bottom side it is moving toward them. Whatever side the section of wood sets down on first will cause the pieces to be thrown away from or at them, depending on whether the climber is backchaining or using the gut of the bar. It is best to backchain when cutting small vertical wood. Start the cut on the right side, main case down, then draw the saw around and toward your left quarter. By cutting with the top of the bar from this stance, you can observe the progress of the cut, how much wood is being cut, how much wood there is left to cut, and when to stop cutting. After the bulk of the cut is made, pull the saw out and do one of two things with the piece you just cut. Pull it over and rip it loose of the cut, or finish the cut with the hand saw. If the piece is particularly small, you're best off to pull it over and rip it loose. If it doesn't simply rip loose, then cut the holding strap a bit with the hand saw. Make sure you keep a firm hold on the wood. This will prevent you from accidentally knocking the piece off the cut with your hand saw strokes, which can happen. After cutting the strap, use both hands to discard the wood to the hole. This is done by throwing or dropping it. Dropping the wood is not always as easy as it sounds. Some drop holes can look pretty small from one hundred feet up. Watch that you don't drop any wood too close to the base of the tree because the root swell can deflect it a long way.

LARGE VERTICAL WOOD

As the diameter of the wood increases it becomes heavier and stabler, which will allow you to cut in the conventional manner, using the gut of the bar. Leaving a little strap to hold the cut open will allow easy removal of the power saw. Pull the saw out and nip the holding strap to free the work. Then put the saw down. If the cuts are large, a climber will often get behind the section and use both hands to shove it off. The shove is not a difficult maneuver unless the sections are of considerable size and set heavy on the cut. Being able to shove them off a particular side can be a problem, at times. A wedge on one side can help by keeping the cut open and reducing the friction. By turning and pushing on the work, you can get it to fall off a chosen side. With big wood, the most practical thing to do is to set a rod or pipe in the cut so the section can be rolled off with the shove. Drive in wedges to pick the cut up. Be sure to clean out the saw chips. Set the rod or pipe in the cut parallel to the side you want the work to fall. Pull out the wedges and get behind it. You can even use ball bearings or marbles, as they are multidirectional. But be careful, any slope in the cut can result in the section sliding off when the wedges are removed.

RIPPING THE TRUNK

When you get down to the big wood, the situation may not allow you the convenience of cutting large rounds or slabs. The lack of room to drop big sections into the hole may require you to rip the trunk of the tree in halves or quarters to render the pieces a manageable size. When it comes to ripping the trunk, carefully watch the position of your safety lines. You must be sure there's a sufficient margin of clearance and no possibility that the line is snagged on a stub behind the trunk, putting it in the path of the rip cut. After the rip cuts are placed, you can go back and finish with more crosscuts. The crosscut can be run all the way through, but the smaller pieces that were ripped are susceptible to being thrown off the cut by the chain and the larger pieces can set heavy on the bar. Therefore, wedges may be needed under some of the larger pieces and care should be observed with the smaller ones.

MANAGING SMALL LEANING WOOD

Three to six inch diameter sections, about firewood size, should be undercut three-quarters of the way through, or more, until they set down

on the bar. The cut can be started on the side but it must not venture into the intended holding strap that will keep the wood from falling. Trees with thick bark can make you think you are leaving more wood in the strap than there really is. Most bark has no real holding qualities and a climber can lose a section of wood if they cut too close to it.

After it's cut, you must pull it up and over, keeping hold of it. If too much strap is left, you may have a tough time pulling the wood over, especially if your position is bad. From here on, any more cutting should be done with the hand saw. Both hands should be used to grasp and hold the section while it's pulled over. It helps to leave some stubs for handholds when managing wood this way. The smaller pieces that you can manhandle can often be ripped loose of the cut by pulling and twisting the chunk to break the holding strap. Be careful and keep a good hold of any sections you pull over like this. The holding strap could break or shear off.

After pulling it over, the next step is to cut the holding strap if it is still intact. This means that you must let go with one hand to retrieve the hand saw. Depending on your position and what side the hand saw is on, you may have to change your hold on the wood cradled in your arms. Exchanging holds is a common and sometimes awkward maneuver in this work. The best thing to do is to have the moves figured out beforehand to save the inconvenience of trying to figure it out in a tough situation. Now, holding on to the wood with one hand isn't so bad while the holding strap is still securing it, but after it's cut loose you may not be able to put the hand saw away without risk of losing the section because now it's loose and being held in the cradle of only one arm or hand. For this very reason you should have a light line fixed to the hand saw that's connected to your belt ring or snap. This way you can afford to let go of the hand saw and not lose it. Handling leaning wood requires these kinds of moves all the time and a light saw rope is handy to keep from losing the saw and to prevent needless fumbling of the section.

The moves a climber makes in order to undercut and pull over small leaning sections of wood can well apply to any other sections they cut and feel that they can manage in a similar manner. You will, of course, find it much more difficult to make the same moves and pull over equally large pieces when the angle of the wood is in the horizontal or pendent attitude. Here a climber is reaching outward and downward to accomplish the same task. But whatever the angle of the wood is, a point will come when you cannot safely pull over any larger sections in this manner.

MANAGING LARGE LEANING WOOD

The level cut can be used to section off lengths of wood that are too big or heavy to pull over in the manner described for smaller leaning wood. In any leaning wood, a true crosscut all the way through can cause the section to slide or fall off the cut. The level cut will prevent this from happening by virtue of its angle in relation to the force of gravity. The sections, as long as they're kept short—one to two times their diameter—will set down on the cut instead of sliding, tipping, or falling off of it. This can afford you the convenience of cutting completely through without the sections falling. But they may fall if they are too tall. It's a good idea to leave a strap to hold the cut open so the saw can be removed. Because the cut is a diagonal slice through the trunk, large sections usually require the use of long bars on the saw. If you observe the power head of the saw, you'll notice that it can be either up or down in relation to the bar when making this cut. If you are restricted to the high side of the trunk, you'll have to make the cut with the power head up. If you flip the saw over, the power head will butt into the trunk and you can lose up to ten inches of the bar's length.

Chapter 19

Truck-Mounted Cranes

Truck-mounted cranes, as well as other kinds of mobile cranes, have been used for years in the removal of large trees. If they can be put in a good position near the tree, it is possible to use them for the removal of the entire tree. Most of the time, you'll just need a crane for the removal of the heavy trunk or spar sections. It's more practical for a climber to do most of the light work without a crane. This includes the removal of all the limbs, brush, and tops that you can handle with your own gear. The time needed by the crane to finish the job can then be cut down to just a couple of hours. This is preferable due to the high operating cost of cranes.

Cranes have enormous lifting power, which makes them ideally suited for this kind of work. They can handle loads weighing many tons. The operators of these rigs can usually tell what they can handle and what they can't, but the climber should try to get an operator who has some experience in tree removal. This is because some operators have never tensioned up on loads that are anchored down one moment and free the next. These large cuts have tremendous momentum, even when they're moving slow. If a large piece of work were to break away too quickly due to poor positioning, poor rigging, or improper tensioning, and you were in the way, you know which one of you would give first.

The climber should have their own choker cables, straps, and slings; most crane operators don't have the rigging to do tree work. You should also make sure the rigging is in good shape and is suitable for the loads it's intended to take.

It's best to have the operator position the boom a little out of lead so the sections will be inclined to pull away from you—but not more than a few inches. Since the boom is positioned primarily overhead the work, everything that will be cut will not swing far. Make certain that each section is properly rigged to keep them from tipping or turning over you.

Review **Chapter 3**. The common method used to cut the sections off is a single, true crosscut. A saw with a bar long enough to make the cut without having to double back will make it easier for you to make these large cuts from a safe position. A saw with too short of a bar may jeopardize your safety by putting you in a tight spot to finish the cut. The cut should be made without an undercut unless it is for a very specific reason. An undercut will cause the sections to break off abruptly if there is any bind. Without an undercut, any bind on the section will start to show gradually as the cut nears completion. The climber should take careful note of the behavior of the section as the cut progresses and signal to the operator to shift the boom or adjust the tension to correct anything not right. You should also have a couple of wedges in your hip pocket to keep some cuts open.

Familiarize yourself with the hand signals that crane operators work by. These signals are standard and used by most crane operators worldwide. Most signals are affirmed with eye contact and a nod of the head which means you must be within the operator's view when giving the signals. If you can't communicate with the operator, you're creating a margin for error that shouldn't be there.

On rare occasions you may have the opportunity to remove an entire tree with a crane. Though it's not the standard procedure, some situations may deem it necessary. Since each is unique, it's impossible to say whether the tree in question should be taken down from the top, the

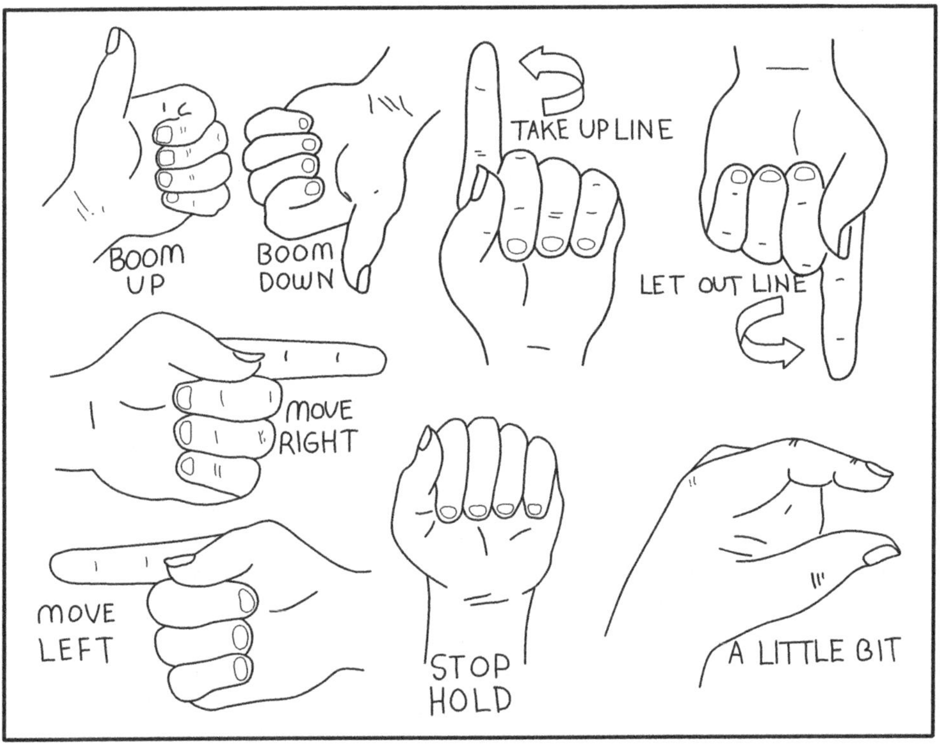

CRANE OPERATOR HAND SIGNALS—Note: "A Little Bit" Is somewhat varied from the standard signal which uses two hands. A climber often needs one hand to: Hold a Saw; Hold a line; Hold their position, etc.

side, or the bottom. It's always best though, to start from a side that is in the open, so room can be made to safely work out the parts that are confined and pose the greatest risk. Any small limbs that might break in the course of removing the larger limbs should be cut first and secured to one or another of the large sections to be removed. This is a more efficient way to work, as you are giving the small limbs a free ride rather than having to contend with them individually.

It's up to the climber to make a good working plan as to where the crane will be set up and what sections will be removed first. One of the better ways to do it is to climb and prepare the tree at least a day prior to the arrival of the crane. Do any minor cutting necessary to untangle the major sections to be rigged out. In removing a large spar or limb with all its brush intact, don't take the chance of breaking any crossed limbs over your head. The preparatory work will clean out the inside of the tree so you can do the heavy work without fighting or worrying about the smaller stuff. While you're in the tree deciding how it'll be cut, you should also have the chokers, straps, and slings ready to install. Then you will have your plan made and the tree at least partially rigged before the work with the crane is actually done.

When removing a large limb or spar, the biggest challenge is to properly rig it so it retains its attitude. Generally, you want the rigging to hold the work fast so it does not tip or fall. It can stress the rigging, jarring the crane. The best way to set the rigging on this kind of work is to secure its extremities. That is, if the spar is long, pick it from two points rather than trying to balance it by placing only one strap near the middle. If a spar is Y shaped, it should have a strap or sling secured to each leg. This will keep it from twisting over as it will if only two of the legs are held in the line. Chain slings can make adjusting the rigging lengths easier in these situations, because standard choker and strap lengths can leave you with excess slack on the far leg of a spar.

The hook is a heavy item to manage in a tree. Small ones are usually five hundred pounds. They are not very easy to reach for, grab ahold of, and pull to where you need them. In tight quarters the hook can be just inches away from the eye of a choker or strap and you can't get the two together. A small block and tackle can be helpful at times.

Cranes do not function well on ground that slopes as the turntable is designed to work only on the level. Shoring may have to be placed to level out the machine. Some rigs have their own leveling outriggers, so that it won't be a problem. Check for the features of the unit you hire.

The booms are often hauled to the work site on separate trucks and assembled there. Some of the reaches are over one hundred feet. Make sure the site has room to set the rig up without having to take down too many fences or power lines. This is a part of your pre-planning. Check to see if there is a separate charge for the truck that hauls the boom assembly.

Chapter 20

Aerial Lift Trucks

Aerial lift rigs are an essential tool for line clearance and urban trimming. Units designed specifically for tree work will vary in their design and performance. The major considerations in choosing a rig are reach, articulation, portability, controls, and safety features.

REACH

Reach is the major limiting factor governing the use of aerial lift rigs. When the booms can't reach the work, a climber will have to take over. Most lifts designed for tree work reach forty to sixty feet which will fulfill most needs. There are units available that can reach up to ninety and one hundred feet. These high rigs are primarily used in utility line construction and maintenance.

ARTICULATION

Double boom units will vary considerably in their range of articulating movement. The lower boom may raise only to the vertical, but some rigs can extend the lower boom farther. The upper boom will extend a little past the vertical when the lower boom is in the same position. Again, some rigs can extend their top boom farther. Rotation is another varying feature of the rigs. Most have endless rotation, with some rigs having stops that prevent the operator from making a complete turn.

Telescopic features are found on the smaller units. The ability to extend the boom by telescopic action is indispensable for cramped area operation. Rigs with the greatest articulation have the best advantage in tree work.

PORTABILITY

Combination lift and chip rigs are too big for tight quarters and limited to what can be reached from a main road. Small extending boom rigs are ideal for trimming in driveways. Trailer rigs can be detached from a tow vehicle, set up to work under their own power, and be set in place by hand.

CONTROLS

The joy stick control is the easiest for smooth operation, incorporating all the articulation of the unit in one control. The operator can raise and lower either boom and use the rotation simultaneously. When an operator learns the joystick, they will be able to run the machine by feel.

Some rigs have separate controls for each function. The control box can have five or more separate levers for upper boom, lower boom, rotation, tools, and sometimes the deadman.

Operators that are familiar with the joystick may find separate controls awkward. Unless the operator has large hands, they may not be able to simultaneously run more than two controls at a time. Separate controls make for more stops when directing the movement of the bucket. The knobs for separate controls are usually the same size and have to be checked to be sure the right ones are engaged. It's easy to activate the wrong one by feel alone, making operation of the rig dangerous in the dark. Carve different notches in the knobs to identify which ones are being engaged without having to look at them.

SAFETY FEATURES

The brush guard that covers the controls protects the controls and operator. It also prevents the risk of accidental operation by keeping limbs from hitting and engaging the controls. Make sure the guard is in place.

SHIELDING

Most rigs have dielectric shielding on their booms and have the major structural portions of the booms made of insulating material. These two features are not foolproof or meant for total protection. An operator should not take them for granted and work casually around power lines. Dirt is a major reason for failure in shields and insulators, along with improper maintenance and installation. Keep them clean and maintained properly.

LOCKOUT VALVES

The hydraulic systems on most rigs have lockout valves to prevent cylinder collapse in the event of line rupture. If you have a rig without lockout valves, install them yourself.

DEADMAN CONTROL

The deadman control ensures movement in the rig will not occur when the controls are accidentally activated. This control itself must be activated by the operator prior to working any other control. The deadman can be activated by foot or hand. Do not attempt to override the deadman control and always keep it functioning properly.

OUTRIGGERS

Mechanical outriggers have to be pulled out and set up by hand. The stanchions are locked in with pins and tightend down to the pad with a large acme screw. They are foolproof but messy and clumsy to work with for frequent set ups. Hydraulic outriggers are the most common. The controls that set the stanchions are often located in a blind area.

It's a common courtesy and safety practice to give warning when setting the outriggers. Many people have had their feet crushed because no warnings were given. On one particular unit, the controls for setting the outriggers could be activated while standing right under them.

The outrigger cylinder seals can wear out and cause the outriggers to bleed off. This can occur when you work the rig at an extended horizontal reach over one outrigger. You might not be aware of a cylinder leaking until you swing to the other side. When the balance shifts to the other outrigger, the slack will be taken up by a quick shift in the motion of the rig. When the boom cylinders start leaking, it will be difficult to maintain position. On sidehill positions, the hydraulic motor that controls rotation can fail to hold the position and the boom will creep downhill. Either one of these situations can cause the operator to lose control of the rig. Recognize these symptoms of hydraulic system leaks and bleed-offs. When you recognize it, fix it.

Many phone company lift rigs lack outriggers. Modification of the truck body or chassis can make these rigs potentially unstable and require the owner to install outriggers. Failure to use outriggers can result in toppling the rig over. Always double check to make sure the outriggers have been set.

The outrigger can be nullified if set on ground that is not solid or secure. Soft ground will require shoring under the outrigger pads to distribute the load over a wider surface. When the ground is particularly soft or uneven, use a series of blocks and shoring. Use thick, wide blocks free of splits or defects. Lay them wide-side down for stability and stack them crosswise for strength. When setting the outrigger, observe how the shoring and the ground settles. If ground settling occurs, the shoring will need an additional base area built under it. Keep an eye on the shoring itself. Rebuild any shoring that cracks, splits, or shifts. After the outriggers are blocked up make periodic inspections for further sinking or settling. Do not take hard ground for granted. The edge of a road can crumble off very easily. How far an outrigger is set from a road edge is a most important safety consideration. Asphalt pavement can get mushed out from a bare outrigger pad and cause a rig to topple. So shore up on asphalt too, especially on those hot days when asphalt pavement gets soft. Private paved driveways are usually more susceptible to being mushed by outrigger pads. The road base compacting requirements for private drives are not as substantial as on county and state highways.

SETTING UP THE RIG

A good operator will know where and how the lift should be set to get maximum use of the reach and articulation of the unit. This greatly reduces how often the machine has to be set up to do a job. It takes

imagination and knowledge of the machine to set up the rig in the right location the first time, saving time and inconvenience of setting it up again to finish a job. Some work sites may have tight quarters between the trees, buildings, and utility lines making it necessary to unfold the rig in one location, then move it to the location where it is to be set. Rigs can be moved when they' re unfolded but only when the booms are bearing on the front or rear of the truck chassis. The ability to set up can be a limiting factor in itself. There will be situations where the rig can reach the work but can't be set up.

RUNNING THE RIG

Experienced operators can guide the movement of the bucket smoothly in, out, and around the tree with a minimum of sharp or jerky moves. New operators can get rough with a rig by banging the booms and the bucket into the trees. Moving the controls quickly in or out will result in rough and jerky operation and cause stress and wear in the pivot pins, knuckles, and rotation components. The components can become prematurely worn out from rough operation. Control response can be adjusted by regulating the hydraulic pressure and flow. If the flow and pressure is set high, the rig controls will be very responsive and move quickly. It may be fitting for an experienced operator to have the rig set as such, but not for the beginner, especially if they're working near power lines. Tame the rig down a little bit if a beginner is operating it. It won't respond as fast but it will be safer.

With double boom lifts, be aware of the lower boom and knuckle position. When the boom is half cocked, the knuckle will move opposite of the bucket position. This is the area of the boom that has been responsible for most power line contact incidents. Keep an eye on the knuckle or you'll run it into a tree, building, or power line. Also, always keep your hands inside the bucket when maneuvering in tight quarters.

POWER LINE SAFETY

The most serious danger associated with the operation of aerial lifts is the possibility of accidents involving electrical power lines. The danger in these accidents is not always to the operator, but to someone on the ground in contact with the rig when it becomes energized.

Persons on the ground should maintain a safe distance from the rig when it is in operation. This rule is seen on placards and warning signs posted on rigs used for powerline clearance trimming. The minimum distance set by the laws governing operation of these rigs is six feet. The laws also set minimum distances the rigs can work near power lines. These minimum distances differ according to the experience of the operator and the voltage of the nearby power lines. All operators are required to know the minimum distances. These laws are regularly changed and can be confusing to understand.

The laws are not the remedy for prevention of accidents involving contact with power lines. Common sense and awareness are a greater aid to prevention. For the operator of an aerial lift rig in the vicinity of power lines and the person that works near the rig on the ground, keep aware of each other and the machine's relative position at all times.

ROAD SAFETY

Most operation of aerial lifts occurs on roadways, so road protection and safety is a must. The requirements for traffic warning, control, and work site protection can vary a lot. Most of the laws dictating specific requirements are based on common sense. You could be found liable of an infraction in court in spite of following the law if you did not use common sense first.

TRAFFIC WARNING SIGNS

In urban areas where traffic movement is light and slow, like a quiet neighborhood street, traffic warning signs are often set less than one hundred feet on either side of the work site. On main thoroughfares where traffic is steady and faster, signs are required two hundred to three hundred feet on either side. This would be common along boulevards in a city. Along highways where traffic volume is high and moves fast, a series of warning signs are required up to a mile or more on both sides of the work site. The requirements for adequate traffic warning set by the state highways is becoming more and more strict. It can require a substantial investment in traffic warning signs and devices.

SETTING UP THE SIGNS

Adequate traffic warning signs include: **ROAD WORK AHEAD, MEN WORKING, LANE CLOSED, FLAGMAN AHEAD,** and **PREPARE TO STOP.** Make sure the signs are set in a visible location, are stable, and will not get blown over by wind or traffic. Sand bags or counter weights placed on the stanchion legs will prevent the warning signs from getting blown over. Setting anchors or using existing road sign bases to support traffic warning signs are becoming more common. In spite of your efforts to set the signs securely, they can still get blown over. If traffic is coming uncommonly fast towards the work site, send someone to check the signs.

TRAFFIC CONES

These devices represent an artificial barrier for traffic to maneuver around. In a quiet neighborhood, you may get by with a half dozen set around the rig. If you are controlling traffic around the work site and closing a lane, you will need many more.

PERSONAL PROTECTION

People working along the roadside are required to wear high visibility vests so traffic can see them. This is very important and should never be neglected. Around the work site, make it a habit to observe the traffic whenever you come around from the blind side of a rig or vehicle. Never walk out into the traffic lane from a blind position. If you are controlling traffic, stay as visible as you can. Don't stand in the shade, on the blind side of a turn, or the blind side of a hill crest. Give the oncoming traffic enough time to react to your position.

TRAFFIC CONTROL

The traffic controller wears a high visibility vest and uses a flag and a stop/slow sign. The flag is waved to approaching traffic to draw attention to the displayed stop/slow sign. When stopping traffic, hold the stop/slow sign high and wave the flag. Don't ever take it for granted that the traffic sees you. Even if you are just slowing traffic, display the stop side of the sign until the traffic slows because many drivers will continue their speed in spite of a slow sign being displayed. When the slow side of the sign is displayed, the stop side can show to traffic coming from the other direction and cause confusion, so watch how you display the stop/slow sign.

SIGNALS BETWEEN FLAGMEN

Flag signals are frequently used between flagmen to control the flow of traffic around the work site. Waving the flag overhead can mean that traffic is coming and you intend to let it through. Waving the flag low to the ground can mean that you have traffic stopped. Waving the flag up and down can be used as a verification signal.

Many signals can be devised between work crew members. Be sure they are well understood by everyone. Walkie-talkies are frequently used for signals between flagmen when they cannot see each other. When using them make sure you have a verification signal before letting traffic through. It's possible for both flagmen to key down at the same time and cancel out each other's call. Be aware of crank calls over the air. Traffic can monitor your band and send erroneous calls. And also, make sure that the batteries are fresh or charged.

OPERATION OF THE RIG IN TRAFFIC

The operator of an aerial lift rig must not project the booms into the traffic lanes unless the traffic has been stopped. This will prevent a collision between the traffic and your boom. Make sure you have an adequate safety margin of room around the rig defined by a line of cones. All work must be within the barrier set by the cones.

Do not allow any brush or trimmings to fall or land outside of the barrier unless the traffic has been stopped.

PEDESTRIAN PROTECTION

The operator of an aerial lift must be aware of pedestrian protection as well as traffic protection. A lot of the time the work site must accommodate pedestrian traffic. It is not wise to route pedestrian traffic around the rig on the traffic side, but sometimes this may be the only way. If a situation forces you to do this, stop the operation of the rig and have the ground man escort the pedestrians around it. Ideally you should clear a route on the non-traffic side. This often requires the ground man to keep the route clear at all times and make sure that it is safe. Again, the operation of the rig should be stopped and the pedestrians escorted through the work site.

MAINTENANCE OF THE RIG

Aerial lifts are highly mechanical units and must be maintained properly. Keep the rig clean, properly lubricated, and adjusted. Periodic inspections of the hoses, knuckles, cables, chains, pins, control lines, cylinders, and dielectric shields must be performed. The owner of a rig should have the service and maintenance manual.

HYDRAULIC TOOLS

Hydraulic tools are available with aerial lift rigs. The hydraulic chainsaw is slow and heavy, but its low noise level makes it useful when working in residential areas. The most outstanding tool is the hydraulic pruner. The hydraulic pruner cannot be surpassed for its suitability in tree trimming and is used in the same way as a mechanical pruner. However, the power of the hydraulic pruners make them much more versatile.

OPERATOR PERFORMANCE

The operator that is knowledgeable about trimming trees will frequently reach inside the tree to make their cuts, often maneuvering the bucket inside the tree. Unfortunately, most operators will trim the tree strictly from the outside. It ends up turning the tree into a big hedge that demands more work to trim each time. Eventually the tree has to be slaughtered to get the required clearances.

I've often climbed and done the cutting in the tree while the lift operator was holding and pulling out the limbs and brush. When I was done cutting inside the tree, the operator would finish the finer detailed trimming on the outside canopy. I've traded off over the years with different climbers and operators doing much of our trimming just like this. The work proceeds very fast because large cuts can be taken and it saves a lot on broken leads.

I've also worked with operators that refused to follow this method. It's not uncommon to hear debates between climbers and aerial lift operators in the line clearing business. Much of the work can be done more efficiently if the operators work with a climber once in a while.

Chapter 21

Introduction to Tree Falling

The trees, techniques, schools of thought, and terminology of tree falling vary considerably from one region to the next. In spite of this, certain basic rules and principles apply.

The main principle being: cutting the trunk of the tree so as to leave a strap of wood that will act as a hinge to hold the tree onto the stump while it guides the tree to a desired direction. With that in mind, it's easier to imagine a hinge in the trunk of the tree acting as a pivot point for the tree to swing on. This hinge may be put in at different heights, depths, and angles, making the tree tilt, fall, and swing different ways. Most trees you will ever fall can be handled according to the guidelines in the coming chapters. That said, I might add that true wisdom will be gained chiefly from your own experiences and from what other people in the business pass on to you. What can be learned from this book is proficiency and insights on what to look for before actually falling a tree.

PRIORITIES

Certain priorities will dictate how a tree should be cut. For the most part, in logging practice, the timber faller will pick the best ground for the tree to lay with the least chance of breaking it; where they can limb and buck the tree; where the equipment can reach and manage it; and away from creeks. In closer quarters around private property, public thoroughfares, and utility right-of-ways, the priority may not necessarily be to save the tree, but rather, to remove the hazard the tree poses.

VARIABLE FACTORS IN TREE FALLING

THE TREE'S FAVOR

The favor of the tree is one of the first things you look for when you walk up to it. A good walk around the tree may be required to find its true favor. It may require using a plumb bob to be sure. The favor of some trees can be deceiving; there are illusions in nature that can throw your eye off. On steep ground the classic uphill leaner is a good example. This tree appears to have its favor toward the hill, but in reality it doesn't.

Even on level ground, where you can walk all around the tree, it can be hard to determine the favor of some; not necessarily due to angular illusion, but by the tree's odd symmetry. A tree's odd symmetry can make it well-balanced, and thus, hard to find the favor. You'll encounter this in many broad trees and some forest trees with sweep in their trunks. Here, a plumb bob may not do you any good. Most trees have a distinct favor that's not difficult to find. The favor may be slight and determined by a subtle lean or limb distribution. Or the favor can be prominent, bearing a lot of strain on the trunk. Such trees are the most concern to fall. **Chapter 28** elaborates on lean and favor of a tree.

THE SPECIES

What species of tree you are working with is one of the first questions asked about a tree falling job. Without even seeing the tree first, just knowing the species tells a lot to a person familiar with it. The species of a particular tree is a clue to its growth habits, it's natural habitat and geographical range, the strength and value of it's wood, and many other things useful in evaluating it. As a person in the business of cutting trees, you should know the species you are working with.

HABIT OF GROWTH

FOREST TREES

Forest trees are predominantly tall and single-trunked. Most trees in this group are not too difficult. Their favor is generally easy to see, and not much work is needed to get them down. The heavy trees in this group, though, can be just the opposite. Any lean combined with their height can exert a tremendous amount of leverage on the trunk, and ultimately, the stump. And that's where you're cutting it. These kinds of trees and forces are featured in the following chapters.

BROAD TREES

The growth habit of many trees will make them broader than they are tall. Even forest trees when growing in the open can grow similarly. A broad tree can have its major limbs low to the ground. Such limbs can make a tree spring or shoot back off the stump when it's felled. They can cause the tree to roll over. Large trees like this can make limbing or bucking particularly dangerous. Many of the limbs supporting the tree, or over your head, will be shattered or inconspicuously broken. They can be deceptive. Evaluate these situations carefully. Over the years I've climbed a lot of trees in preparation to get around the problems their lower limbs posed in falling them.

CODOMINANT TREES

Trees that grow together in a group are commonly referred to as doubles and triples, or multiples. Codominant trees, as they are formally called, can present you with the most interesting situations and possibilities in tree falling, and they can present you with the most anxious moments of your life if you guess them wrong. For the beginner it is advised to carefully consider any multiple tree before attempting to fall it all together with one simple falling cut. The reasons why are discussed in **Chapter 27.**

BIG TREES

Large trees arc difficult for the beginner to cut because they lose sight of the tip of the cutting bar. This can result in mismatched cuts and conflicts in the guiding qualities of the hinge. Always use a power saw with a bar long enough to go all the way through the tree. This alone can prevent over half of the possible errors a beginner can make with a smaller saw. This should be a firm rule for the private tree worker. For the timber faller, it's not always practical.

Codominant Trees

WOOD STRENGTH AND GRAIN

It is beyond the scope of this chapter to say which species are stronger and which are weaker because the amount of wood needed to hold any tree on the stump varies considerably regardless of whether the tree is noted for the strength in its wood or for the lack of it. The wood in some trees is very resilient. That is, it can bend, pull and hold a tree well. Resilient wood will exhibit many fine wood fibers sticking up across the hinge after a tree is felled. This is a trait in younger trees of moderate vigor. On the other side of the coin you'll find trees with brittle, or brashy wood. Such wood when acting as a hinge cannot hold or guide a tree very long before it breaks like glass. You can have two trees of the same species: one can be resilient and the other brashy. One example: vigorous second growth redwood on the river flats are reputedly brashy. The moderately growing ones on the hillside are more resilient. What do you have between or next to someone's house? Unfortunately there is no positive way of determining either. Experience can give clues though. This is a factor of tree falling that periodically reminds us we shouldn't take chances.

One aspect of the wood that a person can learn a lot about, and that can be elaborated on, is how to read the grain and its flow in the trunk where the cut is to be made. This is a very important factor to consider and one that does not necessarily have anything to do with a particular species. The grain flow in the wood is not always uniform and parallel to the trunk. If you don't recognize this fact, you can lose the tree. This has happened before and has been confused with improper technique.

Consider down low on the stump: the grain in the wood does not always run vertical like it generally does higher up the trunk. You would prefer vertical grain to hold and guide a tree, though you don't need it in all situations. You can often determine the flow of the grain by observing the outside appearance of the bark. If there's a definite twist in the appearance of the bark, it is very likely that the grain in the wood runs the same way. If there are any abrupt changes in the pattern of the bark, it may be indicative of a large knot or old injury healed over. These areas are not good choices for placement of the hinge as the hinge wood can pull out and fail to guide the tree. For the same reasons be observant for "bark inclusions." These are areas of the stump that recede their growth, which then form pockets of bark inside the stump. This is not a good area for the corner of the hinge to run through.

ROT AND UNSOUND WOOD

Even if the trunk of the tree appears to be in good condition this does not always mean that it is. Heart rot may be so extensive that the tree could break the moment you begin cutting it. If there is fungus growing off the side of the trunk or if slime oozes out of a knothole, suspect rot. These signs are not always present though; the next best method of testing for rot is to smack the tree with the back side of the ax. In many trees, if there's a hollow you'll hear it. You can check the degree to which a suspected tree has heart rot by boring into the trunk where you plan to place the falling cut. The bore cut will tell you a lot by the feel of the cut and the color or texture of the chips. Remember, dead and rotten wood goes through composition change; it loses its strength and resilience and should not be bet on to hold a tree in a marginal situation.

SHELLS AND GOOSE PENS

Some trees will be quite alive while standing on a mere shell or rind of wood. When this condition is accompanied by an opening on one side

Rot and Unsound Wood

of the trunk, it is often referred to as a "goose pen" or the tree as "goosed out." Of main concern here is the amount of wood left to hold and guide the tree after the necessary cuts have been made to fall it. It's not unheard of for some to collapse their stump after being cut up. What should you do, then, with a tree you can't fall in the conventional manner due to the poor condition of its trunk? Don't fall it if your intuition tells you not to. In some instances like this, the tree can be rigged and pulled after the stump is crippled or squared up. This gives you a chance to get away from the tree. "Crippling" a tree is accomplished by selectively making major or minor cuts in the stump, prompting the tree to break over when the command is given to pull it. This is done only on trees in such poor condition that a regular falling cut might be too dangerous to make; exactly how the tree breaks over is not always predictable. "Squaring up" the trunk means cutting what wood is available to act as the corners for a hinge, even though it may not resemble a typical falling cut when it's completed. The two corners can square up to give the guiding qualities of a hinge but not necessarily its holding qualities.

OLD TREES AND LANDMARK TREES

Old trees around homes, estates, roads, and along old fence lines often have metal fasteners inside the wood attached by someone years ago. Their presence can be hard to detect by the eye alone. Although nails and wire do not affect the wood much, they can ruin or break the chain on the power saw. In codominant trees around old estates, homes, and schools, you'll frequently find rocks and other odds and ends grown inside the seams of the crotch unions. Over the years I have known tree fallers to find everything from coke bottles to horseshoes in these trees. If you have a large old tree to cut that has been in close proximity to humans for several generations, you should suspect trouble at the stump.

TRUNK SHAPE

The shape of the trunk in most trees is anything but round. Their irregular forms can make it difficult to find a good place to cut the stump to fit the situation. It can even void the possibility. Elliptical forms can be most limiting. Odd shapes like root swell, protrusions, or conks can be sawed off to make the shape of the stump more bearable to work with. Don't take this too far, though. Removal of a large root protrusion can significantly weaken the potential strength of the hinge or the tree itself. Sometimes this won't matter, and sometimes it will.

STUMP HEIGHT

Specific stump heights are strictly enforced in all corporate, state and national forests. In California it's a gig on the timber faller to have stumps in excess of twelve inches high measured from the high side of the ground contour. Some areas stipulate lower stumps. Many accidents involving personal injury, loss of control on the tree, and property damage have resulted from following this rule too strictly. You often need a stump of greater height for the room to work safely, to effectively run a power saw, to put specific control on the trees you fall, and to hold a tree from sliding, shooting back or rolling. In the effort to make a low stump you can lose one or the other, or all. Situations arise where a higher than specified stump is required but they should be the product of necessity, not negligence. Once they have served their purpose they should be cut down.

TREE HEIGHT

The approximate height of any tree can easily be determined by visual examination. Exact heights are not necessary to know unless the top of the tree poses a danger to something within its reach. There are a number of hand-held optical measuring instruments available which can be used to determine the height of a tree. Two examples are range finders and inclinometers. Their accuracy is very good. I have used both to find the distances to the first limbs and to the tops of big trees. On level ground, if you can get back and view the top of a tree from a forty-five-degree angle, you'll be as far away from it as it is tall. This should give you a clue as to how the gradient affects your calculations. If there's any doubt whether the top of the tree will clear an obstacle, either the tree should be topped, high stumped, or the obstacle removed. High stumping shortens the fall of the tree from its lower end rather than its top end. Be sure to review **Chapter 16**, particularly when performing the topping at less than half the tree's height.

WIND FACTOR

After you have weighed everything discussed so far in this chapter, you must consider the wind factor. As a pretty firm rule, don't fall trees in the wind. The wind is a pretty variable factor in itself though, and there are times when you can use it to your advantage. I am referring to a gentle, prevailing wind that is not hitting the tree in hard gusts, just working it a bit. This kind of wind can help you in some situations. Be forewarned that the wind can catch you off guard, lose your tree, scare the heck out of you, and require you to run for your life. You will encounter this most frequently in small trees that grow tall. We call them whips where I work because they are prone to sway in the slightest breezes. These little trees can sit ahead or back on you from the most gentle gust of wind, giving you about a second to get out of there alive. The tree tends to split out and fall down on the stump, called barber chair or slabbing out. It's the number one killer of chainsaws and it would be the number one killer of timber fallers if they stuck around to save them.

Chapter 22

Saw Handling

When you are in the business of cutting trees, you're going to be handling the chainsaw a lot. There are right ways and wrong ways to handle a power saw. The biggest concern in handling a chainsaw is your safety. In order to be safe, you need to know a little about handling it.

STARTING THE SAW

The prescribed method of starting a power saw is on the ground with your foot through the pistol grip, one hand on the handlebar and the other hand tugging the starter pull rope. If the saw is cold, pull the choke closed and tug smartly on the rope until the engine pops. After that, push the choke about two-thirds of the way in and pull the rope once or twice more. This will generally get any chain saw started. It's also advised that you engage the chain brake when starting the saw. There is a throttle-lock button on many larger saws which partially cracks the throttle for cold starting. I personally don't care for them because they throttle the engine enough to engage the clutch and get the chain rolling. This in itself can lead to an accident. It is not a concern if you have a saw with a chain brake, but make sure that the brake is engaged when using the throttle lock for starting, and never disengage the chain brake with the throttle lock actively functioning. Release the throttle lock first, then release the chain brake.

DROP-STARTING THE SAW

This method of starting the chainsaw is frowned on in many institutions, but it's the most common method used. It's necessary at times because you're not always on good enough ground to start a saw in the prescribed manner, especially when working on steep ground, up in a tree, on a springboard, or up on a suspended log. The small saws can literally be drop-started by holding the saw by the pistol grip with the right hand and dropping it downward while, at the same time, pulling the starter rope with the left hand. This particular method allows you to manually work the throttle without dependence on the throttle lock. This is a big plus because you can give the throttle that little crack it needs to start the saw without necessarily engaging the clutch and getting the chain to roll. Even larger saws can be started the same way but with the bar supported on a log, limb or stump when doing it. The reason why this method is frowned on is because of the statistical accident rate associated with it. From my own experience I know "When your hands are stiff or numb from cold you can lose your grip when starting a saw this way."

STARTING A SAW IN A CUT

Starting a saw in a cut is frowned upon. However, it is a necessary evil to perform from time to time. Your grip can be on either the wraparound handlebars or by the pistol grip, depending on the situation and your position. On good ground and when making vertical cuts it's easy. Avoid starting a saw in a cut over your head or doing it with the throttle lock on. It can cause the saw to power itself right out of a cut, another tendency of the infamous throttle lock. This is the main concern when starting a saw in a cut. There are also times it is safer than trying to manage a running saw back into a previous cut.

PUSH AND PULL TENDENCIES

Whenever you cut with the bottom of the bar, the saw tends to pull you to the work. The bottom of the bar is often referred to as the gut of the bar. You won't notice this tendency to pull as much on good ground where you have a firm stance, or when the dogs are engaged while cutting. But when you cut at a reach on steep or loose ground, this can pull you right off the hillside. In order to reduce this effect, secure your stance.

When cutting with the top of the bar, called backchaining, there is a tendency for you to be pushed back by the saw. If you cut from a shaky stance while backchaining, you can get pushed over backwards by the saw. In that event, kickback incidents become high. In spite of this, backchaining is frequently used in tree falling and bucking. Make sure you have a proper grip on the power saw when backchaining.

KICKBACK TENDENCIES

The chain movement around the tip of the bar creates the kickback tendency we all know about. It's a deadly example of the action/reaction principle. Kickback is variable by how much inertia is behind it and exactly what part of the tip makes contact. The reaction of the very top actually pushes the saw, and it can push a saw right out of a cut. The very end of the tip and its upper quarter is the most critical part of the tip to be aware of. Avoid accidental contact with this part of the tip. The amount of power unleashed during kickback can cause you to lose control of the saw and become victimized by it, so watch how you move and work with the saw.

The bottom quarter of the tip is regularly used when nipping wood. As a general rule, nipping is done when you can observe the tip as it's

KICKBACK TENDENCIES

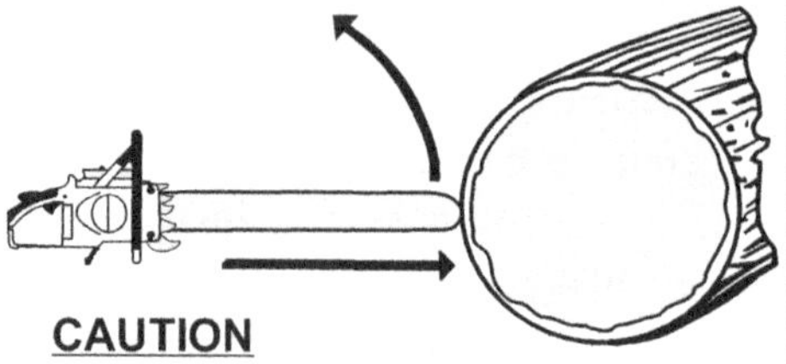

CAUTION

AVOID ACCIDENTAL BAR TIP CONTACT

PUSH AND PULL TENDENCIES

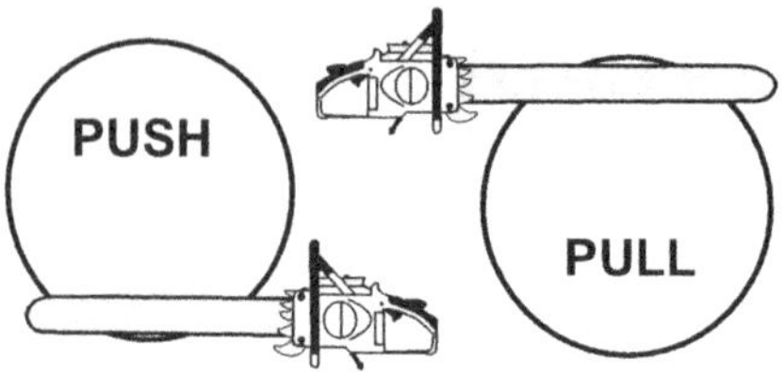

ALWAYS MAINTAIN A POSITIVE STANCE AND PROPER GRIP WHEN OPERATING A POWER SAW.

cutting. However, you can safely nip through a blind cut as long as you nip only while drawing the saw out of the cut. Never nip into a blind cut though! You can't see what the upper quarter of the tip may run into.

STARTING A CUT

On vertical cuts, such as bucking a log on good ground, set the gut of the bar lightly on the mark, align the bar square to the log and begin the cut, easily at first. The saw will start to pull. The more power and pressure you apply to the cut the more you will have to hold back on the saw. Once the cut is on course you can then power into it and set the dogs, if needed. The same procedure is used to start most vertical cuts. But horizontal cuts, used as undercuts or back cuts, are started much differently.

If the cut is lower than your waist, aligning and starting it is generally not too difficult. Your upper torso counterbalances the weight of the saw when you align it. When the cut is chest- to head-level high, it can be more difficult, especially with big saws. To be able to heft up and hold the saw, start the cut and have it properly aligned, takes a lot of practice. In this case, you may need to start the cut immediately upon hefting it into position (See **Chapter 24— Bar Axis Points**).

RESTARTING A CUT

For various reasons you'll have to restart some cuts. This is easiest to do in open vertical cuts. If the cut is closed at the top, insert the tip where the kerf is still open or where you previously pulled the saw out. Lay the tip into the kerf and throttle the saw easily. Maintain a firm stance and good grip. Let the chain pull out the loose chips in the kerf and at the same time pull the saw back into the cut. If you throttle up and jam the bar into a previous cut, you're flirting with danger. The tip could run into the edge of the kerf and kick back out of the cut. It is most important to remember this fact when making horizontal cuts. You don't always have the stance to control the saw if it kicks back as you do in vertical cuts. When you stick a saw into a previous cut to finish it, do it carefully.

YOUR STANCE AND REACH TO THE WORK

Your stance and reach to the work determines how safely you can handle a saw, and the ground you're on determines your stance and reach to the work. There are acceptable combinations of ground and stance, and there are combinations that are borderline or even foolish. On level ground, you generally have your choice of stance and reach to the work, unless the work is up in the air, or when ripping. Even on level ground, most rip cuts require you to heft up the saw and reach over your head to start and make the cut.

When falling trees on steep ground, you may be able to work only from one side of the tree, and catching the far corner can require you to cut at a reach. When bucking the tree on steep ground, even more factors come into play, for example, whether the tree lies up or downhill, or on the side of the hill, plus any binds the tree might be in and how high it is off the ground. In the majority of situations, you can improve your stance and reach to the work so it can be safely done. If you're not confident with the stance or reach where you have to work, don't do it.

Overhead cutting and one-hand operation of a power saw is considered Improper Technique by all institutions.

USE THE PROPER GRIP ON THE SAW

The "proper grip" would be with one hand on the wrap-around handle bar, thumb locked around it, and one hand on the pistol grip. This can be accomplished right or left handed. You are advised to use the proper grip whenever running a chainsaw. This way you can exert the most control on it. It's true, so don't forget it. Unfortunately, emphasis on this rule has overshadowed many of the other hazards we face daily in this tree cutting business. Remember that while operating a power saw you must also remain aware of both your surroundings and what you're working on too.

LONG BARS

When cutting with long bars, keep the cut free of excess saw chips. This is done by frequent reaming and cleaning. The chain will pull saw chips back into a cut too, especially full comp chains which are like chip pumps. The long bars and chain can pack the kerf full of chips. If you make any sudden retreat or pull back the bar, the top part of the chain can grab a wad of loose chips and pack them tight in the cut right at the upper quarter of the bar tip. This can actually jam the bar and chain in the cut. If the chips jam the chain before the tip is reached, it can push the saw out of the cut. Therefore, when you're cutting with long bars, up to half of the time spent on some cuts will be spent reaming and cleaning.

This reaming and cleaning is a method of chainsaw handling in which the operator uses a semi-reciprocating bar action in the cut for the purpose of pulling out the loose chips and keeping the saw kerf open. In big cuts, if you don't ream and clean, you will stall the saw and get the bar and chain stuck (See **Chapter 34: Bucking - Top Bind**, **Reaming**). Another thing to consider with long bars is bar bow. Long bars bow over in the horizontal position and are inclined to throw the chain when the saw is throttled. In big saws, bar bow can tatter the drivers on the chain. Long bars also require a lot of bearing, leaning, and pulling to work, all of which can be very tiring, even on good ground with a good stance.

DOGGING, SWEEPING AND PULSING

The dogs on the saw, referred to as "bumper spikes" elsewhere, allow you to anchor the saw and sweep the bar while cutting. In tree falling, this dogging and sweeping is vital to squaring your cuts. Without the dogs, saw handling would be more difficult and dangerous. The saw would slip during handling and the bar would not sweep through a cut. Between dogging and sweeping you will pulse the power of the saw, that is, you will modify the power output and chain speed to coincide with the moves. This requires that you have a good firm grip on the saw, then pull the saw out enough to break the dogs loose while maintaining enough chain speed to keep the loose chips in the kerf from jamming or stalling the chain. Power pulsing is a highly variable technique used between dogging and sweeping, and it regularly employs some progressive cutting to advance the cut prior to dogging in again. It is not always done under full power but more often employs pulses of light power.

THE HIGH/LOW SIDE

When falling trees on steep ground, there is a distinct high and low side to consider. If the bar on your power saw is too short to reach all the way through the tree, then you will have to cut from both sides of it. In this situation, if you're falling the tree to the sidehill (as opposed to down or uphill), it can require you to work from the low side. In second growth redwood clumps you are regularly faced with having to work on the low side of the clump to fall the trees on that side of it. The concern of working on the low side of a tree or group of trees is that it often puts you in a position to reach over your head to cut with the saw. A springboard can remedy that. However, the low side of some trees can present you with a shear drop off the mountain that even working off a springboard can be dangerous to do. In this case you may have to fix a line that will catch you if a fall is likely. Even if a springboard isn't needed, be aware that the ground on the low side of a tree is often cause for bad footing and slips down the hill. It is not good if this happens while cutting on the tree or when the tree is falling. It's the wrong place to be (See **Chapter 32—Loose Terrain**).

Working the high side can present difficulty when sidehilling the trees. It often requires you to cut a higher stump because the mountain or slope of the ground can cramp your room to work on that side. It can prevent pulling the saw out of the cut without it bumping into the mountain. In the back cut, with wedges or jacks in place, the only way to remove the saw may come only by removing the power head off the bar and chain first. Steep ground makes saw handling and tree falling more dangerous to do. Be sure to make accommodations to keep it safe.

SETTING A SPRINGBOARD

For a couple of reasons the use of a springboard may be warranted. Steep ground or unusual stump conditions may require it. Notching the stump is the first consideration in setting a board. Examine the contour of the stump. Convex areas are easiest places for the notch. Concave areas require boring and whittling. Examine the bit on your board referred to as the shoe. The width, thickness and taper of the shoewill determine the notch you make. The base of the notch must not be negatively sloped or the board will pitch down. Ideally, you want a slightly positive pitch in the board. The top cut for opening the notch should not angle more that 20 degrees; if the notch is shallow then a greater angle could cause slippage. In depth, the notch should engulf the shoe. It will keep the board more secure when pivoting or "tailing" it. For obvious reasons make sure that you do not place the notch under a jack seat or under wedges. Also be aware that placing the notch under the corner of the hinge can cause that corner to pull out. Beginners should practice or experiment in setting and using a springboard before actually using one.

Out in the woods the need for a board is often negated by their unavailability. Many fallers have used limbs or small tops in lieu of a board. Such improvising will suffice at times. However, the use of a limb or top requires you to make a much different kind of notch to secure the implement. How you might do it is peculiar to the situation. What can be said about it is to follow the rules of setting a regular board and make a sufficient notch to keep the limb or top from slipping or rolling out. This also requires some modification on the end of the limb or top. The opportunity to tail or pivot these items in the notch is usually absent. The footing you gain using a limb or top is not as good as a board. Remember that! And be sure you're wearing calk boots (See **Chapter 34 - Calk Boots**).

Throughout the upcoming chapters more will be discussed about handling and using a chainsaw. You'll hear references to squaring, cornering up, dogging, sweeping, reaming, boring, nipping and whittling. After reading through these chapters, you should gain an understanding of how a chainsaw is used.

SPRINGBOARD NOTCH

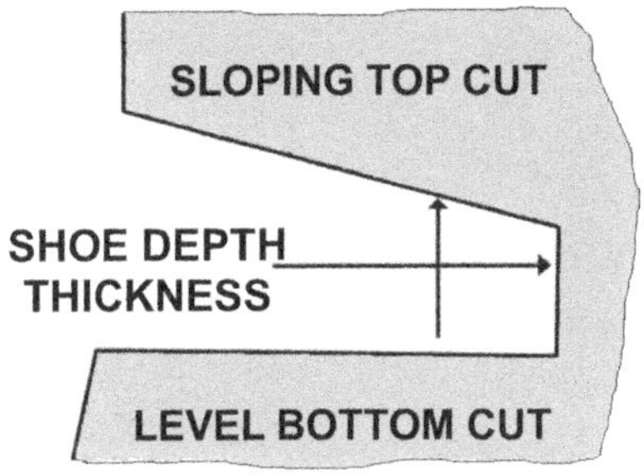

SPRINGBOARD SHOE AND BIT

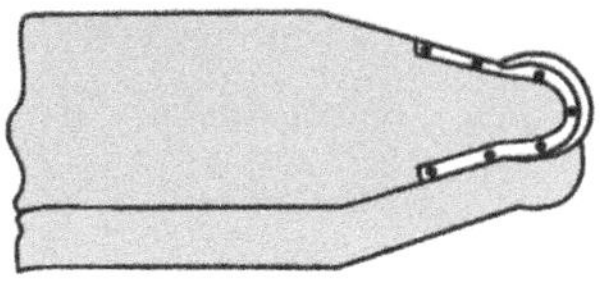

Chapter 23

The Undercut

The falling cuts used most often are based on the old standard "conventional" design. It alone will handle a good percentage of the trees that you will fall. But you'll find out that it is inadequate when used exclusively.

Like most felling cuts, the old standard is made in three major passes of the saw. These are the undercut, the diagonal cut, and the back cut. How they are made in relation to one another determines how the falling cut is applied. In this discussion, the standard falling cut will be applied to a straight, standing tree.

THE UNDERCUT

The first cut you will make in the tree is the undercut. This cut sets the direction the tree will fall. Proper placement of it is very important because it is also the base line the other two cuts will follow. If it is improperly placed in the tree, then it's doubtful that the other two cuts will be properly aligned. In general, for straight trees, the undercut should be level and square to the trunk. It should be progressed into one third the diameter of the trunk. There are many reasons for the undercut to be deeper which will be discussed later. The finish of the undercut must be straight through the trunk without any deviations. When the cut is straight and on the level, it sets the direction the tree is to fall. In this example, the tree will fall over toward a direction perpendicular to the undercut. If the undercut is not truly straight or on the level, it will not indicate the true direction that the tree will fall, but how the other two cuts are made in relation to the undercut can change the course of the tree, too. If everything else follows correctly, the tree will follow the undercut.

CHECKING THE GUN

There are a number of ways to make sure the undercut is aimed in the right direction. One of the easiest ways is to use the sights on the saw. These sights are an embossed line molded into the side cases of most larger power saws. They indicate the right angle, or angle that is perpendicular to the cut. More precisely, the sights indicate where the tree is going to lay. All you have to do is sight down this line and continue, or stop, cutting when the sights line up to the lay. It's actually very simple. It's most straightforward in small trees where the length of the bar extends through the trunk, but there are many factors that can affect how you interpret the indications.

If the saw you're using does not have sights on it, you can scratch some in the side case by placing a square along the center line of the bar studs. You can even use the square to check the gun.

SQUARING A CUT OFF ONE CORNER

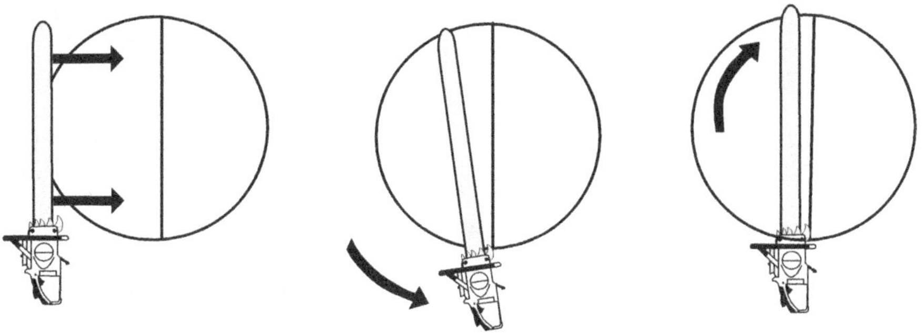

ALIGN AND START CORNER UP SQUARE UP

FOR UNDERCUTS AND BACK CUTS IN SMALL TREES

THE CORNERS

In large trees, mark the corners where the undercut will run through the trunk. The corners are the end points of the hinge. The corner on the other side of the tree from where you start is called the "far"

or "off" corner. In small trees where the bar extends through the trunk, the far corner will be automatically cut and squared to the lay. In larger trees it's not as simple unless you have a bar long enough to go all the way through. This is why the corners are marked first in large trees.

THE GUNNING STICKS

Using the gunning sticks is the best method to find and mark where the corners of the hinge will be. The gunning sticks can be made out of anything having equal-length legs hinged together. I've seen them made out of wood sticks and electrical conduit. When unfolded and pointed to the lay, the ends of the legs will indicate where the corners of the hinge should be on the tree. Aim the sticks to the head of the lay and place the legs against the sides of the trunk approximately one-third of the way in. Keep the sticks level. Then have someone mark the corners where the ends of the sticks lie on the trunk. After the corners are marked, make the undercut up to them. In a large tree, this means squaring the cut from both sides or corners. Wherever you start the cut, you must still use the sights on the saw when coming up to each corner. Each corner must be square to the lay. When done properly, your cuts should run straight from one corner to the other. In theory it's easy, but in actual practice a beginner can end up with anything but a straight cut between the corners.

METAL TAPE

If you don't have a set of gunning sticks, use a metal tape to mark the corners. The fifty-foot logger's tape, or an equivalent, is the best to use. Hammer a peg into the ground where you want the tree to fall. Attach the nail end of the tape to it. Draw the tape out to one side of the tree where you want one corner to be. Make sure the tape is tight and take note of the measurement there. Cut off or smooth the bark where you want to make the mark; then put a mark there. Go to the other side of the tree. Draw the tape tight and mark the trunk at the measure you noted for the other side. These marks will be the corners of your hinge where the undercut should end up.

There is another way to use the tape with the help of a friend. Place the nail end of the tape where you want one corner to be. Draw the tape out to an even-number length, let's say thirty feet. Place that measurement approximately where you want the other corner to be and have your friend hold it there. Then go to the fifteen-foot point of the tape and draw it tight in front of you with your thumb. In this way, the tape will act as a set of gunning sticks. Have your friend shift the thirty-foot measurement fore or aft on the trunk of the tree until the V, where you're holding the tape tightly, aligns to the lay. Then have your friend mark that corner. The next step is to make the undercut to those corners and square to the lay.

INTERPRETING THE GUN

The above methods for sighting the undercut are fairly reliable. But there is a minor degree of error possible in each one.

When using the sights on the saw, remember that the indications you read are for the side of the tree that you're on, plus the distance the sight line is from that side. If you go to the other corner and sight-in,

SQUARING A CUT FROM BOTH SIDES

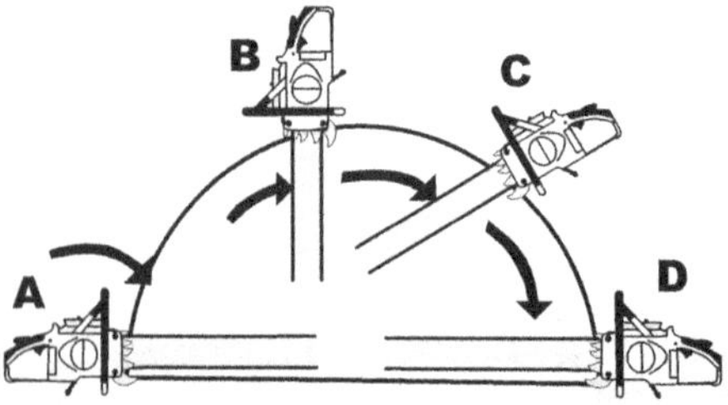

FOR UNDERCUTS AND BACK CUTS IN LARGE TREES

A. CUT UP THE FAR CORNER FIRST.
B. THEN FLIP THE SAW OVER AND REINSERT INTO THE CUT.
C. PROGRESS THE CUT TO THE SAFE CORNER.
D. SQUARE UP THE SAFE CORNER.

Avoid parallax error in your big trees.

you'll find a minor discrepancy in the indications of the undercut. It's called parallax error. Parallax error occurs because the perpendicular from each line of sight is different. An increase in the difference will occur when you use a nearby target to sight-in to. In tight shots, you must account for this difference.

When using the metal tape to mark the corners by yourself, the exact location of the peg is very important. You should sight-in the peg's location from the center of the trunk and peer down the lay in the direction you want the top to land. You can set the peg anywhere in that line of sight. Now go to each side of the tree and observe the peg again. A discrepancy will be observed from each corner. It's parallax error again.

When using the gunning sticks, you're sighting from the center of the trunk and looking to the head of the lay. This makes the indications you observe the most accurate of all. However, parallax error can show up in your cutting, and you must learn to compensate for it. The two-person method of using the metal tape is nearly as accurate as the gunning sticks.

From this discussion, you can see that different factors affect how to find and interpret the indications you observe using each method. These factors can make the difference between hitting the layout or just catching the side of it. There are other factors that can affect where the tree will land. You'll have to consider these factors also in your final decisions when sighting-in the undercut. These factors will be discussed in the context of the situations where they may come up.

GUNNING TO A LAY YOU CAN'T SEE

It happens on occasion that you get down in a hole or behind something that blocks your view of the lay. From the head of the layout you may be able to see the top of the tree but when you get down to the base of the tree you can lose sight of the lay. You could lose you bearings and miss the lay by a considerable amount. In this situation, get a compass bearing from where you viewed the top of the tree. Let's say it's 180 degrees due south. Go down to the base of the tree and gun the undercut 360 degrees due north. You'll come a lot closer to hitting the lay than by guessing. Along with this method you may also have to figure in compensation for side lean if the tree has any (See **Chapter 28— Lean in Trees- Side Lean**).

ERRORS IN YOUR CUTTING

A beginner can end up with anything but a straight undercut between the corners and many errors can be made. The main one stems from parallax error. In large trees, it shows up when you choose too close of a target to gun each corner to. This produces an inverted hinge. In spite of an inverted hinge, most trees will still fall true to the gun, but only if the location of the corners is correct. You can minimize this particular error by sighting-in each corner to a more distant target in the lay. This produces a straighter cut between the corners.

Another error you can make, and a common one, is not leveling the bar. On straight trees, make the undercut level. An undercut that is not level will make the tree swing while it falls. The swinging can change the indicated direction of fall. In other words, the sights on the saw will not show you the true direction the tree will lay if the undercut is not level. There will be a high and a low corner on the hinge. As a rule, a tree will swing to the high corner during its fall. This so-called error is a method often used to get trees with side lean to swing to the lay. In a leaning tree, the undercut will be on a slant if it is placed to fall the tree to the side of the lean. You want to keep all your cuts square to the trunk of the tree. The reasons why at times you may do otherwise will be discussed later.

OBSERVING THE TREE WHILE PLACING THE UNDERCUT

While you make the undercut, observe the tree for movement. This is done by dogging in the saw and cutting while looking to the top. A tree inclined to fall to the lay will be observed to move ahead as the undercut progresses. If the tree is observed to move back while placing the undercut, it indicates the favor to be aft of the face. If the tree does not appear to move at all, the favor may be off to the side. These observations will confirm your suspicions about a tree's favor if you were uncertain about it in the beginning.

Chapter 24

The Diagonal Cut

In this chapter, we will discuss the purpose of the diagonal cut, the different ways to make it, the errors that can occur while making it, and some tips on how to avoid errors.

When the diagonal cut matches up with the undercut, that portion of wood between the two cuts will fall loose and produce an opening. This opening is called the face of the falling cut. The term "face cut" typifies the falling cut. The angle or opening of the face determines to a large extent how far the tree will tip over before it breaks free of its bond to the stump. As a rule, a wide face will hold the tree to the stump for a longer period of time. Let's examine the advantages and disadvantages of a wide face or a narrow face.

WIDE FACE CUTS

A wide angle in the face can capitalize on the guiding qualities of the hinge. In tight quarters, the wide face can give you the control to keep a tree from damaging something in its vicinity, which is not possible if the tree is allowed to free-fall unguided and unattached to the stump. The wide face has a particular advantage when used in trees that have back lean because it allows the tree more room to straighten up and fall over to the lay before the face closes.

To get a wide-angled face, make two diagonal cuts, one above and another below the undercut. However, there is another way to get the wide-open effect without having to cut quite so much wood. It will be discussed later.

FACE ANGLE/WOOD PULL

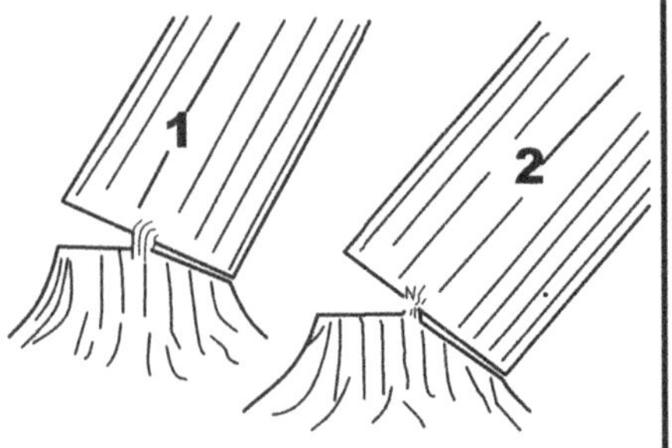

1. NARROW FACE OPENINGS INCREASE WOOD PULL FROM THE TREE AND STUMP.

2. WIDE FACE OPENINGS DECREASE WOOD PULL FROM THE TREE AND STUMP.

NARROW FACE CUTS

A narrow angle in the face will induce the tree to break the hinge wood soon after it tips. Used discreetly, a narrow face has certain advantages in situations where you need the tree to get off the stump soon after it starts falling.

NEGATIVE TENDENCIES OF NARROW FACE CUTS

A narrow face cut can deceive you. They are notorious for concealing errors in the finish of your cuts; whereas, in a wide face most errors in your cutting are more obvious and, therefore, more likely to be corrected. In the wrong trees a narrow face can cause massive splitting, wood pull and barber chair. Knowing when you can get by with a narrow face cut in a tree takes experience. Beginners should stick with the standard, wider face cuts until they learn where the narrow ones can be safely used.

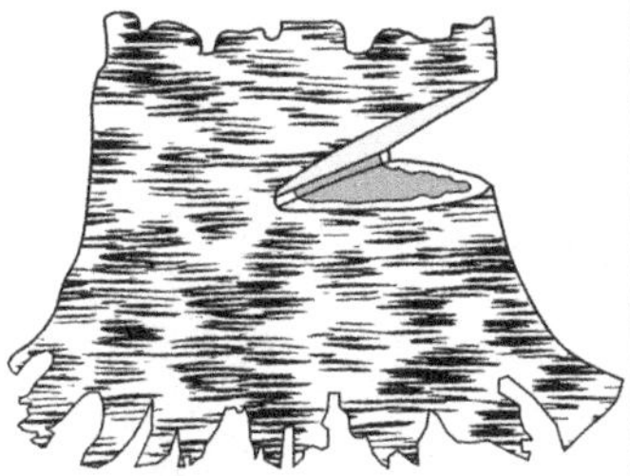

CONVENTIONAL

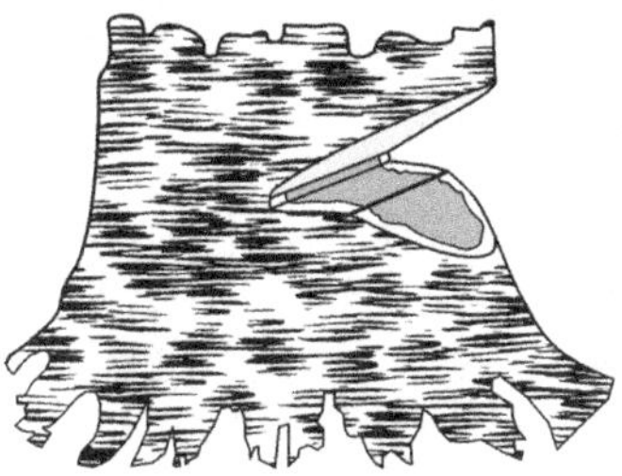

CONVENTIONAL
WITH SNIPE

CONVENTIONAL FACE CUT

The diagonal cut can be placed above or below the undercut. When it's placed above the undercut, the face cut is considered conventional. It is the standard cut which sticks in most people's minds. Novice tree fallers use conventional face cuts as conventional ones seem easier to learn and to place correcdy. The conventional cut stems from the days of crosscuts and axes when the diagonal cut was chopped out by hand. Hand chopping a diagonal cut is always easier when it's done from the top.

HUMBOLDT-STYLE FACE

If you look at many of the large, old stumps the old timers left, you'll see one here and there where the face cut was chopped out from the bottom. Why would someone bend over and chop from the bottom when it's easier to do from the top? It's because the negative slope of the

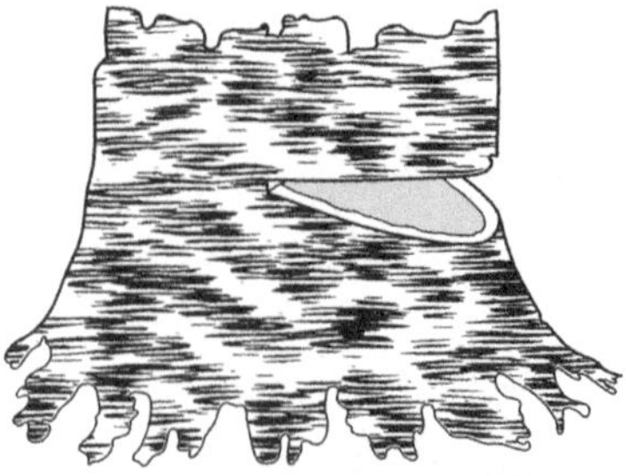

HUMBOLDT
SECOND GROWTH STYLE

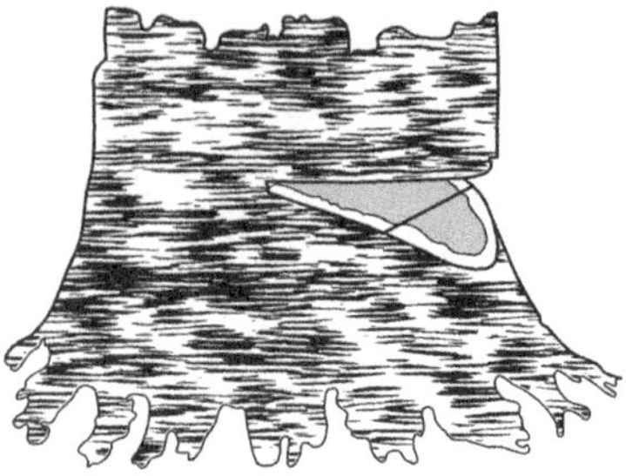

HUMBOLDT
WITH SNIPE

cut greatly improves the tendency of the butt of the tree to slip off the stump during the tree's fall, particularly when the tree is felled to the sidehill or downhill. When the diagonal cut is made from the bottom, it is referred to as the Humboldt cut or the Humboldt version of the falling cut. It's used almost exclusively by professional timber fallers.

On uphill lays, the Humboldt provides more stump shot to hold a tree from shooting back. The Humboldt also leaves the butt of the tree square. It is preferable for a butt log to be square rather than having the diagonal out of it. It would behoove the beginner to learn both the conventional and the Humboldt version of the diagonal cut.

MISMATCHED CUTS

Failure to bring the finish of the undercut and the diagonal cut together correctly will produce a variety of mismatches between them. Some mismatched cuts will need a little correction and others may need

The Gap, The Pinch-You can expect better holding qualities in the hinge wood when there is a gap.

the entire cut started over. The beginner is advised to correct any mismatches in their falling cuts until they understand their functions and where they can be safely used. Let's examine a couple of different ways you can mismatch the two cuts and how the tree will behave as a result of them.

THE GAP

This mismatch can extend the diagonal cut beyond the finish of the undercut. It may mean having to extend both cuts to get them to match up. Monitor the diagonal cut and stop it before it passes up the finish of the undercut. The wood between the two cuts, called the undercut, pie, or cheese, will not drop loose. Rather than extend the two cuts farther back into the tree to get the pie out, you should use the ax to break it out. There are several methods of getting the pie out with an ax; these will be discussed later.

When the pie comes out, there will be a noticeable difference where the two cuts meet the hinge. The corner, or the hinge itself, will be opened with a gap between the undercut and the diagonal cut. It should not be of any concern unless you do not want the effect it has on the tree.

A gap will widen the face. It has a peculiar knack for allowing the hinge wood to bow or fold over with the tree. You can expect better holding qualities in a hinge because of this fact. The opposite of this is referred to as the "pinch." In a pinch, the undercut and diagonal meet tightly, and the opening at the corners is narrow. The hinge wood will break sooner with a pinch.

In small or young trees, the theory of the gap holds truest. This is because younger trees have more resilient wood. Older trees have brittler wood in comparison, and a gap does not always guarantee the tree will stay on the stump longer.

THE DUTCHMAN

This mismatch will occur whenever the diagonal cut finishes short of the undercut. It will leave a portion of the kerf from the undercut in the tree. It can occur on either side of the cut or all the way across. This kind of a miss is called a Dutchman. Dutchmans cause the tree to break the hinge wood prematurely on whichever side they occur. Between the

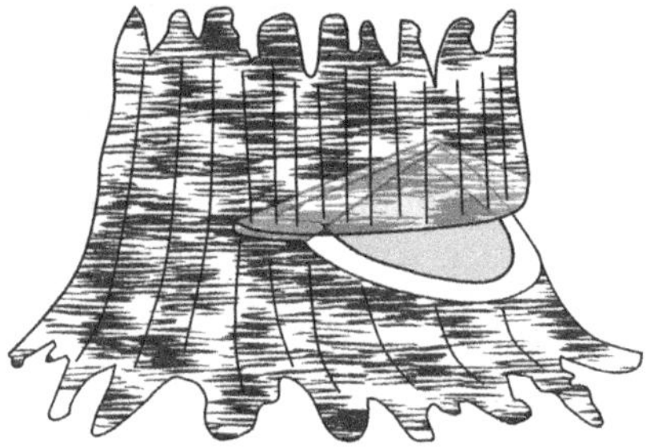

THE DUTCHMAN

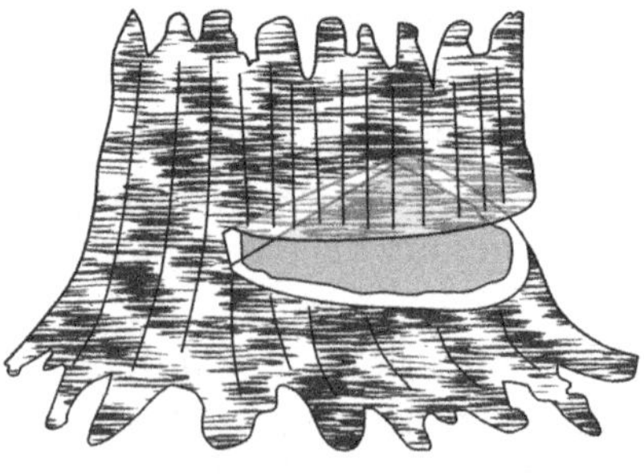

WIDE AND NARROW

depth of the kerf and width of its opening you can tailor a Dutchman to take effect at an exact moment in a particular tree's fall. However, the beginner is advised to not use them. They are more times an error rather than a method and should be treated as such.

WIDE AND NARROW MISMATCH

You can have both a pinch and a gap at the corners. This kind of miss will leave the face with a wide side and a narrow side. It is easily corrected by widening out the narrow side of the face. If the error is not corrected, the tree will not follow true to the undercut. This holds especially true if the overall angle of the face is narrow. It's easy to understand why this is so if you take a look at it. The narrow side of the face will close sooner than the wide side. The result can be a considerable miss to the lay. Ideally, you want both corners of the face to be equally opened. When the face closes, the butt of the tree will break the hinge squarely and theoretically come off the stump square to it. If the overall angle of the face is wide, the effect of the narrow side is delayed. In this case, the miss to the lay may be insignificant. It's a matter of observing what the error is and figuring out where the effect of the narrow side will take place during the tree's fall.

The other mismatches that happen frequently are those that occur when you're not adept at using a short bar length with which to cut large trees. In a situation like this, the combination of misses are too many to discuss. In any tree you cut that is bigger than the bar on your saw, mark the corners of the hinge by using a tape or gunning sticks. This one precautionary measure will eliminate over half of the mistakes the beginner is likely to make. It will ensure that the corners of the hinge will be square to the lay even if nothing else is. It's the location of the corners that ultimately guides the tree. From this point on, it's elementary and up to you to square all your cuts to the corners.

BAR AXIS POINTS

There are three pivots, or axis points on a bar: the tilt axis, the roll axis, and the sweep axis. The tilt and roll axis points are used in aligning your cuts. The sweep is used to square your cuts and is started after the tilt and roll are aligned. The exact pivot points are sometimes elusive or imaginary, but they run along a definite plane in relation to one another. The plane they run along is the bar itself. Understanding the concepts of the axis points will greatly improve your ability to match up your cuts.

BAR AXIS POINTS

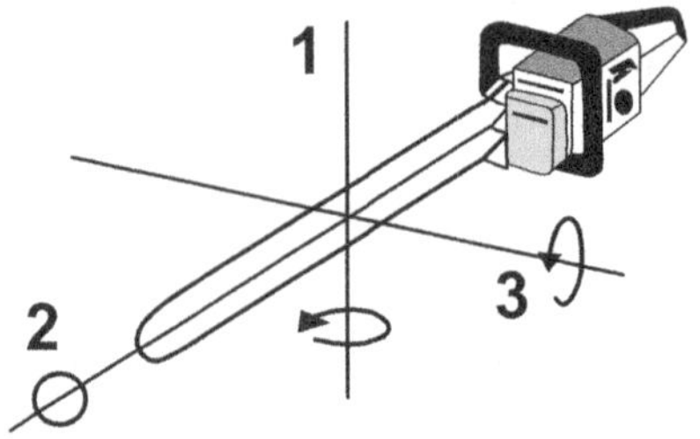

1. TILT AXIS. USED WHEN LEVELING OR ANGLING THE LENGTH OF THE BAR.
2. ROLL AXIS. USED WHEN LEVELING OR ANGLING THE WIDTH OF THE BAR.
3. SWEEP AXIS. USED WHILE THE BAR IS ACTIVELY ENGAGED IN A CUT.

Bar Axis Points-Knowledge of the bar axis points can help you align and match the diagonal cut.

THE TILT AXIS

The tilt axis runs through the width of the bar. Any shift in the tilt axis results in a corresponding change of tilt along the bar's length. Remember, the exact pivot point can be elusive or imaginary at any axis. In the tilt axis, you can observe the overall angle in the length of the bar. Viewed from the right perspective, the tilt is quite observable, like watching the second hand on a clock change angle as it revolves around its axis. The tilt axis is the main axis used in leveling a bar's length to start an undercut in a straight tree.

THE ROLL AXIS

The roll axis runs through the length of the bar. Since the bar is narrow, any changes in it are not so easily observable. If the roll axis is level and the tilt axis is level also, you have a truly straight and level cut across a stump. Any change in either axis will result in an unlevel stump.

You can verify this by placing a magnetic level on the bar along both axis points. You can change either one without necessarily affecting the other.

ALIGNMENT OF AND STARTING THE DIAGONAL CUT

There are three basic ways to start the diagonal cut: from the corner, from the side, and from the front. The ground you're working on will primarily govern how you start the cut. Basically, it comes down to knowing which position will allow you to make the most accurate cut. If you don't feel right about it, change your position to start the cut.

STARTING FROM THE CORNER

When starting the diagonal cut from the corner, position the clutch drum near the corner of the undercut. Align the roll axis of the bar level to the undercut and tilt the bar at the same time. Then start the cut. As long as you don't shift the roll axis when you tilt the bar, the finish of the diagonal cut should match as evenly on the far corner as on the corner where you started it.

STARTING FROM THE SIDE

As described here, it is the front quarter of the stump on your side. At this position, angle both the tilt and roll axis, and then start the cut. This is the position used by most professional fallers. The alignment is adjusted by eye and gut feeling. It's a lot like angling a mirror to reflect a beam of light down the lay. When you feel right about it, you put the bar into the tree and go for it.

STARTING FROM THE FRONT

At this position, rely on keeping the tilt of the bar level and shift the roll axis to converge with the finish of the undercut. This is usually a good place to start the diagonal cut in small trees. Stand to the side and observe the angle of the bar and its position in relation to the corner of the undercut. When it looks right, start the cut.

MAKING THE CUT IN LARGE TREES

Align the saw and start the cut. Progress to one corner and finish the diagonal on that corner. Remember, keep it square to the undercut. Stop cutting when the sights line up to the lay. Pull the saw out, flip it over, and reinsert the bar into the cut, and then progress to the far corner. Be careful when restarting a cut, don't jam the tip in under power. Let the bar settle in with short pulses of power until it's seated safely, and then proceed. If the diagonal cut was aligned properly on the first corner, it should match up evenly on the off corner. But it may not due to a dull chain, worn bar, odd trunk shape, or torquing on the saw. Torquing on the saw is caused by the way you pull or lean on it while it's cutting. You can change the track of a cut quite easily by torquing on the saw.

BUSTING OUT THE UNDERCUT

There are a number of different ways of getting the undercut out of the tree. It's necessary to bust it out when there's a gap at the hinge. You can knock out most small undercuts from one to three feet in diameter in their entirety with a sharp blow right in front with the back side of the ax. Your success depends on whether the tree has straight, vertical, or clear grain, and whether the gap is less than one inch. Be sure you're using safety glasses; the bark and sapwood can spatter from the blows. Some undercuts knock out easily with direct frontal blows and some don't. On tougher ones, the problem is often an old internal knot, wound, or scar making the wood twisty. You can often break the smaller ones loose by striking the blade of the ax into the saw kerfs. If you're not adept at striking the blade into the kerf, you can put a wedge in and drive it in enough to crack the corner. After the corners are cracked, a couple of blows with the ax will usually finish the job. Sometimes though, instead of falling out, it may just wiggle like a loose tooth. This is indicative of an old knot or limb running through the wood that is part of the gap itself. They can be stubborn to break out, and you may have to do more cutting.

SPLITTING OUT THE UNDERCUT

Another way to get a stubborn undercut out is by boring in front at the widest part and driving in a fast tapered wedge. It will split the undercut in half. One of the halves will pop out and the other will often stay and require a little work to break it out. This technique of splitting

Boring the Face to Split out the Undercut

out the undercut in half is often done after one side of the face is made. Thus, half of the undercut will be out and allow you the chance to keep an eye on the tip of the bar while finishing the other side.

SPLITTING OUT LARGE UNDERCUTS

Very large undercuts with wide gaps are usually busted out by placing a series of bore cuts throughout and driving in wedges to break the pieces loose. Along with the boring and wedge-busting, you'll have to use the blade of your ax to crack a lot of the pieces out as well as applying frontal and side blows with the back side. These large under cuts generally require you to crawl inside them and clean out all the chunks and debris adhering to the gap. The best tool to clean out these chunks is the pulaski. You'll find that pry bars and picks work well to help get the chunks out too. When you're swinging a pulaski or pick, be sure that no one is on the other side of where the tool will fling if you miss the chunk. Chunks will fly out also, some with considerable speed, in the same direction that you work the tool. This is a major consideration for bystander safety.

BORING THE CORNERS

Large undercuts can be taken out in their entirety by boring into the corners and driving in wedges. However, this method is frowned upon by people who believe busting and cleaning the undercut out is the proper way to do it. Their philosophy stems from the variable factor of grain interruption. When the undercut is split out, the grain in the wood that is going to be the hinge is continuous and uninterrupted. Boring the corners can lead to inaccuracy, grain interruption and possible shearing of the hinge wood.

Chapter 25

The Back Cut

After the face cut is complete, the next step in falling the tree is the back cut. Before starting a back cut, stop and double-check everything else that may influence the layout. This will be the last chance to do it. Many things can change in the layout during the course of facing up a tree. The noise of the saw can obstruct your awareness of warnings from any persons entering or working in the layout. Safety precautions include giving warnings, listening for them, double-checking the undercut, and

refueling the saw. If the tree is being pulled to the lay, communication between the faller and the person doing the pulling is important prior to starting the back cut. The back cut is the grand finale that sets everything into motion. For that reason it is well worth the time to stop and double-check everything.

BACK CUT HEIGHT

In the old, standard falling cut, the back cut is started just above the plane of the undercut. In small trees that is about an inch. In large trees, it can be as much as a foot or more. In most trees it isn't that important to make the back cut higher, but in some trees it is. For example, in trees being felled uphill that are expected to settle back and rest on the stump, a high back cut can prompt them to stay on the stump rather than shooting downhill off of it. Here the back cut and stump itself may have to be made considerably higher to catch the butt of the tree. In certain trees, a high back cut can give the tree a ledge to stand and teeter on while it's being pulled. This ledge may be referred to as the stump shot. Different people will give you different dimensions for what the stump shot should be. There are a lot of reasons why you would want one or the other. I will explain a few of them.

HIGH BACK CUTS

When the tree starts to fall, a minor split will occur from the finish of the back cut and run down to the plane of the undercut. This split is nothing to be alarmed about. It's just a result of the tree taking the hinge wood. High back cuts tend to delay the formation of this split. The back cut has to be progressed farther for the tree to fall on its own. The reaction of the tree following the face is delayed the higher you make the back cut. This is because of the resistance in the wood to run that long of a split between the back cut and the undercut. In some pull-trees this resistance can help hold them to the stump better. High back cuts are a bad choice when free-falling stubs of trees or poles. When wedging, more work will be required to lift a tree that has too high of a back cut. High back cuts are also inclined to interrupt the grain of the wood in the undercut. For that very reason, the split has more distance to run out of the hinge. High back cuts also leave more protruding stumps and are somewhat wasteful of wood. Unless you have a specific reason for a high back cut, don't use them.

EVEN BACK CUTS

In most of the larger trees I fall, I keep the back cut close to the undercut level, Humboldt style. In many of them you will still find ample stump shot because I leave a gap in the corners of the hinge.

When the back cut is level to the undercut, and there is a gap at the hinge, a split will run from the finish of the back cut down to the bottom of the gap. The tree will pull the hinge wood. The actual break in the hinge wood will occur at, or near, the bottom of the gap. So a face cut with a gap can provide stump shot. If the split doesn't form, and instead the hinge breaks at the level of the back cut, it's indicative of too much hinge wood to break. In trees with resilient wood, the theory of how the gap works can be better depended on.

LOW BACK CUTS

Do not make your back cuts lower than the undercut. Lower back cuts don't follow the rules and concepts of regular falling practices. They have been observed to promote splitting out and barber chair. However, one exception is when you're pulling a heavy, back-leaning, or limb-locked tree with the rigging low on the stump. Normally, I advise anybody to rig their lines in their pull-trees high enough to avoid having to do it this way because the amount of power needed to pull a heavy or limb-locked tree with the rigging low on the stump can be more than the strength of the hinge to hold the tree on the stump. In this event you will pull the tree off the stump and the tree can go astray. The big winches on the Cats can do it easily enough though. In this kind of situation, a low back cut will leave the stump shot on the back of the stump and thus, a ledge for the tree to butt up against and not likely to jump over it. Always rig your pull-trees high enough so you don't have to do it this way. It's risky business working with such high leverages.

MISALIGNED BACK CUTS

There are a number of ways you can misalign the back cut. They involve the back cut's angle in relation to the face cut. Keep all your cuts square to the trunk, especially if you're going to wedge or jack the tree. Any angle in the back cut will cause you to lose some of the force of the implement. This will be explained better later on. In small trees and even in larger ones, you can often get by with subtly mismatched angles in your back cuts without any consequences.

BACK CUT STYLES

The manner in which the back cut is made and progressed is a little different in each tree. The biggest factor governing how the back cut is started, progressed, and finished is the inclination of the tree to fall to the lay. Trees can be put in three categories: trees with little inclination to fall to the lay, trees that do not favor the lay, and trees that heavily favor to the lay. It's not always lean that gives a tree its inclination. Its inclination is also determined by the symmetry or weight of the limbs on either side, the wind, and the depth of the undercut. All of these things will affect the inclination for the tree to fall to the lay.

TREES WITH LITTLE INCLINATION TO FALL TO THE LAY

In small trees, use a bar long enough to reach the far corner, align and start the cut. Set the dogs at one corner and sweep the bar to the far corner while observing the tree. If the tree is observed to move to the

Observing the Top for Movement

DOGGING AROUND TO THE FAR SIDE

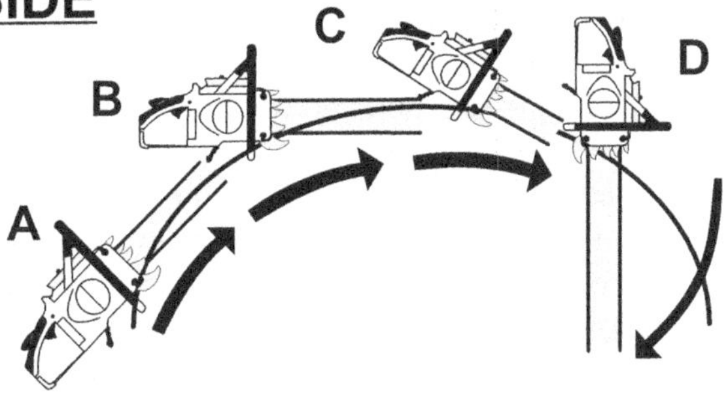

A. ALIGN AND START THE CUT, THEN BREAK THE DOGS LOOSE AND RESET THEM AT (B). PROGRESS AS DESCRIBED ALL THE WAY TO (D). THEN SWEEP THE CUT BACK TO (A).

FOR UNDERCUTS, BACK CUTS AND BUCKING

face, continue to cut up to the intended hinge. A tree like this will generally stop moving to the lay when you stop progressing the back cut. This means that there is too much hinge wood and more will have to be cut for the tree to fall. Look to the treetop to observe it for movement. Be careful if there is cloud movement in the background sky; it can give you erroneous indications of the tree's movement. While observing the top for movement, it's sometimes necessary to steady your position with one hand against the trunk If the tree is observed to not move while the back cut is progressed, set a wedge to keep it from setting back. Then cut up to the intended hinge, pull the saw out, and drive the wedge.

In larger trees like this, the back cut can be started and progressed in much the same way, with the exception of having to make it from both sides. Cut up the far corner first in large trees. In most cases, the far corner will be the low side of the tree or the most difficult and dangerous side to work. This is the reason you cut it up first.

If you are on ground that is difficult to work from though, you may have to line up and begin the back cut on the easy or safe side of the tree first. Then dog the saw around gradually to cut up to the far corner. To dog a saw around the back of a tree, line up the cut and start it on your side first. Before the tip of the bar is inside the cut, pull the dogs loose and reset them farther around the back without taking the bar out of the cut you just started. Do this until you can reach the far corner with a full sweep of the bar. Then work back, completing the cut to the safe side. Be careful whenever dogging around. You could lose sight of the bar tip on the far side at times, and could run it into something you can't see. If you're on good ground, you can cut up the far corner in any fashion; then go to the safe side and finish the cut.

TREES THAT FAVOR BACK FROM THE LAY

Unless these trees are excessively back-heavy, most of them will be fairly simple and safe to fall. You will, of course, have to pull the tree, wedge it, or jack it. No matter how you prompt the tree to fall to the face, the back cut can be similarly placed as in the above trees. That is, progress and complete the back cut and then prompt the tree to fall. Pulling, wedging, and jacking trees is elaborated on later.

TREES THAT HEAVILY FAVOR THE LAY

These trees are referred to as head leaners. They can be the most dangerous to fall. In the other trees you can start, progress, and complete the back cut in a conventional manner, with head leaners it's not as easy. In small trees you may have to progress the back cut as fast as the saw is capable of making it. Such a technique is referred to as keeping ahead of the split. If you don't do this, it is likely that the tree will split out. That's why these trees are so dangerous. They start falling before you can get the back cut properly finished and too much wood breaks. Many of these trees are lost out of the lay because you don't have enough time to square the back cut to the undercut. You may only get one corner cut up when the tree starts falling.

BORING THE BACK CUT

Large trees have more room to make the back cut and you can start it by boring. Line up the saw like you're going to start the back cut, but stand back a ways to bore in just behind the hinge. Remember, all boring commands a solid stance and proper grip on the saw. When you start a bore cut, use the bottom quarter of the bar tip. Once started, straighten out the saw and plunge the bar through the back of the tree. Progress the cut up to the intended hinge or corners. The wood left in the back of the tree will keep the tree from falling while you square up the cut; this is the nice feature of boring the back. Finish by cutting the remaining wood in the back. This must be done prudently because the tree will often pull some wood out of the stump which can grab your saw away from you when the tree falls. If there's a lot of wood left to cut, you should flip the saw over, reinsert it into the bore cut, and cut towards the back of the tree with the gut of the bar. Leave enough wood to keep the tree from falling. Cut that last bit of wood from outside. In small trees you can nip the holding wood with the tip of the bar. In large trees the gut of the bar is socked into the holding wood below the back cut which helps prevent wood pull from taking the saw. Wood pull can take the saw if you sock the gut of the bar into the holding wood above the back cut. In either case, you may prefer to nip the holding wood.

Boring the back cut is generally accepted as being one of the safest ways to trip a head leaner. However, don't get too relaxed while doing it. Many such trees have fallen over in the course of making or finishing the bore cut. It can result in the back of the tree and the roots pulling out of the ground, giving you little warning to bail out without having to leave the saw and run for your life. This is to be expected in trees that have rot in the stump. But even sound trees can similarly surprise you. That's why you should practice great care when cutting head leaners down.

There is another way to trip a head leaner that is discussed in the variations of the falling cut. It's called the Coos Bay cut. You may prefer to use it on certain head leaners.

BORING THE BACK

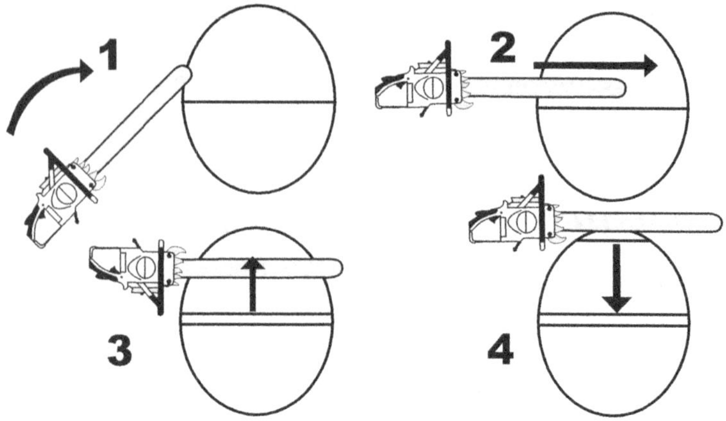

USE CAUTION: Heavy head leaners can pull out their roots when boring the back.

Chapter 26

The Hinge

The hinge is the result of facing and backing up the tree and is ultimately the guiding force that will see the tree to its lay. Its placement and the distribution of holding wood should always be predetermined.

HINGE PLACEMENT

The placement of the hinge has a pronounced effect on the trees you fall. There are three locations in which you can place the hinge: forward, middle, and rear.

FORWARD PLACEMENT OF THE HINGE

This is about one-third or less of the way in the stump. In small trees, forward placement of the hinge gives you the room needed to set wedges or jacks. It also gives you the advantage of leverage on back-leaning trees. This is because the implement is farther from the hinge, or pivot point. Forward placement will require you to lift the back of the tree farther in order to get the tree to fall, which will often require you to double up your wedges or shim the jack. In straight, balanced and free standing trees, forward placement of the hinge will always require the use of wedges or jacks to prompt them to fall because the hinge is ahead of the tree's center of gravity.

MIDDLE PLACEMENT OF THE HINGE

This offers you the maximum amount of hinge across the stump unless the stump is oddly shaped. If you're going for strength and

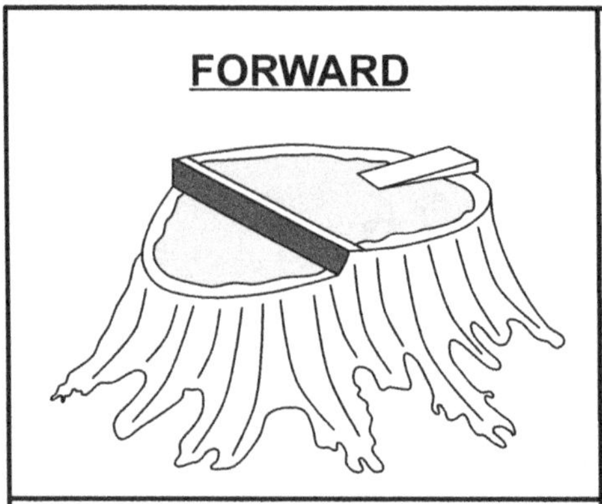

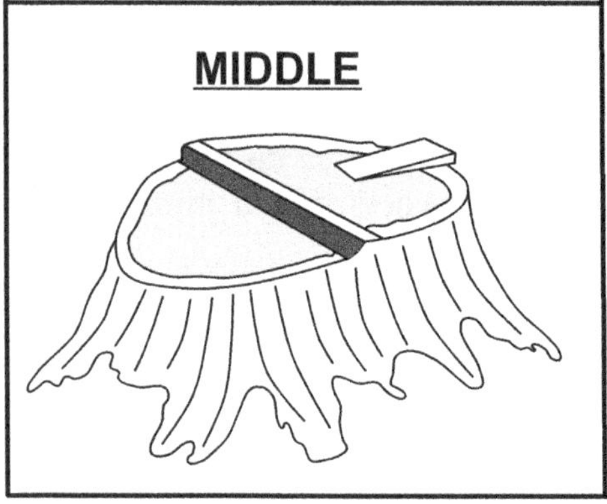

holding potential of a hinge, middle placement is often your best choice. Middle placement of the hinge will give you more lift out of your wedges and jacks because the fulcrum point is closer to the implement. However, if the tree has back lean, it can exert more force on the implement when the hinge is in the middle. In straight or balanced trees this will be just the opposite. In fact, many trees will free-fall to the lay if the hinge runs through the middle of the stump. The same trees would have to be wedged or jacked if the hinge were farther forward. You can approximate the location of the tree's center of gravity by closely observing the tree while placing the undercut. If the tree appears to move ahead while placing the undercut, the center of gravity of the tree will be forward in the stump. If the tree appears to move back, the center of gravity will be aft in the stump. If the tree doesn't appear to move at all and the undercut is nearly halfway in, you can assume the center of gravity is off to the side or in the middle of the stump.

REAR PLACEMENT OF THE HINGE

This placement of the hinge will get many trees to fall over on their own by undermining the center of gravity in the trunk. It is called "sawing lean" into the tree. Rear placement of the hinge is a technique used by many professional timber fallers. However well it works for them, the private tree worker will not have much chance to use it except in falling poles or stubs of trees. In most private tree work, there is not a lot of room for error. You cannot very often afford to cut a face into a tree this deep for the convenience of getting it to fall on its own. In certain trees the timber faller will keep on cutting until the tree is observed to move ahead. Most of the time it works, but some factors can turn things around on you. A gust of wind or limb-lock condition can hold a tree from moving ahead or setting back until it's too late. A certain percentage of such trees are lost by these factors.

This is a very suitable hinge placement if you are falling stubs of trees or poles that stand straight and balanced. Such stubs or poles will have little inclination to fall unless they are undercut deep enough to undermine their center of gravity. Whether in tree, stub, or pole, you must be certain of their balance. If you're not, don't try to saw a lean in any of them.

HINGE WOOD DISTRIBUTION

THE BEEFY HINGE

Too much wood in the hinge will cause even a head leaner not to fall until more wood is cut. It often results in massive splitting in the tree. If a tree is being pulled to the lay, it will pull harder with too much wood in the hinge, and it could cause enough resistance to fail the rigging. Even in pull-trees, too much wood can cause massive splitting. If you are wedging or jacking the tree with too much hinge wood, you will have to work harder to succeed. As a rule stay away from a hinge that is too beefy. However, in pull-trees with side lean a beefy hinge with a high back cut will help carry them over better while minimizing side drift.

THE THIN HINGE

Trees will wedge, jack, and pull easier with a thin hinge. But a thin hinge, especially with jack trees, can be risky. Too thin of a hinge may

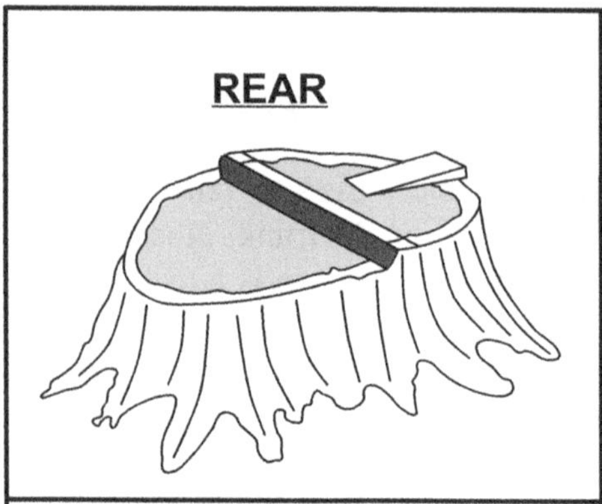

fail to hold a tree on the stump, particularly if the tree is rocking in the wind. A thin hinge is suitable for well-balanced trees or trees that lean to the lay. A tree will fall much faster with a thin hinge, too, compared to a tree that is pulling and breaking a beefy hinge. A thin hinge gives a tree more momentum to drive itself through the limbs of other neighboring trees. The beefy hinge can cause the same tree to get hung up on its way down.

THE UNEVEN HINGE

A hinge that is uneven will tend to pull a straight tree to the side that has more wood. The tree will land somewhere between the gun of the undercut and the gun of the back cut. This is an applicable hinge for controlling trees with side lean or offset limb weight, providing that the beefy side is on the tensioned part of the stump. See **Chapter 28**. Trees that start falling before a faller can square up the back cut (head leaners) commonly end up with uneven hinge wood. Uneven hinges are easy to avoid in most trees that give you time to square up the cuts before they start falling such as wedge, jack, and pull-trees.

TOO LITTLE ?

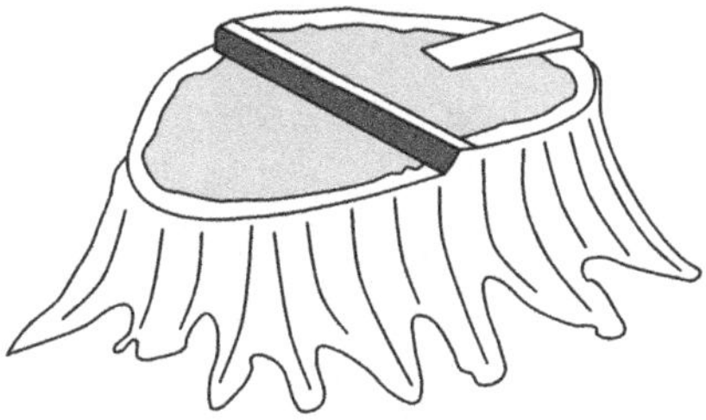

UNEVEN

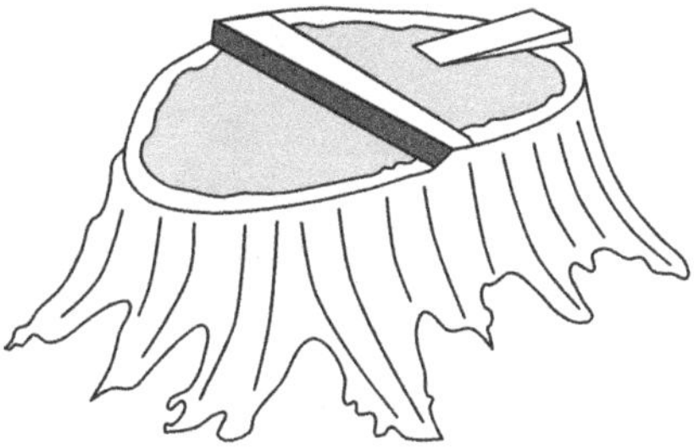

THE UNCUT CORNER HINGE

This error in the hinge is all too common when falling trees with too short of a bar on the power saw. When the bar is too short, you may have difficulty getting around to the far corner to cut it up. This is most frequently associated with falling trees on steep ground. The uncut corner can hold the tree fast to the stump, preventing all efforts to get it to tip over until you get around and correct it. Do not believe that the tree will go over if you continue cutting on your side. If you are wedging the tree, you will work yourself to exhaustion and get nowhere. Hydraulic jacks can sometimes crack an uncut corner loose. A jack can even bust the wrong corner loose first. If you have to get around to an uncut corner on the dangerous side of the tree, the tree will frequently fall immediately after it is cut, putting you on the wrong side of it when it does.

THE CUTOFF CORNER HINGE

A hinge with one corner cut off lacks continuity and results in a high percentage of lost trees. In leaning trees, it's usual for the

compression side of the tree to set down on the stump when that corner is cut off. It can be observed in the tree and can pinch the saw in the cut. Cutting the high corner off a side leaner will result in a Coos bay scenario (See **Chapter 27— The Coos Bay**). In jack or wedge trees, a cutoff corner can be unforgiving. On a rare occasion, a cutoff corner can be of benefit to you if you know how to use it. A faller may cut off a corner to get the tree to respond to it at a specific time after it is guided over by the hinge. You may need a tree to be guided through other trees and then roll or break to one side. A cutoff corner can provide this, but it means staying at the stump during a fair part of a tree's fall.

THE DIAGONAL CUT-THROUGH HINGE

This type of hinge is not much of a hinge at all. It results when a faller progresses the diagonal cut past the undercut into what is supposed to be the hinge wood. The diagonal cut-through hinge is prevalent when you fail to monitor the diagonal cut. Since the tip of the bar is out of sight at times, this will happen now and then. Be careful not to take the diagonal cut past the undercut. In extreme cases, the better part of the holding wood in the hinge will be severed by such an error. Unfortunately, this type of error is hard to detect sometimes because the kerf of the diagonal cut will fill with saw chips and conceal it. This is most likely if the diagonal cut meets the hinge at a pinch. If there is a gap at the hinge, such errors can often be detected before sending the tree over. Many trees with this error will still fall true to the lay. This is because the corners are usually still intact, and, as you should recall, it's the corners that ultimately guide the tree. But remember, many trees need more than just the corners to see them to the lay. This error is easy to prevent if you keep an eye on the saw sights and stop the diagonal when it lines up to the lay that the undercut was sighted to.

THE BACK CUT-THROUGH HINGE

This is essentially the same type of error as the diagonal cutthrough hinge and prevented in the same way.

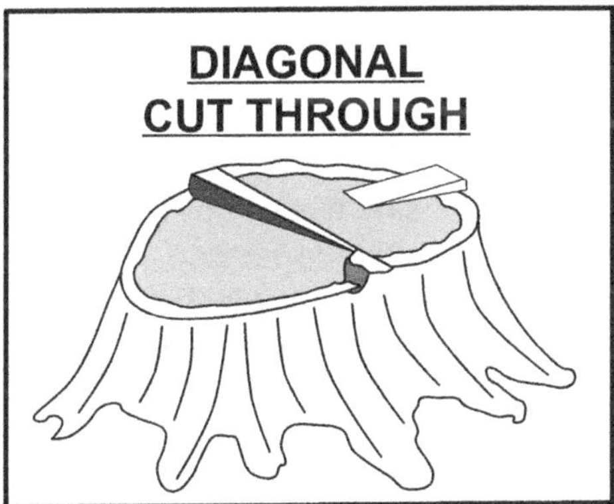

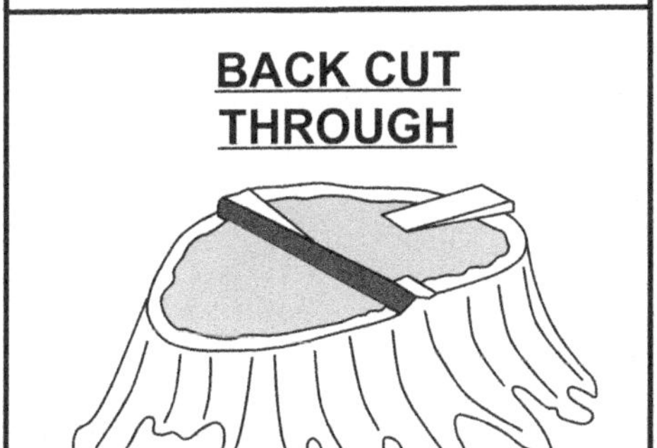

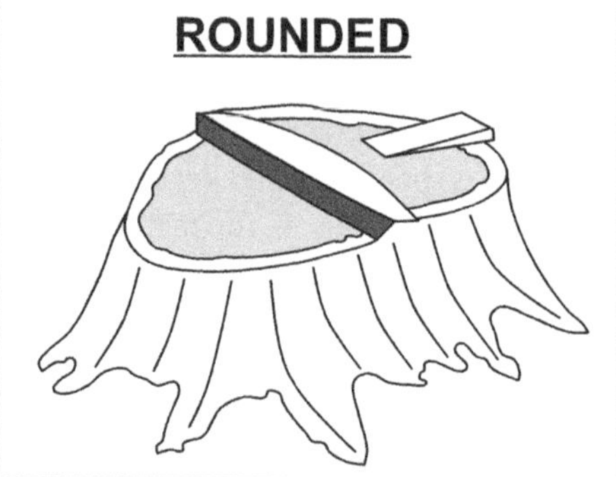

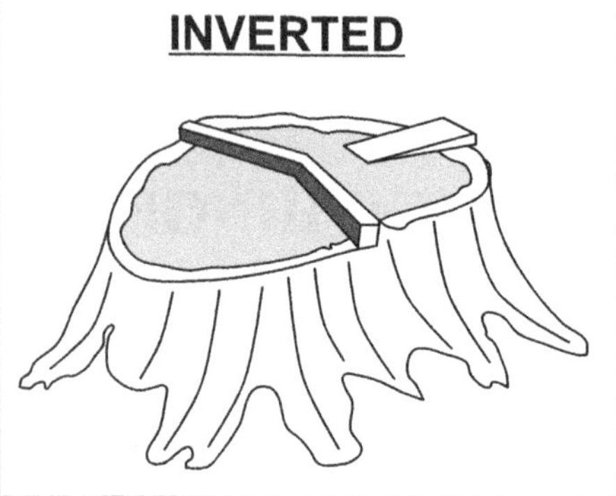

THE ROUNDED HINGE

This hinge is common when cutting with a saw that is not equipped with dogs. Dogs are necessary to anchor the saw at the corners so you can sweep the bar and square your cuts. With a rounded hinge, it can appear that the tree is cut up properly to the corners. The center of the hinge will actually be thicker, giving it a rounded aspect. This can still occur even if you have dogs on your saw. They may be too short to grab the tree or the bark may be loose and sloughy. Even a saw with dogs will slip at times and give you this kind of hinge. The rounded hinge has a lot of resistance and can make getting a tree to fall difficult. It's found most frequently in the back cut because its finish is out of sight until the tree falls. If you are adept at using the sights on the saw, you will recognize this error and correct it.

THE INVERTED HINGE

An inverted hinge has a lot of resistance at first; a tree with an inverted hinge will stall or lift hard until the inside wood breaks. Then it will go over surprisingly easy. The degree of the error will be more pronounced the closer the target to which you gun each corner. This is parallax error. It's easily preventable as long as you use a more distant target to gun each corner to.

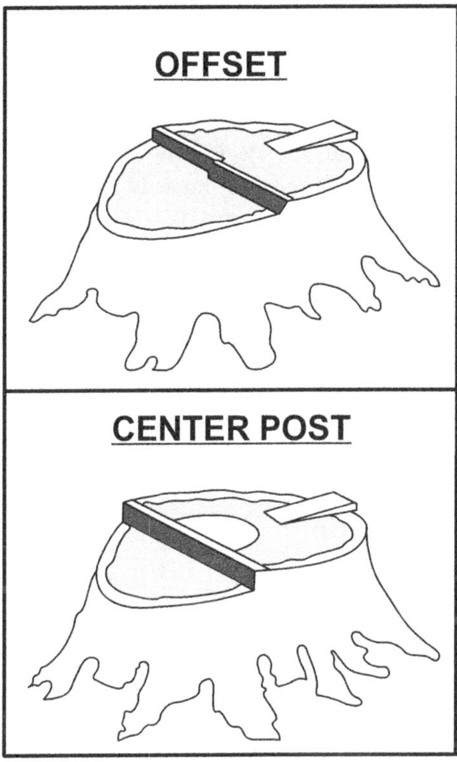

THE OFFSET HINGE

This kind of hinge is a result of not properly marking the corners. The problem is that one corner or half of the hinge can be positioned ahead of or behind the other. Such a hinge will have drastic conflicting qualities in spite of the fact that the gun of the two corners is the same. The only way the tree may go is for the aft portion to break loose. If it doesn't, the tree will follow the corners and not necessarily their gun. The offset hinge has no beneficial aspects in getting a tree to fall where you want it to. It's easily preventable by correctly marking the corners and seeing that the undercut runs straight through the stump between them.

THE CENTER-POST HINGE

If the diameter of the tree is more than twice the bar's length, you'll have a center post of wood in the hinge. The post or plug of wood can create enough resistance to hold a tree from falling. It can even cause massive wood pull out of the center of the tree. If you're aware that a post is going to be created, remedy it by reaching inside the face and cutting it out from that position before making the back cut. Of course, the face will have to be wide enough for you to reach in with the saw and bore out the post. Shy away from doing this in heavy forward leaners. If the tree is cut up and won't go over because of the post, the only remedy is to have a saw with a bar long enough to reach in and cut it.

Chapter 27

Variations and Multiple Trees

It's been said that necessity is the mother of invention. In tree falling, necessity has come up with a myriad of variations of the basic falling cut. Many of the variations have come about in a relatively short time since the introduction of the power saw because only by virtue of its ability to bore its tip into the tree are some of these methods even possible.

THE ULTRAWIDE FACE

This is a good face to use in pull-trees that lean back. Use two opposing diagonal cuts to the undercut, one conventional and one Humboldt. Purposely overshoot each diagonal cut without going past the undercut. The pies will not fall loose. They will need to be knocked, busted, or chipped out. After opening and cleaning out the face, you will notice the hinge will be gapped where the two diagonal cuts finished. The wider this gap is the farther the tree will carry over before the two diagonal cuts meet. This is the feature of the ultrawide face.

THE SWINGING FACE

At times you will need to swing a tree. To do this, the entire face and back cut is purposely placed in the tree out of pitch or out of level. In many situations it should be accompanied with a wide face. Note when using this cut that the tree will always tend to swing to the high side of the face. The amount of pitch in a straight tree shouldn't exceed more than thirty degrees. After that, you really don't gain much more effect. Trees that lean will have an out-of-pitch trunk anyway. Any time the falling cut is placed square to the trunk in order to fall a tree sideways to its lean, the resulting face will be out-of-pitch and tend to swing the

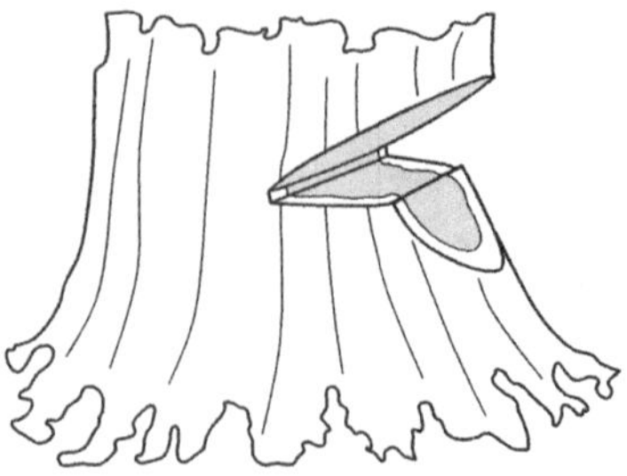

STEEP SNIPE

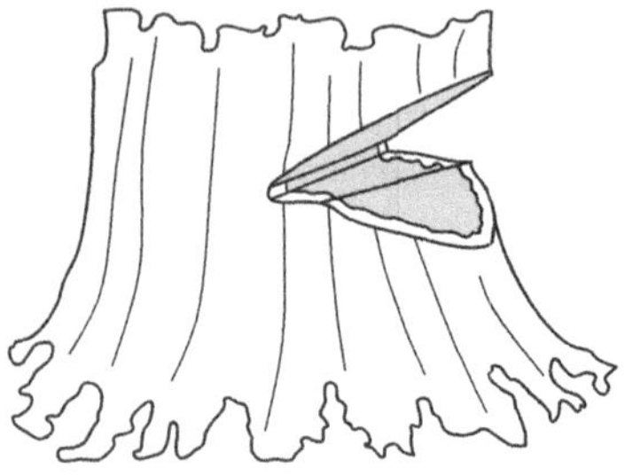

OBTUSE SNIPE

tree. If you use a Dutchman in the low corner and hold extra wood on the high corner, you can amplify the effect. But always remember that when swinging trees the success and fail rate is about even.

THE SNIPE

In many regions, particularly in small trees and second growth timber, the diagonal cut is often referred to as the snipe. However, the true snipe stands on its own merit and is a dynamic element in the falling cut. It's placed after the face cut is opened and cleaned out. It usually entails a minor diagonal cut taken off the lip of the stump, or butt of the tree. It can also occupy a major portion of the work and time in opening and finishing a falling cut. It can give the butt of the tree a square ledge from which to break off rather than breaking off at the natural contour of the stump's edge. This can have a very substantial effect on how a tree breaks off the stump. When it's placed at an angle to the hinge, it can have the effect of a Dutchman and kick the butt of the tree off on the side where it's placed. In this application it's called the obtuse, or rolling snipe. When it's placed at a steep slope off the front lip of the stump, it

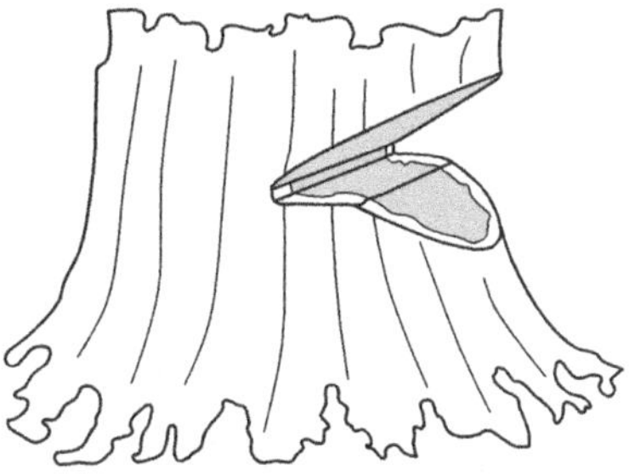

PARTIAL SNIPE

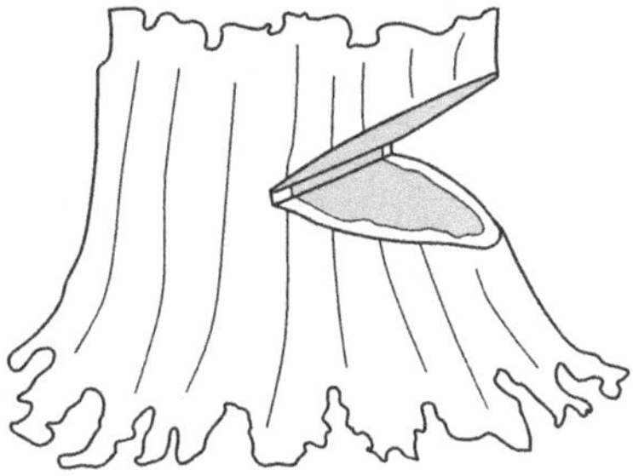

FULL SNIPE

can prompt the butt of the tree to drop off.

In face cuts that have a gap at the hinge, the snipe can widen the face and give the tree more room to fall before the face closes. The snipe does not necessarily do this if the hinge is tight or in a pinch. The amount of snipe is often governed by gut feeling rather than any precise formula. Where it is placed and how much is taken out of the undercut, or diagonal, is sometimes debatable.

THE BLOCK-OUT FACE (HUMBOLDT)

In Northern California this falling cut is routinely used in the large and valuable trees there. It has a high success rate. It capitalizes on the gap and snipe attributes. In a ten foot diameter tree a gap of eight to ten inches at the hinge would be about right. The undercut and gap are accomplished by two converging undercuts. They should be an inch or two wider apart in the front. This makes it easier to get the undercut out and get inside to clean and inspect the hinge.

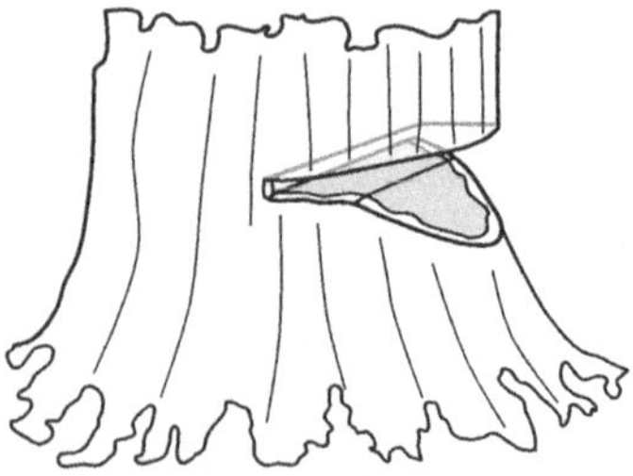

HUMBOLDT
OLD GROWTH STYLE

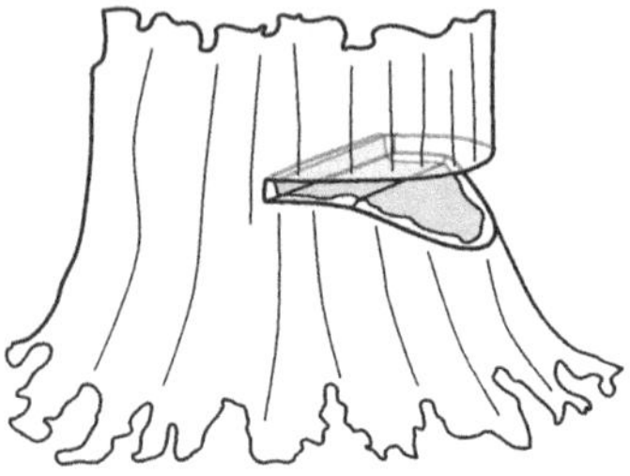

HUMBOLDT
BLOCK OUT STYLE

Boring is always necessary between the cuts to render the undercut block into manageable sections. Break loose the sections by driving wedges in the bore cuts and using picks and pry bars to get them out. The use of a snipe is mandatory to widen the face and give the tree a square ledge on the stump to break off ol. The type of snipe used depends on the situation. But whatever kind is used, it is always calculated to fit the situation. By the time this face cut is done, it can resemble a typical Humboldt cut.

EARLY DEPARTURE FACE

At times, you need to get the butt off the stump soon after the tree starts falling. On steep ground this can get a tree to drop into a gulch instead of across it. It saves breaking a lot of trees. There are many variations of this type of cut, but each utilizes a steep snipe off the lower lip of the stump. The hinge should be in a pinch since you don't want the effect of a wide face slowing the departure. In one variation, there is a Dutchman all the way across the face of the hinge. As a rule, the Dutchman shouldn't be wider than half of the hinge width. This will minimize wood pull and still give the effect you need: to break the tree free of its bond to the stump. It's wise to only use this cut on trees that lean to the lay. Boring the back cut is strongly recommended.

THE COO'S BAY

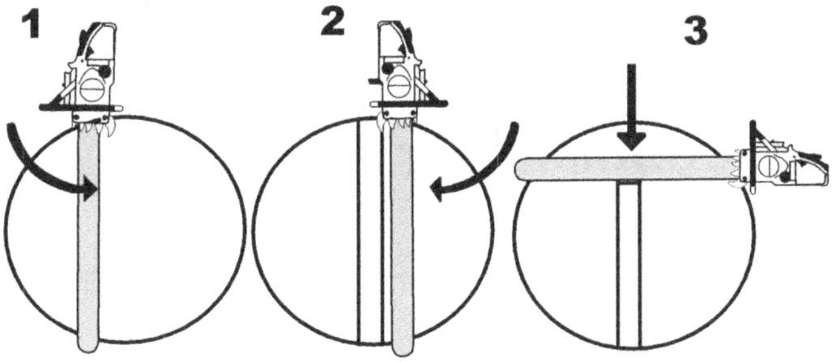

FOR HEAD LEANERS ONLY

THE COOS BAY

This cut is used as a precautionary procedure in tripping heavy head leaners. It has no directional control, but minimizes major splitting and wood pull. Place a crosscut a little more than one-third of the way in on each side of the trunk, square to the trunk and parallel to the favor of the tree. These two cuts leave the tree with a strip of wood running from the tension side of the stump to the compression side. If the tree is inclined to shift to either side, it's necessary to snug a wedge in one or both of the cuts to compensate for it. The tree has had an "undercut" and a "back cut" placed in it, but without a diagonal cut to open either side. The tree is standing on a center strip, or post, that you may choose to bore through in the center from side to side creating two posts. The post can be considered the hinge of a side leaner, and when you cut the top corner off a side leaner, you're going to lose the tree to its favor. This is a safe way to deal with heavy head leaners.

Holding wood may also be severed following advice and precautions on Tripping a Set Back Tree in **Chapter 29—Freeing a Stuck Saw**. Beware! Relative side favor or offset weight in the tree can result in the tree twisting and splitting! *Also*! A sound stump is necessary when using the Coos Bay!

The basic falling cut and the variations discussed can be tailored to fit a wide variety of trees and situations. The situations vary as greatly as do the trees. At times you'll have to make up your own solutions to a particular problem tree. When falling trees individually, most of the cuts talked about will work more or less the way they are designed to. This is not necessarily true when you fall multiple trees, rotten trees, and trees that are limb locked together. Several solutions for handling problem trees are discussed in the ensuing pages.

FALLING CODOMINANT TREES

FALLING A DOUBLE BROADSIDE

What makes falling a double broadside a tricky situation is that there's a strong tendency for the two trees to separate while in the course of cutting on them, and especially when they're falling. The major factor

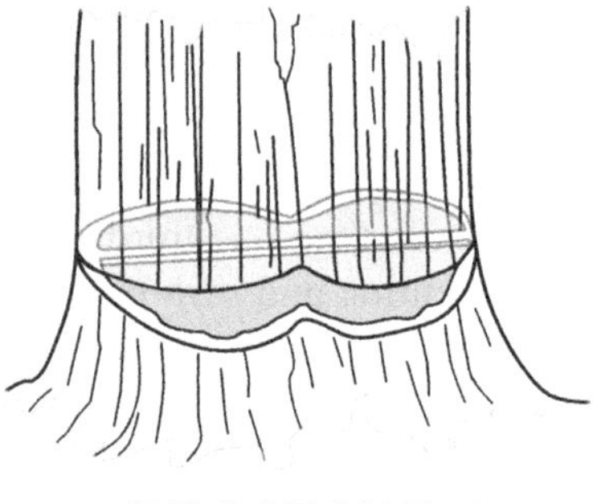

BROAD WAYS

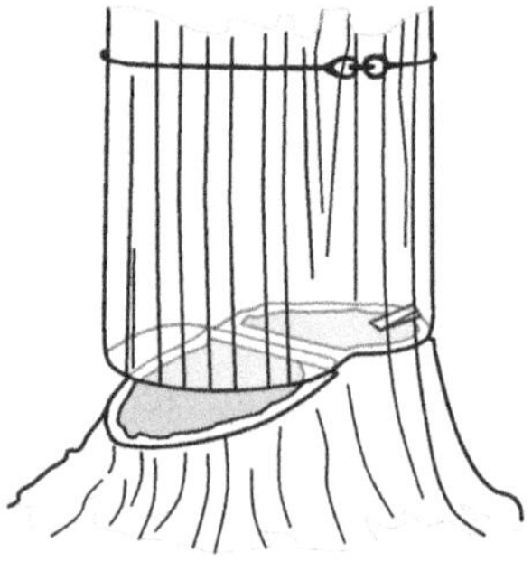

WITH THE UNION

governing whether the trees will split apart or not is how well they are grown together at the crotch union. Outside appearances are not always indicative of what's inside. Even if the union appears to be strong, such trees regularly split apart when they impact. If it is bad for the trees to split apart, they should be bound together. Binders and chain work well to do this. Up higher in the trees, you can use lighter rigging to hold them together. It is advised that you bind both top and bottom because lower binding by itself does not always guarantee that one tree won't shift from the other. It can happen in a fair percentage of cases.

The hinge must be straight and true through both trunks or there will be conflicting qualities that can force the two trees apart. If wedging or jacking, the force delivered by the implement can separate the two trees if it is too great on one and not on the other. If pulling the trees, rig both of them so they will pull together rather than pulling on just one. There are exceptions.

FALLING A DOUBLE WITH THE UNION

The hinge wood is located to provide each tree some support along the union seam. Should the hinge be fore or aft, one of the two trees could lose its bond to the stump and be left hanging onto the other tree by just the crotch union. For obvious reasons that is not a good situation, because at any time the unsupported tree can set down and fall away without warning, especially if you're delivering the force of a wedge or jack on the loose member. With the hinge located properly you should still bind the trees together. It's also recommended to use a wide face in this application.

In another scenario, you can use one of the two trees to pull the other. Set rigging in the tree to hold them together. Leave some slack in it so you can fall one of the trees away from the other, not far, but far enough so that it can bear a pull on the back tree. You can then cut the back tree and use the forward tree to pull it. There are considerations to this method. Down low the rigging would have to be quite substantial and set with a minimum of slack. It must also be set so it won't slip. Up higher you can use lighter rigging, but it will have to be set with more slack to let the lead tree move ahead and bear a pull. In utilizing this technique follow the procedures for ripping and falling a double apart.

SLIDING A DOUBLE APART

If you're going to fall one tree so it slides by the other at the rip cut, keep a few things in mind. Crossed limbs between the trees become a potential problem. Another problem is that the far corner of the hinge is going to be out of sight, inside the union, so use the sights on the saw when placing the back cut to make sure it's squared properly. A strong possibility of an error exists since you can't see inside the union.

If you use an over-length saw bar in this situation, you won't be able to dog up to keep from cutting into the other tree. Not being able to dog up, especially in a big cut, makes saw handling difficult. You'll need a firm stance and strong grip on the saw. Whenever the tip of the saw runs along the inside edge of a cut, the saw is likely to kick back. Be careful and keep a firm, proper grip on the saw.

When falling trees apart like this you may sever a lot of wood in the stump of the trees you leave; weakening them; or creating a condition that can cause complications later. For this reason, observe the stumps carefully for this condition in the trees you fall that were left out of a group.

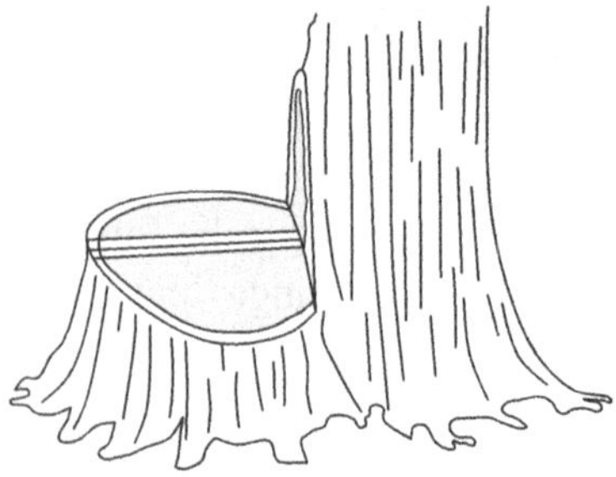

RIP AND SLIDE BY

RIP AND FALL AWAY

Before placing a back cut in this situation, double-check the angle of the hinge and the angle of the rip cut. The trees may rub or bump each other at the rip cut if it doesn't angle properly to the hinge. This can result in a considerable miss to the lay even when everything else is correct.

Note also that the inside corner is often a weak counterpart of the hinge in this situation. On occasion it will be responsible for the tree to drift to the outside corner. The reason for this is twofold; lack of sapwood there and composition change from compression where two trees grow together.

RIPPING AND FALLING A DOUBLE APART

In this situation, the crotch union is ripped and one of the two trees is felled directly away from the other tree. In large trees of this type, the ripping may have to be done from both sides and sometimes at heights great enough to require climbing.

Look to the tops for crossed or grafted limbs so common in double and multiple trees. The hinge is often positioned to accommodate falling the tree a certain way so it will slide through any crossed limbs between the two. To set the hinge any other way may force the tree into a bind by aggravating the condition. Wedges or jacks can force such limb conditions apart if they are not heavily locked together.

The back cut will have to be bored when the trees are being felled directly apart. When placing the back cut, be sure that it intersects fully with the rip cut. If it doesn't, a plug of wood may be left in the back and hold the tree fast to the stump. This goes for the rip cut too. Make sure that both cuts fully intersect each other.

A variation of this uses the rip cut as the back cut. The face cut is made all the way to the union and then the rip cut is used to trip the tree into falling. Make sure the union is strong, since the act of placing a face that deep could cause the tree you are cutting to split off the other. For the same reason, care should be used when making the rip cut that trips them apart.

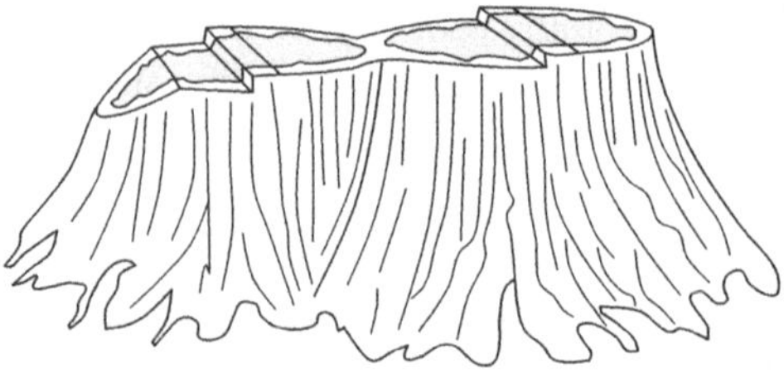

FACE AND FALL BOTH
BIND OR TIE TOGETHER ?

RIP TO TRIP

FALLING A PAIR OR MORE

The trees may be far enough apart to walk between them yet have some conflicting crossed limbs that makes it necessary to fall more than one at a time. You may want to aim all the face cuts in the same direction; that way you can get the momentum of the group working together. But some exceptions are in order if you don’t want the trees falling on top of one another.

In this situation the limbs between a front and back tree can lock together after they start falling. If the limbs are of a substantial size, it can stall the trees from falling. It can present you with a new situation that may require cutting the back tree completely off the stump to get the two down.

In groups of limb locked trees you should start at the front trees and work your way to the back. It may even be better if you faced up all the trees first and then went back through and placed the back cuts. It all depends on the situation.

THE TEEPEE

Getting trees hung up in one another is a common occurrence in this business. For your safety there are a lot of considerations on how you deal with this situation. Observe the hung-up tree. Is it well crotched in the one that's holding it? Has it broken free of the stump? Is it bearing hard on the tree that's holding it? A well crotched tree is generally going to stay hung up. If it's not well crotched, it could fall at any time. Cutting the hung-up tree off its stump will often prompt it to roll out of the supporting tree's limbs. If the tree is well crotched in the other, and free of its stump, then cutting the supporting tree is another option. In many situations it's recognized as being a deadly option.

Sometimes another tree can be felled into the hang up to remedy the situation, but this can further complicate things by involving more trees in the hang up. If you have the equipment to pull the trees out, that may be your only other option. OSHA has set guidelines on dealing with hung-up trees that may differ. You should review them.

DOMINO FALLING

This is a strategy of hitting and knocking down trees in a progression. Beware that *it can be a very dangerous procedure*, especially when applied to knocking down a set back or back-leaning tree with one behind it. Why? If you fail to successfully knock down these particular target trees they can rebound and break over backwards! Plus the tree you use for ammo to knock over the other can be deflected, broken or shot back! That's where you're at. For these reasons and more I advise not to engage in domino falling (See **Chapter 32— When the Tree Falls**, for more insight).

LAYING OUT THE TREES

A timber faller receiving a new strip of trees walks through it first to evaluate the possible ways to lay it out. This is important because there may be hundreds of trees to lay in a limited area. Failure to lay the timber correctly in the amount of space provided can result in much breakage, loss of product, undue risks, and loss of job.

LAYING TIMBER IN LEAD

To lay timber in lead requires long ground and relatively straight trees. You then have an ideal situation where you can lay the trees side by side and in between one another without crossing them. This is a good lead for big trees, but once you get going you'll probably have to keep it. One tree crossing the lead can result in much breakage thereafter.

LAYING THE TIMBER OUT OF LEAD

More frequently you'll not have the ideal situation. The ground may be shot. That is, it may be broken up by skid roads, ravines, rock outcrops and landslides. Moreover, the trees may have lean that defy desired order. At times it can seem chaotic. Still, certain rules apply, and

a thorough evaluation is always required. First, pick the low spots and any roads to lay trees in first. This will prevent breakage in the timber you lay over it. By filling in the low spots first you can also improve the ground for laying other trees on. It's usually prudent and makes for less breakage to work with the bigger trees first and then lay the smaller trees over them. In spite of crossing the timber over itself, it's done in such a way that actually prevents breakage. But even here it's possible to cross yourself up.

STAGE FALLING

You may run out of ground to lay more trees in and have to stop falling until it's logged out. Although you'll be working with the knowledge that you're coming back later to finish it up, you still need a good plan because you don't want to come back more than once if you don't have to.

LAYOUT TREES

Here you're falling large and valuable trees into a lay that has been built by heavy equipment. As a rule, have the operator take out the high spots in the lay, and use them to fill in the low spots. Have the operator dig out any stumps that your tree could hit. This may be all that is necessary, but if the ground is hard, have the operator break and fluff it into mounds. Mounds offer cushioning on hard ground, but their size and frequency are important. If the mounds are too far apart, trees can break. Where the tree top will land, mounds should be closer together to absorb the impact. Avoid crowns in the layout, for this may cause breakage. A minor bit of belly in the lay is tolerable. Once you're satisfied with the lay, you can proceed with falling the tree, taking care not to miss the layout.

Chapter 28

Lean In Trees

Of all the factors to be considered in tree falling, no single one can match the importance of lean. There are two factors of lean to consider. One is the degree of the lean and the other is the direction the tree is felled in relation to it.

THE DEGREE OF THE LEAN

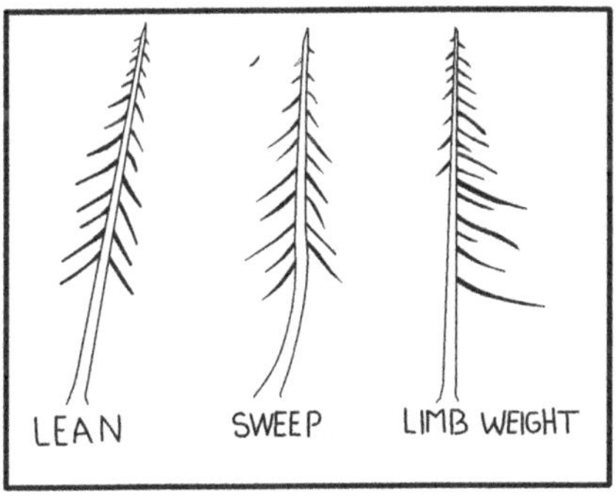

The existing lean in the tree is a good indication of the amount of tension and pressure exerted on the stump. But limb distribution and any sweep in the trunk of the tree can add to or subtract from the amount of tension and pressure exerted by any lean.

SWEEP

Sweep is a pronounced curve in the trunks of many trees. Most trees with sweep will be found to hang or lean to the side of the sweep. I have seen many exceptions. On occasion, you'll find trees that straighten or lean back over the sweep, which can, in effect, neutralize the strain and pressure on the stump. These are odd trees; they are the kind that can get you to believe their favor is other than what it seems.

LIMB WEIGHT

Trees that lean a little bit can be balanced out by their limbs. If the limb structure is uniform, any degree of lean will surely produce a certain amount of tension on the stump. Should all the limbs be primarily on the side of the lean, then the strain on the stump from even a slight lean can be significant. Limb weight alone can cause drift in a perfectly vertical tree. Account for it in your hinge wood distribution and/or the gun of the undercut when the limb weight is predominantly on one side.

PLUMBING THE TREE

The lean in most trees can be determined using the plumb bob. The plumb bob is a simple weight hanging off a string, and used in many applications as a reference line for the vertical. Using the plumb bob for forest trees is most straight forward. Plumb the tree from several different angles. If the tree is straight, the string will fall in a line running from the stump to the top. Any lean in the tree will become apparent by a difference in the line. If the line passes through the trunk and not the top, or visa versa, there is lean in the tree. It's commonly expressed in the amount of feet out; for example, the top of this tree is ten feet out. If the tree is one hundred feet tall and uniformly balanced by its limbs, it can be considered a light leaner. If the tree has more limbs on the side of the lean, it can be considered a moderate leaner. If the tree has all its limbs on the side of the lean, it can be considered a heavy leaner. If the tree has sweep to the lean and hangs or bows over by the weight on that side, it can be considered very heavy and very dangerous.

THE ANGLE THE TREE IS FELLED RELATIVE TO THE LEAN

There are real and relative considerations here. When a tree is plumbed while standing directly fore or aft of the true lean, it may not appear to lean at all. The real lean in a tree will be found only when you view it at a direct right angle to it. At any other angle, the lean will appear to be less than what it really is. This is called the relative lean. Its importance will be discussed when we talk about compensating for lean in the undercut.

When you fall the tree forward to the lean, it's called a head leaner. When you fall the tree against the lean, it's called a back leaner. When you fall the tree sideways to the lean, it's called a side leaner. Let's discuss briefly how you might handle some head leaners, back leaners, and side leaners.

HEAD LEANERS

Getting these trees to fall is no problem. However, getting them to do it without splitting or ripping themselves apart can be. These two things are cause for accidents and injury, so you've got to know how to minimize them. It makes a big difference whether a tree is a light, moderate, or heavy head leaner. A heavy head leaner is the most dangerous. However, if you treat even a light head leaner without respect, it can result in much the same consequences. Large or small, with most you want to get an ample undercut. Make it as deep as you can without getting the saw stuck in it. If the cut gets tight, pull out the saw and open it up with a snipe. After that, nip and cut carefully to deepen and widen the face. That's the first step. The second is the back cut. When you start the back cut in a small head leaner, don't hesitate or stop until it's cut up adequately. A slow back cut in a head leaner is recipe for major splitting and barber chair. In the larger trees you can elect to bore the back which is the best way to do it for minimizing wood pull and gaining directional control. Consider using the Coos Bay cut in the bad head leaners where directional control is not needed as much as just getting the tree down safely. A seldom used but valuable technique that has directional control is rigging the tree to hold it while the undercut and back cut are made. After that, the rigging is then released to let the tree fall.

BACK LEANERS

These trees will need to be wedged, jacked, or pulled to the lay. Wedge the light ones, jack the moderate ones, and pull the heavy ones. The procedures for performing any of these tasks are described in the chapters on wedging, jacking, and pulling trees.

One thing that head leaners and back leaners both have in common is if you're falling them directly fore or aft of the lean there will be no relative lean apparent in either. The real lean will still be working and exerting the tension and pressure on the stump which requires you to deal with its influence. Other than that you really don't have to make any adjustments or compensations in the gun of the undercut, but when you begin falling trees sideways to the lean some compensations are necessary.

The terms "back" and "side" are applied to these leaners because they want to go where you don't want them to go. If you lose a leaner to its favor it may hit a house, cross a road, take out some power lines, hang up in or damage other trees, or simply fall into a regulated area.

SIDE LEANERS

Let's say you have a tree that is one hundred feet tall. The main stem of this tree is straight but the top doubles out. When plumbing the tree from the lay, it is noted that each top is ten feet out from the butt. The tree is straight and for the most part balanced by the tops opposing each other. If you set a marker in the lay at one hundred feet and square the undercut to hit it, what do you think will happen? You won't hit the marker. If the tree had a single, straight top you would, but this tree has a double top that is spread twenty feet apart at the top. Each top will lay ten feet to each side of the marker.

In another example using the same tree, let's say for the tree to fit inside the lay, the relative right side top must hit the marker. In this case, it would be the top on the right side of the tree as you look towards the lay. How would you do it? Simply by squaring the undercut ten foot to the left of the marker. Then the right hand top will hit the marker. It's rather simple in this kind of tree because it doesn't really lean; the tops are just spread apart. If you view the tree from any other angle, the tops will appear to be closer together. This is the relative distance for which you must compensate.

The same school of thought is applied if the top of a side leaner is observed to be ten feet out from the butt at one angle and fifteen feet out at another. Compensate for the amount of feet out from where the tree is viewed at the head of the lay. The main difference here is that the leaner desires to fall to the side of the lean while it's headed for the lay. This desire to fall off to the side of the lean is referred to as side drift. You don't have to be as concerned about it in trees that have just a slight lean, but in moderate leaners you do. It should automatically be expected in heavy side leaners.

OTHER COMPENSATIONS

Besides compensations in the gun of the undercut, there are other kinds of compensations you can use such as wood distribution in the hinge, pitch in the hinge, and Dutchman in the low corner.

WOOD IN THE HINGE

It's a fairly standard practice to leave more wood on the tension side of the stump, or hinge. It helps quite a bit to control drift. How much more wood to leave is governed by gut feeling more than anything else.

As a rule of thumb, leave half as much in a light side leaner and twice as much in a moderate side leaner.

PITCH

Another compensation is to place the undercut out of pitch to swing the tree. Most side leaners will have an out-of-pitch trunk anyway. You should recall that a tree will always tend to swing to the high corner of an out-of-pitch face. In effect, it can compensate the gun.

DUTCHMAN'S

Employing a Dutchman in the low corner as a compensation for side lean has been used by many fallers over the years. You'll never find two persons agreeing on how much of a Dutchman it takes to compensate for side lean. Many people don't believe in using them at all.

Using any of these compensations is no guarantee with side leaners. Sometimes they'll oversteer a tree and you'll miss the lay from over compensation instead of side drift. The variables affecting a side leaner most are the strength and soundness of the wood, the tension and pressure on it, and the mechanical features of the cut you use. Any one of these factors can cause compensation errors and drift.

HOLDING AND SWINGING SIDE LEANERS

If you can keep a side leaner on the stump long enough to follow the face, you can work with them more effectively. The best way to keep a side leaner on the stump is by rigging a holding line to swing the tree. To gain an understanding of how it works, demonstrate to yourself this simple principle.

Take a broom and tie about six to eight feet of string on the comb where it connects to the handle. Go outside on the grass, stand the broom upside down, and stick the handle in the ground about one or two inches. Kick the broom out at an angle to simulate a lean. Position the string on the ground to hold the broom steady and from falling to the lean. You'll find that the location for the string to hold the broom steady will be directly behind the lean and in lead with the butt. While holding the line tight, let the broom fall to one side or the other. Make a note of where the broom lands and stand it back up. As long as you keep everything constant, the broom will fall in the same area each time. As will a tree when you hold it the same way.

In trees, it's not as easy to find a suitable location directly behind the lean from which to hold them. Sometimes the line will be positioned fore or aft of the ideal location. The concern here is that you may get some drift if the line is forward, and you may get an excess of swing if the line is aft. But either way, you can find the location of where the tree will land if you measure the length of the line from its anchor point to where it's attached to the tree. Then measure the height above the hinge where the line is fixed in the tree. Take these two measurements and draw them out to the lay. Where the two intersect is where the tree will land, providing there is no stretch in the holding line.

STRETCH IN THE HOLDING LINE

Line stretch can cause side drift when swinging side leaners. To eliminate the possibility of drift from stretch in the holding line, tighten it up to the point needed to pull the tree against its lean. If you don't tighten it, the tree can drift out of the lay. If you're using hard rigging, such as steel cable, this won't be a major concern; with rope, it is.

POSITION OF THE HOLDING LINE

The anchor point of the holding line ideally should be behind, or in lead with, the lean. Forward of that point a little is acceptable when it helps lead the tree to the lay. If the anchor point is too far forward though, the tree can drift. Aft of that point can cause the tree to draw over. The height, angle, and run in the line also bear consideration.

PATH OF THE HOLDING LINE

The holding line follows the tree. Because it follows the tree, it can cross with something. If there are obstacles in its path you may have to change your tack. For example, the holding line can break if it crosses with a stout obstacle such as another tree. If it doesn't break, the tree you're pulling can lunge over and bear a hard pull on the line. A stout line can even break trees down in its path as it follows the tree it's holding. Anticipate obstacles in the path of the holding line. You may have to make room for it.

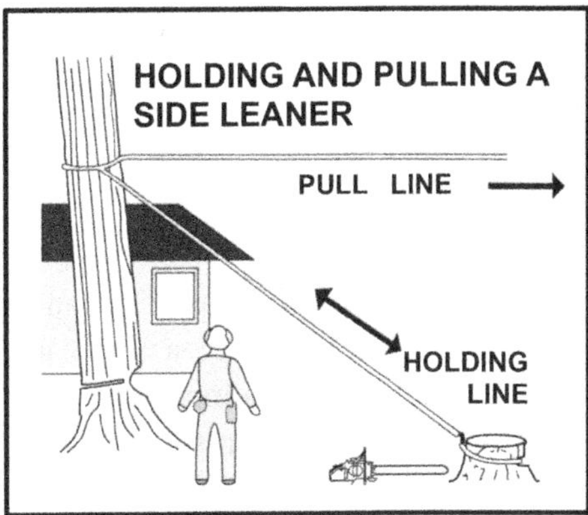

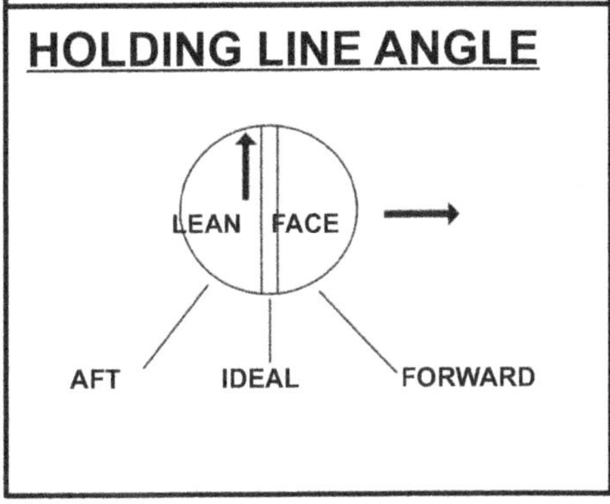

PROMPTING A SIDE LEANER

It's often necessary to prompt the tree to the lay if it lacks the inclination to go on its own. If the holding line is aft, or if the tree has relative back lean to the lay, it will be necessary to prompt it. You can wedge the small ones, jack the larger ones, and pull the bigger ones. Generally, though, it's easier to set another line to pull the tree when you're up in it setting the holding line. The line used to pull the tree does not always have to be as strong as the line used to hold the tree. Make sure, though, that the line you use is adequate for the job.

TETHERING THE HOLDING LINE

After everything is set up and you have a plan, there is one more thing you can do to ensure success, and that is to precisely pull and release the holding line during the tree's fall. This will make a big difference in the outcome of swinging a side leaner. For instance, if the anchor for the holding line is forward, you may want to take it up as the tree starts moving. If the anchor is aft, you may want to release the line after the tree is guided over so far. Tethering the holding line allows you to get down to the nitty-gritty of controlling a tree's fall.

OBTUSE TRUNK ANGLE

A pronounced sweep or lean can bring the position of the trunk to a near-horizontal attitude. Such angle in the trunk of a tree can make cutting them down difficult. This can be further complicated by working on steep ground. In combination it accounts for a fair percentage of misses to the lay. Trees with a lot of sweep in the trunk can rock, teeter, or roll more pronouncedly when they hit the ground, even on level ground. Thus, it's wise to leave the stump when they go.

OTHER REASONS FOR MISSING A LAY

Side lean and obtuse trunk angle are two recognized reasons for side drift and missing a layout. Improper technique at the stump of the tree is a big cause of misses to the lay and the reader should realize that it's not excusable. There are other factors not so readily apparent that can result in misses to the lay. A person should be aware of them before considering falling a tree in a lay that is in close proximity to potential liabilities.

If the tree you fall rubs hard through the limbs of another, they can shove the tree you just fell off its course and out of the lay. In another situation the tree can be pulled over to the side by its limbs grabbing onto another tree in front of it. The so-called "parachute effect" or wind resistance of the limbs on one side of a tree can result in a similar miss to the lay. As mentioned earlier, off-sided limb weight alone can result in a miss to the lay. Your tree can cross the top of another tree that leans over into the lay, causing your tree to slide down the trunk of the leaner resulting in a considerable miss to the lay. Bark inclusions and other defects in the stump that escape detection are also a main cause of misses to the lay. All of these factors periodically remind us that we shouldn't take chances in tight quarters, and sometimes it might be best to hire a qualified climber to remedy these uncertain situations.

Chapter 29

Wedging the Tree

As a tool, the wedge is unsurpassed for its suitability and convenience in tree falling. Nothing else can be inserted or driven into the cuts, cracks, and crannies that occur so frequently in this work and which need such a device to lift or keep a cut open.

As a safety measure, seat the wedge in the back cut when there is enough room to allow it, then go ahead with the back cut and observe the tree. If a tree favors falling to the face, movement will be evident as the

back cut is progressed. A tree's movement is best observed by looking through its limbs toward the top. If it is accurately observed to be moving toward the face, you can safely continue the back cut. When the tree is observed to not move, the back cut should be stopped. A subtle breeze can hold a tree from falling; too beefy of a hinge can hold a tree; limbs from neighboring trees can hold the one you're falling. If none of these factors are holding the tree from falling, then the true favor of the tree is resting on the wedge. Remove the saw if the tree is cut up properly, and then finish driving the wedge. For each smack on the wedge, the top of the tree should clearly show movement toward the face. If it takes more driving of the wedge to get the tree over, it's a good thing you set a wedge in the first place.

Unless the tree obviously favors the lay, the insertion of the wedge in the back cut should be a regular habit.

THE SET BACK TREE

Not all trees will set back the same. Some trees will set back quite easily and can even rock back and forth on the hinge. If you cut more wood, such a tree can then set back hard. If or when a tree does, be ready to race out of there because a hard set back tree can break or twist over the wrong way. Difficulty is encountered setting wedges in a set back tree. The cut may close up tight in the back of the stump while still being open forward of that point, so you may be able to start a wedge there. In large trees you may be able to reopen part of the back cut by boring. This will make an opening to start a wedge where it should be. The wedge should be of a fine taper and have a sharp leading edge. Be extremely careful when starting a wedge in a tight or closed cut. Drive it in easily at first and don't start walloping it until it's in a couple of inches; it can shoot out, especially if not hit square! With set back trees it's best to use an alloy or steel wedge, because their leading edge can take the abuse of being driven in a tight cut better than the plastic wedge. Plastic wedges are easily mutilated when picking up a set back tree. They can get hot and roll over, break and fly apart, cause the ax to recoil violently when driven that hard.

After you get a tree back up, you may have to cut more wood. This can be a problem in small trees because there is often not enough room to get the saw in the back cut without it running into the wedges. You may be able to remedy this by boring in ahead of them, but you risk hitting the wedges with the saw. One remedy may come by cutting into the face. Cutting into the face can relieve the pressure from a beefy hinge.

You're advised to do this with caution and be very observant. Don't use the gut of the bar, but use the lower quarter of the tip to nip the hinge wood. Draw the tip across the hinge in an even pass out of the cut. If an excess of hinge wood is holding the tree from falling, then movement of the tree towards the face will be evident when you nip the hinge wood. This is often all it takes to get some trees to fall, so be ready to get out of there. At times you may have to drive the wedges a little and nip a little.

Nipping the hinge wood is a long time, old practice but care should be taken to not cut the tree off the stump or negatively alter the face while doing it. It can present you with a new and potentially dangerous situation.

TIPS ON WEDGING SMALL TREES

There are a few tricks to wedging over small trees because there's not always enough room to make the back cut and set wedges at the same time. In small trees it's best to make the cuts close to the ground where the stump is larger. It gives you a little more room. You could also try driving the wedges in sideways. It's not uncommon in small trees for the

SETTING THE WEDGES FIRST

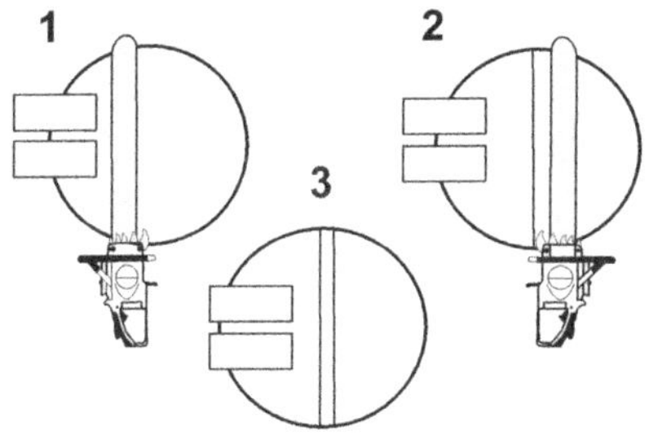

PROCEDURE IN SMALL OR BACK HEAVY TREES

1. START THE BACK CUT AND SET THE WEDGES WHEN THERE'S ROOM. CUT UP TO HINGE AND SNUG THE WEDGES.
2. FACE UP THE TREE TO THE LAY.
3. FINISH DRIVING THE WEDGES AND DOUBLE UP IF NECESSARY.

beginner to set their wedges up against the bar and chain. This results in shredding your wedges, damaging your chain, or both. A good way to avoid this problem is to make the back cut and set the wedges prior to making the face. Under normal circumstances, start the back cut and sight it to the lay as you progress it. When there's room to set the wedges, do so. Progress the back cut a little more and set the wedges snugly. Pull out the saw and make your face cut. Face up the tree square to the back cut and leave the proper amount of hinge wood needed for the tree. Take note, be extra careful to not cut into or through the hinge wood. After the face is complete, drive in the wedges. Once you have done this a few times, you'll become accustomed to the procedures.

A word of caution on the practice. If you misjudge the favor of the tree, or a breeze moves the tree ahead, it can set ahead on the undercut, or diagonal, while it's being placed. Setting the wedges too tight can prompt this also. Evaluate the favor of the tree carefully before attempting to place the back cut and wedges first. A repercussion on the light side is to get the saw stuck in the undercut or diagonal. On the heavy side, the tree could split out and barber chair. If it does, leave the saw and get out of there fast!

TIPS ON WEDGING LARGE TREES

In large trees there is plenty of room to set your wedges while starting and progressing the back cut. But these trees will need ample wedges to keep them from setting back. Their weight can make the wood compress over a single wedge or a set of small wedges. Under normal circumstances, after you start the back cut, place the wedges as soon as there is room. Snug up the wedges and progress the back cut. Observe the tree. If it moves ahead, continue progressing the back cut and driving in the wedges. If the wedges get tight, place more of them to share the load. Continue this routine until the tree is cut up to the hinge and then stop cutting. Set your saw aside in a safe place, then drive in only the wedges needed to lift the tree. In spite of having four or five wedges in the back cut that were needed in the beginning, you may be able to finish the job with just one or two. This is a good sign. It means the tree is beginning to favor the face and you are not working against a beefy hinge. If the tree is cut up and you still have to drive in all the wedges, it may mean a need for more. Sometimes you can gain additional lift from your wedges by chopping off the bark and sapwood of the tree and driving them in farther. This is only done if the tree is lifting easily and you know it's not going to take too much more to get it over.

WEDGING THE TREE

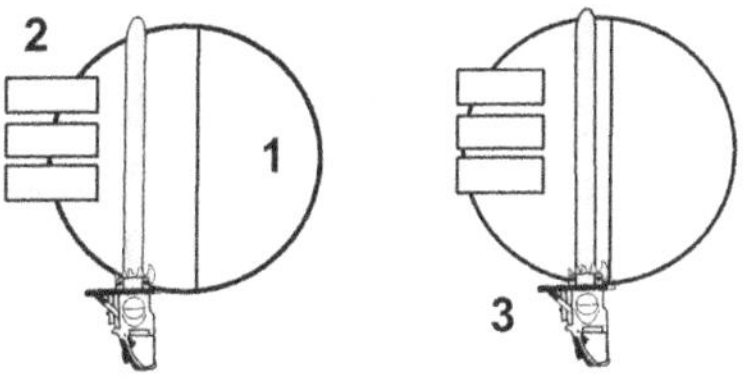

PROCEDURE IN WELL STANDING MODERATE TO LARGE TREES

1. FACE UP THE TREE TO THE LAY.
2. BEGIN THE BACK CUT AND SET WEDGES.
3. PROGRESS THE BACK CUT AND WEDGES TOGETHER. CUT UP TO HINGE, REMOVE SAW, FINISH DRIVING WEDGES, DOUBLE UP IF NECESSARY.

DOUBLING THE WEDGES

When doubling your wedges, use the fine taper variety. They stack and stay together the best. Fast tapered wedges don't double or stack well; they shoot out of the cut if they're hit unsquarely, and a tree sitting hard on them can spit them out. Whenever this happens, a tree can set back. Always advise bystanders to stand back when starting a set of doubles. If you can drive a full set of doubles, it's a good sign. The tree is beginning to favor the face. If they're driving hard, position yourself to smack only one at a time in the stack. They'll drive easier this way.

If the tree has yet to go, set another pair of doubles in the back cut where it's a little narrower closer to the hinge. Do it this way, rather than stacking the wedges up three high. Stacking wedges over two high is risky because they can't take much pressure without spitting out of the cut.

WEDGE COMPLIMENT

You'll find that certain combinations of wedges will compliment each other. In small trees. I'll sport three to four wedges in my pouch. One double taper 7D, two double taper 110s, and one ten-inch Scottsco. If a tree is going to be easy to wedge, I'll start with the 7D. If it looks like more work, I'll drive in a 110. If the tree takes all of the 110 and half of the 7D, I'll then set the ten-inch Scottsco and drive it home with the help of the 7D. This will loosen up the 110 that I have in the tree already. I can then double up both 110s which will loosen up the 7D and the Scottsco. If the tree has yet to fall, I can take the 7D and flip it upside down and mate the bottom flat part of it to the Scottsco and get more lift. With this combination of wedges, you can keep lifting the tree in a very gradual sequence of trading and mating their tapers.

In the large trees, the combination of wedges I use will be something like this: two double taper 112s, one double taper 114, and one double taper 115. I'll start off with the thinnest and build up to the thickest match.

WEIGHT-OF-A-BIRD FACTOR

There have been times when my combinations didn't work simply because I ran out of wedges and needed one or two more. A couple of times it's been so close, I believe that if a bird landed on the tree, it would have fallen to the lay. It's these times when a little gust of wind will finish the job.

On that note, don't ever walk out in the lay with a tree standing on wedges. A number of people have been killed doing it. Pick a path well off to the side of the lay if you have to leave the tree to get more wedges.

CONTRARY FACTORS IN WEDGING

There are a number of factors that can nullify the effectiveness of your wedges. These are the bark on the tree, wood compression, wood buckling, stray kerfs, too much hinge wood, and limb-lock conditions.

TREE BARK

As a rule, take the bark off the back of the tree so the wedges are set in sound wood. If the bark on the tree is thin this may not be necessary to do. However, a lot of trees have thick bark and by all appearances, the wedges will be sufficiently seated. These trees can set back as a result of the bark compressing, so get in the habit of removing the bark off the back of the tree.

WOOD COMPRESSION

The effect of wood compression is much the same as bark compression. Big trees that are rocking in the wind, with only one or two small wedges in the back, can compress the wood over the wedges and set back. More, or larger wedges, will prevent wood compression by distributing the pressure over more wedge-surface area. Some trees have soft wood and will compress over wedges without the help of any wind.

WOOD BUCKLING

Wood buckling can also nullify the lift in your wedges. What happens is that the wood splits off the back of the tree as the wedge is driven in. The wedge enters the back cut but the tree will not lift. Instead, the wood buckles. You will encounter this most often if you set your wedges in the vicinity of root swell. The grain there does not always run vertical to the trunk, so the force of the wedge can cause it to split and buckle before lifting the tree. I have found that you can sometimes chop the buckling portion off the tree until you get the wedge in better wood.

STRAY KERFS

The stray kerf occurs when you start a back cut and realize you have lined it up wrong and then have to restart it. The problem is, when you set your wedges and start driving them in, the wood will split and collapse between the two cuts. Sometimes the lesser of two evils is to work with a misaligned back cut rather than to have a stray kerf collapse the wood. Evaluate the placement and depth of the stray kerf and its relative position to where the back cut should be. If the stray kerf is shallow, you can get by with chopping out the back part of the tree where it occurs and then start the new back cut.

A BEEFY HINGE

If you have too much hinge wood, it will be apparent by observing the tree while wedging. The tree will shake when you drive the wedges, but it will hesitate moving ahead. The remedy is to cut the hinge up a little finer. In small trees, this may only be possible by boring in ahead of the wedges or by nipping the hinge from the face. In large trees its fairly easy to remedy. But in large trees, there may be some conflict in the hinge or the face rather than too much wood in the hinge. Check and see if that's the problem. You may or may not be able to remedy that problem.

LIMB-LOCKED TREES

Limb-locked trees can sometimes be wedged apart. Many limb-locked trees will lift in the back as you wedge, but they will not always pull out. Here, you may have to cut the neighboring tree. Be very careful when forcing limb-locked trees apart. The limbs can break and fall on you at any time.

TYPES AND SIZES OF WEDGES

PLASTIC WEDGES

The kinds of plastic used in wedges will vary in hardness and determine their quality and lasting characteristics. The soft plastic wedges are the cheapest and get beat up easily. They're meant for low-impact use. The hard plastic wedges are the choice of the pro. They can be driven in briskly without deforming the head, as long as they're struck squarely. The head on even the hard wedges can deform in a session where you can't get in the position to hit them squarely. This gets expensive at six to ten dollars each. You can ruin two or three in one bad tree. Uneven blows to the hard plastic wedges can also break them, but usually not until telltale signs of hairline cracks appear. If you notice cracks in your wedges, throw them away. They will, however, make good shims. If you do use them, warn innocent bystanders, because many people have been struck by them when they break.

There is a new type of plastic wedge with a steel head called the Hard Head. It shows promise of having the durability of a steel head and the forgiveness of the plastic taper. It's a good combination to have in a wedge. They drive excellently and ax recoil is practically eliminated.

ALLOY WEDGES

The alloy wedges are more expensive but well suited to drive into a closed-up cut without the tendency of bending over the leading edge. These wedges may be the only thing that will get a tree back up after setting back. Even they can still break though, from uneven blows and sheer punishment. For their weight alone I've used them to drive in the plastic wedges when the ax wasn't handy.

STEEL WEDGES

The steel falling wedges are a different matter. They were the main machine to fall big timber before the advent of the hydraulic jack. Even today they are relied on for bringing down a lot of big trees. The effectiveness of the steel falling wedges cannot be denied. Their disadvantage is their weight and brutality to the cutting chain. Most steel falling wedges are of fine taper and pronouncedly longer than you will find in the alloy or plastic wedges. I have seen some over twenty inches long. They are often accompanied by a pair of thin steel plates called shims that are placed within the cut to achieve additional lift and reduce the friction of driving them in. They are extremely durable; I have seen them driven clean through the hinge wood and out the face. Do not confuse the steel splitting wedges with the falling variety. The splitting wedges taper too quickly to use for tree falling; they are too easily spit out of the cut.

SIZE AND TAPER OF WEDGES

The kinds of trees you're cutting will greatly determine what kind of wedges you will use most often. Small trees will of course require short wedges and large trees will require long wedges, short meaning around six to ten inches and long meaning around twelve to fifteen inches. Besides the length of the wedge, their width and overall taper is an important consideration when choosing what type to buy or use. The thin wedges drive in the easiest because of their fine taper and they pack a lot of power on the stump. They also stack and double up much better without being spit out of the cut. Always use the fine tapered wedges when doubling or stacking them.

Take a close look at the leading edge of the wedges you buy. In small trees, a thin wedge with a fine, leading taper will reach far inside the back cut and get cut off very soon because of it. Before you know it, your ten inch wedge is eight inches long and its leading edge is too thick for tight cuts. You can buy wedges with blunted leading tapers that are made exclusively for small trees. There is one especially, called the 7D and made by the Double Taper Wedge Company. This particular wedge is wide in the front with a blunt leading edge and overall fine taper for the first three inches; then it increases its pitch in the latter half of the wedge. When you buy wedges, consider the length, overall taper, width, and leading edge.

WEDGE MAINTENANCE

All wedges should be groomed periodically to keep the heads square and mushroom edges from forming. A wedge with an unsquare, mushroomed head will not drive straight. They don't double up very well either. Wedges in such a condition are difficult and unnerving to work with. The plastic wedges are easy to groom by using a few careful strokes of the ax over a stump. Or you can use the saw to cut their heads square when they are still in the cut. The alloy and steel wedges need grinding to square them cleanly. This is most important on the steel wedges because pieces of the mushroom head can break off like bullets and pierce the skin or put out eyes. The leading edge should also be maintained. It's nice to have at least one wedge with a good leading edge, although, every once in a while, a short, blunt, and quickly tapered wedge is just what you need, particularly if the back cut is shallow and you wish to avoid contact with the bar and chain.

WEDGING IN THE WIND

As a rule, you shouldn't fall trees in the wind, but it can help when you're wedging some trees. I've left a few trees here and there expressly to wait for a prevailing northwesterly wind to help me take them down. I once had a tree cut up to the hinge with a wedge started in the back. The wind came up and rocked the tree forward to the lay and the wedge fell out. I turned to leave thinking the tree was headed for the lay. But when I looked again it was setting back and ready to barber chair. From that incident, I learned that you never assume a tree is headed for the lay and walk away from it without making sure the wedge is fully seated in the cut.

THE AX

Your ax is an important element in wedging. Every faller has their own opinions on the matter of their axes. Some fallers like to keep their ax sharp. You don't need a sharp ax out in the woods unless you have to chop your saw out often. If you fall on a sharp ax you could cut yourself. Many fallers don't sharpen their axes for that reason. The head of the ax is the most important part of the ax because it determines the life expectancy of your plastic wedges. You want to have a good square flat head. Some axes have small and rounded heads which can mutilate your wedges. This can be fixed with a little bit of welding and grinder work on the head to make it bigger and flatter.

The weight of the ax is important too. If you're falling big trees, get a heavy ax that weighs four to five pounds. You can get by quite well with a three-pound ax in small timber. The length of the handle is a matter of personal preference. You can smack the wedges much harder with a long handle. But the length can be a nuisance in cramped situations. Axes are easily lost out in the woods when you toss them. They frequently get under the leaves and are never seen again, so it's a good idea to paint your entire ax with a contrasting color. Fluorescent is popular. However, the color blue shows up very well in a dark woods when brighter colors won't.

FREEING A STUCK SAW

If your saw is stuck in a set back tree, put a line in the tree and pull it. Out in the woods, there is often no property at stake and the remedy to free up a saw that is stuck is to use another saw to cut the tree off the stump and let the tree go astray. You can also use your ax to chop out one corner of the hinge to achieve the same effect. Remove the power head off the bar and chain before doing it. The most you will lose is the bar and chain. One option to save it is to tie a string or bungee cord to it, or bend over a little sapling tree and tie it to the bar and chain. Either of these ways will help save your bar and chain. You may find some difficulty in removing the power head if the unit is dogged tightly against the stump. There may not be enough slack in the chain to separate the power head from the bar, particularly on units with external clutch drums. In this case, use the clutch drum removal tool supplied with your saw. All it does is jam the piston so you can break the clutch loose. If you don't have one, you can stuff the starter pull rope in the cylinder to

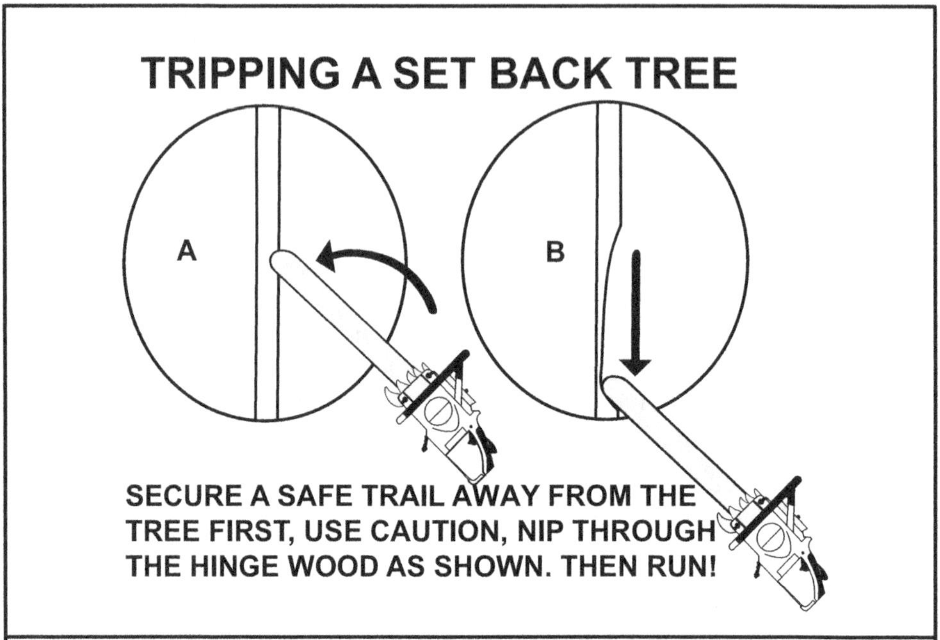

Tripping a Set Back Tree—Review the precautions before electing to trip a set back tree.

jam the piston. The only other alternative is to break the chain with a file or your ax. It works, but it's hard on the equipment.

Whether you choose to trip the tree backwards or sideways depends on the situation and the tree. You may elect to sever a corner or nip through the remaining holding wood on one side or another. In either case, it's a dangerous act to perform because most trees like this will shoot off the stump, especially if they graze or roll off another tree. This is because they're rocking over the back cut and there's no stump shot to hold them to the stump. It's a definite get-out-of-there-quick situation. You must have a good path of escape. As dangerous as it is, it is necessary to do at times because it can be more dangerous to leave the tree standing. Beginners are advised to get help.

Chapter 30

Jacking the Tree

The tree jack is primarily used in the logging industry. Few people in the private sector use them. In spite of that, there is ample reason to use these machines in the private sector. One of the main advantages of the tree jack is the lift it has over wedges. Jacks can easily lift a tree four inches while wedges normally peak out at two. The jack is not a total replacement for the wedge, though; there's a limit to its capabilities. The wedge is really the ultimate tool for holding a tree; the jack is just more

convenient for its power and lift. Learning how to use the jack is not as hard as being able to tell the difference between where it can be used and where it cannot.

Practice using the jack in easy trees first, trees that are within the capabilities of wedging. These are good trees to learn how to make the jack seat and use the jack. Once you develop the knack of placing the jack seat properly, you can work up to using the jack in heavier trees. By then you'll have developed a feel for it and be better at accurately judging the situation.

TYPES OF JACKS

HEIN WARNER AND DUFF NORTON TREE JACKS

These tree jacks have been the standby of many tree fallers over the years. They are ruggedly built of steel and cast iron and weigh over fifty pounds.

DUFF-NORTON / HEIN-WARNER TREE JACKS

IDENTIFY;
RAM AND CUP, BARREL, HOUSING AND RESERVOIR, PUMP ASSEMBLY BASE PLATE, CHECK VALVES, BLEED VALVE, HIGH AND LOW PRESSURE OIL PASSAGES, TOP NUT AND PACKING

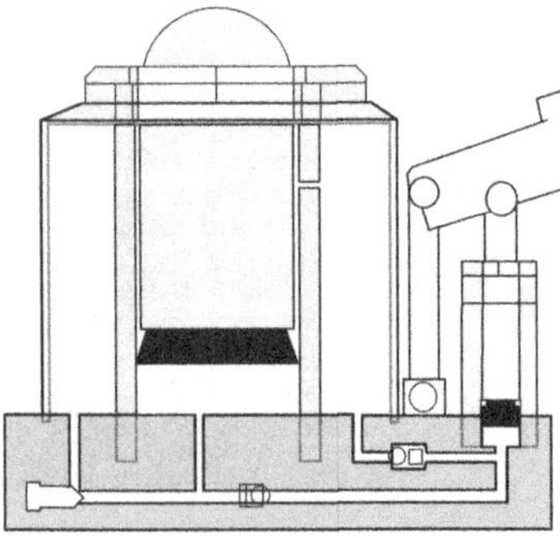

The Duffys and Heinys have their pumps built into the base plate in the conventional manner of most hydraulic jacks. As a result of this, the faller has to get right under the tree to pump the jack. The pumps are direct drive; that is, they have a single-pitch hinge for the handle to work on. With Hein Warner and Duff Norton jacks, a faller can only monitor the pressure by how hard the tree is jacking. In order to retract the ram, the faller must stand or jump on it after the bleed valve is cracked. This can be especially difficult if the packing gland is set too tight. The top jack plate on these machines should have a short chain connecting them to the main unit to prevent losing the plate. In fact, the entire unit should have a lag and chain to keep it on the stump. Tree jacks often fall off the stump and roll down the hill.

These jacks are rated at about twenty-five to thirty tons. But some fallers will testify that they're more powerful than that. When using the Duffys and Heinys in the horizontal position, make sure to set them with the pump on the low side so it can pick up the oil.

SILVEY TREE JACKS

These jacks are made of aluminum alloy which has taken care of the weight factor to some degree. The big Silveys are still a heavy item to pack around. The pump and reservoir are a separate part of the big Silvey jacks. They are incorporated in a pack frame used to carry the rams. The rams are connected to the pump by a quick-disconnect hydraulic line that allows the faller to pump the rams away from the tree. The big Silveys are interconnected so multiple rams can be used for almost an unlimited source of power. All of the Silveys have analog pressure gauges which a faller can monitor as they cut the tree. By monitoring the gauge, they can tell whether or not the tree is setting harder on the jack or getting lighter. The Silveys all have retraction springs on their jack plates which compress the jack back down after the pressure valve is bled off. The pumps on the Silveys have an adjustable pitch hinge that allows a faller to pump the jack in high or low range depending on the amount of pressure needed.

JACK BLOWOUTS

Most blowouts occur when jacks are used in trees that are rocking in the wind. For this reason, don't jack or fall trees in the wind. Sometimes, though, the wind will come up in the middle of what you're doing. If you have a tree standing on a jack and the wind comes up, get

SILVEY TREE JACKS

IDENTIFY;
RAMS AND CUPS, BARRELS, PUMP ASSEMBLY AND RESERVOIR, HIGH PRESSURE HOSE AND PASSAGES BLEED VALVE, CHECK VALVES, PRESSURE GAUGE, RETRACTION SPRINGS, DISCONNECT FITTINGS, JACK BASE AND PLATES, RAM SELECTOR VALVE

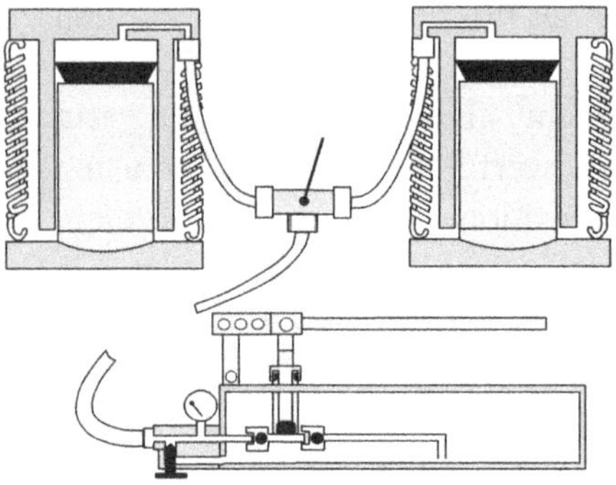

some wedges in the back cut and keep them tight. I've seen the pressure gauges on the Silveys go from zero into the red line, back and forth, from the tree rocking in the wind. Don't try to pump the jacks if the wind is rocking the tree back, but when the tree rebounds ahead, pump like crazy while the pressure is low on the unit and keep those wedges tight. The pressure on the jack from a tree setting back can expand the barrel and the oil in the barrel will be expelled out the top packing gland. The extreme pressures that come as a result of a major blow-out can permanently expand the barrel. This will cause the unit to forever blowout before it reaches full operating pressure. If a blowout occurs, replace the barrel. In the Silveys, blowouts can also occur in the hoses. This can happen if a faller steps on the hoses with their cork boots, or it can happen when using unrecommended hoses and fittings as replacement parts. There are horror stories of people losing their arms from blowouts and/or suffering major infections from the oil getting through the skin and into their body.

JACK MAINTENANCE

Basic care of all jacks is simple. Keep them full of the recommended hydraulic oil so air space in the reservoir doesn't accumulate condensation. Hydraulic jack oil is thin and rather watery to work through the jack's passageways and check valves. Oil other than hydraulic jack oil can cause the check valves to not seat properly. You'll also have a lot of difficulty retracting the rams if you use the wrong kind of oil, especially when it's cold. Keep the jack fully retracted, upright, and covered so the rams don't become oxidized and score the packing seals. Don't overload your jack by using cheater bars on the pump handles. If you reach the red line, set wedges in the cut and get another jack to share the load. Check the oil level in the jack before using it. Many fallers have gone to work with a jack, only to find it was low on oil after they set it.

HIGH- AND LOW-PRESSURE LEAKS

HIGH-PRESSURE LEAKS

High-pressure leaks occur when the jack is under a load. They are most often internal leaks within the unit, but they can also manifest themselves as an external leak. Ultimately, they will result in the jack bleeding off and the tree setting back. Most high-pressure leaks will be found at the check and bleed valves. The main cause of leaks at the check valves is contamination between the ball and seat. When the high-pressure check valve fails to seat properly, the pump and handle will extend. It can extend so much that it will pick you up if you're hanging on the handle. People have had their jaws and arms broken from being struck by the handle when the check valve fails. Leaks at the bleed valve tend to result from wear in the seat. Contamination can also be responsible for leaks at the bleed valve. Such leaks can be very slow and sound like water running through a faucet. You can still use the jack with minor bleed-valve leaks but you'll never hold a tree for long with one. A leak in the bleed valve, however slow, will eventually cause a tree to set back. High-pressure leaks can also occur at the service plugs threaded in the base plate. These pipe-threaded plugs are removed when you service the check valves. Improper installation of the service plugs by cross-threading and failure to use seal compound or Teflon tape will result in a leak in the base plate.

LOW-PRESSURE LEAKS

Low-pressure leaks are most commonly found in the base plate where the outside housing fits into the machined groove. This housing is the oil reservoir for the jack. The large nut on top of the jack secures the housing. When the nut becomes loose the housing will too. And then you'll lose your oil. Wrestling with the jack in a tight seat by pulling on the carry handle will often result in the housing slipping its fit in the groove, starting a leak there. If you have a jack laying around the garage and notice it's all wet with oil, don't be alarmed unless you spot a puddle next to it. It's generally seepage from a housing leak. As minor as this kind of leak is, it can deplete the reservoir over time and leave you short on oil in the middle of jacking a tree over. Before you go out in the woods with your jack, check the oil level and keep it full of clean hydraulic jack oil.

INSPECTING THE STUMP

It's extremely important that the jack seat be in sound wood. Observe the stump above and below where you plan to place the seat. Both sides must be able to take the pressure required to raise the tree. There must not be any rot or defects in the stump that will cause the wood to collapse. Boring is recommended to check for unsound wood in a suspected tree. Sometimes the wood in a tree will be sound but soft. In such stumps the jack may never lift the tree; instead, it will bury itself in the wood and be totally ineffective.

Additional jacks and wedges will help pick up trees with soft wood by using more surface area to share the load, if you can get them in the stump. If you're jacking heavy trees made of soft wood, get some jack plates with a lot of surface area. You may have to make them yourself. If there are any obvious signs of the stump being unsuitable to take the pressure, consider pulling the tree. Also make sure that you don't place any notches or other cuts under or over the jack and seat, for example, don't put a springboard notch under the seat. These can cause the stump or tree to collapse and render the seat ineffective.

MAKING THE SEAT

A straight trunk generally has vertical grain and both the seat and back cut will be level if calculated correctly. If the seat angles outward from the stump, the jack may kick out from it. In trees that lean, the rules of keeping the cuts square to the trunk and to each other still apply. This means that the cuts and the seat will not necessarily be level in trees that lean. An unlevel seat is subject to a jack falling out when there's insufficient pressure to hold it in place. This can happen at a bad time when a tree first commits to the face. Such a time is when a tree is teetering between setting on the jack and going over to the face. If the jack falls out, you can lose the tree over backwards. Small lags and chain can be used to hold the jack tight in the seat and help remedy this contingency. Consider securing your jack plate also.

Until you develop a good eye, mark with chalk or crayon where the cuts will run in the trunk. This is very important in the jack seat because you don't want to make it too wide. If you do, you'll lose some of the lift in the jack, requiring you to set shims.

Stand back and look at the stump: visualize it with the jack, jack seat, back cut, undercut, and diagonal cut in it. If you don't consider the relationship of all of the cuts to each other, you may run short of room to place the jack seat or the face.

In all jack seats, a partial crosscut is made below the back cut the same distance as the jack is tall, when fully retracted. This cut is the base of your jack seat. It's a good idea to scribe that measurement on the side of your jack, so you don't forget it. This measurement will vary between

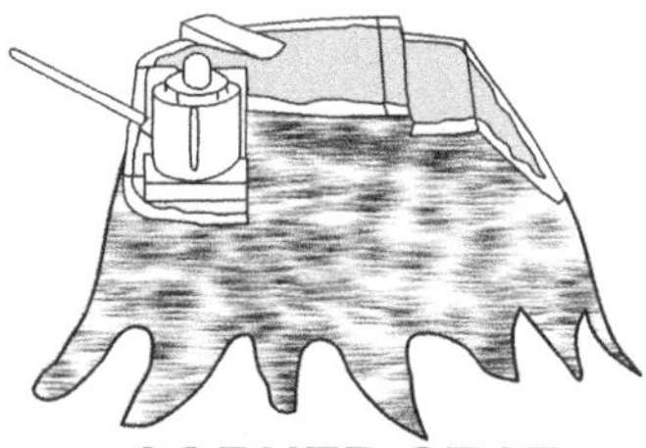

CORNER SEAT
SIDE POSITION

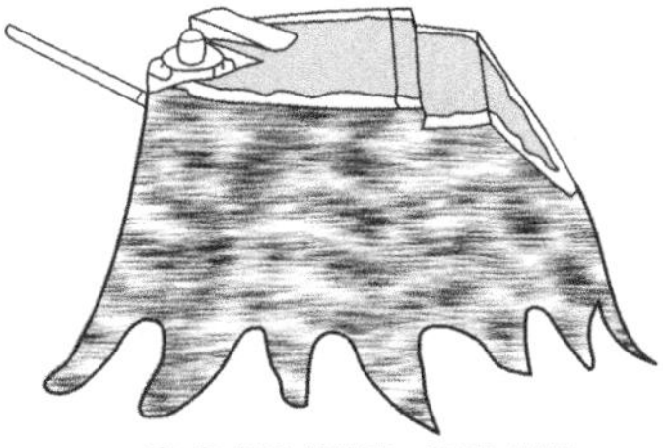

CORNER SEAT
REAR POSITION

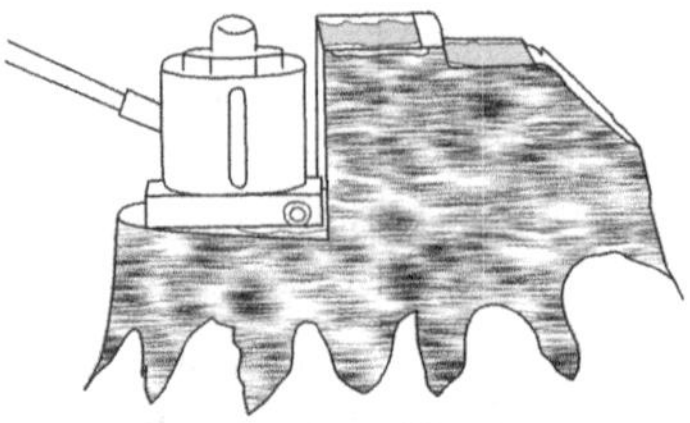

FULL SEAT IN A SMALL TREE

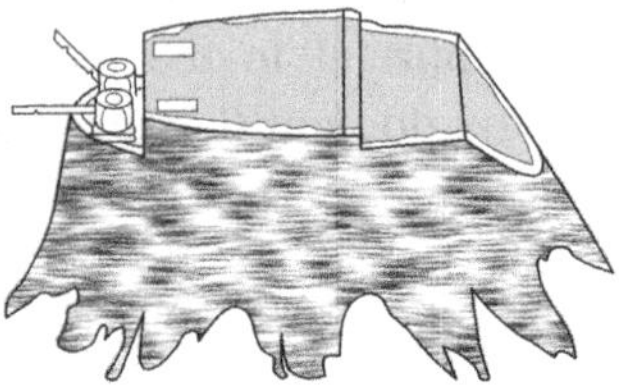

FULL SEAT IN A LARGE TREE

jacks depending on the top plate and whether or not the jack has been modified in any way. The seat is opened by placing a rip cut between he back cut down to the base. The rip cut is started by boring. Be sure to maintain a positive grip and firm stance when starting the bore cut. After that remove the block of wood.

THE CORNER SEAT

Make two partial bore and rip cuts perpendicular to one another and between the back cut and the base of the jack seat. The block of wood should come loose without too much trouble if the cuts intersect one another. This is a rather easy seat to make and it leaves more of the stump intact which allows you to use wedges if needed.

THE FULL SEAT

The full seat is made by running a full-length bore cut through the back of the tree and running it down to the base for the jack. The block of wood is large and frequently you have to use a wedge to pop it loose in order to get hold of it to pull it out. This is the most common jack seat in small trees. In small trees you don't have a choice of seat; you must make a full seat. Making the bore cut off a springboard can be difficult and dangerous to do. One remedy to negate the bore cut can come by making a series of cross cuts from the jack base up to the back cut. The wood between can then be broken out to open the seat.

USING THE JACK

Once the jack seat is made, set in the jack and tighten it up. You'll observe some movement in small trees when bringing the jack up to operating pressure. If the jack has a pressure gauge on it, take note of the pressure it's holding. If the tree is light, 2,000 psi should be sufficient. Heavier trees may require you to set the pressure up to 5,000 psi. Once the pressure is set, leave the jack handle up. The reason for this will be explained shortly. If the tree has been faced up, progress the back cut a little bit and check the pressure again. If the pressure drops, it's a good sign. Pump the pressure up to where it was before and continue the cut. As long as the pressure keeps dropping between pumping the jack and making the back cut, you're in control of the tree. If the pressure raises after the back cut is progressed, it could be a bad sign. Stop and observe the pressure and the tree. If the wind is moving the tree, there will be some fluctuation in your readings. If this is the case, you may still have control if you pump the jack during the low pressure stages. If the tree starts setting harder on the jack, set wedges and knock them in tightly. Observe the pressure. If the pressure dropped while the wedges were being set, increase it again and knock the wedges in further. Observe the pressure and continue the back cut as long as you can keep the tree from setting too hard on the jack. If the pressure increases as the back cut is progressed and the wedges are tight, stop and get another jack in the seat to share the load. Do not keep cutting. If you do, the tree could drive the jack and wedges into the stump and set back. You will lose the tree over backwards.

There are two reasons to leave the jack handle up. One is for your safety in case the check valve fails. If the check valve fails while the pump handle is down, the handle will raise with extreme force and speed. As long as the handle is up this cannot happen. The other reason to leave the jack handle up is to monitor movement in the tree. If the tree should move ahead while you're cutting the face or back cut, the handle will drop from the release of pressure on the pump. This could happen from the wind moving the tree ahead or the tree favoring the face. You would not notice either, though, if the handle were down. Sometimes I will hang some weight on the handle, like my gas can or oil jug. The extra weight on the handle makes it respond much quicker to any drop in pressure in the jack, and you can better monitor what's happening to the tree while you cut it.

TIPS ON JACKING SMALL TREES

The jack is placed first in small trees, then they are faced up. This is much the same procedure as setting wedges in a small tree prior to the face cut. In small trees the jack seat can take up a good proportion of the stump, not allowing you the chance to set either wedges or other jacks if you need them. If you have a small tree setting hard on the jack, stop cutting and get a line in the tree and pull it. If you continue to force the tree over with the jack, you may end up breaking the hinge wood before forcing the tree over to the face. This is called jacking the tree off the stump. In small trees, the jack is regularly placed close to the hinge and you lose leverage on the tree. Even a small tree can exert tremendous pressure on the jack. The force on the hinge can be very great, great enough to break it. As a rule, the hinge should be forward to gain leverage and so you won't stress the hinge wood. A couple of inches can make a big difference between getting the tree over to the face or jacking it off the stump. This is one of the dilemmas of jacking small trees. If you're not sure about it then leave it, or pull the tree.

TIPS ON JACKING LARGE TREES

In large trees, the jack seat can be placed anywhere that is incidental to the back cut. Be sure to leave yourself enough room in the back cut, ahead of the seat, to reset the bar so the back cut can be finished without running the chain into the jack plate.

SHIMMING THE JACK

Shimming is the process of taking up slack in order to set something snugly or in line. There are a number of reasons to shim the jack. For instance, if you cut the seat too wide. Running low on oil is another reason to shim the jack. A jack that is low on oil may only raise the tree an inch or two instead of three or four, thus requiring you to set shims. Large trees with the hinge forward often require shimming.

When shimming, set the tree on wedges and then retract the jack. Make sure that you set sufficient wedges to hold the tree before bleeding off the jack. Insufficient wedges or surface area to hold the tree could result in the tree setting back when the jack is bled off. The best shims I have found are one-inch-thick aluminum plates, but I have seen some fallers cross stack wedges in the seat and use them for shims too. If you use wedges, use only the finely tapered ones without defects, so they will mate up properly.

Chapter 31

Pulling the Tree

If a tree cannot be safely felled by free-falling it, wedging it, or jacking it, it should be pulled. Whatever the reason or the situation, if you have any doubts, pull the tree. This is the best way to get any tree where you want it.

HEIGHT THE TREE IS RIGGED

The line should be rigged high in the tree. This is for leverage on the tree. If you have strong rigging and ample power, you don't have to rig the line quite as high in the tree to pull it. This is truest in trees that stand straight. In back-leaning trees, you must keep the major weight of the tree under the rigging. That means rigging it at least halfway up the tree. If most of the weight of the tree is over the rigging, you could pull the tree off of the stump before you pull it over to the face, especially in heavy back leaners.

DIRECT PULLING ANGLES

A direct angle of pull is most important in back-leaning trees. The more direct the angle of pull on the tree, the more effective the power you apply to it. If the tree is rigged high, you'll begin losing your effective pulling power the closer you are to it. A point is reached where the power in the line will be pulling more downward on the tree than outward toward the lay. In straight trees, you have a lot more room for inadequate angles of pull. In trees that lean back, you don't. For every degree of back lean from the vertical, and every degree of line angle from the horizontal, you lose your effective pull by one percent. By the time the line angle and tree angle match one another, you will have lost all outward pull on the tree. In situations like this, it takes a great deal of

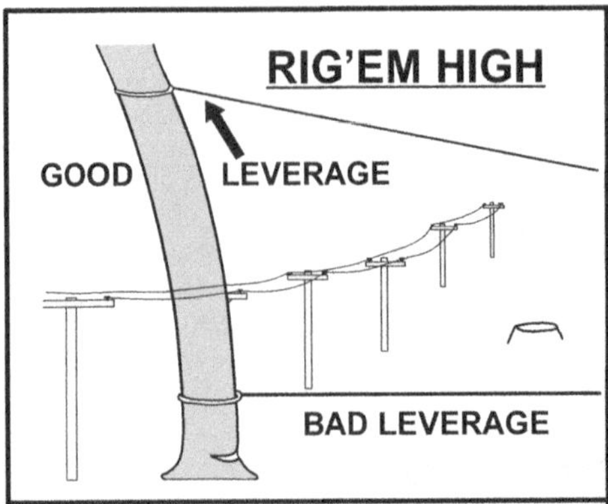

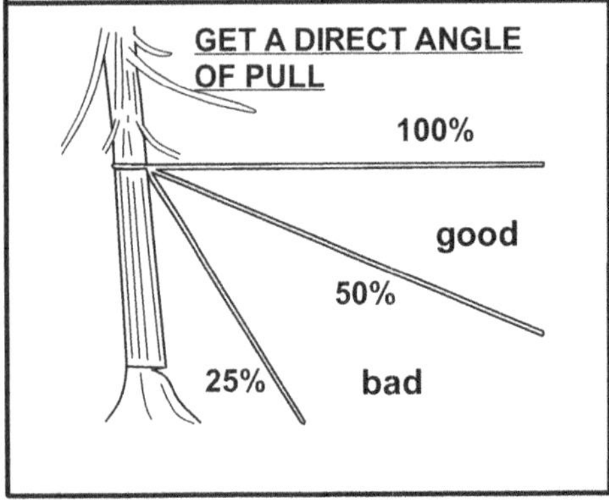

power to upright a tree, even if it is small. In my area, we have a lot of steep ground to get up on to improve our line angles. On flat ground, you may be at a loss to pull any tree that leans back more than forty-five degrees.

HINGE ANGLE TO PULL ANGLE

Another angle to consider is the angle of pull in relation to the direction the tree is felled. This pulling angle is most effective when it's in lead or square to the face. The effectiveness diminishes the more you pull on the corner of the hinge. It is acceptable at times to pull on the corner of the hinge if you are going to hold any side weight to prevent the tree from drifting, but it takes a lot of experience to know where this angle is. It's best to pull most trees in lead with the lay. If you don't have enough line to get out of the lay, you'll have to pull from the side. One of the better ways to get the direct angle you need and stay out of the lay is to run the pull line through a block set in the desired location. This way you can pull from a safe position outside the lay and have the angle of pull you need. A lot of people don't consider using a block to do this, and they'll take an unnecessary chance by pulling the tree from a dangerous location near the head of the lay.

LIGHTWEIGHT TREES

Lightweight trees are those trees that can be "pulled by hand" using a rope or light line.

Fix a throw line over a suitable limb or crotch in the tree. A suitable limb or crotch is one that is high enough, strong enough, and at least at a right angle to the direction of pull. This is so the line will not roll or crawl off the limb or crotch it's fixed in. With a little practice, you can become proficient in tossing the throw line to limbs up to sixty feet high or more. If you cannot find a suitable limb or crotch to throw to, climb the tree and place the line securely. If there are limbs and brush in the way, it may be more practical to climb the tree and throw the line out over the limbs in the direction of the pull. The three-eighths inch polypropylene throw line can withstand the loads a single person can generate, about one hundred pounds of pulling power. If two or more persons plan to pull on the line, it would be wise to go to a heavier line, such as half-inch nylon. Heavier lines can be pulled into the tree with the throw line after it is over a suitable limb or crotch.

After the line is fixed, test pull the tree before cutting it. Lean back in the line with your heals dug in and pull on the tree. This is a prudent thing to do for a number of reasons. If the line is fixed over a marginal limb or crotch, it could slip or break off the limb during the test pull. Your power to pull the tree will be observed in the movement of the tree when you pull on the line. If the tree moves ahead significantly, you have control of it and have accurately judged it. If the tree moves little during the test pull, there's not much power on it. It is not meant to be pulled by hand.

MEDIUM-WEIGHT TREES

Medium-weight trees require a mechanical advantage to pull them. Hand winches, rope come-alongs, and block and tackle coupled with one-half-inch nylon rope will generate five hundred to one thousand pounds of pull. This is enough to get most trees in this category over. If a sling is used to anchor the implement, it should be stronger than the tool's maximum pulling power. If the sling should break before the line, the tool could take off with deadly force.

If the tree has an inclination to drift, these tools cannot always keep up with the rate at which the tree wants to go with it. If you can speed up the rate of pull, drift may not be a concern. The best way to pull trees with an inclination to drift is with a vehicle. Vehicles are ideally suited for pulling medium-weight trees as long as they have room to run and the traction to pull. Be sure that the angle in the line is not pulling upward on the vehicle, or it can lose its traction. Ideally you should run the pull line through a tail-hold block. This will put the run of line that the vehicle is towing at or near ground level. Thus, it will not distract from the vehicles traction. You may want to put some weight over the drive wheels too; this will help improve the traction if the ground is loose.

You can pull trees that are marginally medium weight using several come-alongs and a block and tackle. Combining these tools, it's possible to generate a couple of tons of pulling power. It can be done in a few different ways. The tree can be rigged with several lines that run to each implement. Or, the tree can be rigged with one heavy line run through a tail hold, each implement then being fastened to it. In the course of events, tighten one come-along up to its limit, then tighten each of the other come-alongs the same. By the time you get back to the first one you'll be able to draw up more line with it. It's a bit slow for one person to do, but it gets the job done.

HEAVYWEIGHT TREES

Heavyweight trees need power equipment to pull them. The use of hard rigging is recommended. Rope has too much stretch to pull heavy trees. Although you can use rope, I advise against it. Hard rigging is steel cable, straps, and chokers. Even with hard rigging, be sure there's no bite, otherwise you'll break it, too. Chokers are adequate for most heavy trees you'll ever pull, but they can bite into themselves and break at the bell if the pull becomes too great. The angle you set the bell on a choker determines the bite it has. Set the bell so the line pulls through it and not against it. Straps, on the other hand, can take nearly twice the load a choker of equal size can, but the nice thing about chokers is that they'll stay where you put them because they bite into whatever they're set on. When you set a choker, though, it wont bite until there is a load in it. They can slip, too, if you set them on a bare trunk. To hold them in place until the line gets tight, shove a stick into the bell to jam it. Straps will slip down the side of a tree if there's nothing to hold them there. This happens most often when the angle of pull on the tree is

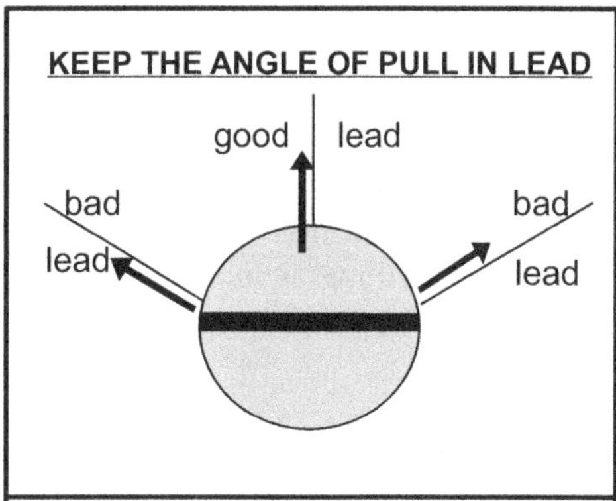

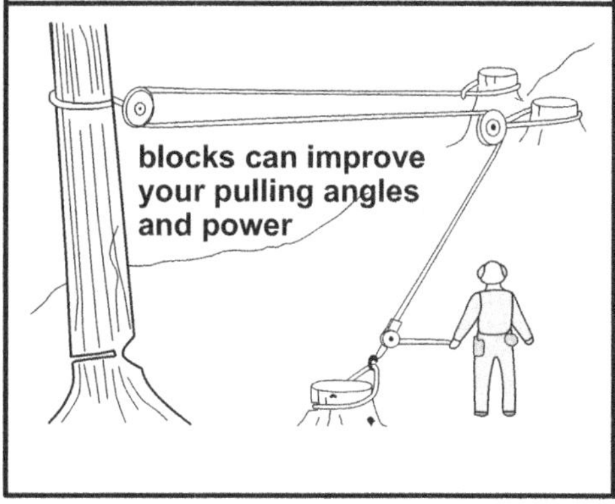

more downward than outward. If you use a strap, be sure to set it in a strong crotch or over limbs that will keep it from slipping. If you have neither, you'll have to drive spikes in the trunk to hold the strap in place. One good way to increase your pulling power is to rig a block in the tree and run the line back to the anchor you're pulling from. You'll lose pull speed, but the gain in power may be the greater benefit. Rigging a block in the tree will effectively double the pulling power of any implement.

Heavy rigging is not something a climber can hang off their belt and take up the tree with them. The usual way to get heavy rigging up in the tree is for the climber to hang a pass block and line in the tree and let someone on the ground pull it up. If manpower is lacking on the ground, a climber can set a rope come-along in the tree to pull up the rigging themselves. If there's not a lot of rigging, you may be able to pull it up into the tree by hand, but it can get heavy awfully fast the higher you pull it up in the tree. This is especially true if you're pulling up a belly in the line. We rigged one tree with two hundred feet of three-quarterinch cable. I am not sure how heavy it was, but it took a truck to pull the end up. It also took over four hundred feet of pass line, two tail holds, and the pass block. Usually, heavy pull-trees only require you to get eighty to a hundred feet up in the tree. Once a climber is in the tree, they'll hang the pass block and pass line. The ground crew pulls up the strap or choker and then the climber sets it. The ground crew may then hoist up a long strap and shackle, followed by the bull line and hook off the Cat to fix it all together. If you have everything you need and encounter no problems, the whole ordeal will take about an hour.

COMMUNICATION AND SIGNALS

Communication between the person doing the pulling and the person doing the falling is essential. It's wise for the person doing the falling to sit down and talk, beforehand, with the person doing the pulling. Oftentimes you'll need to get out of the area before a tree is pulled and you must explain to the person pulling the tree to not pull it until you are in the clear. A lot of pull-trees will need to be pulled just so far, and then let go. Timing the pull and release of the tree is critical and has to be understood perfectly. At times you will be out of sight and need to use walkie-talkies.

PULLING PROCEDURES IN MEDIUM AND HEAVYWEIGHT TREES

After rigging a tree, certain procedures should be followed to tighten the line, cut the tree, and pull it. First of all, the weight of the tree should be picked up by tensioning the line. This brings the tree, or the strain it exerts on the stump, to a neutral point. Each tree's neutral point is different. In straight trees, you may only need to pull the line enough to take the belly out of it. For example, a one-hundred-foot span of one-half-inch nylon line, running at a forty-five-degree angle, will have approximately forty pounds of pull on it by the time it's pulled tight enough to take the belly out of it. In hard rigging using three-quarter-inch steel cable with the same lengths and angles, the pull will be approximately five to six hundred pounds. In either case, the belly in the line is often enough to pull a straight tree over. Any more tension than that may be too much.

In back-leaning trees, observe their tops when tensioning the line. The tops of lightweight trees in this category should rise a couple of feet. The tops of heavy back leaners should rise more. In either, the height at which the line is rigged in the tree will affect the movement in the top when the line is tensioned. If the line is rigged low in the tree, more power will be needed to tension the line in order to observe any movement in its top. I've seen some Cat operators tension the line so hard I thought they were going to break either the rigging or the tree. There is no reason to tighten up on a tree that hard if everything else is correct. A tree that is pulled too hard will set on the undercut while it's being made. If it's not tensioned enough, the tree will set on the back cut while it's being made. In either situation, you'll have to make an adjustment to correct the over- or under-tensioning of the pull line.

Once the tension of the line is correct, make the face cut in the tree. If the tree leans back, be sure to widen out the face adequately. Narrow face cuts on back-leaning pull-trees are an omen for disaster. Don't use them. If the tensioning was done properly, you won't notice anything peculiar while making the face cut. But if the line is too tight, the tree may move ahead and set down on the undercut. Tell the ground worker pulling the tree to slack off a little. Once the face is complete, you may desire that the ground worker tighten up the line a little bit, but just a little. This the prudent thing to do in heavy back leaners before starting the back cut.

Before starting the back cut, let everybody know that's what you're going to do. This is part of the game plan in falling any tree. If the tree has back lean or sweep in the butt, be sure to utilize a high back cut. If the line is tensioned properly, the tree will stay where it is while the back cut is being made. If the line is not tensioned enough, a back leaner will set back. If this happens, tell the person pulling to take it up a little. Once everything is finally set, cut the tree up to the intended hinge. For some reason, many people leave a beefy hinge in the pull-trees they cut. It's really not necessary unless the tree is rotten or has some other defect that warrants a beefy hinge. However, a beefy hinge can help control side drift in trees that lean to the side.

TIGHTLINING

When a person is rigging and falling trees by themselves it is referred to as tightlining. In the normal course of events, the faller will rig the tree and set the tension in the line to hold it. Then they'll go to the tree and cut it up. After the tree is cut up, they will leave it and go to the location from which it can be pulled. This kind of single-person operation is quite efficient for the most part. There are never any communication problems.

As mentioned earlier, the belly in the line is often enough to pull a tree. If you're tightlining trees by yourself, let the belly of the line do most of the pulling. This eliminates the need to go back and pull the tree after cutting it. You can increase the belly weight of the line simply by hanging extra weight in its span. The handiest weights to use are rounds of wood or short logs. After rigging the tree, attach the weight to the line approximately mid-span and then draw the line up. As long as the weight is in the air, even while it's falling, it's always pulling on the tree. In some trees it can even keep up with drift.

LINE HEIGHT AND SIDE DRIFT

If you can keep pulling a tree as it's falling, you will be able to control side drift to a good degree. This is where logging winches fail because they're so slow, they can't always keep up with the tree when it's rigged high. Down low, the tree is not falling as fast, and the winches can often keep up with the tree if they're rigged low. If you think there may be a problem with side drift, set another line to hold the tree from drifting. See **Chapter 28** for details on holding and pulling.

Chapter 32

When the Tree Falls

Of everything that has been discussed so far, nothing is more important than having a way to safety when a tree starts falling. A lot of brush clearing is involved in falling trees, for more reasons than making room to work. You must also clear room to see the situation better. This helps ensure you a safety margin. Take a good look around you and visualize the chain of events that may occur when the tree falls. Then clear yourself a trail so you can leave and avoid any danger. Some trails do not fulfill this purpose and the situation turns into a run-for-your-life affair. Some of the dangers in falling trees are almost invisible to the eye. Only experience may be the key to detecting their presence. The following are ten classic hidden dangers that can go unnoticed until the tree starts falling. The beginner is reminded to keep a sharp eye out for these things and to keep an eye on the tree as you depart; don't take for granted that your trail will take you to safety every time.

BARBER CHAIR

This hazard is mostly associated with improper technique used in tree falling. But it can occur from natural causes such as the wind or structural irregularities in the tree. Occasionally you can anticipate it, but more often it catches you by surprise when it happens. It's a common hazard in heavy head leaners. Whenever gusts of wind rock the tree, barber chair should be anticipated. Get out of there fast because the tree will split in half and flop right back down on itself in a matter of seconds. Never run straight behind the tree to get away from it because the trunk of the tree is often shot back toward that direction. The safest route is stage right or left of the tree. Barber chair destroys a lot of power saws. It would kill more people, too, if they stuck around to save them.

BREAKING OTHER TREES WITH THE ONE YOU'RE FALLING

For the most part, avoid hitting other trees with the one you're falling. Keep in mind that it doesn't necessarily take a direct hit from your tree to break others around it. Limbs are the worst for catching and pulling over tops and other trees. It's very common to see broken limbs, tops, and chunks of wood propelled back over and beyond the tree that was felled. The neighboring trees can be compared to a sling-shot, or catapult. They can throw broken limbs well over fifty feet. If a tree is hit hard enough to snap its top out, it'll generally fall back toward the tree that clobbered it. This happens in a lot of snags. If you anticipate trees breaking as a result of the tree you're cutting, cut down the trees in its path first.

WEAKENED NEIGHBORS

After the tree has fallen and everything settles down, the danger is not over. Standing trees in the vicinity may be substantially weakened by the tree you've just felled. Keep an eye on them. These kinds of trees will hang or lean over the one you have just felled and then fall seconds to minutes later. Don't work under these trees! Cut them down first.

TREES SHOOTING BACK

This term may be unfamiliar to people who have never worked on steep ground. Those who have worked on steep ground will tell you it's something you must be wary of. When falling a tree uphill, it has an inclination to settle back and rest on the stump. If the stump doesn't catch the tree, it can shoot back over and well beyond the stump. This is guaranteed to happen when a tree is felled uphill and across logs or other trees on the ground. The logs act like skids for the felled tree to slide on.

As a rule, your trail should lead you away from the tree, never behind it. Even on level ground, trees can shoot back over and past the

stump when they collide, bounce, or slide off one another. A tree's own limbs can cause it to shoot back over the stump if the tree is not big enough to break the limbs when it falls. Many fallers have been injured or killed by trees shooting back because their escape trail led them right behind the tree.

FISHTAIL

Fishtail, or side swing can happen when the tree you fall becomes side-bound between other trees while in the course of falling. How much ground a tree can cover when fishtailing cannot be overemphasized. Your only chance to avoid the tree may be to get behind another tree, if there is time. This is a bad one for the area covered by the tree when it swings around. Many injuries and deaths are attributed to it.

LIMB-LOCKED TREES

When forcing limb-locked trees apart, pay particular attention to the area where any limbs may fall and clear a trail for yourself away from this area. When wedging any tree, you have to keep your eye on what you're doing. When jacking a tree, you will have the luxury to observe the tops pulling apart while you're doing it. Do not wear earplugs if you're listening for the sound of limbs breaking or falling overhead.

Many fallers have been clobbered by the limbs they broke out of the tree themselves; either by going back to try to finish the job, or when the limbs became dislodged after the tree began to fall.

STRUCTURAL FAILURE

Anybody who cuts trees for long will one day experience structural failure. Structural failure is mostly associated with trees that have extensive heart rot, but I've also seen it occur in trees that had splits, breaks, or cracks in them. Heart rot is not always easy to detect. A good smack with the head of the ax will, in the majority of cases, tell you if a tree is rotten. It's easy to forget this precaution. The hazard of heart rot is that the tree may go astray while it's being cut. If the tree goes astray, it will often render the faller's escape trail useless. The faller will have to scramble and run for their life in any direction they can go. There's usually not enough time to pull the saw out to save it.

THE SPLITTING APART OF MULTIPLE TREES

Never let this hazard catch you off-guard. You should anticipate separation of multiple trees in the course of cutting them, especially as they start falling. Not uncommonly, each member of a multiple tree can go its own way as it falls. There is the possibility of hitting a double tree at the head of the lay with the tree you are falling, causing both halves to split apart. These can go their separate ways and stretch out well beyond the lay, or come back at you. Review **Chapter 27** on Falling Codominant Trees.

MOUSETRAPS

Old windfalls, cull logs, and fresh logs lying on the ground will become covered with brush, dirt, leaves, and mulch. Escape trails can put a faller right on top of one of these hazards. If the tree you fall hits the end of a suspended or teetering log, you can get launched right off of it or hit by it. If you see the possibility of this happening, cut the culprit log at or near its pivot point; this will nullify its teetering capabilities.

POOR TERRAIN (BAD GROUND)

The ground around the tree can prevent you from leaving the tree you've just felled. On more than one occasion, I've lost my footing on steep ground and fallen or slid out of control in my effort to leave the scene. From those experiences I recommend that if you're working on steep or loose terrain, spend a little extra time clearing or making an escape trail. And that includes the ground immediately around the tree that you work from.

WIRES AND VINES

Wires and vines are responsible for many accidents because their presence often goes unnoticed. If you're aware of overhead lines, be particularly cautious of guy wires, too. Guy wires are often set in places where you would never suspect them; for example, hidden by branches in the tree you're falling or ahead of you in the layout. If a tree knocks a guy wire down, the pole and wires it supports usually fall down too. If the tree you're falling knocks down wires, treat the wires with the utmost respect, even if you're sure they're not power lines. They may have electricity flowing through them from somewhere else in the line. Fire is likely when power lines are knocked down. If you have to put out a fire, be sure you don't get tangled in the lines, and when lines get knocked down, keep your wits about you and don't panic. If public thoroughfares are involved, get out and stop any traffic or persons who might enter the area. Have someone call the fire department and the electric company.

Vines are another potential hazard. If you spot vines, follow their trail around the tree and cut them if necessary. I've seen vines steer trees out of the lay and yank limbs and tops out of neighboring trees.

Chapter 33

Dead Trees

Periodically, both the faller and climber will work with dead trees. Whether falling or climbing dead or rotten trees, an assessment must first be made in order to determine the tree's soundness. There are five factors to consider in an evaluation of a dead tree's soundness: how long the tree has been dead, how old it was when it died, how it died, the species of the tree, and the environment it is in. Let's discuss these factors, how they relate to one another, and what to expect when working on a dead or rotten tree.

HOW LONG THE TREE HAS BEEN DEAD

If the tree is near residences, you can find out when the tree died from the people who live there. If the tree is out in the wild, you can tell by observing the overall appearance of the tree. If the tree has all its limbs, branches, twigs, and bark intact, it has not been dead for long. Signs such as the bark slipping are an excellent indicator of how long a tree has been dead if you're familiar with the species. A tree whose limbs and bark are falling off has been dead for some time. Such a tree may not be suitable to climb or fall without taking special precautions.

HOW OLD THE TREE WAS WHEN IT DIED

Older trees retain their soundness much longer than younger trees. This is because older trees have more heartwood in their structure. Younger trees rot much more quickly because they are comprised mostly of sapwood. Sapwood rots much faster than heartwood, but older trees can live long enough to develop extensive heart rot. It's a good practice to check for heart rot in older dead trees. An old tree that had heart rot and has been left standing long enough for the bark to slip and the sapwood to rot is a bad tree to reckon with.

HOW THE TREE DIED

If the tree died quickly, all of it will be evenly dead. A tree can die slowly or quickly from fire, disease, or pestilence. Any rot in a tree that died quickly will be uniform throughout the tree. A tree that died slowly, on the other hand, may have sound wood within parts of its structure while other parts may be in an advanced state of decay. This is commonly found in trees that die over a period of time from the top down. Forest trees often die in this manner. Root disease can cause one side of a tree, broad trees especially, to die back years before the other side does. Drought and freeze can have a devastating effect over broad areas of trees in certain locales. If you are in an area where a drought or freeze has occurred, you may be cutting down trees that died during that period for many years to come.

THE SPECIES OF THE TREE

This is a good barometer of a dead tree's soundness. Certain species of trees are known for their rot resistance while other trees are known for their lack of resistance. When you're in the business of climbing and cutting trees, you'll become familiar with the species of trees native to your area and their various characteristics. In my area of coastal Northern California, the alder and willow can become unsafe to cut or fall in just a year or two after dying. The tan oak in this region rots relatively fast as well. The white fir and the Douglas fir last much longer in comparison, depending on the age of the tree and the other factors mentioned. The redwood in Northern California is known for its resistance to rot; some older dead redwoods stand for hundreds of years.

Within cities, you'll work with many introduced species. There is much to learn about them and how well they resist decay. I've worked in a few dead Lombardy poplars that vibrated badly though they'd only been dead for a couple of years. I have worked in blue gum eucalyptus that had been dead for ten years and the wood was still very sound. Thousands of introduced trees died in Northern California in 1972 and

1990 from an unseasonable freeze. It will be a long time before all those trees are removed.

THE ENVIRONMENT IN WHICH THE TREE GROWS

Study the microenvironment in which the tree you are cutting lived. As little as a few hundred feet can make a big difference in environment, and environment affects the soundness of a dead tree. The biggest factor is the ambient moisture content of the environment. Is the tree in deep woods where it's dark and damp? If so, it will develop an advanced state of rot as compared to a tree that has grown and died in the open where sun and wind keep it dry. Dead trees in dark woods are particularly dangerous; if they are rotten they can absorb a lot of moisture and become very heavy. Rotten trees in this environment often break up from their own weight during a rainy period. Be particularly cautious of younger trees that have died in dark woods. They can break up and fall apart just from you bumping into them.

SLIPPING BARK

Generally speaking, if the bark is still intact and sticking to the tree, the wood will be sound. The bark on certain species of dead trees will slip within a couple of years, particularly on the younger trees. The bark of older trees can be loose but still hold on to the tree by its rigidity and contour around the trunk. Such shells of bark can persist for many years on older trees. Loose bark causes a lot of kicking-out for the climber. Entry into a tree with loose bark using spurs may not be possible. A fixed line is a better way to get up and over the loose bark. A climber must often remove the bark as they climb and work. Be careful not to break off too big of a slab. I have seen climbers break off pieces of bark that were beyond their ability to control. If losing pieces of bark poses liability problems because of structures you're working over, it is best to stipulate, prior to doing the work, that it may be beyond your control to prevent it from slipping off. Slipping bark can also cause rigging knots to slip off the work. It can fall out of the tree while you're cutting it down and clobber you.

WOOD ROT

This is something no climber likes to see in the trees they climb. In spite of its presence, many trees will still be safe to climb and work in certain circumstances, for example, if the sapwood is punky but the heartwood is sound. The sapwood can get punky and eventually rot away under the bark. In younger trees in this condition, their structure is not sound enough to safely climb because they are primarily made up of sapwood. Older trees in this condition can have a substantial amount of heartwood making them quite safe to work in. Make an evaluation of the heartwood structure within the tree. It exists in the primary structure of the older trees. The secondary, or outer, structure can be unsafe to enter and work even if the primary is safe. You can tell where the sound wood is according to how far into the tree your spurs go. If your spurs stick and hold in the sapwood, even if it is punky, it's a good sign. If it's rotten and you're burying long points without reaching sound wood, perhaps you shouldn't climb it at all. Older trees in this condition should have the bark removed and the sapwood chipped or sloughed off to find out if the heartwood is also deteriorated. It doesn't take too much work to find out if the tree is suitable to work in.

A climber must use extraordinarily smooth technique when climbing rotten trees. It's easy to shake the limbs and tops out of them if your climbing technique is jerky and makes the tree move unsteadily.

WEATHER-HARDENED WOOD

In certain trees that lose their bark early, the sapwood dries out and gets bone hard and bleached out from the sun and weather. You can see this in the heartwood structure of old snags that have lost their bark and sapwood. It's necessary to use short, sharp pole points on your spurs in dead trees like this. Hardwood is not always indicative of sound wood. Wood can lose its resilience and become very brittle. Brittle lengths of wood will shatter into pieces when they hit hard ground. Brittle wood is difficult to cut and doesn't hold well either. Don't try to swing spars or tops unless you know for sure the hinge wood can hold it. Weathering can cause extensive cross-structural cracks in wood. Careful examination will reveal hairline cracks running through and across the wood. This is more frequent in the dead limbs of old trees. Weathered deadwood is also extremely light in comparison to a live tree.

ROOT ROT

Rot in the roots can progress faster in certain kinds of dead trees than rot in the upper structure of the tree. It is difficult to assess root rot; the only way one might suspect it is if one is familiar with the tree or trees one is working with. Many younger trees will topple over before their upper structure shows signs of major decay. Older trees may persist for many years without toppling over. It is advisable to use guy lines to support a dead tree suspected of having root rot. If the tree is known to have died as a result of root disease, you can assume root rot to be of more potential danger than any rotting in the upper structure of the tree. You can shake small trees to see if the base, or stump, of the tree moves in the ground. In larger trees, you may notice the same thing from higher up. Your movement is amplified up higher and will stress the stump of the tree. I noticed this in a half-dead live oak once. The whole tree was moving in the ground, ready to topple over. If it toppled over, it would roll down the hill into a private residence. We secured the tree with guy lines and promptly removed it.

FALLING DEAD TREES

Professional fallers may work in areas where fire has killed thousands of trees and spend months or even years falling them. Prudence dictates harvesting trees in an area like this quickly, before they rot. Oftentimes you will enter an area after a burn and work amongst dead snags scattered here and there through live timber. Many of these snags will be in an advanced stage of decay and be very dangerous. They can fall as a result of the ground shaking from heavy equipment working and from other trees smacking the ground. They can crumble when a tree glances by them. Fall the snags first if they pose a hazard. On steep ground, while bucking above a snag, be careful that the logs don't roll down and hit them. It can snap their tops out over you. Conventional falling cuts are sometimes useless or dangerous in badly rotten trees, such as shell and goose pens. Fall rotten trees in the direction of their lean or favor. Don't attempt to force a badly rotten tree over with wedges. The jarring on the tree from driving a wedge can break its top out. The jar on the tree from a dutchman closing can do the same, so you really must be careful. Also, don't expect a rotten tree to hold on to the stump if you attempt to swing it.

Crippling the stump and pulling the tree may be a safer way to fall some snags if a regular falling cut can't be made. Crippling is the act of placing major or minor crosscuts and bore cuts in the stump to prompt the tree to break over. If you're pulling the tree, be very careful when tensioning the pull line. You can easily pull the top out of a snag or rotten tree. It is advisable to leave the area when the line is tensioned. If the tree is going to fall apart, that's when it'll do it.

Chapter 34

Limbing and Bucking the Tree

WIDOW MAKERS

In the forest, before jumping onto the tree to limb and buck it, observe the neighboring trees for signs of suspended broken tops and limbs. Limbs and tops hanging in nearby trees are referred to as widow makers. In the private sector they are often referred to as hangers. Some widow makers can be removed by falling the tree in which they hang. Small ones can be removed with a throw line if they're within reach of it.

Bucking the Tree

A high-powered rifle can even be used to remove them if the situation permits. Widow makers in trees that are on or around public and private property may have to be removed by a qualified tree climber if the trees in which they are hanging are to be left standing. Leaving widow makers in trees where the public will venture is a serious liability that a faller can be held responsible for. In forest lands where production timber falling occurs, widow makers only jeopardize the faller who works under them. Fallers who keep scale on their hard hats take an extra chance of serious injury by widow makers every time they remove their hat to record their scale. Don't take for granted that widow makers will stay in place, especially if the wind starts blowing.

CALK BOOTS

Walking on the tree can be a hazard in itself if you do not have the proper footwear. Calk boots, or corks, as they're often called, are an important safety tool for the timber faller. These boots have many short spikes, like cleats on athletic shoes, sticking down from their soles for non-skid traction. The private tree worker can usually get by without them because the ground they work on is generally good. But there will be times when even they should use them, especially in the spring when the bark slips off the tree and logs. The exposed surface where the bark slips or gets broken off is the active cambium; it's as slick as a greased skillet until it dries out. Don't ever step or walk out on a log if you're not wearing calk boots, and be particularly cautious not to step on any bark that has shaken loose. It's like stepping on a bar of soap in the shower. Even your corks won't be effective on loose bark. Some kinds of bark, loose or not, are notoriously slippery when wet.

There are different kinds of calk boots to choose from: long or short point, permanent or replaceable point, plus the option of a foul- or fair-weather boot. If you're working on steep ground and walking up and down a lot of logs you will need a longer nail than when working on flat ground. But you have to watch the long ones because they can pick up a lot of sticks and be the cause of some bad footing in themselves. In time, the points on the corks will dull, resulting in more slipping. If they're replaceable, get a new set. If the points are short, dull, and irreplaceable, invest in a new pair of calk boots.

Safety manuals for arborists specify that a person is never to walk or work while on top of the tree. This may be fine for the arborist who works on good ground, but on steep ground, the timber faller regularly uses trees and logs as a means of getting around and doing their work.

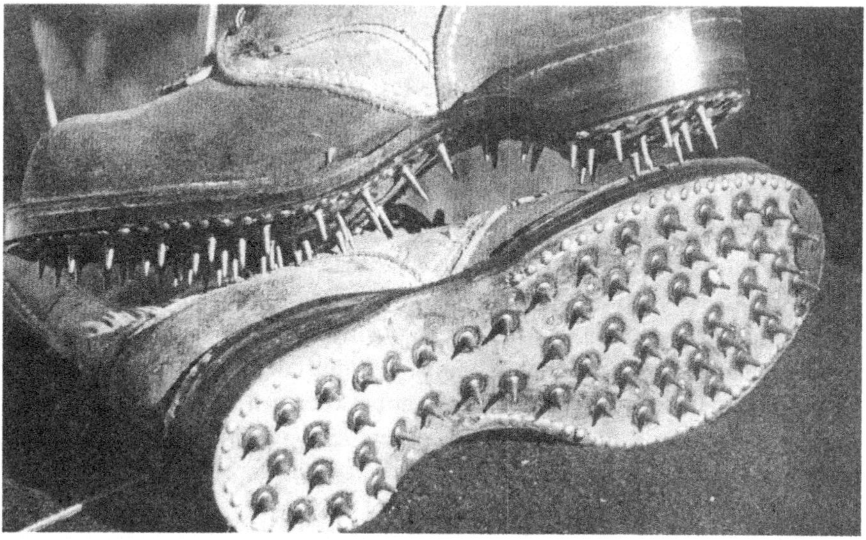

TREE STABILITY

Not all trees will fall flat onto the ground. Many trees will be supported by their limbs. Careful selection of the order in which they are cut is very important. How to treat supporting limbs depends on how stable they hold the tree and if they pose a benefit, a handicap or a hazard. At times, a supporting limb can keep the tree from rolling and be of benefit while you work on the rest of the tree. Such limbs will be the last ones cut, if at all. If they prop the tree in the air, beware that any cutting on them could result in the tree toppling or rolling. If you leave a supporting limb beware that the other limbs you remove could relinquish more load on the limb you've chosen to hold the tree. So if you leave a supporting limb, pick a strong one, or several. If other persons are working on the same tree, they should be given warning of any unstable conditions as well as the position of any supporting limbs. Instruct them not to cut the supporting limb without notifying others first. Communication is very important between all concerned; cutting a supporting limb without warning others can result in a very serious accident.

LIMBING PROCEDURES FOR FOREST TREES

Limbing procedures in forest trees are fairly simple. But it can get more complicated when dealing with more than one tree at a time. In the ideal situation, you begin the limbing at the butt of the tree and work towards the top. If you're on steep ground, you will work on top of the tree. On flatter ground, you may find it easier to walk beside the tree to remove its limbs. In the logging industry, the amount of limbing required by the faller varies. Most of the time a faller will remove only the limbs on the top and side of the tree that they can reach comfortably. Some contracts between the faller and the logger may stipulate a full limb and buck on the trees they fall. In most private work, the faller will do a full limb and buck if it's specified, and that may include the limbs under the tree as it lies.

THE ANGLE OF THE LIMBS

The angle of the limbs off the side of the tree can determine the difficulty rating of the limbing procedure in forest trees. If they angle sharply back to the butt of the tree, you can expect the limbing to be difficult. This angle puts you under the limbs as you work towards the top. Limbs on the top side of you often need to be cut several times before you get to where they're attached to the tree. You can also expect some difficulty if the limbs angle sharply away from the butt. The difficulty lies in the limbs you cut falling on top of and in the limbs you're working towards. Limbs that project vertically off the trunk are the easiest to work with. You can side-hinge many of them which you can't with limbs that angle sharply fore or aft.

THE DISTRIBUTION AND FREQUENCY OF THE LIMBS

This aspect also determines the difficulty in limbing a forest tree. Some forest trees are thickly limbed, from the base of the tree to its top, and you may go through a couple of tanks of gas with your saw before you've finished cutting them all. Thickly limbed trees grow out in the open. Other forest trees are sparsely limbed with the main concentration in the top. It may only take a quarter of a tank of gas to cut them. Sparsely limbed trees grow deep in the woods. Still other forest trees have all their limbs growing on one side. This type of tree grows in a group or on the edge of a deep woods or opening. Trees like this will often fall with their limbs up in the air even though you directed the tree to land on them. It's due to a phenomenon called the parachute effect. The wind resistance of the limbs can cause the tree to roll over during its fall to the ground. When such a tree rubs by another, it will frequently roll over and lie the same way. Most timber fallers prefer the tree to land on its limbs. This is because they're only obligated to cut the limbs off on the top and sides of the tree. The private tree worker prefers to have the tree lie with the limbs up because much of the time they have to dispose of them and it's difficult to clean up a bunch of broken limbs that the tree has driven into the ground. You can have a fair degree of control over the so-called parachute effect by the width, or opening of the face. A wide face with a gap at the hinge will delay the effect of the tree rolling over. In many cases, it will completely stop it. If you're aware that a tree will roll during its fall, it can be a clue to what side of the stump it will fall off of.

UPHILL LIMBING

If a tree is felled up a steep hill, it can be a lot of work climbing up and cutting the limbs off, especially if the tree is tall. When you're working uphill, the butt of the limbs will be up and in front of you making it easy to reach them with the saw. However, if they are large and hang over you, it puts you in a vulnerable position. In that situation, it is best to get above them to cut them off. If the limbs angle toward the top of the tree, or are bent over toward it, the butts can spring towards you, which means toward your upper torso or facial area.

SIDEHILL LIMBING

When a tree is felled sidehill on long ground, you can position it much like it would be on level ground. It's much easier to work toward the top of a tree lying like this, especially if the ground is steep. On bad ground, trees felled sidehill are often up in the air spanning draws or resting over knolls. If the ground is particularly steep there can be a long fall off either side. A tree that lies sidehill will have the desire to roll if it's not held by another tree or stump. If it's held from rolling only by the limbs, you need to know one important thing about cutting them off. Some of the limbs will hold the tree fast and some might be prompting it to roll. Cut the limbs that are prompting the tree to roll and leave the ones that are holding it. The limbs on the upper quarter of the tree, hanging in the air, on the downhill side, will prompt the tree to roll. So will the limbs the tree rests on, on the uphill side. The limbs that hang in the air on the uphill side can keep the tree from rolling by their counterbalancing effect. The limbs bent by the tree on the downhill side will hold the tree fast. If you cut the uphill-side hanging limbs, the other two opposing forces will exert more pressure on the lower limbs on the downhill side that hold the tree.

Keep in mind the forces that the limbs have on the tree and the importance of cutting them in a manner that neutralizes or keeps the tree from rolling.

DOWNHILL LIMBING

If the tree is felled downhill, a faller will have the most difficulty cutting its limbs off. This is because you have to stoop over to cut them. If the limbs are frequent and angle towards you, you can look forward to hard work. In fact, no matter how the limbs angle, downhill limbing is very taxing. Don't limb a tree going downhill unless it's for a good reason. It's very easy to take a fall if you step on a loose stick. If you have to limb a tree downhill, it's better to go down to the top and remove the limbs while working toward the butt of the tree. If the tree is sparsely limbed, you may find it practical to limb it going downhill. If the ground is long, you can often do the limbing by walking beside it.

SWEEP IN THE TRUNK

The sweep in a tree can determine what you should do during the limbing and bucking. If the sweep lies on its side, flat on the ground, you don't have to worry about it too much. But you will if the sweep is overhanging a bank. If the sweep is up in the air, it will position the belly of the trunk higher than the butt and top. Generally speaking, a tree like this will roll over and lie on its side when all the limbs are cut off. Sometimes it will stay the way it is if you leave a few supporting limbs to

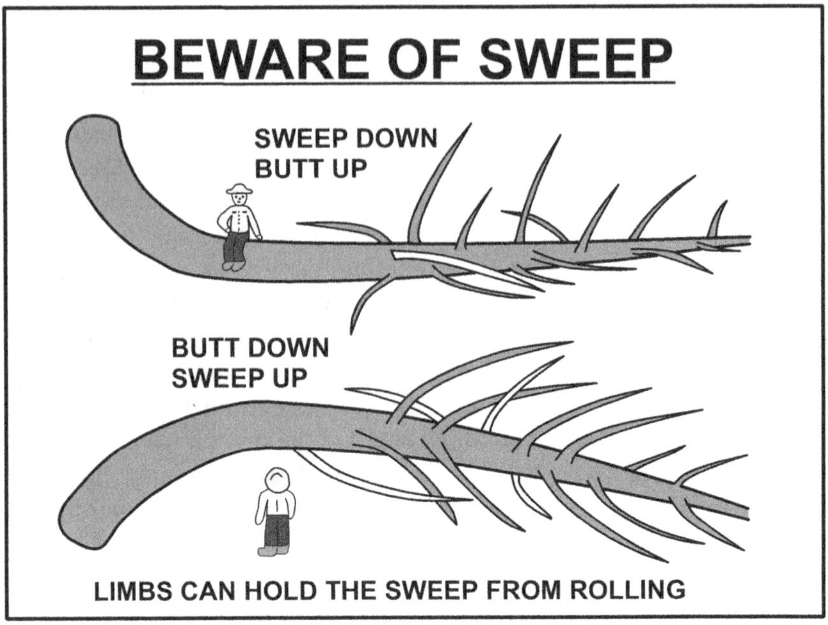

hold it. This is something you have to keep an eye on while limbing the tree. On level ground, a tree with its sweep in the air can still roll over on you. If you observe the tree carefully, you can determine its favor. You can even prompt it to roll to a desired side by the order in which you cut its limbs off. Sometimes the sweep, or belly of the tree, will be on the ground and the butt of the tree will be up in the air. The tree will still desire to roll because its butt is higher than the rest of it. The difference between the two is in whether the butt or the belly of the tree settles.

CUTTING THE LIMBS

Most limbs on forest trees can be removed using the simple hinge cut. Enter through the tension side on the limb. On limbs that hang out, follow the rules of the drop and slice cuts (See **Chapter 13**). If they're big limbs you may want to undercut them to minimize splitting or you can cut them off in a couple of pieces to achieve the same effect. This is sometimes the best thing to do.

FREESTANDING LIMBS ON TOP

These deserve special thought, especially if they're large and hang over you. The face cut works much better than the simple hinge cut for directing their fall. It's difficult to cut these limbs flush to the trunk when you're standing on top of the tree. Pig ears are the stubs that result. Pig ears are generally frowned upon if they're over an inch and they'll spear you, too, if you fall on them. It's wise to remove any stubs and pig ears that result from your limbing procedures.

LIMBS ON THE LOW SIDE

These limbs can be bent by the tree lying on them. The binds can be radical. Before you cut any limbs like this, check to see how the tree is going to settle as a result because it will to a certain degree when the binds in the limbs are relieved. Limbs on the low side are inclined to split and jump when you cut them. Be ready for this and leave the bad ones alone for that reason. You can cut most of these limbs with a little thought and care. Enter a crosscut on the tension side of the limb right against the trunk. Other binds may indicate another location for the crosscut. Don't attempt to sever the compressed side or you'll get the saw stuck.

LIMBS DRIVEN INTO THE GROUND

These limbs have end bind and need to be cut with a diagonal or salami cut. If you try a crosscut on limbs driven into the ground, the tree will set down and close the cut. The diagonal will allow the cut to slide apart. Be careful, even with the salami cut. You may have to do some nipping on the limb to prompt the salami cut to function, or place another diagonal cut at a little different angle than the first cut to achieve your goal. After that, remove the resulting pig ear.

DANGEROUS LIMBS

The shape of the bend in a limb will tell you a lot about where you should cut it or if you should cut it at all. It will tell you where it's going to spring and what side you should be on when cutting it. If a limb is being pushed on and bent over at the same time, it can spring at you when you cut it. Many people have received bruised ankles and shins, major cuts, and broken noses, jaws and teeth from bent limbs striking them.

Beware of any limb that is holding something else from springing. If you're not careful, that something else may strike you. It may be a smaller tree under the limbs you're cutting. The limbs you're working under may be holding a wad of broken limbs over you. Several

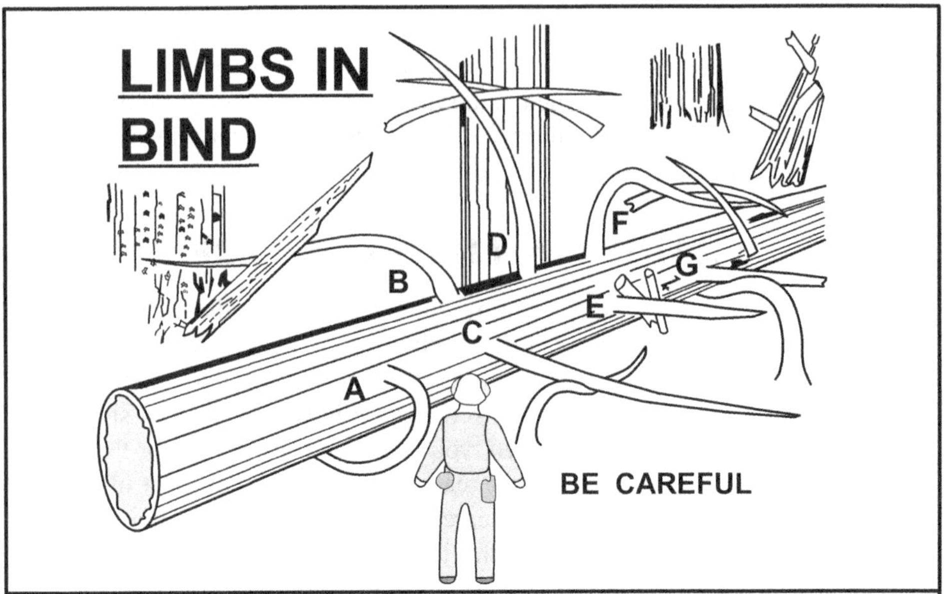

conditions can promote this. One condition, called "the slammer," occurs when the limbs on your tree are pinned against another standing tree. The confluence of the two frequently suspends fallen limbs broken off of both trees. It's the classic mousetrap scenario where a cut on any limb may flatten you.

One notorious trait common to cutting limbs off forest trees, is the frequent broken limbs that fall down and rest on the trunk, right in the crotches where you need to place the bar of the power saw to cut the others off. These broken limbs slow your work down because you have to cut each of them several times in order to get them out of the way. In the long run, it's often easier to put the saw down and pull the limb out and get rid of it. The little limbs, sticks, and twigs that lie on the trunk amongst the ones you're going to cut off are trouble too. The chain frequently grabs and throws them at you. When the chain grabs a stick like this, it will often kick the bar up. Many kickback accidents have occurred as a result of uncontrolled bar-tip contact after or during the grabbing of a loose limb. Large sticks kicked up like this can bruise you in the shins and small sticks can strike you in the eye. I strongly advise eye protection.

LIMBING PROCEDURES IN BROAD TREES

The limbing procedures in broad trees are a little more involved than in forest trees. This is because a broad tree's form can be so varied. If it's a large tree, you can spend half a day just cutting it's limbs. A large Monterey Cypress is a good example of a fully limbed tree that will keep you busy for a long time. However, not all broad-tree forms are difficult to work with, especially in the younger trees. You'll find a lot of the younger trees in this category will start out with a basic form similar to the forest trees. Most broad trees don't start broadening until they are of age. The older trees can become gnarled and twisted, without a single straight limb in the bunch. If you have to chip or haul the brush, you can expect the worst in these old broad trees.

Most of what has been said about cutting the limbs off forest trees also applies to limbing broad trees. However, in broad trees you will have to contend with much more of the tree's structure propped on its limbs and over your head. Small broad trees will often fall without breaking many of their limbs. The bigger trees are a lot heavier and crash hard when they fall. A lot of the limbs will fracture, break, and split on the tree, ready to break or fall off. Be cautious of trees like this. Don't work with broken limbs over your head or holding the tree up. Work from the outside in. If the tree is a double or a triple, the major unions that hold the spars together are frequently split and will unfold or come apart when you cut the limbs off.

Long-sparred trees like the eucalyptus can put long binds in its limbs. If you see an unbroken spar, or long limb, with a hard bend in it, leave it for last. It's best to work with the lesser limbs first and leave the bigger, or most dangerous limbs for later. You can often relieve a hard bind in a potentially dangerous limb by cutting off other limbs around it first. This can relieve some of the major binds in the tree too.

BUCKING THE TREE

If you're cutting firewood lengths from the tree, you won't have to deal with the potential danger of major binds, sweeps, or imbalances as you will when bucking long log lengths. When a faller is cutting firewood, they work on the ends of the tree, where bind is minimal, unless the end itself is pinned. But as a rule, when you take short lengths off the end of a tree, you gradually relieve any bind in it. It's when you step into the middle of a tree to cut a long log, that any bind can be triggered abruptly and sometimes violently. If you're going to cut long log lengths, you should know what bind is, how to recognize it, its effect on the tree, the types of bind a log or tree can be in, how to cut the log to relieve the bind, and how to do it safely or know when not to do it.

FACTORS CONTRIBUTING TO BIND

Gravity is the major contributing factor to bind. The amount of bind in a tree is governed by how much of the tree is suspended in the air by draws or knolls. Balance and pivot points play a big role in how the bind triggers the tree to settle or straighten. You can control the action to a great extent by taking the balance and pivot points into consideration. Outside influences, though, can overwhelm the influence of gravity or balance. Binds from outside influences can be extreme, for example, when a tree pins itself into other trees during or after its fall.

There are four major types of bind: top bind, bottom bind, side bind, and end bind. Regardless of the type of bind it is, with the exception of end bind, the only difference between them is the relative angle of the force.

Other forces to consider when bucking the tree are torque and shear. Torque is the tendency of the tree or log to roll while you're bucking it. Shear is the tendency for a cut to slide apart, all cuts do not part in the same way. The forces of bind, torque, and shear can all be combined in a tree, creating unusual bucking situations.

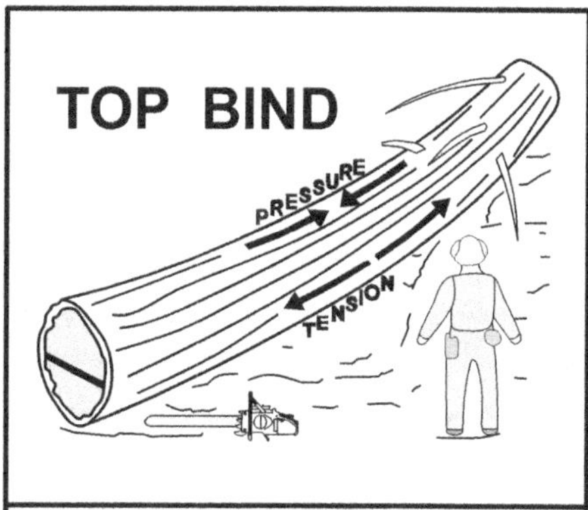

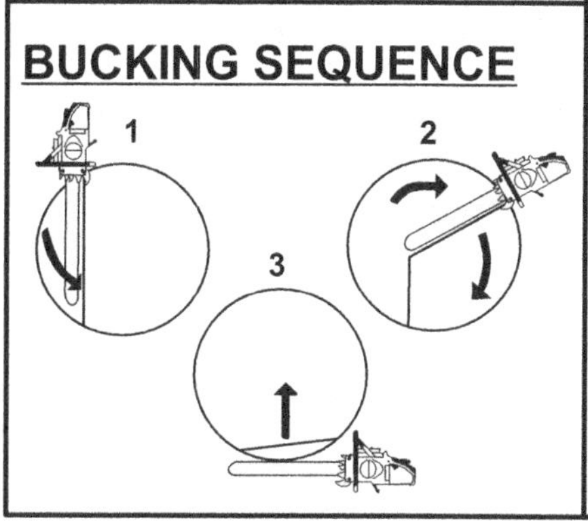

TOP BIND

This bind will be present whenever a tree spans a low spot. Gravity will make the trunk heavy, and it will have the desire to lie down when you buck it. First sever the pressure side, which is the top, in this case. It is called the top buck In small cuts of six to twelve inches, make the top buck carefully. It is often made by nipping. This is because small cuts tend to close quickly when the pressure side is severed. The next step is to cut what wood is left holding the tree together. It is called the bottom or under buck. The bottom buck is easy to cut when the trunk is off the ground enough to get the bar under it. Without exception, backchain the bottom buck When the wood is severed, the trunk will settle. Because of this, the bottom buck is often called the trip cut.

If the tree is lying close or on the ground, you may not be able to get the bar under the trunk to make the bottom buck In small cuts you can get through by using the multiple cut technique. This is a rough form of reaming where you make another cut right next to the top buck In minor binds, you may only have to do this once or twice to get all the way through. In heavier binds, cut out a small face in the trunk and work it in deeper by prudent nipping with the tip. You can spoil the cutting chain if you're not careful when making small bucks close to the ground.

In larger cuts of twenty to thirty inches, it is easier to make the top buck by reaming. The top buck can often be carried all the way through by reaming. It takes a powerful saw and sharp chain to ream efficiently. Align and start the top buck with the gut of the bar. Progress on through until the cut begins to close or get tight. Draw the saw back while

REAMING THE CUT

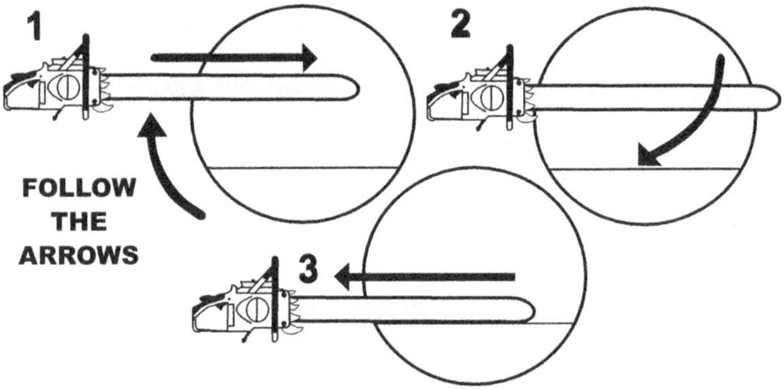

keeping the chain speed high; then plunge it back in. Repeat as necessary as you progress through the log. The start of the top buck will begin to close. As you progress it will close up tight. Your reaming will keep the current part of the buck open. Some will advise that you use wedges to keep the top buck open. When you become adept at reaming, you'll find it the better way to go.

As mentioned earlier, in large cuts you can carry the top buck all the way through the tree by reaming, but you may prefer to pull the saw out and trip the cuts apart from the bottom. The nice thing about making a top buck this deep into the tree is that you won't need much of a bottom buck to trip the cuts apart. The bottom buck may only amount to a nip of the saw to settle the logs. In this instance you will backchain the bottom buck. Be sure to maintain a positive stance and good grip on the saw when tripping the bind. When the logs drop, either one could pull the saw down. This could result in damaging the saw if you're bucking between other logs. Out in the open the saw can push back and drive the pistol grip into your groin. This is due to the push force on the saw while backchaining and tripping an underbuck. Be prepared for it.

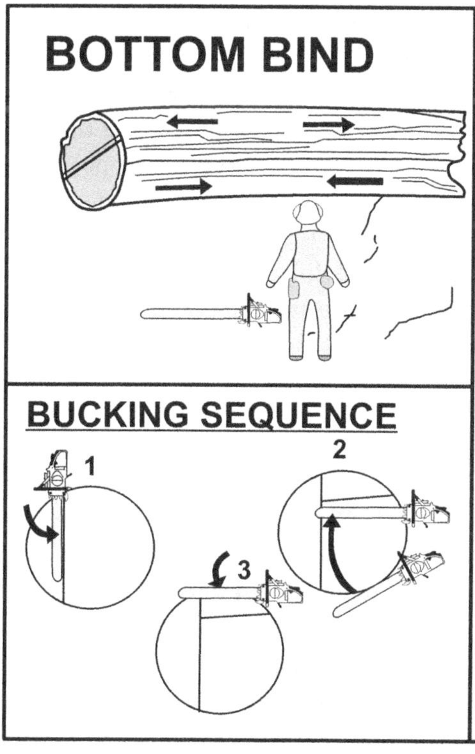

BOTTOM BIND

This bind is present in trees that lie over a hump or knoll and whose end, or ends, are suspended. It is sometimes referred to as being rainbowed over. Underbuck the tree first. In small cuts, the underbuck is done by backchaining and/or careful nipping. It's easy to do in trees with bottom bind because most of the time the trees are up in the air. After an adequate amount of wood is severed by the underbuck, finish by tripping the bind with the top buck. An overhanging top or butt of a small tree will usually drop right off. If you failed to underbuck sufficiently, a pronounced split can run through either log.

In the larger cuts, the bottom buck must be sufficiently deep. It can require rigorous reaming by backchaining. While reaming a bottom bound tree, apply a firm, upward pull on the saw to backchain the underbuck. This can be difficult, depending on your stance and reach to the work. In a light bottom bind, a sufficient underbuck is about halfway through; in a hard bind, progress the cut farther. If you fail to sufficiently underbuck the tree, a major split will run through the logs when you execute the top buck. For safety reasons, stand well to the side when tripping a cut that has bottom bind. A sufficient underbuck will leave a minimum of wood left to sever and make it safer to trip the bind.

With bottom bind, one or both logs can rise. You can determine how much they will rise if you observe how far the overhanging end has to drop, where the pivot point will be, and how far on the other side of it you're making the buck. The farther you are from the pivot point, opposite the overhanging end, the more one end, or both, will rise when you trip the bind. The closer you are to the pivot point, the less the end or ends will rise. This is one situation where a preferred log length may have to be sacrificed in favor of your safety. The unpleasant thing about bottom bind is that you can get hit by one of the logs when they rise up. Be careful.

SIDE BIND

This bind can be deceptively dangerous. It is the number one cause of broken legs and other body parts in this business. The forces of side bind can exert more pressure on a tree than any of the other natural forces. This is because a tree can drive itself into a harder bind from the momentum of its fall. Such a tree can also have the added binds of other trees working on it. The action from tripping a side bind can cause the

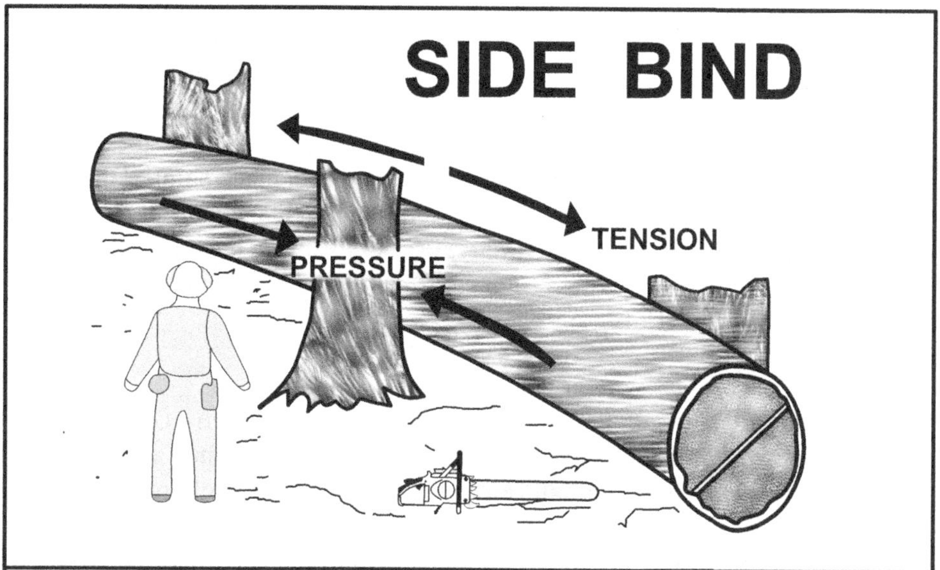

ends to spring ten to twenty feet. Don't fool with a tree in this condition. In lesser cases, side bind is possible to work with safely. If the tree you're working on is side bound around other, smaller trees, you may be able to reach under from the safe side to cut them off. This is a good and fairly safe way to relieve a side-bound tree.

By careful observation, you can determine whether the tree has a compounded side bind or a single side bind. The number of contact points that hold the tree in its bind will tell you if it's single or compounded. Single contact side bind can be tripped without the ends springing if the bind is tripped right at the mid contact point. This is similar to tripping a bottom bind at a pivot point. This is not possible in compound side bind. For the beginner, I strongly advise to leave any side bound trees and get some help from someone experienced.

END BIND

This is a peculiar type of bind in that it's made up of only one force: pressure. End bind is frequently found in trees that are felled straight up on steep ground but can also occur on more level ground. It's commonly found in trees that fall with their sweep in the air. The butt and top can be driven in the ground, preventing the sweep from settling. A tree with end bind tends not to separate when it's bucked. In fact, I've seen a number of trees over the years that were bucked all the way through in several places and did not settle or drop.

With end bind, you run the risk of getting the saw stuck in the cut. Judicious reaming will prevent this from happening most of the time. Sometimes it's necessary to put a couple of wedges in the cut so you can get the saw out. In smaller cuts you may not be able to do this. In this case, cutting a diagonal, salami cut, through the trunk will relieve the bind. Movement in one or both parts of the trunk will occur when you make the cut. If you choose to cut a diagonal through the trunk, do it knowing the direction of the movement and keep yourself out of the way.

SHEAR (STRIKE / SLIP)

The funny thing about shear is that the log can split on either side, unlike other binds where a split runs from the tension side only. The main characteristic distinguishing shear from other binds is how the cuts separate. Under the influence of a shear, they slide or scrape apart. With the other binds, the cut opens to the tension side of the bind which is also the general direction of the log's movement.

Shear is unusual because it comes from a combination of a top bind and a bottom bind trying to balance each other out. If you go to one end of the tree, you may have a distinct top bind situation, while on the other end, you may have a bottom bind situation. What you'll have in the middle is shear. Between the middle and each end will be a diminishing

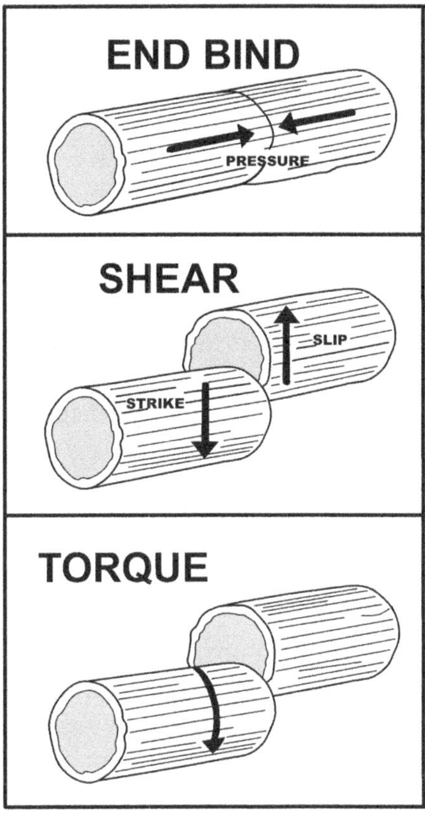

force of shear turning into a top or bottom bind. Shear also occurs when one log can settle and the other can't. Generally speaking, shear is an easy bind to relieve. In its pure form, it doesn't matter which side you relieve first. But on either side of it you'll have to account for the influence of the major bind and buck accordingly. Failure to relieve shear often results in getting the saw stuck in the cut. This happens because the unrelieved side will slab and hold the logs tightly from sliding apart. With shear, it can happen on either side, binding the saw tight in the cut.

TORQUE

This force results from one end of the tree wanting to roll while you're making the buck. It happens most frequently in sidehill bucking. But it can occur on flat ground when a tree is supported by its limbs in an odd manner. It can catch you by surprise as you're finishing a buck. Torquing has the unpleasant tendency to close the far, or low, side of the cut, resulting in the saw getting stuck. Torquing can also cause major wood pull or slabbing off the side of the log. You'll find it primarily in trees absent of other binds. This is because other binds will often hold the parts of the tree from rolling until they're tripped loose.

COMBINATION BIND

You may encounter trees that have a combination of binds working on them at the same time. It would be impossible to elaborate on every situation you might come across. What can be said, though, is to take the primary bind into consideration first and then the other binds. Look at the situation carefully and don't assume that the primary influence is the only influence. If you're ever bucking a tree, anticipating a particular reaction, and it's not happening, stop and look at the tree again. You probably overlooked something. Don't make a habit of bucking without evaluating the tree. You could be in for a big surprise!

BUCKING CROTCH UNIONS

In multiple trees, the crotch unions can hold the binds and the trees from splitting apart. An unwise decision to buck at a crotch union can trigger it to open violently, splitting the trees apart. It's also easy to get the saw stuck in the crotch union when bucking. For this reason, it's generally safer to buck a multiple tree from its tops down toward the unions.

BUCKING BREAKS

Don't buck right at a break. There's a high chance you'll get the saw stuck in the buck. Breaks in the tree that are still held together are the worst for this. Amongst the broken and split chunks, often twisted and still holding the tree together, you may find a combination of binds. Make the buck in the least broken or split part of the tree first and make it well to the side of the break. If you can make the buck there, you can buck on the other side of the break with some confidence that you won't get stuck. In most breaks, you should nip through the buck and be very cautious about using the gut of the bar. There's just more of the bar in the cut to get stuck. You can often pull the tip out in a situation where you couldn't pull the gut of the bar out. In small breaks, all you can do is cut with the tip. In clean open breaks, you can buck with the gut of the bar with confidence.

Bucking Crotch Unions and Breaks

LEAVING COUPLINGS

A coupling is a strap of wood left in a buck to hold the cut from opening up or coming apart. There are many reasons to leave couplings. The number one reason is for your safety. In the woods, many fallers leave couplings because they would be struck by one of the logs or by something else in the vicinity if they tripped the bind. For instance, other logs lying nearby may be set in motion when you trip the buck. Be observant of your surroundings. If either case seems likely, don't complete the buck; leave a coupling. There is an art to leaving couplings. Large couplings can be the cause of a number of problems. For one thing, couplings are notorious for causing splitting in the logs when the equipment pulls them out. They can ruin the logs. For another, couplings that don't break easily can strain the rigging, causing it to break before getting the logs out. Leaving large couplings in your bucks can result in split logs and broken rigging. Needless to say, this can really make people mad at you. Think before leaving a coupling. You'll be surprised at how little wood can hold a bind, depending on the bind and where the wood is left. There is no firm rule as to how much wood to leave—you must apply your experience and judge each situation. If you know which way the logs will be pulled out, you have a clue for which side to leave the coupling on. As a rule, leave couplings on the tension side. You can break your couplings later with another tree you fall, remedying the hassles they present when the equipment pulls the logs out.

Another reason that people leave couplings is because they don't want to spoil the sharp on their chain. When bucking close to the ground, you can spoil your chain if you hit the dirt. If you're careful, you can complete the majority of your bucks on the ground without leaving couplings or spoiling your chain. It may require that you dig the dirt out where the buck is coming through. If the tree lies on pavement or on rock, you have to nip that last part very carefully with the tip of the bar. In many trees, the color of the chips coming out of the cut will indicate how close the cut is to the finish. When the color changes, it is indicative of the saw just cutting bark. Don't cut through the bark, you'll see sparks come out of the cut if you do. The time span between the color changing and the cut going through the bark, may be only a second. If the bark is thick, you'll have a slightly greater margin.

LOG SETTLING AND VEER

Beware of how a log will settle in its surroundings. Logs will roll, drop, shoot back, raise, shift and veer. Veer is the act of a log swinging to the side as it settles. The importance here is that you do not want to be in the way of a log doing this. Several conditions can promote log veer. Uneven ground, stumps or other logs that the tree rests on, or over, can

Log Settling and Veer-Log Raise, Log Shoot Back, Lod Drop, Log Gone!

cause the logs you trip to veer. Your technique of tripping a bind can also be the cause of log veer, particularly in top bind situations where the buck is chest to head high. When underbucking to trip the bind in this situation beware of how you sever the holding wood. If you sever through your side first the logs can veer toward you; severing the far side first can cause the logs to veer away; severing the holding wood squarely will prompt the logs to drop straight down. This works if no other binds are present! In these circumstances the depth of the top buck plays an important role. Leaving a minimum of holding wood to sever at the bottom can alleviate the majority of veering tendencies. This school of thought can be applied in all of your bucking. Remember, in many bucking situations you must observe how you sever the holding wood to keep log veer in your control.

BUCKING ORDER

Sometimes you have to go from one end of the tree to another in order to buck it. For example, let's say you just felled and limbed a 120-foot tall tree and marked it in twenty-foot segments. On good ground you would limb the tree out, snip the top off, and buck the tree back to the butt. Most of the time you won't have an ideal situation, and you may have to go back to the butt and buck toward the top. This is done to maintain your safety or to keep from splitting the tree. A balance and bind situation may require that you buck the tree in a certain sequence, which, if you don't follow, could result in your being struck or rolled over by the tree. To discover the correct order, you must observe the tree and gauge the results from bucking it in this or that place. If you buck it in the right place first, the tree may settle in a convenient spot to buck the rest of it rather than settling into a more difficult situation. Your faculties for gauging the results of bucking the tree in different spots will become highly developed over time. The beginner can gain a fair understanding of it if they exercise their imagination.

PREFERRED LENGTHS AND TRIM

Preferred lengths are set by the log buyer or customer. Sometimes preferred lengths have to be sacrificed in lieu of your safety.

Actual log lengths include a certain amount of trim. Logs under twenty feet, called short logs, will include six inches of trim in their length; logs over twenty feet will include one foot of trim in their length;

and logs over forty feet will often include one-and-a-half feet of trim. The trim length will vary depending on who you're cutting the logs for. When I bucked trees for the Forest Service and the state, they required five inches of trim on short logs, and ten inches on long. They are very strict about it. When I bucked logs for Georgia Pacific, they wanted short logs to have eight inches of trim and long logs to have fifteen. Wherever you work in the woods the logger will tell you the trim length and will often give you a card with the preferred lengths and trim printed on it. The trim and preferred lengths can change on the basis of the diameter and species of the logs, too. Tempers get riled and fingers are pointed from the forester to the logger down to the faller for inaccurate trim or lengths, even an inch under or over! These are called mismanufactured lengths. If a faller consistently makes mismanufactured lengths, that's a problem. One mismanufactured length out of a hundred or more logs ought to be permissible. There are many different reasons a mismanufactured length may occur. Even in the private sector, the faller has to abide by certain lengths. Do the best you can to keep the mismanufactured lengths to a minimum.

WINDFALLS AND UPROOTED TREES

These are a common occurrence during stormy weather periods. Whether they are by themselves or in combination with others will dictate how to handle them. By themselves, you may have the option to buck them from either end. If a windfall or uprooted tree is lying on the ground, the best thing to do is to remove all the limbs first so you can see it better. If you start bucking from the top back, beware that the root wad can make the tree stand back up because of its counterbalancing effect. If you buck the root wad off first, beware that it can flop back into its hole after the buck is complete. A lot of shear will be present in the butt of the tree when you buck it loose of the root wad. It's generally best to make a sufficient underbuck first and then trip the wad loose with a top buck.

If an uprooted tree is hanging in another tree, the first step is to buck the root wad off. This often sets two things in motion: the root wad settling in its hole, and the tree falling out of the one in which it's hanging. So watch it. If you buck the root wad off and the tree is still hung up, then you'll have to buck short lengths off of it as you work towards the hang up. The bind in a hung up tree like this is generally top bind, though it can be accompanied by some end bind as well. The tree can fall out of its confines at any time while you're bucking it down,

Windfalls and Uprooted Trees - During stormy periods the tree worker deals with lots of wind-fallen trees.

especially as you buck closer to the tree in which it's hung.

Oftentimes, you can take a hung-up windfall, that is still attached to its root wad, and rig a line in it to pull it back up. This usually doesn't take much work. After it's standing back up, you have the option of falling it to a more desirable location or you can guy it with lines and wreck it out by climbing it if there's no room to fall it.

FREEING A STUCK SAW

The best remedy to free a stuck saw is to use another saw to get it out. For the private tree man, another saw is usually in the truck, not far away. For the faller who works in the woods, the closest saw is usually farther away than that. The faller may have to resort to chopping the tree with an ax to get the saw out. People more often get stuck in small bucks with top bind or shear. Some fallers pack an extra bar and chain for these occasions, particularly when they're working far from the truck.

If you cut your saw out with another saw, don't cut in the same kerf to free it. You can spoil the chain on the saw you're using and wipe out a couple of cutters on the stuck one. Make the cut on either side of the kerf and you'll save both chains. I carry a small folding hand saw in my pack that comes in handy for cutting the power saw out of limbs and small tops. If you try to pull or pry the saw out, you'll break the isolastic mounts on the power head. This is the number one cause of mount failure and broken chains. Beware that freeing a stuck saw can put you in a bad position. Sometimes it's best to take the power head off and leave the bar and chain until you can get the proper equipment to remedy the situation.

BIG BUCKS

In bucking any tree, you need a saw with a cutting bar long enough to go at least halfway through the buck, otherwise there will be a plug of wood left in the middle holding the logs together. The hardest part about big bucks is keeping them square: don't use salami cuts here. If you're not careful, you can miss being square by a number of inches and end up with a mismanufactured length. Leave more trim on your big bucks in case of error in your bucking.

A true-cutting saw is a prerequisite for big bucks. Your alignment in starting the buck is the second. It's a good practice to mark the tree on the top and sides of where the buck will run. It's also a good practice to step back periodically to view your progress. Aligning a big buck on level ground is not too difficult. But on steep ground it can be difficult to gauge the angles, especially in a bottom-bind situation. A big buck with bottom bind on steep ground is not beginner material.

Whether you're in a top or bottom bind situation, you will start most big bucks in the same manner. Sever the far, low side of the tree first. The far side is generally the downhill side. Sever the far side enough to finish the buck on the safe side without leaving a plug.

RIPPING THE LOGS

Sometimes you have to rip the logs to make them more manageable. In California, the maximum legal width on the highways is eight feet. All logs over eight feet that are to be trucked over the highways are ripped in half. The larger ones are even quartered. With a special permit, these big logs are sometimes hauled on low-bed trucks and ripped at the mill. Logs are also ripped so they can be moved. If the equipment can't pick them up, often they will have to be ripped.

In big rips it's wise to lay out the line where you're going to run the cut. Some people will even tack a board on the top of the log and follow

Ripping the Logs - There are many ways to split a log.

the edge of it to keep the rip running true. If you're not careful, you can be off at the far end of the rip. The rip is usually started on the end by cutting straight down with the full length of the bar. This kind of ripping follows the grain in the wood. You will end up with long strings of wood instead of chips. If you dog up tight to the end of the log, these strings will clog the discharge, requiring you to stop and clear it out.

Don't dog into the end of the log when you rip like this. Hold the saw back a little and give the strings room to pull out of the cut. In some logs, this may be all the ripping you'll have to do. The forks on the loader are often rammed into this cut to split the logs the rest of the way. Sometimes, a large steel wedge is fastened to the blade on the Cat and used for splitting the logs. It saves a lot of ripping. You can often saw a jack seat in the end of the log and use the hydraulic jack to run the split. In doing so, you may have to shim up the jack a couple of times. Be sure to throw some chunks of wood down into the rip to keep it open. If it's a stubborn log, you might split the jack seat before you split the log itself. Before you chance to do this, hop up on the log and progress the rip cut further. Then try jacking a little more.

Chapter 35

Stumps

Dealing with stumps is an incidental part of tree work. In metropolitan areas most stumps are dug or ground out. In urban and rural areas, people will frequently keep stumps in place, as a reminder, pedestal, foundation, or even for carving. Such stumps are cut to heights specified by the owner.

In utility right of ways, thousands of stumps are cut to ground level for the purpose of access and improved work environment. In timberland Cat ground, a stump is just a stump. The only time they are shown any attention is to dig them out of the way for a layout or a road. In the yarder ground, stumps are looked at with some favor. They are regularly notched to secure straps and blocks for guy lines and tail holds.

Some stumps are highly valued for their wood. A stump can be worth more for the unique grain in its wood, making some stumps more valuable than the tree they supported. Wherever you work, you'll find that the treatment of the stump can be highly varied.

FLUSH CUTTING STUMPS

Flush cutting a stump is sawing them down as low to the ground as possible. Cutting a stump this low will remove its obstructive features in your own back yard and open access in remote areas.

Large stumps can be a problem to flush cut. Root swell can make a stump-cut two or three times as large as the cut that was used to fall the tree. When cutting as low as possible, dig a trench around the stump for the handle bars of the saw to clear the ground. If the handle bars bump into any root protrusions or the ground, it can cause a well lined up cut to veer off track.

Before utting any stump, check around its base for pockets of dirt, rocks, and metal. A screwdriver works well to clean the dirt pockets out,

or better yet, use a garden hose and high pressure water nozzle. After cleaning around a stump, you may elect to peel the bark off. This will ensure you do not run into any dirt or rocks that might have been left from a casual cleaning.

Very large and high stumps may need to be cut down into blocks through a series of cross and intersecting rip cuts; use this method if you are managing the removal by hand. Make a preliminary survey of the stump's size, shape, and ground level contour. Pick locations to dog the saw in and get maximum use of the bar's length to sweep through the stump. Avoid cutting in places where the saw's handle bars bump into the stump. Pick places to cut where the dogs on the saw can stick firmly in the stump, making for the straightest cuts. Big stumps are a good opportunity for a beginner to practice saw handling in making and matching up large cuts.

The usual tools will include pry bars, wedges, hydraulic jacks, come-alongs, winches, and even spar poles. Hydraulic jacks work well to break out blocks whose center cannot be reached with the tip of the power saw. Jacks can also be used to pop open overlapping and other mismatched cuts. Don't wrestle with too large or awkward a chunk. Get some help or cut the pieces smaller.

On sidehill or steep ground, flush cutting a stump will not necessarily be on the level and instead the cut may follow the contour of the ground itself. A sloping cut on the downhill can make a stump slide off the cut when completed. A large stump can slide off and roll down a mountain side knocking down everything in its path. Even a small runaway stump can cause a big accident. Don't work below a stump that you are expecting to shoot off the cut. Leave a strap of wood on the high side to hold the stump until the major part is cut; then position yourself to the side or above and cut it loose.

REGENERATIVE STUMPS

Many stumps will sucker back new growth if they're the type that have adventitious buds or burl in the roots. Flush cutting cannot stop a stump like this from growing back. However, flush cutting a stump greatly reduces the maintenance cost of dealing with the regenerative growth. High stumps have a large three dimensional surface area above the ground for regenerative growth to occur. A good flush cut will render the stump down to a flat plane. Recurring growth is restricted to the perimeter, making it easier to deal with on repeated occasions. The perimeter of a flush cut stump can be stripped of its bark and regenerative tissue quite effectively with an ax. On small stumps new growth will end in just a couple of treatments over a year's time. Larger stumps will take longer. Each treatment with the ax to chop and strip the active perimeter on the stump will increasingly deplete its ability to regenerate. This method has an advantage over the use of chemicals to control suckering stumps in the vicinity of standing live trees. It's also much more effective, and definitely cleaner than the hydro-ax.

DIGGING OUT STUMPS

A shovel, pick, and ax are all that is needed to remove stumps up to about ten inches, depending on the species. This is often the only way to remove some stumps if the work area is not machine accessible. After removing a few stumps like this, you'll become familiar with the rooting habits of younger trees and learn where the main supporting roots lie. Do some preliminary digging to expose the roots that anchor the stump. The pulaski works well to chop out dirt. A five pound ax is recommended for chopping the roots. After the lateral roots are chopped

Digging out Small Stumps

through, the stump should wiggle enough to indicate if a tap root is present. Tap roots can be a problem to reach and more digging may be required to get at them, though usually only on one side.

PULLING OUT STUMPS

Vehicles and trucks can be used to pull out small stumps, but vehicles usually do not have the inertia to rip stumps out of the ground unless they are small. Most of the time you have to do some digging and chopping on the stump so the vehicle can pull them out. If you are jerking out small stumps, make sure you use steel cable or chain when you do it and not rope. On a long tight run, a rope pull can result in a stump flying out of its hole when the last root breaks. People have been killed by it.

Using heavy equipment to dig and pull out stumps is more practical if you can get the equipment on site. To pull the stumps, leave them high for the factor of leverage. A flush cut stump is difficult for even heavy equipment to pull or dig out.

Even with heavy equipment and powerful winches, some stumps will have to be dug around prior to pulling. Split very large stumps prior to the digging operation. Splitting will greatly reduce the time and work it takes to get the stumps out of the ground. Large wedges specifically designed to fit on heavy equipment for splitting stumps are available. However, it would not be difficult to build one yourself.

If you have access to heavy equipment, you can uproot entire trees. This is a practical approach with smaller trees and solves the problem of falling the tree, then dealing with the stumps afterward. With larger trees, I watched a Cat D8 pushing over some Douglas fir trees that were five feet in diameter. For safety reasons, that should be the maximum size, even for a Cat D8.

GRINDING STUMPS

In urban and metropolitan areas the modern stump grinder is used to handle most stump work. Many of the small stumps ground out are within the range of removal with a shovel and ax, which may be the only way if underground service lines lie nearby. With larger stumps, flush cut them before grinding. Stump grinders reduce the stump down to chips and mulch; there's usually no need for further handling of the stump after that. With digging and pulling, you are still faced with doing something with the stump after it is out of the ground. Survey the area where you will be grinding for underground services. This is one of the biggest liabilities that come with owning or operating a stump grinder. The residents of the property may be of some help in locating underground services.

CHEMICAL STUMP CONTROL

The use of chemicals in dealing with stumps is a highly controversial subject. If you choose to use poison to kill any stump, be

educated in the proper use and application of the type of chemical you're using. Isolate the stumps that are to be affected and make sure they do not have any connective ties with other trees of the same species standing in the same area. Many poisons can be transmitted from a stump to other trees you may not wish to poison. For all the possible ill effects and liabilities that can occur, don't use poisons. But used discretely and properly, chemicals may have a place in regenerative stump control.

BURNING STUMPS

There are commercial products available to use as an aid in burning out stumps. The main active ingredient in these products is potassium nitrate. It has many uses in other products and has not been recognized as being particularly harmful.

Potassium nitrate can sustain a burn in whatever it mixes with or permeates such as cigarette paper and gunpowder. The effectiveness of potassium is governed by the size of the stump, the amount of potassium used, and the amount of time it's allowed to permeate into the stump. Follow the directions on the product labeling. However, burning out stumps is one of the less effective ways of dealing with them. Stumps seldom burn completely and often have to be dealt with by some other means.

If you have a pile of dug out stumps to burn, clean out the dirt from the roots and the bases first. This in itself can be a lot of work, but stumps will never burn well with dirt in them. If you burn a pile of stumps, get the equipment to push them tightly together. This eliminates voids and cold spots in the stump pile and ensures a clean burn of the pile.

MILLING STUMPS

The unique grain of some stumps makes them quite valuable as decorative furniture and laminates. Many people earn a modest living cutting stumps for such purposes. The digging, pulling, loading, hauling, cleaning, and cutting of a stump is heavy work. It's not something the average person will jump right into without considering the investment in time and tools. Stump brokers will buy stumps direct; if they think your stumps are what they want, they'll hand you a check and do the rest. There's getting to be quite a lucrative market developed by these brokers. The stumps are sent overseas where they are heated in pressure cookers, then turned on a lathe to peel the stump into laminates.

To cut a stump into table slabs, clean the stump thoroughly. This includes picking and water blasting the dirt and rocks out of it. If the stump is not as clean as possible, you'll rock and dirty a lot of chain. You might consider using the more expensive carbide chain for this reason. Survey the stump for yield of the best cuts possible. There's a lot of thought that goes into it before you start cutting. It's not always a matter of getting the most cuts as it is to get the best cuts. The grain will show better by cutting at a certain angle than others, especially in stumps with burl.

Use a big saw, set up with rails and a guide, to mill the slabs straight and true. A saw so outfitted is called a mill, or an Alaskan mill.

Chapter 36

Introduction to Trimming, Training, and Pruning

TRIMMING

Trimming is a world apart from pruning and training practices. In the broad sense of the word, trimming is cutting the tree to the customer's order, or to one's personal taste. It does not follow specific

Trimming-A Monterey cypress that was trimmed. It involved heading back, thinning and removal of dead and broken limbs.

guidelines like pruning and training practices. Most trimming consists of cutting the tree for clearance around homes, power lines, and roadways. Other trimming consists of cutting the tree to let in light or to open views. The last bit of trimming may be for the tree's sake, as in selective thinning, drop crotching, or heading back. Such cutting practices fall into the realm of tree trimming. Compared to pruning and training, trimming is an arbitrary way of cutting trees.

Trimming does not follow any rules and is often done on a whim or how one feels it should be done. For this reason, trimming can have disastrous effects.

TRAINING

Training systems begin in the early development of the tree and set the lines and form the tree will have later in its life. The purpose of training trees in landscape, nursery, and agriculture is to develop a strong primary and secondary structure that is both aesthetic and functional. A properly trained form can facilitate fruit and flower production, harvesting, cultivation, and future pruning systems. In production orchards, uniformity is a must, and only through proper training can it be obtained. Most trees in orchards are not in their natural form. In the wild, fruit trees don't resemble the cultivated counterpart that most people are familiar with.

In landscape areas and parks, the planted trees will often reflect some degree of training that gives them the form they exhibit. In any situation, the initial training of the tree will have a direct bearing on all future work and maintenance.

PRUNING

Pruning systems used in tree work are capitalized in the agriculture industry for fruit and flower production. In most private tree work, the trimmer will not get involved in too much pruning. But learning the pruning systems will greatly improve one's understanding of tree growth and in turn make them a better trimmer by it. Unlike trimming, pruning is done for a specific purpose and follows strict guidelines for when it's done, what is cut, and what is left. Pruning systems come into play after the tree's initial form is established by training. Pruning systems will maintain a tree's form and keep it contained in such a way as to facilitate all other required horticultural practices. Pruning systems follow the tree's annual growth cycles and must be adhered to without deviation.

Pruning is done in the young growth or young wood of the tree. On an established tree it is combined along with other trimming or cutting. In pruning you must be able to distinguish the basic units of plant development and current growth from year old growth and two year growth. It can get down to counting individual buds on a stem and picking certain ones to leave or remove.

Depending on the type of trees you have to work with, you may have a choice of several different pruning systems to keep them contained or to create unique flower and foliage effects. The keys to pruning are regularity and adhering to the system the tree is trained with. It is a skill that can take years to learn and understand. Once you understand what pruning is and how to use it, you can turn your work into an art form that reflects your knowledge and manipulative skills.

The question of trimming, training, or pruning is wholly academic as to when it should be done, how it should be done, and does it really need to be done at all. Living in close proximity to trees makes it necessary to do. Except for production orchards, the best thing to do for any tree is to let it develop naturally and step in only when it shows need of corrective work for its preservation.

GROWTH HABITS OF TREES

Before learning about trimming, training, and pruning practices you should have at least a layman's knowledge of the different growth habits of trees, basically the tree's form.

CENTRAL LEAD

Trees with central lead habits of growth will include most of the conifers such as firs, pines, spruce, and redwood. In these trees the habit of growth is clearly defined into a single central lead with radial branching. The young trees in this category will be practically identical in their form. They will be thick with branches and foliage with an ascending habit. As these trees become older, their forms will become increasingly typical of each species. The lower limbs will become longer, heavier, and begin to even out or droop. The amount of limbs may be reduced significantly in the older trees with much of the space between them filled by the lateral growth of the remaining older ones. This habit of growth can be maintained all the way to maturity in large proportions. In the middle life of other trees, more lateral growth may be exhibited. In some cases doubling of the lead will occur and result in

Central Lead—A mature stand of Redwood.

multiple trunks and tops. When you observe such a tree, you'll find the habit of growth to be retained in each individual member of the tree. What causes most of these changes are hereditary traits and environmental factors. Central lead trees need little intervention other than to see they do not develop and mature with structural defects.

MODIFIED LEAD

This group can be broken down into two different categories: ascending and spreading.

ASCENDING MODIFIED LEAD

Trees typical of this growth habit will include poplars, alders, beeches, some oaks, and even some conifers. Many of the trees in this group will start out with a main central lead. As they get older their form becomes more typical for the species. The branching of the tree into spars will be ascending in habit all the way to maturity. These trees will regularly be taller than they are wide. Environmental conditions can make some grow squat and spread out. Genetic variants can also occur.

SPREADING MODIFIED LEAD

Maples, oaks, and walnut trees will spread and become at least as big around as they are tall, sometimes a lot bigger around. Trees in this group often lack any particular main trunk and the branching and lateral development will make up the particular form of the tree. These trees make up the better part of most familiar shade and fruit trees. They are also the most manageable to train and come out with any desired results. Because of their manageability, many will be found to be trained into unusual and atypical forms. Hybrid and genetic variants in this group have been cultivated for years and used extensively in landscaping. Such variants usually require a minimum of training and pruning to establish the desired form we would like. The natural wild trees in this group will require more work and time to train or maintain.

G.F.B. ON A TREE'S GROWTH HABITS

Don't try to change a tree's habit of growth. Any cutting done to the tree should be to augment its growth habits. Any trimming that disrupts a tree's natural habit of growth will result in a disfigured and high maintenance tree. A good example of this will be found in the topping of central lead trees. Landscape design is where much of the mistakes in tree trimming begin. When trees are planted where they'll overtake the space they are allotted, heavy cutting on the tree will inevitably occur. There will be no need for heavy cutting on trees chosen in a well thought out landscape design. Because of this, the trees will retain their natural growth habits and always be beautiful.

TREE FORMS

The forms in trees vary from wild, domestic, and cultured.

WILD FORM

In the wild form, the tree's growth is a result of the natural processes of the environment. Wild tree forms vary from symmetrically perfect to grotesquely beautiful. Injuries from natural forces can transform wild trees into mature forms that are totally atypical. Some wild forms can be extremely exaggerated. A close observation of the tree and immediate area can often tell the story of time and events that caused

Wild Form—An exhibit of beautiful wild form. Give the tree space to grow and look what you get

such a notable form. Most wild trees fight for their space to grow in, changing them considerably from ones that don't. In the woods, the availability of light means life or death for the trees and it is light that the tree seeks. In a conifer forest the trees grow so close together that the only light available comes from directly above. Their natural habit of growth is perfectly suited for growing straight up to it. In a hardwood forest the trees can grow with openings to the sides and above. Hardwoods grow in broad forms and often lean or favor a certain side. The natural forces that many wild trees endure cause a high percentage to show wounds and scars from breakage in winds, mechanical damage, lightening strikes, fire, floods, slides, pestilence, and disease. All this can create some really wild forms that would be interesting to have near a home if only they weren't harboring some defect that would pose them a hazard to have near by.

DOMESTIC FORM

Domestic trees are usually clones from hybrids and genetic variants that prove themselves to be well suited for landscape areas. Well suited means that the tree is adaptable to an area and will prove to be low maintenance and long lived. Domestic forms are set by initial training in commercial wholesale nurseries. After sale and planting, their growth is usually monitored and managed. This is why we see such uniformity in the trees planted in cities, parks, and along boulevards. Most of these trees in the cities are well kept up and managed. You can also find mistakes in the choosing and planting of certain domestic trees. Much trouble can result from these mistakes and the recourse may come only by the removal of many trees where they were misplanted.

CULTURED FORM

These trees will exhibit a high degree of care and training. Cultured form can be seen in private gardens and exotic parks. Trees in these forms will start with early training as are most domestic trees, with the training carried out through the tree's entire life. A tree thirty or forty years of age can reflect a much greater age with this type of care and often imitate wild forms. Shrubs are regularly used to imitate trees of great age by this cultured care. Shrubs are small trees and offer a good chance for the beginner to learn ornamental and cultured form. What can be done to many shrubs can also be done to many trees in this respect and often is. But trees are more challenging and larger. Some of the design you can impart to a tree can be very beautiful and rewarding for years and even generations.

Chapter 37

Tree Growth

Trees regenerate their new growth by three different means: from active buds, latent buds, and adventitious buds.

ACTIVE BUDS

Active buds are found on the terminal ends of growing stems and are active all through the growing season, from bud break in the spring to bud set in the fall. When they set in the fall, there is very little difference between them and the latent bud except for their position. The position of an active bud keeps it active and many other buds behind it latent. In a full season's growth, the active bud will grow a certain amount in length. On the stem that is generated, other buds will appear at the base of each leaf. Some of those buds will take on an active role the next season and others will become latent buds. Active buds keep latent buds what they are. The latent bud will only become active in the event of losing an active bud.

LATENT BUDS

These are developed during the annual growing season and will remain dormant until some stimulus prompts them into active growth. Latent buds can persist for many years on older parts of a tree without ever coming into active growth. In some trees they can be difficult to find. Generally speaking, latent buds will be more frequent in the younger parts of the tree and diminish in the older parts. They become active whenever the tree loses a part of its structure through natural or man-made causes. Once latent buds are dead there is no bringing them back. If a branch is cut back behind the region where viable latent buds appear, no new growth will occur from that branch unless the particular tree has adventitious qualities. In pruning or trimming a tree with latent buds, be aware of their location and work within those areas that have a good supply.

ADVENTITIOUS BUDS

This type of bud can occur in just about any part of a tree. There may not be any indication of their presence, and they can pop up wherever any cutting is performed, or even where it is not. The amount of new growth from an adventitious bud seems to be unlimited. They can multiply to such a degree as to form what is commonly known as burl. Burl occurs most often in the stumps of trees that regenerate by adventitious behavior but can also be found in the upper structure, though not as prevalent or in great quantity. Upon close observation you can locate the regions where adventitious buds might persist. Those regions will generally be old crotch unions. If the buds can be seen, but not actively growing, one might expect them to be latent. In all respects they are, but they arise from adventitious tissue. Trees use both types of buds the same way with few exceptions. How these buds are stimulated into active growth and how they express it in new growth is highly variable and worth further discussion.

SUBDOMINANT LEADS

In between major laterals along a branch and between branches on the trunk of the tree are smaller limbs and leads that never amount to much. In the normal life of a tree, these smaller or subdominant leads will die out and constitute a minor part of the dead wood in moderately aged and older trees. When green and alive, they're often used as leads in trimming. But more times than not they will remain subdominant and any new growth will come from latent or adventitious buds in the vicinity. This does not hold true in all cases, but happens enough to raise some questions as to the exact role of the subdominant leads. One notable feature of subdominant leads is that as long as they persist there is usually a good supply of latent buds in the area.

Knowing this is helpful when considering cutting a primary limb back to such a lead. Most subdominant limbs are fragile and will break off the main lead very easily. For that reason they don't always make for a good lead to cut back to. If one is used as a lead and broken off by accident, there will probably be latent or adventitious buds very close to the cut that can carry on the role of the broken lead. If you pay close attention to this, there will be little reason to cut the limb farther back to another lead. Though it may appear to be a stub to the layman, it is a good location for a bud to start a new limb before the subdominant lead was broken. As mentioned, this is often what happens anyway, even when the subdominant lead is still intact. Should there be an absence of latent buds and the tree lacks adventitious qualities, then you would have a genuine stub. Young and vigorous leads are always a good choice to cut back to because of their ample supply of buds. Older leads usually lack vigor and their buds will be small and few, making them a bad choice to cut to in trees that only have latent buds. The tree will shed older subdominant leads if the primary lead is left uncut. If the primary lead is cut to a weak subdominant lead, the whole limb will die if the tree lacks adventitious qualities. The species of the tree has a great deal to do with the activity of the subdominant leads. Many conifers are pretty reliable in this respect, particularly in the older wood. The subdominant leads in the younger parts of the tree can be depended on for renewal purposes, and the weaker ones in the older parts can't. These small leads are good for protection from sunburn after many primary limbs have been cut back or removed. They can often cover up noticeable cuts made in the tree and disguise any cutting operations. Their presence also seems to keep down the amount of unwanted sucker growth in parts of the tree where it's not desired.

UNIT OF GROWTH

In one season an active bud will generate one unit of growth, or one season's growth. This growth is highly variable in different trees and even in different parts of the same tree. In young trees the tops will show more vigor in a season's growth than the lower limbs. It's a pretty firm rule in most trees except the older or mature ones.

A person learning about trees must be able to distinguish units of growth. A single branch can consist of many year's growth. Each year's growth is hallmarked by a bump or scar along the stem of a branch. These bumps are produced by active buds setting in the fall and then coming back into active growth the next season. In the younger parts of a stem, they can easily be identified. You can count back the years or units that make up the stem. Once you develop a sense for it, you'll see how a branch grows the way it does. Symmetrical conifers produce limbs in whorls around the trunk and each whorl of limbs is the mark of a season's growth. You can find the age of the tree and the limbs at any given point by counting the number of whorls from the top down, beginning with the current season's growth. There are minor exceptions. Once you learn to distinguish the current season's growth from one year growth and two year growth, you will begin to understand how to manipulate the entire tree by trimming, training, and pruning.

Considering the way that trees grow, their development could be demonstrated in a computer generated imaging program from seed to mature form. Add a menu of species selection, genetic variation, environmental effects and trimming, training and pruning practices and you'll be able to observe in minutes what it takes a tree years to do.

VIGOR AND CAPACITY

In a small sapling, there is a larger proportion of leaf area to actual wood. This abundance of leaf area and lack of tree bulk is why young trees are so vigorous and grow so fast. The young tree can utilize more of the sugars manufactured by the leaves for active growth.

In a hypothetical example of the vigor and capacity relationship, let's look at a sapling tree that has fifty active buds and five hundred square inches of leaf area at the end of the growing season. At bud break in the spring there will be a near doubling of active buds and a proportional increase of leaf area generated. The tree is gaining more capacity to generate new growth each year. During the next season the tree will set about one hundred active buds and have all the remaining sugars from the leaf area generated in its store. Should the tree be pruned back to fifty buds, or its previous seasons stature, then the vigor and capacity of it will change dramatically. The tree developed the capacity to push one hundred active buds, but only has fifty. The vigor of those remaining will be increased.

What happens to the capacity of the tree is much different. While the tree will appear to be growing faster by its increased vigor, its actual capacity to produce new growth for this season has been reduced. At the end of the season, the total amount of growth for the tree will be less than if it was not pruned at all, although it will appear to grow faster. What would happen if the tree was pruned down to ten active buds? The vigor of the buds would be rampant and the capacity of the tree would fall off dramatically.

When left alone the tree will grow at a steady rate in its vigor and capacity throughout its juvenile life. As the tree ages, vigor drops off and an enormous capacity develops. There is an uncanny balance in how the sugars produced by the leaves are utilized for active growth, sustenance, and as a seasonal store. The older tree will have much more bulk to sustain along with many thousands of active buds to push into growth. This balance can be altered by pruning and trimming.

In the training years of a sapling tree, heavy cutting can stimulate vigorous growth. If the tree is left to grow for a few years to build up its capacity, then pruned down to a few chosen buds or leads, those chosen will be very vigorous. If their position is thought out carefully, they will develop into a primary and secondary structure of good form. After such initial training, any more heavy pruning is usually unnecessary. When an annual program is continued, some very interesting tree forms can be developed, but only if the location of the buds, or leads, you leave is chosen wisely. There seems to be no end as to how far you can take this pruning, from the juvenile tree on throughout its life. If a regular program is maintained as described, the tree's vigor and capacity will remain at a fixed level. The total capacity of the tree will be greatly reduced but the vigor of the tree will be strong. Trees that grow to be very large and grow quickly can be contained almost indefinitely by judicious pruning. A pleasing aesthetic form can be developed through the life of the tree while keeping it manageable and within its space. Once a program like this is started on a tree or plant, it must be adhered to or the tree will grow wild and out of its space. Pruning programs are used extensively in orchards and vineyards to maintain the plant's vigor, capacity, size, and productivity. However, around our homes we can be much more creative with it.

An older tree can have thousands of active buds with an enormous overall capacity. The vigor of each stem will be much less compared to the younger tree. When heavy cutting is performed on an older tree, the resumption of new growth will be "out of phase."

On the old tree, suckers and water sprouts will arise from the main structure and essentially be young trees growing off parts of the older one. Heavy cutting on older trees rudely throws the vigor and capacity out of balance and results in out of phase sucker growth. In young trees, heavy cutting will also stimulate out of phase growth, but it doesn't take long for the young tree to get back in phase with itself. Older trees take many years in returning to being in phase. Be careful about how much and where you cut a larger and older tree whose vigor is much less and whose capacity is much greater.

An older tree can be moderately cut with good results in directing its new growth if you are careful in choosing where the cuts are made. Any out of phase growth will or should fill out the tree in a symmetrical or aesthetic form. However, the heavier the cutting, the harder it will be to control it. The section on pollarding trees elaborates on this in better detail (See **Chapter 39**).

Be aware of a plant's regenerative abilities and the vigor/capacity relationship. Also, be aware of how the vigor and capacity of the tree can be influenced by pruning and trimming. Last, you should have an idea in spotting bud and lead location in trimming and pruning. All this is paramount when training an aesthetic form and maintaining a tree that is regularly trimmed or pruned.

Chapter 38

Structural Defects and Tree Preservation

Trees, whether in the wild or your backyard, can develop major structural defects that will cause breaking or splitting apart. Most structural defects in a tree can be easily prevented from developing. An experienced person in the business can point out what makes a tree strong or weak, but many people will leave a tree to break rather than take the advice of someone experienced. In contrast, some people will cut down a perfectly strong tree that is free of defects because they're afraid of it, even after being advised that the tree could persist without being a threat. It's either cut it down or leave it alone with many people. Whether or not any advice is taken should not discourage you from offering a professional opinion; it's in everyone's best interest that a professional opinion be offered, for the tree's sake as well. In order to present a qualified opinion on this subject, learn to recognize structural defects, their prevention, and their remedies.

RUB AND GRAFT WOUNDS

Adversely crossed limbs will develop wear spots from the mechanical action of the wind. If corrected early, no damage will result, but if left too long, permanent structural damage could develop in either the limbs, trunk, or both. When the wear spots are so bad as to pose a hazard, then the entire removal of the limb, top, spar, or tree may be warranted. This defect is common and should be corrected early by acutting the crossed limbs out.

Graft wounds will begin as crossed limbs. They may rub early in the life of the tree and become rigid as the tree grows. During the rigid period, grafts can occur and be broken loose many times from mechanical action before bonds become permanent. In those cases the wound could exhibit areas of bonding and deformed callus growth, which could mature into a major weak spot in the tree's structure. If bonding occurs early, the graft can develop into sound structure when the polarity of it is not crossed. Polarity is the flow of nutrients in woody tissue. For successful and strong grafts the polarity must match. At times, grafts with crossed polarity may appear well knit. Look at the form of the graft carefully for seams and irregularity in the grain. This defect can be corrected early in the tree's development.

TIGHT CROTCHES

Many species of trees grow with tight crotches. This type of crotch cannot hold together well in the buffeting of strong winds and will frequently split apart. Preventing development of tight crotches is possible in most trees and should take place early in the life of the tree by removing one of the leads.

WIND CHECKS

Longitudinal cracks in the limbs and trunk will vary from slight to gaping. When they persist, mechanical action from the wind can keep them open and prevent satisfactory healing. If caught in time, the crack can be drawn together with bolts and healing can occur. Cracks in the trunk of the tree may not be as readily apparent as those in the limbs.

Peculiar vertical seams or ridges on the trunk of smooth barked trees can be a good indicator of possible cracks, especially if sap or dark water oozes from them. Trees can survive for long periods of time with cracks in their trunks. A crack or wind check may not always be a viable reason for destruction of a tree. There are degrees between minor or major cracks and the possibility of threat from a wind checked tree. If you can hear a tree popping or creaking inside of the trunk, this is indicative of a check actively working. It would be hard to convince anyone that a tree like this would be safe to leave near a home. Not all wind check trees will creek or pop in the wind. Such a tree may be worth the time to drop crotch (See Chapter 39) for less wind resistance on the cracks and bracing with bolts to draw the cracks together.

VINING PLANTS

Structural damage from vines will vary considerably. The degree of damage depends on the age of the tree when the vine infests it and how long after that the vine persists. Young trees that become infested with vines never get a chance to develop or mature before the vine adversely affects them. Older trees that have developed sound structure before infestation can be within the realm of saving. The vine can even have a certain aesthetic appeal by the way it hangs or grows over the trunk. No matter how nice vines may appear, most trees do not do well together with them. It does matter what kind of vine it is and if the vine has a choke hold on the tree or is taking over its canopy. Some vines are less aggressive and may be tolerated so long as they don't choke the tree. Other vines can be very aggressive and should not be allowed to persist where it is hoped a tree will grow.

Choke holds will occur where a vine encircles the trunk or the limbs. They can cause major deformities in the structure of a tree and the possibility of breakage. A choke hold on the tree can be prevented by early observation and removal of the vine. If the vine takes over the canopy, it can starve the tree of sunlight and kill it. If a vine taking over the canopy in a small tree doesn't kill it, it can still set the tree back in its development to become a strong tree. If the condition is recognized in older trees, the vine should be eradicated as soon as possible. The tree must be climbed and the vine removed. An older tree cannot keep up with the vigor of an aggressive vine and will die long before its time.

VERMIN AND STRUCTURAL INTEGRITY

Rodents, squirrels, and other vermin often use the bark and cambium of trees for nest building and food. On trees with vertical structure, the wounds they create may encircle the entire trunk and cause extensive girdling. Trees that branch out laterally will have the damage confined to the top side of the spars and limbs, making it difficult to spot the defect from the ground. Break up the nests and persuade the vermin to leave. If the wounds are large and encircle the trunk, bridge grafting may be the only way to save it, but only in the most valuable of trees. Cable or brace limbs and spars that have damage. Drop crotching can lighten the load. Reduced leverages exerted on the spars will lessen the susceptibility of breakage at weak points. Old wounds that have developed into cavities may call for the removal of the affected parts.

CAVITIES AND HEART ROT

Heart rot and cavities are common in mature trees. Many trees in the wild can be found standing for hundreds of years with cavities and supporting heavy major structure. There usually isn't much you can do to correct the problem. So how do you evaluate any threat or hazard associated with it? There are a few factors to consider: degree and location, vigor of the tree, balance of the tree, and proximity to infrastructure.

The degree: Slight, being the development of a cavity. Moderate; a developed cavity but not exceeding the majority of structure. Extreme; a hollow, the tree is supported by a rind. Location: what side of the tree does the cavity occur on? This has significance if the tree is in a lean. In what part of the bole does it occur? That could be the very base of the tree or somewhere else in the main stem or crotch unions.

The vigor of the tree: Many trees have successfully healed over large wounds that once covered the whole side of the trunk. Only a vigorous tree can do this. As a rule, young trees are more vigorous than older ones and stand a much better chance of healing over such a wound. Don't let the size of a tree fool you into believing it's old or not vigorous because some large trees can be quite vigorous. How do you determine vigor? Look at the tree. A vigorous tree will be full of foliage and look robust. The annual growth on a vigorous tree will be long and healthy. In a vigorous tree the seams in the bark will show active expansion, and any wounds will exhibit an aggressively advancing callus.

The balance of the tree: A tree that is out of balance puts stress on the trunk. How do you determine balance and stress? Look at the tree. If the tree leans there is a certain amount of stress on the trunk that is determined by the degree of its lean. A tree that develops large branching spars can put a lot of stress on the crotch unions. In combination with a cavity, such a trunk or crotch could fail at any time.

Proximity to infrastructure: If the tree is beside, or over roads, utilities, dwellings or other structures it could pose a risk This is the factor that generally decides the fate of the tree. For safety and liability reasons most trees are removed when they exhibit a cavity defect. But drop crotching, cabling, through-bolt bracing, guying, and cavity work can save most trees with cavities. Few people will spend that much money on a tree, but on occasion you'll find some people who will.

CAVITY WORK

Cavity work is cosmetic and of little benefit in repairing what has been lost in the structure of a tree. However, upon a conversant evaluation, cavity work can hasten the closing of the wound, have aesthetic value, and reflect a caring for the tree. You will find many contradicting opinions on the matter of cavity work and wound preparation. The beginner can find what has been written about the subject of cavity preparation, sterilization, and filling at the library.

CABLING AND BRACING

The worth of cabling and bracing in tree preservation is well known and within the beginners abilities to understand and do. Cabling and bracing relieves stress on the structure. Both of these procedures can be avoided by relieving the stress on a limb or crotch by prudent heading back or drop crotching. Combined together, these procedures can turn a once weak tree into a strong one.

The tools for cabling and bracing are minimal. A brace and bit will do. In small trees, a cordless electric drill may suffice. In large trees, you may have to rent a big reduction drive drill or gas augur and use a boring bit specially made for large holes. Add a come-along and a few wrenches, and you will have everything for the work.

The materials for cabling and bracing are obtainable at most hardware stores and horticultural supply outlets. In some trees, consider having hardware, like brackets, specially made. It adds a little touch of class to the finished job. You may even decide to make the through-bolts yourself, especially for the big trees. The material you use should be heavy duty and corrosion resistant. If it isn't, it won't last. Account for the weather, the time, and the beating the hardware is going to be subjected to. Go first class with the material.

Cabling is done in the higher and spread out structure of the tree. The main idea is to relieve the stress on the crotches and limbs by balancing and holding them together. Some trees will be quite simple to design a support system; one cable may be all that's needed to hold a double tree together. Other trees will require a substantial amount of both aerial cabling and through-bolt bracing. It is important to pick a design that is both functional and aesthetic. If it's not planned with that thought in mind, the work will be of little benefit. In the upper structure, aerial cabling does not need to be drawn very tight, just enough to get the slack out of it. Down lower, the cabling will be drawn tighter.

With aerial cabling the tree and the supports are always going to move or flex to some degree.

Through-bolt bracing is used to strengthen crotch unions. With through-bolt bracing aerial cabling may not be necessary. When installed properly, through-bolts have little or no visual impact. As mentioned earlier, you may desire to make your own through-bolts for certain large trees.

SWAY

As much benefit that cable and brace work is on the crotches of a tree, it is no guarantee that the tree will not break beyond it from sway. The only way to relieve the stress put on a tree from sway is to lessen the wind resistance of the tree. This is possible by drop crotching, thinning, and heading back.

Chapter 39

Application of Trimming, Training, and Pruning

DROP CROTCHING

Drop crotching is most effectively used in young to moderately aged domestic shade and fruit trees that have ample leads to drop the main back to.

Examine the tree's outer canopy and fix in your mind another canopy within the existing one. Trees are fractal; the form in the minor parts resemble the form of the whole. Walk around the tree to get a full picture. Different possibilities become obvious from different viewing angles.

Done properly drop crotching will have little effect on the growth habits of most trees. The form of the tree may be changed moderately in bringing it down or compacting. Drop crotching can be done in any part of the tree or performed throughout. It is effective in bringing balance to a tree that has none, has lost its balance, or to moderately change the form of the tree.

Quite often it is barely noticeable that some trees have been drop crotched, even when fifty percent of the tree's bulk has been removed. Little sucker growth results because there is usually enough uninterrupted active and latent buds on the leads left to resume and suppress it. Sucker growth can be expected when the lead is weak and not able to fulfill its role. Healthy leads are ascending and at least a third to half the size of the main lead. More sucker growth can be expected when the leads are even or descending in habit.

Drop crotching is not detrimental to the tree if it's well planned and done properly. The only real effect it has on the tree is in reducing the capacity of the tree and increasing the vigor of the chosen leads. An individual tree can be drop crotched quite a few times over the years, as long as there are internal laterals to cut back to. This can be achieved by pruning and thinning the tree to keep it open so light can enter and sustain the internal laterals and buds.

HEADING BACK

When a branch lacks a suitable lead to cut back to, head (cut) the limb back to a desired spot with buds. It happens often in trimming, but should only be done when there is no other alternative. Before deciding to head a limb back, consider the position of the limb and its role in the structural symmetry of the tree. If the limb doesn't play a vital role in the symmetry of the tree, take it all the way out. Stand back and look at the tree and the limb in question. The absence of a small limb among many others may not even be noticed. Visualize the limb's absence and position after heading back. If its removal would negatively offset the form of the tree, it may be best to head it back, especially if the limb constitutes more of the tree. The amount of viable buds on the limb is another consideration. Younger limbs will frequently be covered with an abundance of buds and small, shoot-like limbs. When you head a limb back in these areas, you'll get what you expect.

An older limb will not have an abundance of buds. Observe the limb in the area you wish to cut and encourage new growth. If you spot viable buds you may be in luck if they are healthy. If the tree has adventitious qualities you would even be luckier because you can't always find them where you want them. Having new growth occur in this situation is a gamble, sometimes it doesn't come back the way you hoped.

TOPPING

Topping is sometimes confused with drop crotching. The distinction lies in the form of the tree and where or how it is cut. Topping should be used with caution as it can be a major detrimental form of trimming.

HEDGING

Hedging affects the sound structure of a tree and any structure that does develop will be unsound and weak. Defects such as split crotches, crossed limbs, grafts, and rub wounds are common results of hedging trees.

Trees that have been hedged early in their lives and then allowed to grow wild will harbor many defects and be highly susceptible to breakage. Constant trimming of the tree from the outside will result in hedging, even if it was unintended when such trimming began.

Hedging is one of the biggest trimming errors in the line clearance business. To keep a tree in its space and at the same time not form a hedge, use a system that includes drop crotching and thinning. This will promote lateral lead and bud development in the structure that is left. If a hedge is desired, plant a shrub and never use a tree for that purpose.

THINNING AND SKINNING

Thinning is not required in a tree that develops on its own. Natural thinning consists of the tree's dominant leads suppressing the subdominant leads by shading them out. Trees will grow into an untangled form unless something alters the natural thinning process, such as cutting back the top or main leads of a tree. Many leads that normally would be shed as dead wood will continue growing and could be mixed with sucker growth, causing you to have to thin once in a while.

Thinning can be performed in any part of a tree regardless of its age and generally will have no detrimental effects. Thinning is important during the training years of a young tree's form. Certain leads have to be thinned and removed to control and direct the tree's growth. After the initial thinning, you may have to further thin the tree later in its life to stimulate growth. The very act of thinning the number of leads in a tree will stimulate lateral bud development in the remaining chosen leads and give you the opportunity to cut those leads back later. Use thinning to relieve congestion and crossed structure in a tree. If you watch what thinning accomplishes, you'll begin to understand how the natural processes work.

A rough form of thinning is skinning, or stripping. It's used a lot in moderately aged and older trees to show off their trunks and lead structure. In effect it can make a tree look older or more mature for its age. In practice you quite literally strip out all the subdominant leads, minor shoots, and sometimes even the existing latent buds out to the canopy line. While the effect is pleasing to the eye, the practice can be quite detrimental to the tree. In many cases it can totally void any future chance of heading back without death to the leads or tree. The practice can also be very depleting to the health and vigor of the tree, and it can outright kill certain species of trees. In training young trees the practice can hasten development of the chosen structure while having a low impact on it. The worst can be expected in older trees that regenerate only by active and latent buds. Trees that have adventitious qualities can have a better chance of recovery after a treatment of skinning.

LIMB RAISING

The raising of limbs in most trees is not a detrimental form of trimming. All trees in the wild go through a natural limb raising process. In coniferous forests, trees shed their lower limbs by the upper canopy shading them out. Animals contribute by constantly browsing on a tree's lower limbs. Trees that are born in the open will not follow suit, but they still go through a limb raising process of the upper limbs spreading and drooping to the ground over the lower ones. The upper limbs will take over the canopy that the lower limbs once occupied. In an urban tree, the limb raising may go on through the life of the tree. This often results from limbs becoming long and drooping into roads, access ways, or views.

There is a degree of how far you can go with limb raising before the tree loses proportion or symmetry or the trunk is exposed to hard sun. Trees with pendent and drooping limbs will fair better from a heavy limb raising. A tree with ascending leads will have its trunk exposed to possible sunburn from any amount of limb raising. Gradual limb raising will give a tree a better chance of adapting to its lower limbs being removed or raised.

POLLARDING

Pollarding is one of the most misunderstood forms of trimming used and misused today. Pollarding consists of heavy cutting and stubbing back the leads. It can be considered a brash form of heading back. This is almost a traditional way of trimming trees in some locales. In natural events, trees will be pollarded by wind, lightning, and other trees falling against them. Trees that survive these events can grow into hideous, unusual, and unique forms. A person deciding to pollard a tree can create any one.

A tree that has its main lead divisions evenly spaced throughout can offer an excellent chance for a so-called light pollard. In this case it would be more like heading the leads back. If such a pollarding is thought out properly, it can actually have some beneficial results in developing the tree's future form. In top working fruit trees, the main leads are all headed back in the vicinity of the third, fourth, and fifth divisions and the variety is grafted to the stubbed off ends. The variety is managed into the tree's new outer divisions where the fruit is born. This is an old practice in agriculture and the trimmer can apply it to landscape trees when re-establishing a tree that has grown out of its space.

Pollarding is sometimes done to trees on an annual basis. Each year's growth is cut back to a big ugly knob that eventually develops from the practice. Since this is done on an annual basis and only one year's growth is removed, it could be considered a form of rogue pruning.

Observe how any tree grows back after being pollarded. The resulting growth is the most vigorous you will ever see generated in a single season. Sucker growth will grow straight up and frequently in places where it's not wanted. When looking at the tree and then the suckers, the sucker growth will be out of phase with the rest of the tree, (i.e. young shoots on an old tree—See **Chapter 37**—Vigor and Capacity).

SPUR PRUNING

Spur pruning is used to contain many deciduous vines and trees. It can also be used on some evergreens. Unusual and pleasing effects can be created with it. I learned spur pruning when working in the vineyards. In order to understand how spur pruning is applied to a tree, look at how it is applied to an individual arm on a vine. In this example I'll use a single stem, or cane, of one year's growth. The cane is four feet long, of moderate vigor, and has set a dozen buds at the end of the growing season. During the dormant period, the cane is pruned down to two buds. This is called a two bud spur. At bud break in the spring, two new canes grow out of the spur. During the next dormant period, the outer-most cane is removed entirely down to the bottom one, and the bottom cane is pruned to a two bud spur. This pruning is repeated on each arm of the vine.

With grapevines, spur pruning is an annual system that has to be strictly followed. If the vine is strong and vigorous, increase the number of buds left on the spurs or increase the number of spurs on the vine. Attempts to convert an established tree into a pruning system are not impossible but will involve a little more thought and work to get started.

CANE PRUNING

Cane pruning is also used on grape vines. With cane pruning, spurs and entire canes are managed on the same vine. In this system the canes are used for bearing the majority of the fruit, and the spurs are used solely for cane renewal.

Canes that are two years old at the time of pruning will have a full rank of one year old canes growing from them. Remove entirely the two year old canes. What is left on the vine are one year old canes that came from spurs from last year's pruning. Some of those canes will be chosen for bearing fruit the next season and others will be pruned down to spurs.

Deciding which to use for canes or leave for spurs depends on their location on the vine. The outermost canes on the vine are left for bearing fruit the next season and then tied to the trellis. The inner most selected canes are pruned to spurs. Since future canes will come from those spurs, they will keep the entire vine closer to the trellis. Pruning the vine any other way will increase its size away from the trellis and into the vineyard row. In no time, the vine would be out of its place and get broken from cultivation and harvesting equipment.

If you are questioning what this has to do with trimming a tree, you are not understanding the main intent of the system. The system functions as a producer of fruit and keeps the vines in their place longer than any other system. This knowledge used in choosing positions for canes and spurs is also vitally important to the tree trimming industry.

ON PRUNING FRUIT TREES

Many of the pruning systems used on fruit trees are very similar to the spur pruning principle. On an established apple tree the fruit will be born on little knobby branchlets called fruiting spurs. These spurs persist on older wood inside the canopy of the tree. With an established tree you'll spend most of your time pruning the outer leads of the tree back and performing regular maintenance such as thinning and minor drop crotching. There is a distinct line between the growth that occurs outside of the pruning and where the fruit is born. The growth born each season as a result of your pruning is vegetative. You will actually spend little or no time managing the fruiting spurs. However, a fruiting spur can also grow vegetatively but only if the tree is pruned or cut too hard. Over-pruning will throw an apple tree out of phase and result in low production of fruit. Some fruit and nut trees are periodically cut heavily to stimulate out of phase new growth as this is the only way to get some species to produce a crop in abundance.

BUYING ORNAMENTAL AND FRUIT TREES

When purchasing ornamental shade and fruit trees, look at the initial training they've had. Inspect the crotch unions to make sure they are smooth, strong, and not too sharp. If the tree is a grafted variety, make sure the variety is knitted strongly to the stock. Crotch spacing is particularly important. In broad leaf domestic shade trees, too many primary branches from the same location is a negative quality. There should be some space between the leads so the crotches can form smoothly and not tightly. Thinning can provide this. With central lead coniferous trees, chose a tree that is thick with primary branches. Look inside the branches to see if the tree has single or multiple leads. Depending on the species of conifer, multiple leads could be a negative quality. Most irregularities found in container trees can be corrected after planting. Get your money's worth and be picky when buying trees.

MATURE TREES

With few exceptions, the form of most mature trees will be permanently set. There is seldom any possibility of training an established mature form into a new one. You can change or enhance the form of a mature tree by prudent trimming. Anything you do to a mature tree will be permanent. If you make a mistake, it'll show as long as the tree stands. Mature trees don't have a lot of growth left in them although they can persist as they are for long periods of time. Be careful when the work involves mature trees.

There's a dire need in the private sector, municipalities, and utility industries for qualified people to trim, train, and prune trees. Many of the people involved in the work don't know or don't care how to do it right. The customer can also be the cause for the wrongs in a lot of tree trimming. Institutions that govern and oversee the work are often responsible for ignorant or neglectful practices done by those practicing the craft. In the line clearing business, the companies hate to see a worker spend too much time on any particular tree. They say it's not cost effective. Trimming a tree incorrectly will make it more costly to maintain in the future. This is a widespread problem that leaves many ugly and deformed trees along our highways and even in our own backyards.

The most important task is to educate the private owners, companies, and institutions that oversee the work and the crafts-people that perform the work in the true art of trimming, training, and pruning trees so that the next generation of trees will be beautiful and less costly to maintain.

Chapter 40

Managing Brush and Wood Disposal

Clean up operations constitute a major part of the time and cost in tree work, and in many cases it determines how a job is done. It's not mindless work and actually requires a good deal of experience and thought. My first six years of line clearance work involved trimming and removing trees along the roads and in people's yards where a thorough clean up was part of the work. Then I spent the next twelve years clearing some of the most overgrown and neglected cross country right-of-ways in Northern California.

After eighteen years of cutting, stacking, chipping, burning, hauling, and running a crew, I got to know the clean up part pretty well. Since it can be the biggest part of any job, knowing how to do it keeps the cost down.

CHAINS

Forming chains of people to pass brush, wood, or whatever, is an age old practice. It relieves the burden on the individual and spreads it out to everyone in the chain. In chains where the brush is passed by hand or thrown on its way to a chipper, everyone will be stopped if the last person feeding the chipper tries to work with a difficult piece of brush. In such chains, the last person should set aside any awkward pieces of brush to keep everyone in the chain working. These difficult pieces can be dealt with later.

Maintaining the synchronization of the chain is very important. If someone in the middle drops a piece of brush that's tossed to them, have them leave it for the piece coming next. Once you stoop to pick up a dropped piece, the timing can be lost and you may have to stoop to pick

Clean up is a big part of tree work.

up the rest. Such a break in a chain will result in everybody bending over to pick up brush when originally it was a catch and throw operation. Before starting a chain, examine the situation carefully and see if there's an alternative to moving the debris some other way. Chains in their own right are effective, but only when the correct number of people are used.

DRAGGING THE BRUSH

Dragging is best suited in open areas. It is most easy when the haul is on level or downhill ground. Dragging brush sidehill is difficult and sometimes dangerous because of the tendency for it to roll and wrench a person's arm or wrist. Uphill dragging is only done over a very short distance. Whenever dragging brush, pull with the butt end leading. If the haul is downhill, larger pieces can be dragged.

Large pieces of brush can be used as a sled to haul the smaller pieces that abound in disposal work. In the course of dragging one large piece of brush, you can tote a number of other smaller pieces with it.Pull with your toes dug in and arms extended back or heals dug in and arms extended forward. Take care of your back: warm up your muscles by starting easy and then build up to heavier hauls.

CARRYING THE BRUSH

Carrying brush by hand can be the most tiring and time consuming for the amount of debris moved. It's often the only practical method to move bush and debris through landscaped yards without damage to shrubs and flower beds. Carry the brush in areas occupied by pets or livestock to keep it from being contaminated with undesirable substances. Carrying will keep the debris from becoming dirty or muddy, saving considerable wear on chipper blades. There's a lot of stooping, bending over, picking up, and turning around to carrying. There's the front carry, side carry, over the shoulder, and overhead carry. Knowing how to manage the balance points of what you carry makes a big difference in how hard you make the work on yourself. When lifting the loads, remember to start out by stretching and carrying light loads. Use the proper lifting technique, using your legs more than your back.

USING A SPAR POLE TO MOVE DEBRIS

Whenever you can, use a tree as a spar pole to assist your movement of debris. It only takes a little time to set one up, and it can save you a lot of hard dragging and carrying over rough terrain. We used them all the time in the cross country right of ways; the ground was steep and hard to work on. Some schemes were small: two and three man power, thirty foot spar, half inch bull line, sixty foot of reach. Some were quite elaborate: one ton truck power, 90 foot spars with tail holds and guy lines, one inch bull lines, hundreds of feet of reach. Be sure the tree you use as a spar is substantial enough to handle the loads you intend to put on it. Set guy lines to bolster a marginal spar. You can break or up-root them if you don't. The discussions in Chapters 1,2 and 3 will enlighten those who want to know more about rigging, theory, and safety when using it.

MOVING LOGS

The best way to manage logs is with logging equipment. Steel rigging and powerful winches make moving logs pretty simple. Such equipment is usually not a regular tool of the private tree man, but it's easily available for hire in most places when it's needed. Spar poles can be set up to move logs too.

When rolling logs, observe the taper of them. This is an important point as the taper of a log will greatly influence the direction it will desire to roll or how to compensate for the roll. The larger end of the log will always overtake the smaller end in its movement. Quick taper logs can nearly turn around before they roll a distance equal to their own length. After you get an eye for the taper of a log, you can position or aim it so that when it's allowed to roll the taper will carry it to a specific area.

BRUSH CHIPPING

GENERAL POINTERS TO CHIPPING BRUSH

Here are some simple rules to follow whenever chipping:

1. Always wear protective gear. Eye protection, gloves, ear protection, and a snug-fitting, long-sleeve shirt without conventional cuffs. Cuffs are notorious for brush to catch on. For the same reason watch the work gloves you use also.

2. Don't work close to the chipper. Maintain some distance from it. Throw the brush into the chipper and do not hold on. Once the brush touches the blades it can be pulled into the machine very quickly. Some models of disk chippers have feed rolls that govern the rate the brush is pulled into the machine. They take the brush in a slow but steady rate.

3. When larger limbs are run through, small branches and leaves are regularly shed off and fall under the feed chute. Periodically pick up a handful of this small stuff and run it through with a larger piece. Always reserve a few larger limbs on the side to help the final clean up of the small debris. Don't scrape the ground clean when picking up the smaller debris. You will incidentally pick up dirt and gravel which will damage the chipper blades.

4. Run the chipper only at the RPM that is suitable for what's being chipped. Don't run it all out if all you have is small light brush. But make sure you have the chipper cranked up if you are running heavy brush or you could stall the machine. Most chippers have governors that increase the power automatically when the heavy limbs are run through. However, in many cases the governors can fail. It's up to the operator to act as the governor by watching how the crew feeds the machine. If the chipper bogs down, don't throw any more brush into it until it recovers and revs back up.

5. Stand to the side of the chute when you throw in the brush. Don't ever stand directly in front of the chute because the blades can kick back chips, wood chunks, and cones.

6. If you're chipping with someone opposite you, make sure you don't side wash them with the brush you throw in. Side wash is caused by throwing brush into the chute from the side position. When the brush is pulled in by the blades, the side motion is amplified. It can cause some smart stings and bruises if you are caught on the receiving side. Make a conscious effort to throw the brush straight into the chute to minimize the side wash effect.

7. Always give your partner warning whenever you have dead brush or long whips to throw in. Dead limbs and brush can shatter or explode when they're pulled in. Long lanky limbs can whip around and cause some smart stings and bruises.

8. Be especially careful if the brush has any hook crotches. Such crotches have pulled people into the machines before. If you are feeding any short chunks of wood or pine cones, be aware that these two items are frequently kicked back out of the chute, especially when the blades are dull.

9. When cranking up the chipper, engage the clutch slowly with the engine a little above idle speed. Do not engage the clutch too quickly or the engine will stall. Engage it lightly and give the drum and blades time to speed up to the engine speed before fully engaging it. Then crank the engine speed up to the necessary RPM for the brush that is being chipped. Do not crank up the engine speed too high before engaging the clutch. When shutting down the chipper, turn the engine down to an idle and let it slow down the chipper drum and blades. This sometimes takes a minute. When the drum has slowed down to the idle speed of the engine, then disengage the clutch and shut the rig down.

CUTTING THE BRUSH FOR CHIPPING

Learn how to cut the brush properly for chipping. There's really a talent to it. How exactly you would do it depends on the brush, the machine you're using, the man power to manage it, and the area it must be managed through. If you don't cut it just right, you can create unnecessary work. Cut the brush to straighten out any undesirable features that could pose problems: hard angled Y or L crotches. These crotches do not feed through the chipper easily and will often jam in the feed chute. The brush should not be cut too small; this will slow down the handling and feeding of it into the machine. Cut the large limbs into manageable size pieces that won't drag the machine down. A bogged down machine will clog its discharge chute with chips and have to be shut off to clear it.

TO STACK OR NOT TO STACK

Stacking is sometimes a prelude to chipping or burning. Whenever the brush can be managed directly to the chipper after being cut, stacking may not be necessary. This will save the step of stacking and unstacking the brush and much time.

STACKING THE BRUSH FOR CHIPPING

Keep the butt ends of the brush laid in the same direction and evened up. If the butt ends on the bottom of the stack project out, they will hamper your leg room and ability to pull brush off the stack. Avoid throwing brush into a stack from behind. It's notorious for binding the brush together and making it difficult to pull apart. Keep all the small pieces in a pile or stack off to one side. Do not mix them with the larger and more uniform pieces of brush. This also applies to any dead wood and chunks. Keeping it separate facilitates handling during the chipping operation. Throwing it all together in one pile creates a tangled and confusing stack to pull from.

There are different ways of stacking brush. You can layer it from the ground up and all the brush will pull off the "top" of the stack If the brush is straight you can get a large volume in a relatively small stack this way. If a stack is built from one side, you must remember that it will always pull apart easier from the same side it was put together, otherwise many problems will arise when pulling the brush from any other side.

Avoid too large a stack because the brush tends to tangle more from its own mass and weight which can make pulling the brush from the stack more difficult. Try arranging the brush in manageable size stacks, or piles, all pointed toward where the chipper will be working. This works the best when dealing with gnarly and tangled brush.

DULL CHIPPER BLADES

When the chipper blades are dull, the performance of the chipper will be greatly reduced. Dull blades will not pull the brush in efficiently and require the operator to work close to the feed chute and push and jab the brush in. Dull blades kick back short pieces of wood and pine cones. Dull blades make chipping more difficult and more dangerous. Dull blades will shred the brush in long stringy pieces that do not compact so less brush can be hauled in the form of shreds. Dull blades require more time and fuel to chip any amount of brush. When the symptoms of dull blades become obvious, remove them and install sharp ones.

SHARPENING CHIPPER BLADES

Properly sharpened blades are necessary for the efficient operation of the chipper. Properly sharpened blades are honed to a uniform straight edge and matched in pairs that are set opposite each other on the drum or disk. Honing the blades is done on a planner blade sharpening machine. Honing keeps the blade from getting hot and preserves its temper and also maintains the proper profile and angle of the blades. Grinding the blades hollows out the cutting edge making it more vulnerable to chipping or nicking. Grinding will also heat the blade in the process causing the blade to lose its temper and remove more metal to get an edge than is really necessary. However, grinding may sometimes be necessary to even out any large nicks or breaks in the blades. When a lot of grinding is done to any blade, its mate must also be ground down to the same weight and installed on the opposite side of the drum to keep the balance even. Improper balance will cause excessive vibration in the machine and result in bearing wear and loosening of vital parts.

CHANGING THE BLADES (DRUM TYPE)

Prior to disassembly, clean the drum with a steam or pressure cleaner. This will remove pitch and fine organic particles from the socket head bolts and other parts and make disassembly quicker, easier, safer, and cleaner. When breaking down the drum to install the sharp blades, remove all incidental adjusting screws, wedges, bolts, etc. and keep them in order of disassembly. Clean all parts and threaded portions. The mating surfaces of the wedges, drum, and blades should be scraped clean of any organic residue that accumulates between blade changes. Clean out the residues before breaking loose the bolts. Residues will keep the wrenches from seating properly and cause broken knuckles and wallered-out bolts. Don't reuse any wallered-out bolts; you may not be able to remove them during the next blade change and have to use a torch to burn them out.

When reassembling the parts, make sure they're all clean and put a light coat of anti-seize compound on everything. This will make future disassembly much easier and lessen the chance of broken knuckles, twisted bolts, and frazzled nerves. Keep the new blades paired up so they'll be assembled in the proper order. Handle them very carefully as they are heavy and extremely sharp. Wear strong gloves when handling blades. If you fumble or drop a blade, do not try to catch or save it. A blade can be replaced easier than a hand or fingers. The new edge on the blade chips very easily so be careful about bumping or knocking the edge into other parts of the machine. Install the adjusting screws and set one blade in place. Rotate the drum so the blade will be near the bed knife of the chipper. Check the clearance and adjust to the recommended clearance suggested by the manufacture.

A match book cover inserted between the blade and the bed knife works as a good gauge. If the bed knife is hollowed out, the clearances should be checked at the corners of the blades. It would be wise to grind the bed knife square if the hollow exceeds one eighth inch. Once the proper clearance is set, put the wedge in place and secure it down lightly at first. Recheck the clearance and then tighten. After the first blade is installed, turn the drum to install its mate on the opposite side. Repeat the procedure of adjusting and tightening down the wedges that secure the blades. Go around the drum like this until all blades are installed, then check the bolts for proper tightening. Snug them evenly to draw the wedge down squarely against the blades. Do not over tighten.

FIRE SAFETY, PREVENTION AND THE LAW

The laws overseeing controlled burns set most of the standards a person will have to follow. But even abiding by the rules and regulations set by state and local authorities is no excuse in a court if it is deemed that the person doing the burning was not using good common sense. Even in optimum conditions, controlled burns may not be allowed in more and more districts. The issues of air quality and pollution can stop any burning a person may have planned. Be aware of any and all updated new laws and regulations governing controlled burns.

Fire safety requires only good common sense, like not burning on hot, dry, or windy days. Any one of these factors can cause a wild fire. In combination with one another, they can create a condition comparable to an inferno. Besides these more obvious factors, there are others that must be considered. Know the location and extent of ignitables around the burn area. Scraping down to mineral soil in the burn area is not a guarantee of total fire safety if the ground covers dead roots, stumps, or logs. These can smolder underground for days or even weeks. They have been responsible for many a wild fire that cropped up days after the controlled burn was finished. Look around the burn area for their presence and any snags or old stumps down wind where sparks may fly. These are another source of fuel that can start a wild fire.

Once you have ascertained favorable controlled burn conditions, make sure that you have the necessary fire prevention tools. This will be a legal requirement that varies from state to state. Common items are a shovel, ax, chainsaw, and pitch fork. Other tools that may be necessary or required could include a pulaski, McCloud, water back packs, and extinguishers. If a garden hose is available have it handy too.

FIRE SIZE

In many areas there are laws governing the size of fire you can build. In our burn control district, the size of burn you can have around a residence is a maximum of four feet in diameter. However, right over the ridge the state will allow the timber companies to burn acres in one day.

Out on the cross country right of ways our fires are hand fed, but quite large. Look into what size fire you're allowed to build before doing it.

PREPARING THE BURN AREA

Clear the burn area before you start burning. Mineral soil should be exposed in the immediate burn area. In some places this may entail a lot of scraping of duff before mineral soil is exposed. The organic layer can be over a foot thick in some wooded areas and can easily be ignited by sparks. Even a surface that is sufficiently damp to permit safe burning may cover a dry duff that is flammable. The duff layer can burn underground and crop up to the surface days later. Some areas will have to be cleared more aggressively if there is a thick mat of duff and you may have to water the exposed strata. Be particularly aware of the standing trees in a wooded area. If there are limbs from neighboring trees overhanging the burn area, cut them off before starting a burn. The heat from a fire can dry out overhanging limbs and ignite the entire tree. This can be the start of a crown fire that can spread to other neighboring trees.

CONTROL BURNS IN GRASSLAND

A grassy field can dry in a couple of hours after burning begins. Sparks can get annual grasses that have already set seed burning very quickly. A two-acre grassy field can burn in a few minutes and spread into wooded or residential areas. Don't let green grass fool you! Perennial grasses have a substantial amount of dry matter under their green cover. Even in an open field, you may have to clear a larger area than specified by the law. In either wooded or grassy areas, dampness is the major consideration governing whether it would be safe to burn or not.

STARTING A FIRE WITH FLAMMABLE LIQUIDS

There are a lot of ways to start a fire, but only a few may be considered safe. Flammable liquids are responsible for most of the accidents incurred while starting fires, especially gasoline. Gasoline is very dangerous to use for starting fires. Its vapors build, travel, and ignite with amazingly explosive power. Most accidents with gasoline have occurred when a person attempts to douse a stubborn fire.

Starting a fire with gasoline is not advised or recommended. In spite of all warnings, most fires are started with gasoline. You can start a fire with gasoline safely by burying a small tin can up to its rim in the soil where you'll burn the brush. When you're ready to start burning, carefully fill the tin two-thirds full, about five to six ounces in a small bean can. Set the gas container away from the burn area, and then light the tin. The small surface area of the opening will prevent any excess vapors from building to explosive levels making it safe to light, much like a can of Sterno. Do not overfill or get sloppy. Once the tin is lit, begin layering small sticks and brush over it.

DRY MATERIALS AND KINDLING

An age-old method to start fires begins by gathering any available dry material, though today we use a disposable lighter and wad of paper to start it burning instead of flint and rock. Dry materials may seem scarce at times in a damp woods. If you look around a bit you can usually find some, even in the dampest conditions. Check under old logs that are suspended off the ground and even an old log itself may be dry within. A cut and split old log can be the source of dry fuel for many fires.

COALS

The coals from another fire are the easiest and safest to use. Clear the new burn area and place several shovel loads of coals where the new fire will be. Building the coals up to an active fire takes only a few minutes, even when burning green brush.

STARTING THE FIRE

Start off using small sticks and twigs like you're building a little camp fire. Lay the material close together with a minimum of space so the fire can grow evenly throughout. In damp conditions these steps are most crucial. Don't get in a hurry. Start small and build the fire up. Begun properly this way, you should have a fire that will consume anything within an hour.

PROPER STACKING AND BUILDING FIRE

Many dampened fires are caused by a large cockeyed piece in the stack holding the brush off the coals. This is why the proper assembly of the stack is so important. Cut and stack all the limbs, brush, and wood so it lies parallel and close together. Criss-crossed stacks tend to hold the burnables over the coals and results in voids that the fire cannot spread through. You can have a successful burn by cross stacking the limbs, brush, and wood, but only by layering. Random criss-crossing results in voids and stuck fires. Look at each piece before you place it on the fire. If you place it one way, it may pose problems with the burn. If you place it another, it won't. Like a jigsaw puzzle. Maybe you should cut it before throwing it on the fire. Planning is the key ingredient to successful burns of green and any other debris.

BURNING DRY BRUSH

There is a certain element of risk in the direct lighting of dry brush piles. If they're large the fire can spread and get out of control very quickly. To keep on the safe side, feed the dry brush and debris to a smaller and more controllable fire. If you have it in mind to light a dry brush pile make sure there's plenty of room. The flames from a ten foot dry brush pile can leap sixty feet in the air and scorch nearby trees and shrubs. Direct lighting like this does not always end up with a clean burn unless the brush was cut and stacked properly. Improperly stacked, the larger material will never burn and instead will settle down, smolder, and require further handling and time to obtain a complete clean burn.

BURNING GREEN BRUSH

The burning of green brush is prohibited in many areas. In the past, it was a standard practice but now it should be dried out before burning. Green brush burns smoky compared to dry brush and the growing prohibition is an air quality and pollution control measure. In some areas the burning of green brush is not yet prohibited. The important thing to know about burning green brush is cutting and stacking it on the fire properly which is the same as with starting a fire. Build it up to proportion gradually. Cut the brush and limbs so they are straight and lie down well without a lot of voids. Use a set of loppers to cut the brush when starting the fire and add whatever dry material is available. As the fire builds, place the large material a little at a time with ample amounts of smaller material between. This will require you to cut and sort the material as you build the fire. If this procedure is followed you should have a well established fire about an hour after starting. You should then be able to burn whatever you have without fear of dampening the fire. The main problem beginners have with burning green brush is they get hasty and throw too big material on too soon. It results in dampening the fire out. If the fire goes out, disassemble it and start over. This dirty and frustrating chore can run you short of dry material.

BURNING LARGE DEBRIS

When burning, the larger material will burn better close together, especially when a fire burns down and the larger material, be it logs or stumps, is all that is left. When the fire is burned down, throw the large material close together in the heart of the coals. In such a position, the large pieces will keep each other burning. If it's not done this way, larger logs and stumps will persist and you won't get a clean burn.

BURNING FINE DEBRIS

The twigs, leaves, and duff that accumulate in the burn area while the fire is being built will have to be raked up and burned before the operation is over. Most fires will leave a ring of unburned material around their perimeter that will need pitching in. Do not throw in this ring of material until it's burned free of the fire, for then it will pitch in easily. When you do it, rake the outer area and throw on all the other accumulations. This is usually the final step to obtain a clean burn of all combustibles in an area. The fine organic debris will smother out the coals if placed directly on top. Always place some brush on the coals first and then the fine debris. This allows air circulation between the coals and fine material so it can dry and burn.

A CLEAN BURN

The end of a control burn should end in a clean burn. A clean burn will be absent of any material that is unburned or still burning. After raking and cleaning around the burn area, there should be nothing left but coals and ash. At this point it's advised to spread and stir the coals so they will burn quicker. A pile of live coals can persist for days after a burn. When they are spread out, they will usually burn and extinguish themselves in a matter of hours, depending on the size of the coal bed. You can hasten it by spreading the coals and sprinkling with water. But you would be surprised how much water it takes to extinguish a bed of coals. As mentioned earlier, the coals are a good source material to use for starting other fires.

IN CLOSING

I would like to add how this book can be used as a format for instructional purposes. I would also like to express my personal feelings about the current status of the tree care/work industry and the environmental issues surrounding it.

The information in this book, up to chapter 12, can be taught in a classroom through discussions, lectures and model demonstrations. Knots, rigging tools, rigging theory and tools of the trade should all be familiar to the beginner before ever entering a tree with the intention of working in it. Only after being proven proficient in those respects by exam and tests should a beginner even be allowed to start applying it in a tree. The theories and techniques discussed in the latter chapters about climbing and cutting the tree can also be taught by the same means prior to actual field exercises. You don't put a person up in a tree first and then start yelling to them how to tie a knot, set rigging, balance a load or cut limbs and tops out of a tree. That should all be learned first. Only through education and qualification standards can the craft of the tree care/work industry expect to get the benefits and recognition that other trade professions have been getting for a long time.

Tree work is probably one of the oldest professions in the world. Writings and descriptions of it go back thousands of years. In spite of this, it is one of the least understood professions by most people. Over-population and urban sprawl is a worldwide problem that we're all becoming more aware of. It has created a huge tree industry covering planting of trees (native and introduced species), care and trimming of trees (maintenance), as well as wide-spread removals and harvesting of trees (logging). Environmental issues and organizations have cropped up and are spearheading much scrutiny against the timber industry. Even in the cities, urban and rural areas, the private tree businesses are facing more and more of the same kind of scrutiny when it comes to the pruning or removal of trees.

The forested and pristine wooded areas of the Pacific Northwest are becoming inundated by people moving in from the cities. Many of these people hire services to: remove trees for a building site, build roads to get there, let in sun light, open up views and remove any hazards the native trees might present. The purchase of commercial forest products to build their homes usually follows. The protests against logging in the northwest are frequently funded and organized by many such people that move up from the cities and claim to be environmentalists. They too easily forget what their impact on the environment is and are quick to point the finger of blame at the industry.

Bureaucracy has splintered into many new agencies that now attempt to regulate how the small private owner cuts or manages the trees in their own front and back yards, even to the point of not allowing the removal of a hazardous or nuisance tree by one's own home. Private organizations, many old and some new, are also on the bandwagon and pushing for more regulation on what the private owner does with their own trees. The cutting of trees has become a hot political issue now and much rhetoric is slung between factions. The laws resulting from these confrontations have been conflicting and indefinable, resulting in lots of finger pointing and squabbling but not many good solutions. The tree worker is caught right in the middle of it all with everybody insisting on their version of how tree work should be done. Let's try to review things and reach a useful consensus of opinion.

Trees can be replanted over and over and harvested indefinitely, other resources can't. When mineral and petroleum resources are used up what will we have left? We will always have trees. With trees it's like having your cake and eating it too. The current practice of the over cutting of trees is the market-driven result of over-population and consumer demand.

I believe the industry should promote the planting of more small trees and shrubs in crowded urban areas because they would stand a much better chance to reach mature form than a full size tree would. They would be long-lived, pleasing to look at, less costly to maintain, enhance property values, and pose less liability problems. Full size trees in the same places have little chance to ever do the same before heavy cutting and eventual removal remedies the problems they present. The industry should also promote educational programs concerning tree care, growing requirements and forest management practices as relating both to environmental preserves and forest product lands. A more informed public can help make better regulations.

All that said, the ultimate goal of the tree work professional is to do the best possible job for the client, be they a private homeowner or a large forest products corporation. Their primary concern should be for the health and safety of all those involved in the tree work being performed and their secondary concern should be for the tree, whether it is being trimmed to look good for many years to come or it is being felled for forest products. Hopefully the contents of this book will assist the reader in attaining these goals. Good luck and safe climbing!

G. F. BERANEK

Appendix A

Topic Reference

Appendix B
Recommended Reading

"If you are going to get anywhere in life you have to read a lot of books."

- Roald Dahl

An Illustrated Guide to Pruning (Third Edition). Edward F. Gilman. Cengage Learning, 2011.

Arborist Equipment (Second Edition). Donald F. Blair. International Society of Arboriculture, 1999.

Best Practices for Rigging in Arboriculture (Second Edition). Tree Care Industry Association, 2012.

Groundie. Jeff Jepson. Beaver Tree Publishing, 2021.

High Climbers and Timber Fallers - From Old Growth Logging to Second Growth Management. Gerald F. Beranek. Beranek Publications, 2005.

Knots at Work. Jeff Jepson. Beaver Tree Publishing, 2013.

Professional Timber Falling: A Procedural Approach. D. Douglas Dent. Self published, 1974.

The Art and Science of Practical Rigging. Peter S. Donzelli and Sharon J. Lilly. International Society of Arboriculture, 2001.

The Art of Felling Timber - Comprehensive Edition. Roy W. Hauser. www.theartoffellingtimber.com, 2020.

The Tree Climber's Companion - Second Edition. Jeff Jepson. Beaver Tree Publishing, 2000.

Tree Pruning: A Worldwide Photo Guide. Alex Shigo. Shigo and Trees. 1989.

To Fell A Tree. Jeff Jepson. Beaver Tree Publishing, 2009.

Glossary

ABSEILING: Technique used by a climber during a descent down a single or double line. To abseil is to wrap the upcoming line around your foot, leg or waist for the purpose of creating drag on the line to slow or aid your descent.

ACESSORY RINGS AND SNAPS-(Climbing belts): The auxiliary hardware on a climber's belt. Used to secure tools, lines and convenience items.

ACTIVE BUD: On the tip of any growing stem there is an active bud.

ADVENTITIOUS QUALITY: Pertains to a plant's ability to spontaneously regenerate by vegetative means, adventitious tissues, buds roots or burl.

ADVERSE: To move or work in an opposite or contrary direction. As in setting and fixing lines during climbing and working you must consider setting your lines adversely when the situation deems it. That is, to set the line behind and below your position for its steady or its adverse support.

AERIAL: Pertaining to what is aloft, or up in the air. As in aerial lift trucks.

ANCHOR-(Rigging and tools)**:** Natural or man-made device use to secure lines and tools. A stump is a good anchor.

ANGLES AND DANGLES: A loosely used term implying the theory and application of rigging work.

APICAL DOMINANCE-(Tree physiology, pruning, trimming): A phenomenon in plant growth in which its energy, vigor and regeneration occur predominantly in the highest buds, leads and tops.

ARBOR: Prefix meaning tree, as in "arborculture" being the scientific care and planting of trees, or "arborist" a person who is in the business of planting and maintenance of trees.

ASCEND: In climbing to ascend is to go up. To enter a tree you must ascend it. A tool called the "ascender" is a rope-gripping mechanical device of various designs used to aid a climber in ascents up a single line. -{Morphological): "ascending" pertains to the rising structure of a tree's form, opposite of descending, descents etc.

BACKCHAINING: Saw handling technique utilizing the top of the cutting bar. During back chaining, the saw chips are expelled away from your position, in which a strong "push" force is exerted on the saw, thus requiring a firm and proper grip on the power saw.

BACK CUT (Tree falling): After facing up a tree, you place the back cut to fall it. Usually the last cut used in falling a tree.

BACKING UP: Tree cutting term indicating the procedures of placing the back cut to fall or top out a tree.

BACK LEAN-(Tree falling): A tree that leans back away from the layout is called a back leaner.

BACK PULL-(Climbing): Refers to the tension force exerted in the climb line by the climber working at angles to the tie-in point. Increased angles increase back pull in the climb line. Sometimes referred to as side pull.

BACK SPLICE-(Rigging and knots): The back splice is used to terminate the ends of twisted rope. It prevents the line from unraveling and produces a knob or "stop" on the end of the line that a climber's knot (tautline hitch) will not slide past. Certain "plaited" ropes can also be back spliced.

BACK SWING: An object held by a line can swing back and forth like a pendulum. Back swing can have negative connotations.

BAD BOUNCE: Accident when free falling limbs, tops and wood. Depending on how cither land, tliey could take a bad bounce and damage something.

BAD GROUND: Tree falling term indicating the undesirable contour of a lay to fall trees in. Falling trees on bad ground results in breakage.

BAR AXIS: Relative planes and pivot points along the width and length of a chainsaw bar. Knowledge of the bar axis is elemental to well aligned cuts.

BAR BOW: Long saw bars will bow when held horizontally. This can cause the chain to be thrown off the bar.

BARBER CHAIR: A tree falling term indicating an undesired and dangerous massive split running through the trunk of a tree.

BARKING UP-(Climbing): Using the climbing spurs and having the unfortunate occurrence of the tree bark fouling and getting stuck to the point. Barking up causes "kicking-out" and the inability to reset the points until the bark is removed.

BASE LINE-(Tree cutting and falling): The climber and tree faller will frequently use a base line to line up, start and finish the cuts they use. Such base lines are often scratched, scribed or marked on the tree with chalk or crayon. Most experienced people will use an imaginary base line as reference for their cuts.

BELAY-(Climbing origins): In particular, the act of holding fast a load in a line. In single-line techniques, a figure eight descender, or similar friction device, is anchored and utilized by one climber, for its braking effect, to hold or lower another climber. A method of aerial rescue used to lower an injured climber to the ground.

BELLY-(Tree form, rigging): In trees, their spars and limbs, most will be found to have some belly, or sweep in them. The belly is important to consider in many situations. Long spans of rigging will have belly. The point where a line is tight enough to take the visible belly out of a span can be called the belly point.

BIND: Common pressure and tension force encountered while cutting trees. Gravity is the major contributor to bind. Resting, pivot and balance points will shift the relative angle of the force creating recognizable distinctions in it. Top bind, bottom bind etc.

BITE-(Rigging term): In rigging, the bite has several synonyms. The "line of bite" refers to that area in which rigging will cover in the event of its failure. Stay out of the line of bite. A "bite" in a line in one sense has negative connotations when it refers to a line cutting into itself. Many knots will cut into themselves from a hard bite where the lines cross. In another sense "setting a line with a bite" would be for the purpose of fixing a line's position from slipping. A bite can keep a line from slipping around or from an object. Bite is also referred to as the drag force on a line when it runs over a limb or through a crotch.

BITE AND BIND DEVICES-(Climbing gear, safety lines, lanyards); Simple but often crude devices used by some climbers to assist adjustment procedures in the length of the safety line.

BLEED OFF: Term used to imply the release or loss of oil out of the high pressure side of a hydraulic ram or jack.

BLOCK-(Rigging tools): A pulley used specifically as an axis point to change the angle of pull in a line. The design in the frame housing, pulley and attachment apparatus gives blocks certain specialized features and names. Examples: snatch blocks, gang blocks, high lead blocks etc.

BLOCK OUT: A descriptive term, but often wrongly used, that indicates a certain style of undercut used in large trees. Rather than a wedge shaped undercut, a block shaped one is made that requires knocking, splitting and cleaning out. After that the stump is sniped. Synonymous with the Humboldt cut.

BLOCK AND TACKLE-(Rigging tools): A near ancient design rope and pulley system used to increase the power of pull you apply to it. Gang blocks are used in this application. Block and tackle design, in spite of its age old concept, is actively used in modern industry.

BLOW OUT-(Tree falling): Term indicating a massive rupture in the high pressure side of a hydraulic jack Usually as a result of the wind working the tree. Blow out is also synonymous to the action of structural failure in a tree. In this case the side of a tree can blow out from undue pressure exerted on it.

BODY BELT:-(Climbing gear): This is a common support belt used by utility line men, often referred to as a "back belt." In climbing trees the body belt has been used but is not recommended because of its inability to properly support a climber from a single line.

BOGGED DOWN-(Chipping brush): When you stall a chipper with too much material in its chute, Don't bog down the chipper. -(Saw handling): Long bars can bog down in a cut if you don't keep the cut clean and free of chips.

BORE CUT-(Tree cutting): Saw handling technique of driving the tip of the power saw into the tree, vertically or horizontally. The cut is best begun using the bottom quarter of the tip.

BOS'N'S CHAIR: Nautical origin pertaining to rigging. Specifically a makeshift belt or saddle of sorts used for climbing and support. Many people have contrived a bos'n's chair from a "hank" or spare piece of line for the purpose of fulfilling a certain task or duty related to climbing.

BOTTOM BIND: A tree lying over a hump, or whose ends are suspended in the air, is known to have bottom bind.

BRAKE-(Rigging): To stall, hold or tether a load in a line by wrapping it around a limb, trunk or other suitable object. Wrapping a line creates bite and drag on it, and thus the ability to brake a load. There are many specifically designed tools capitalizing on the principle and used as "line brakes".

BREAK AWAY-(Tools, rope and rigging): Introduction of a weak link (a lighter line) into a rope or rigging scheme for fail-point control in the system.

BROAD TREE: A wide category of trees that grow in a squat manor, or spread out by a series of multiple leads. More broad than tall.

BRUSHING OUT-(Tree climbing and cutting): A phase in the removal of a tree by wrecking it out. You will begin the removal by brushing out the tree first by removing the tree's limbs, usually from the bottom up.

BUCK BACK: Method of bucking the tree by which a faller will first limb the tree out to the top while measuring and calculating the best yield of desirable log segments. Then they will buck back.

BUCK DOWN-(Tree falling): Method of bucking short lengths off the butt of a hung-up tree in order to get it down or out of the tree it's hung up in.

BUCKING-(Cutting the tree): Cross sectional cuts through a tree's structure, after it has been fallen, to render it into specific segments or lengths.

BUCKLING-(Tree falling): A term indicating the failure of the wood in the stump of a tree to support or hold the pressure of a wedge or tree jack.

BUD BREAK-(Tree physiology): The commencement of a new season's growth by active buds. In contrast to bud set.

BULL LINE-(Rigging): A generally heavy line used to pull, hold and lower limbs, tops, logs and wood.

BULL SAWS-(Rigging): Typically a crosscut saw in design featuring tooth and raker principle.

BURL: A mass of adventitious tissue and buds occurring in the stumps of many trees. Burl is highly valued for its unique color and grain patterns.

BURNOUT-(Rappelling): A fast descent out of a tree using the climb line. If you descend out of a high tie-in quickly with synthetic rope the tautline hitch can melt and fuse to the climb line. The knot can be pried off but will probably be so melted it will need to be discarded. Fusing can be avoided by descending slow or using arborist grade Manila rope for the tautline hitch.

BUSHWHACK-(Tree trimming): A loosely used term indicating improper technique or style in trimming a tree. A work style reflecting negligence. For example: That guy bushwhacked that tree! and it looks terrible!

BUTT BELT-(Climbing gear): A climber's belt or saddle. The butt belt supports a climber by their waist and fanny.

BUTT FIRST: In rigging and lowering you may desire that the work lead in the descent with its butt first. Limbs and tops on a line will lower through other limbs and brush more consistently without hanging up when they are lowered butt first.

BUTT HEAVY-(Rigging application): Refers to how a line holds a particular piece of work. For example, you may fix the line to hold a limb, top or piece of wood so it is butt heavy, in contrast to its being top or tip heavy. This has significance in how the work settles or lays into the line.

BUTT LOG: Usually the first, or largest log out of a tree is the butt log.

BUTT TIE-(Rigging application): To fix a line to the butt of the work. Butt tying is frequently used by a climber to hold the work by its butt end. The purpose is either to steady the work, secure it or lower it by the butt tie.

CANOPY: In a tree, the outermost envelope of foliage that gives the tree its form is known as its canopy. In a woods a number of canopies can coexist. Upper and lower canopy lines.

CAMBIUM: The active living and growing tissue located between the bark and sapwood is the cambium. Undifferentiated tissue that is the engineer and builder of the tree. Referred to as meristematic tissue.

CALK BOOTS-(Tree falling tools): A work boot with nails, or spikes, in the sole that enables the timber faller to walk on trees and logs without slipping. Synonymous with "corks," or cork boots.

CAPSTAN-(Rigging tools): A rotating drum or spool powered by PTO, hydraulic or hand lever with ratchet and pawl. With wraps of line taken around the capstan you can pull, tension, hold or lower loads. This essentially makes the capstan a line winch and brake in one unit.

CATH-(Heavy equipment): A short version name of the Caterpillar tractor. The term "CAT" is regularly and loosely used synonymously when referring to other makes of heavy equipment also.

CAT FACE: A loosely used term indicating a localized defect in the trunk of a tree. Most cat-face defects are a result of the tree's inability to properly or neatly heal over a wound or scar. Often believed to be caused by bacterial infection.

CHAIN BRAKE: Clutch drum brake mechanism used on most larger power saws to stop the cutting chain during kickback incidents. Mostly inertia activated.

CHOKER-(Steel rigging): In simple description, a wire rope snare used primarily to pull logs with. Chokers utilize a "nubbin end" and sliding "bell" to gain their bite and holding power. They are ultimately handy in tree work for their quick set and release.

CLASH-(Climbing gear, rigging): Dee ring arrangements on some climbing saddles can clash, or attempt to mesh together and be culprit to snap roll out and disengagement. Crossing of lines or fasteners in certain rigging schemes can bring clash and possible maladies.

CLEAN BURN: A clean burn will be absent of any unburned ignitables. The end of any control burn should be a clean one.

CLEANING OUT: Method of saw handling where the operator uses the bar and chain to pull out or remove excess saw chips in a cut. Correction of a dutchman occurring in one corner is known as cleaning out the corner.

CLIMB LINE-(Climbers rope)**:** Generally 1/2 inch diameter twisted or braided firm nylon line. Used primarily for support while working in the tree.

CLINCHING A SAFETY: Climbing technique used to hold oneself to the tree by holding the safety line tightly to the tree with both hands when changing footholds. Also used as a means to arrest a fall in the event of losing footing. Clinch the safety tight around the tree to hold you.

COLLAPSE-(Tree falling): A term indicating the inability of a tree to support itself. Massive structural failure in the trunk of a tree.

COME-ALONG-(Heavy equipment): A simple spool or sheave with ratchet and pawl used primarily for pulling and tensioning lines.

COMPENSATION: Tree falling term indicating a change in the gun of the undercut or distribution of holding wood in the hinge for the purpose of correcting, or steering, an offset (side leaning) tree to a lay.

COMPRESSION: Tree falling term indicating the inability of the wood in the stump to hold the pressure of a wedge or tree jack.

CONFLICTING HINGE: A hinge aggravated into a bind from misaligned, mismatched and unsquare cuts. A hinge in conflict can stall a tree from felling.

COOS BAY-(Tree falling cut): A nondescriptive term implying the particular unconventional technique used as a safety precaution in cutting heavily forward leaning trees.

CONIFEROUS: Meaning to bear seed born in cones. Also indicates a large class of trees; redwood, fir, cedar, pine etc.

CONTROL BURN: A contained fire used for the purpose of brush, slash and debris disposal.

CONVENTIONAL-(Tree falling): When the diagonal cut is taken over the undercut, it is referred to be conventional.

CORNER: Tree falling term indicating the outside points of the hinge wood.

COUPLING-(Tree falling, bucking): A plug or portion of unsevered wood in a cut that keeps the cut from opening or coming apart. Sometimes intentional, sometimes not.

CREEP-(Rigging and knots): This is the event when a line is under load and the securing knot begins to untie itself. Many knots, particularly hitches, when improperly finished will creep and pull through.

CRIPPLE-(Tree falling and cutting): The placement of certain selected cuts varying in depth and angle to serve the purpose of promoting breakage at that point.

CROSSCUT-(Tree cutting): The crosscut is one of the five basic cuts used in tree work. As in bucking the tree, you must cross cut it into lengths. The crosscut is also synonymous to the old saws used in early logging and tree work.

CROTCHING THE LINE-(Rigging): A technique used by a climber to lower work out of a tree on a line. The line is run through, around or over a suitable limb, crotch or stub. The particular configuration depends on the braking force needed.

CUT OFF-(Tree cutting error): In any cut utilizing the guidance of hinge wood. The error is severing the hinge wood before it performs its function. Example: The faller lost the tree because he cut it off.

CUTTER-(Tools): A saw chain is made up of cutters, straps and drivers. Also pertains to the operator of a power saw. That guy is a cutter.

DEAD ENDING-(Rigging): The act of fixing or securing the end of a line that is under, or will experience, a load.

DEADMAN: In rigging, the deadman is a suitable anchor used to hold a vehicle or winch that will be used for pulling. Aerial lift trucks utilize a deadman control as a safety feature. This deadman control must be engaged for the other controls to function.

DEFECT: Term indicating an undesirable trait in a tree. Trees that have a defect are generally removed.

DIAGONAL CUT-(Tree falling): The diagonal cut is the second cut used to open the face of the falling cut. -(Tree cutting): The diagonal is sometimes referred to as the salami cut.

DIEBACK-(Tree trimming): The event of a lead, spar or limb dying after being cut back. An unfortunate event to the tree for the beginner trimmer who cannot anticipate the results of their ignorant trimming.

DIELECTRIC SHIELDS: Aerial lift trucks, line clearance trimming. Electrical insulation material used in the construction of tools and machines. It is nonconductive when clean and diy.

DOGGED UP-(Saw handling): Those sharp points on the front of the case on a power saw are called dogs, bumper spikes elsewhere. In most large cuts you will use the dogs to anchor the saw to the tree. While doing so, you will be dogged up.

DOG AROUND-(Tree falling, bucking): Method of saw handling where a cut is aligned and started on one side of a log or tree and the faller uses the dogs on the saw to pivot, sweep and progress the cut to the far or off side.

DOG LEG-(Climbing)**:** The dog leg is a crook in the trunk of a tree. Mostly associated with the resumption of a new top recurring where an old one died back It can present itself as an obstacle in both climbing and working.

DOUBLE-LINE-(Climbing): A line fixed in the tree in which both ends are utilized for ascending and descending. In double-line technique there is a fixed end to the climber's belt and a running part, or free end, that the climber's knot (tautline hitch) is fashioned to. Double-line technique is the most common and practical means of entering and working in the average tree. In contrast to single-line.

DOUBLE SAFETY TECHNIQUE-(Climbing)**:** Synonymous with double crotching in that one line is securing you while you are fixing the other. Such technique is regularly used to overcome most obstacles in average climbing situations.

DOUBLE STUMPING-(Tree falling): A rare circumstance in falling trees where it becomes a necessity to place an alternative undercut over the previous one. Experience has shown that most successful double stumping is only possible by placing the secondary falling cut well over the first. Grain interruption, shear and collapse of the wood between the two cuts can occur, foiling the alternative attempt.

DOUBLE UP-(Wedging the tree): Stacking wedges on top of one another is known as doubling them up.

DRIFT: Tree falling term indicating the undesirable inclination of trees with side lean to miss the lay through fault of the lean and/or offset limb weight.

DROOPING-(Tree form, morphology): Structure in the tree that has negative angle to it. It hangs down or is pendedt in nature.

DROP-(Ropes, climb lines): One half of a climb-line length has been referred to as its drop length. It is the length of the line when set in double-line configuration. When climbing tall trees the amount of drop you have can be short of what you need.

DROP CROTCH-(Trimming and pruning): Term indicating a main lead being cut back, or down, to another crotch, or suitable lead.

DROP LINE-(Climbing and rigging): A line that a climber uses to check the plumb, or favor, of vertical work. Also synonymous with a light line used to reach the ground. Similar to a throw line but lighter in weight. The term has also been used to indicate a piece of line used as rigging to catch loads that are dropped.

DROP START-(Saw handling): A technique or method of starting a power saw. The saw is held by the right hand and dropped down while the left hand tugs on the starting pull rope. Such technique is frowned upon by many institutions.

DUFF: Nutrient rich decomposed organic material that forms a strata layer under a tree's shed leaves and woody debris. Highly flammable when dry.

DUTCHMAN-(Tree cutting, tree falling): Any amount of saw kerf left in front of the hinge. Usually resulting from failure of the diagonal cut to properly meet with the undercut. Generally recognized as an error.

DYNAMIC LOADING-(Climbing, rigging): Momentum gained from centrifugal force or fall. Avoid situations where dynamic loading exceeds the safe working load in a line.

EASE OFF: In tethering and lowering a load you will frequendy ease off on the line that supports it. You will also ease off certain pieces of work into a line for the purpose of minimizing dynamic loading.

END BIND-(Tree falling and bucking): Pressure or compression force in a log or tree. Logs with end bind will often stay together after being bucked through.

EXCHANGING HOLDS-(Climbing): A common maneuver, but often awkward, where a climber will change their hold on a piece of work, wood, limb or top, to retrieve or put away their hand saw or work line.

FACE CUT-(Tree cutting, falling): Term used to indicate the undercut opening of the falling cut. When you place the falling cut, you face it to the direction of fall. Example: I faced up this tree to fall that way.

FALLER: A person actively engaged in the business of falling timber. A person who is hired by the logger to fall trees.

FARMER JOHN-(Knots and splicing): The farmer John is a simple wrap spliced eye in steel cable. Synonymous with "wild eye splice".

FAVOR-(Tree falling): The direction a tree would naturally fall is its favor.

FIRM LAY-(Ropes, knots and splices): The firmness in a particular grade of rope. Manufacturing process can produce soft, firm and hard grades of rope.

FIXED BACK-(Ropes and climbing): A method of securing the free tail end of the tautline hitch in order to prevent it from creeping through the knot. In this case the tail end must be sufficiently long enough to knot, or fix back, to the saddle ring.

FIXED LINE-(Climbing): A climb-line set in the tree for the purpose of using it to assist entrance into the tree.

FLIPLINING-(Climbing): Technique by which a climber works a stout rope safety (flipline) around and up the trunks of large diameter trees.

FOLLOW THROUGH-(Saw handling): In much of handling a power saw you must calculate follow through of the bar and chain through a cut. Failing to monitor or consider the follow through can result in bar tip contact, kickback, severed lines and personal injury.

FOOT LOCK-(Climbing): An ancient method of rope climbing where climbers utilize their feet to assist a vertical ascent up a fixed line.

FORCE FEED-(Rigging and running ropes): A line under load will fail to run through a crotch if the bite or wraps are in excess of the load's ability to pull the line. The load will stall and the line will have to be force fed through the crotch to get it to run.

FOULED-(Rigging and climbing): A tangled or hung-up line is a fouled line. Blocks can also become fouled.

FREE END-(Throw line and ropes): The running part of the climb line and throw line have been referred to as the free end. That is the end that is not fixed or working.

FREE FALLING-(Cutting the tree, tree falling): Falling a tree without the aid of a "prompt" is known as free falling or falling it off the saw. No other tools or help is needed to accomplish getting the tree to fall.

FREE STANDING-(Cutting the tree, climbing): To a faller a "tree," to a climber "parts" of a tree, that stand vertical and absent of any favor are known to be free standing.

FREE STYLE-(Climbing): The most natural way to climb in small structure or to get past many obstacles in climbing is by utilizing the available hand and footholds. Quite often referred to as the "three point method".

FULL PROFILE-(Climbing): Refers to the cross sectional profile of a cutting blade. A blade with a full profile is a thick blade.

FUSING-(Ropes, climb lines): Extreme pressure and friction can produce sufficient temperatures to fuse, or melt, the fiber in synthetic rope. A drastic loss in line strength can occur during fusing.

GAP-(Tree falling): A term indicating a wide opening immediately in front of the hinge wood.

GIRDLING: A malady in the trunk or stem of a tree where the flow of nutrients is interrupted or blocked. Vines, varmints and vandals contribute to girdling.

GOOD FORM: A tree free of defect is a tree of good form.

GRIP-(Rigging tools): Any number of devices designed to grab lines, wire and cable by jaw, lever and cam action.

GROUND MAN: A person working on the ground serving the needs of aclimber is known as a ground man.

GROUND RUN-(Rigging): Any run of line that parallels the ground while actively under a load. Opposite of aerial run.

GULLETS-(Cutting tools): Recesses in the blade of a crosscut or bull saw used to aid in cleaning out the excess saw dust in the kerf.

GUN: Tree falling term indicating the perpendicular of the undercut, or the direction the tree is intended to fall.

GUNNING STICKS: A pair of folding sticks that a tree faller uses to verify the gun of the undercut.

GUT: Term indicating the bottom or broad side of a chainsaw bar. When you cut with the gut of the bar, the saw chips are expelled out of the clutch and sprocket side case, and by such action the saw can pull you to the work.

HAND LINE: A light line used aloft by a climber to haul up tools and materials. Synonymous with "pass line".

HAND OVER HAND-(Climbing): Pulling oneself up a line over a short distance primarily using handholds on the line.

HANGERS-(Trimming, timber falling): In trimming, the hanger refers to the limbs and leads that were cut by the climber which did not fall out of the tree. In tree falling the hanger (widow maker) is a byproduct of the work and seen hanging in neighboring trees.

HARD RIGGING: Steel cable, chain and associated hardware.

HEAD BACK: Trimming and pruning term indicating the manner in which a limb or lead is cut back. It is generally stubbed off with intention of new growth occurring in the region of the cut.

HEAD LEAN: A tree that leans to the lay is known as a "head leaner".

HEART ROT: Wood rot occurring within the heart of the tree. Peculiar to older or mature trees.

HIGH CLIMBERS-(Climbing gear): Specifically a boot with tall tops that lace to the knee. The high tops are preferred by some climbers for their shin and leg bone protection against wear from the shank of the climbing spurs.

HINGE-(Tree falling): The wood left in the stump used to guide the fall of a tree is known as the hinge wood. In tree cutting, implying action, a climber will hinge or "swing" many of the limbs they cut out of the tree.

HOISTING-(Climbing): Having a double-line set in the tree and utilizing persons on the ground to pull the climber up by hoisting on one end of the line. In another sense, "body" hoisting, the climber pulls up on the line and then heaves their lower torso up and over an objective limb or spar, much like pole vaulting.

HOLDING LINE-(Tree falling): A line rigged to hold a tree with side lean from drifting. The holding line swings the tree.

HOLDING STRAP-(Tree falling): An uncut portion of wood immediately in back of the stump used for the purpose of holding the tree from falling while the back cut is being placed.
-(Tree cutting): A climber will often leave a holding strap to act as a hinge for the purpose of guiding or holding limbs, small tops or sections of wood.

HOLE-(Climbing and logging term): In climbing, the hole is the area that is available to a climber for discarding their trimmings. In logging, the term indicates the workplace where logs are pulled from.

HOLLOW GRIND-(Cutting tools): The profile of a cutting blade that is carved out between the cutting edge and the back. A narrow or thin blade. A blade with a hollow sharpens quicker and cuts with less pressure than one with a full profile.

HUMBOLDT: A County on the coast of Northern California. Tree falling term implying that the diagonal cut is placed below the undercut. The action of the Humboldt cut induces the butt of the tree to slip off the stump.

INVERTED POSITION-(Climbing): In climbing, to be inverted is to be upside down.

JACK PLATE-(Tools): A broad and heavy steel plate with a gimbaled socket that fits on the top ball end of a hydraulic tree jack.

JACK SEAT-(Tree falling): The jack seat is a notch you cut in the stump that serves the purpose of supporting a hydraulic jack.

JAM KNOT-(Tree climbing): A wad of rope that is coiled, wrapped and tucked together that a climber uses as an aid in his climbing and work. The jam knot adds terminal weight to a line and is useful for throwing and securing a line in a remote limb or crotch.

JOY STICK: Hydraulic control that incorporates all articulation of an aerial lift rig in one control: XYZ axis control. In contrast to separate controls.

KEEPER: The gate or sliding mechanism in a snap or carabiner is often referred to as the keeper. Always make sure that the keeper functions properly, has a strong spring and does not ever become fouled.

KEEPING AHEAD OF THE SPLIT: Tree falling and cutting term indicating the ability of a climber or faller to progress a crosscut through a part of the tree faster than the present tension in the cut can promote splitting.

KERF: The width, thickness or opening of a saw cut is known as its kerf.

KICKBACK-(Saw handling): Refers to the action of a chain saw when its bar tip makes unintended contact with an object. The action is to have the bar kick back at you. -(Tree falling): Refers to the action of a fallen tree settling back on or beyond its strump.
-(Climbing): Kickback refers to an uncomfortable occurrence of the shank on the climbing spurs losing its preferred position and settling back behind the calf of the leg.

KICK-OUT: Tree climbing term indicating the inability of a climber's spur to support their weight, usually as a result of loose bark or poor penetration into the wood. This term connotes the unfortunate events that preclude a probable fall.

LATENT BUD-(Tree physiology): As all buds are capable of new growth the latent bud can persist on a tree without ever coming into active growth.

LATERAL-(Tree morphology): When a main lead of a limb sprouts and matures, an offshoot that aligns at an angle to the side of the main lead is called a lateral. Example: You will often prune or cut back a main lead to a lateral.

LATERAL POSITION CHANGE: This term is best described by how a mirror can alter left and right lateral images. In climbing it holds some significance as to your left or right angled position to do certain work in those situations where you can work either side.

LAY-(Tree falling): The ground that a tree is to be felled to is referred to as the lay. There are good lays and there are bad ones, or difficult ones. The lay is all important for saving the tree.

LAYOUT-(Tree falling): This term indicates a lay for a tree that has been built to save the tree. The building and preparation of a layout is highly variable. Lays are predominantly built with heavy equipment to alter the ground for a "good lay." In casual conversation the layout often refers to an opinion or idea of the workplace or company.

LEAD: Tree falling and cutting term indicating the direction and order a timber faller will lay out the timber. Example: My lead for the trees on this slope will be up and down the hill.

LEG LOCK-(Climbing): In much of tree work a climber will rely on a leg lock for a hold on a limb or crotch. In actual practice you will lock your knee around such limb or crotch.

LIFE LINE-(Climbing): A loosely used term that is synonymous with many lines a climber will use. Climb lines, safeties, lanyards, etc.

LIMB LOCK-(Tree falling): This term refers to a tangled limb condition between neighboring trees or different parts of the same tree. Limb locked trees can present certain inconveniences in tree falling.

LIMB RAISING: Tree trimming term that indicates the removal of a tree's lower limbs.

LIMBING: The procedures used in the removal of a tree's limbs by a climber or faller.

LINE CLEARANCE TRIMMER-(Climbing): An individual who is actively engaged in the profession of power line clearance trimming, a person who trims trees away from the power lines.

LOG-(Timber falling): The segments that a professional timber faller bucks or renders a tree into are called logs.

LOG VEER-(Bucking the tree): The act of a log swinging to the side as it settles is called veer. In most situations a faller can control veer by how they trip the bind to settle a log or logs.

LOGGER: An often misused term improperly indicating anybody who works in the woods. The logger is the company owner, or operator, who supplies the means, heavy equipment and manpower to harvest timber by private, State, Federal or corporate contract. All other persons who work for the logger have their own descriptive titles: faller, choker setter, Cat skinner, loader, driver etc.

LONG GROUND: Timber falling term indicating the desirable feature of the terrain to lay trees in. Long ground is good ground to fall and save trees in.

MANILA-(Climbing and rigging): Old style rope. Refers to the fibers of the abaca plant used for the manufacture of Manila hemp rope, not to be confused with hemp rope made from the fibers of Cannabis sativa, or marijuana. Manila has been used throughout the ages.

MIDLINE-(Rigging)**:** Within a span of line or between load and anchor points there is the midline. Its significance implies an operation in the rigging within its midline. The forming of certain knots is often done midline in the rigging.

MISALIGNED: Tree cutting term indicating improper matching of two converging cuts. Synonymous with mismatched.

MISMANUFACTURED: Term used in professional timber falling indicating an inaccurate log length.

MOUSE TRAP: Timber falling term implying certain danger in the falling or bucking of a tree. Domino like mechanical events similar to those of the Rube Goldberg contraptions that work down a line or through an obscure course. Example: I will decline to fall this tree because it's a mouse trap.

MULTIPLE: An often used term indicating a group of trees that are well grown together at the stump, or where the main lead of a tree divides into multiple tops.

NAIL KNOT: Fisherman's knot used to join a lighter line to a heavier line. The way the knot is made has been used for ages in the "serving" of a line's end.

NAP FINNISH-(Rope): Through the course of normal use a rope will develop a nap, or fuzzy finish to it.

NIP CUT: One of the five basic cuts used in tree cutting. When nipping you use the tip of the cutting bar.

OFF CORNER-(Tree falling): The opposite side, or corner, in a tree falling cut. More often referred to as the far corner.

OUT OF PHASE-(Tree physiology): Term suggesting the rank and over vigorous growth that occurs as a result of heavy cutting, or over trimming, in moderately aged trees. As compared to the normal or average growth in the same.

OUT PULL-(Ropes, climbing and rigging): A rarely used term implying the obtuse, negative or adverse direction of pull in a line.

OUTRIGGER-(Aerial lift trucks): The stanchions that give a lift device its stability are known as the outriggers.

OVERHANG: Line clearance trimming term used to describe the position of a tree's limbs or trunk over high voltage power lines. Line clearance trimmers remove lots of overhangs.

PASS BLOCK-(Rigging): A small lightweight block that a climber sets in the tree used for hauling up heavier rigging and tools. Sometimes referred to as a "hand line block."

PASS LINE-(Rigging, line): A light line that runs through a pass block. A hand line.

PASSING THE LINE-(Climbing): A loosely used term indicating the chance or ability for a climber to maneuver a sefety or climb line over an obstacle without having to unsecure it from the belt.

PARACHUTE EFFECT-(Tree falling and topping): A term that indicates how the wind resistance of a tree's limbs can cause it to roll over during its fall.

PEAVEY-(Tools): A hand lever device with a point and swivel hook on one end used for turning or rolling small logs and poles. Also called cant hook.

PEEL OUT-(Tree climbing): This term indicates the inability of the point on a climbing spur to stick to the wood. It results in the point peeling a strip of bark off of thin skinned trees.

PENDENT: Term used to describe how a tree's limbs may droop or hang downward.

PIE CUT: Tree falling term referring to the undercut chunk that falls out of the face cut. This product of the face cut has also been referred to as the cheese, the undercut, the block, etc.

PIG EAR: Tree falling term indicating an improper flush cut when limbing the tree after it's been felled. Rather than a true stub, the result is a pointed one resembling a pig's ear. Hence the name.

PINCH: Tree falling term indicating the tight mergence of the diagonal cut to the undercut, or, the lack of a gap where the two cuts meet in front of the hinge.

PLUMB: Tree falling term indicating a straight and vertical standing tree that is absent of any lean.

PLUMB BOB: The plumb bob is simply a weight on the end of a string that a faller uses for a vertical reference when checking or plumbing a tree.

POLARITY: Pertaining to the "direction of flow" of nutrients through woody tissue. For successful grafts the polarity of the stock and scion must match.

POLE PRUNER, SAW-(Trimming tools): An extendible pole with a pruner head or saw attachment used to cut small to medium size limbs at far reaches in the tree.

POLLARD: Tree trimming term indicating a brash form of heading back a tree's limbs and spars. A generally heavy cut on the structure of a tree. Often detrimental.

POLY: Prefix meaning many. Also used to refer to plastic rope.

POSITION LIMBS: Tree climbing term indicating a choice of limb or limbs used for the purpose of bringing the static and running part of the climb line on a chosen side of the trunk. Often used synonymously with "stopper" limbs.

POWER HEAD: The main case (motor) of a chainsaw is referred to as the power head.

PREFERRED LENGTH-(Timber falling and bucking): The professional timber faller is obliged to buck the trees they fall into preferred lengths specified by the buyer or owner of the trees.

PROFILES-(Cutting tools): The profile refers to the side, or cross sectional view of an object. The blades or cutters on all cutting tools have certain recommended profiles to adhere to when sharpening them. The points on the climbing spurs also have specified profiles to follow when sharpening them.

PROMPT-(Tree falling and cutting): To initiate the fall of a tree by wedge, jack or pulling implement.

PULASKI-(Tools): An ax in design with a spade or pick integrated on the back side. Useful for cleaning around stumps, chopping and digging. The pulaski is often used by the timber faller to pick and dean out the undercut in large trees.

PULL: Tree falling term with many meanings. In one sense the term can mean the high corner of the hinge being used to pull, hold or swing the tree during its fall. In this case the corner can fail and "pull" out. In another sense pull indicates the undesirable event of wood pulling out of the tree from improper falling technique or uncontrollable circumstances. In the obvious sense, to pull, is to put a line in the tree and pull it.

PULSING-(Saw handling): How an individual throttles or pulses the power of a chainsaw. Much of saw handling consists of a wide degree of pulsing. In the majority of cases, you can identify an individual by the sound of how they pulse their saw.

QUARTENING-(Timber falling, climbing): Falling a tree diagonal on a hill side or slope is known as quartering it. Quartering is also synonymous with falling or topping trees within 45 degrees either side of their favor.

RAINBOWED OVER: A loosely used term indicating bottom bind in a tree, whose top and butt are suspended in the air from the tree resting on a knob or knoll. A tall tree so suspended will be bowed.

RANGE FINDER: An optical device used for determining the range or height of a tree.

RAPPEL-(Climbing): An old world trade term implying a climber's descent down a fixed line.

REAMING: Saw handling technique whereby the operator keeps a cut or saw kerf from closing by boring and repeated cleaning with the saw bar tip and chain.

RECOIL: Rigging term indicating the tendency of a stretched out line to spring or snap back after breaking.

RED LINE-(Tree falling, jacking the tree): The red line is the maximum operating pressure shown on the gauge of a Silvey hydraulic tree jack.

RENEWAL SPUR—(Pruning): A one year old shoot, or season's growth pruned down to a two or three bud spur for the sole purpose of using those buds for future shoots or stems to prune again.

RIG: A loosely used term implying the setting, or fixing, of a line or block to a stump, tree or whatever. For example: I rigged that tree. Aerial lift trucks are often referred to as rigs.

RIGHT OF WAYS: In line clearance trimming, right of ways refer to the deeded area in which urban or cross country power lines run.

RIPPING-(Tree cutting): A longitudinal cut (rip cut) through the crotch unions of multiple trees for the purpose of splitting them apart. Ripping is also synonymous to a longitudinal cut used to split logs or wood.

ROLL OUT: Rigging term indicating the action of a snap keeper, or snap hook, becoming tripped loose by an undesired twisting and pressure on it.

ROLLING LOOPS: Climbing technique whereby a climber uses a forearm thrust on a slack line to induce loops to travel through it. A method of working slack over, or through, a crotch or limb.

ROLLING OVER: Climbing technique where a climber commits themselves to be drawn over to the low side of a trunk, limb or spar.

ROTATE-(Rigging): The tendency of a line to turn, or impart a turn to what it's fastened to or supports. A generally undesirable trait of twisted rope, or other rope, that has some inherent twist in it.

RUN: Rigging term implying the length and course of a line that is set for doing some work.

RUNNING PART: Climbing term indicating the loose, or free, end of the climb line that runs through the tautline hitch.

RUN OUT-(Tree cutting): Failure to keep a saw cut running true to course is known as run out. The term also indicates a method of shaking a line to get any twist, or tangles, to run out of it.

SAFE WORKING LOAD, SWL-(Rigging and tools): The maximum rated load for a fastener or line is known as its safe working load rating.

SAFETY LINE-(Climbing gear): A generally short, but stout, piece of rope that a climber uses around the trunk or spars of the tree for the purpose of its support, or safety. The safety line has many synonyms such as lanyard, scare strap, flipline, daisy line.

SALAMI CUT: A term indicating the slope or angle in a cut running through the trunk, limb or stem of a tree. Often used to get each part of the cut to slide by one another. Also synonymous to the negative quality in an improperly angled buck.

SAP CUT: Tree cutting term referring to the technique of severing the sapwood from the comers of the hinge wood. The purpose is to prevent wood pull or splitting in a cut.

SAPWOOD-(Tree physiology): Term indicating the woody and nutrient conductive tissue just under the bark of the tree. Properly referred to as xylem tissue. White in color and regularly distinguishable from the heartwood of most trees.

SAVE: Tree falling term implying the falling of a valuable tree without breaking it. Example: The faller saved the tree.

SAWING LEAN: Tree falling term indicating a deep undercut within the trunk of the tree for the purpose of undermining its balance, or center of gravity, to promote a favor in the tree.

SCION: The variety grafted to the stock is called the scion.

SCOPE-(Climbing and rigging): The length, range or sweep of a line or cable is known as it scope.

SECURITY KNOT-(Climbing and rigging): The so-called security knot is merely a half hitch in the end of a line used to jam, foul or prevent the end of the line from pulling through a knot.

SEIZURE-(Ropes, rigging and knots): A knot drawn so tight that it cannot be untied is seized.

SELECT CUT: Term used to describe the practice of cutting and logging select trees from the rest. Specific criteria in the mode, style or type of selection can vary the practice considerably.

SERVING-(Ropes, rigging): To wrap the end of a line with a lighter line for the purpose of keeping the line from unraveling.

SET-(Ropes, rigging): Set is the desire of a line to stay kinked or twisted. Many lines and cable will form set from being knotted and drawn up to tightly.

SET BACK-(Tree falling and topping): The act of a tree or its top settling on the back cut. Set back has many negative connotations in tree work.

SET DOWN-(Tree falling): Severing the hinge wood in a limb locked tree will result in it setting down and binding the saw.

SHAKEN: Tree falling term that refers to the particular way a tree breaks, or more precisely "splits," but still stays together. This term is also synonymous to how the bark can shake loose from the sapwood on a freshly fallen tree.

SHEAR: Shear is one of the five forces encountered when bucking the tree. With shear the cuts slide by one another when they come apart. See also **BUCKING THE TREE** in **Chapter 34**.

SHIFTING THE BALANCE-(Climbing and topping the tree): By removing the limbs on one side of a treetop you can shift the balance of it to a desired side.

SHIM-(Falling the tree): A steel or aluminum plate used to take up excess space. When jacking trees you will place shims to gain additional lift over the jack's maximum lift.

SHIMMY: An old climbing technique where a person uses only their legs and hands to grasp and maneuver their way up a tree.

SHOOT BACK-(Tree falling): Indicates the action of a fallen tree settling back beyond its stump. This could be hazardous to the faller.

SHORING-(Rigging and equipment): Usually wide and thick timbers used to build a secure base area to set outriggers or stanchions on.

SHORT GROUND: Falling term indicating the undesirable contour of the ground in which to lay trees in. Short ground is bad ground to lay trees in and results in breakage.

SIDEHILL: Falling term referring to how a timber faller lays the trees on a slope. In this case the timber will lie on the slope, parallel to the contour line, much like it would on flat ground.

SIDE ANGLE-(Climbing): Refers to any time a climber is working at a hard angle to the tie-in. With hard side angles you begin losing the tie-in support.

SIDE BOUND-(Falling and bucking the tree): Refers to the relative angle of the pressure, or tension force (bind) in a log or tree. In this case the bind is to the side.

SIDE DRIFT: Tree falling term indicating the undesirable tendency for trees with side lean or heavy offset limbs to break off from the hinge and drift to that side as they are falling toward the lay.

SIDE LOADING-(Climbing and topping the tree): A method of shifting the balance of a top by which a climber will remove the limbs off one side of it and load them in amongst the limbs on the desired side they wish the top to fall towards.

SIDE STEPPING: Climbing technique used to circle around the trunk of the tree using the safety line and spurs.

SIGHTS-(Tree falling and equipment): On the side cases of most larger power saws there are embossed lines that indicate the perpendicular of the cut, called sights.

SILENT BIND: This refers to a felled tree being put into a bind that is not obvious by the lay, but that nonetheless puts the tree under enough bind as to be a hazard to the person bucking the tree. For example, a tall tree can appear to lie "flat" on a gently curved slope.

SINGLE-LINE-(Climbing and entering the tree): Term indicating the particular techniques, more often rock climbing, used by a climber to enter the tree by means of a single fixed line. In contrast to double-line technique. Single-line technique is synonymous with fixed-line technique.

SKINNING: Tree trimming term indicating the removal of a branch's minor leads, shoots and buds. The practice is often carried throughout the tree. An often detrimental practice to the tree. Synony mous with stripping.

SLABBING OUT: Tree falling term synonymous with barber chair.

SLACK LOADING: Rigging term that implies how the rigging works in between slack periods and loading. It's often a dynamic period of rigging alignment in which many maladies can occur. Lines can foul and hooks, pins or snaps can be tripped from slack loading tendencies.

SLACK OFF: Climbing term describing the procedure of slacking one line to gain the reliance, or support, of another. Example: Before I put all my weight in the climb line, I'll slack off the safety first.

SLING-(Rigging, tools): A short, stout line, or strap, with eyes fabricated on each end used to anchor blocks and other tools to stumps, trees or whatever. In climbing, to sling a line is to propel it.

SNAP-ON GEAR: Small slings used by a climber to attach limbs and other pieces of work to a bull line.

SNIPE-(Tree falling and cutting): A rather loosely used term at times that indicates a wide variety of style and proportion of diagonal cuts taken out of the face cut, stump or tree. Any particular snipe can have a pronounced influence in the outcome of a tree's fall.

SPAR: The main divisions of a tree into separate trunks are often referred to as spars.

SPAR POLE-(Rigging): Generally a tree chosen for its ideal position and elevation to set rigging in. Used for pulling.

SPEED LINE-(Rigging, climbing): A system of rigging used in the tree, which in some design and concept follows that used by the "shot gun yarders." Basically a static line spanned between a spar in the tree and a tail hold on the ground which supports a traveling block. The traveling block (carriage) carries the loads and is controlled during its travel back and forth by another line, appropriately called a haul back.

SPREADER SNAP-(Climbing tools): A double snap in the form of a wing designed for and used exclusively on the lower belt dee rings on seat saddles for a climb-line attachment.

SPRINGBOARD-(Falling tools): A board of specific design and purpose that a timber faller uses to work off of and to help them to reach and cut the downhill side of trees growing on steep ground. The board has a shoe, or bit end, that's placed into a notch, cut into the tree to hold it.

SQUARE UP-(Tree cutting and saw handling): Term pertaining to the procedures of properly matching two cuts. In the usual case it involves bringing the back cut up square, or parallel, to the undercut. Squaring up is synonymous with a timber faller keeping the line of trees that are cut square and true to course with the timber harvest boundary, property lines and strip lines.

STAGING-(Falling tools): Planks, or stout boards, that a faller uses to lay between one or more springboards.

STALL-(Falling and rigging): Basically a hesitation in the fall of a tree from limb lock or some conflict in the falling cut or hinge wood. In rigging, a line will stall, or fail to run, if there is too much bite at the tether end.

STATIC LINE: Rigging term with many synonyms. In one sense a static line is one that doesn't stretch, or stretches very little. A single line set semi-permanently that doesn't run but is used to carry or hold loads is also referred to as a static line. On the climber's line, when set in the conventional double-line configuration, one side is referred to as the static side because it does not move or run relative to their position.

STOCK: The variety of tree used as the roots in a grafted tree.

STOPPER: Climbing term implying the limbs or stubs used to hold a climb line in a preferred position, or side, of a tree trunk.

STRADDLE: A common climbing term indicating a particular position a climber will assume to do some of their work in the tree. In position, to straddle a limb or spar is much like being on horseback.

STRAP-(Rigging and timber falling): In design and use a strap is much like a sling, but generally longer and used in extending the reach in a run. The term strap is also used loosely in the trade when referring to a certain corner, chunk or portion of wood used in a cut to hold or pull the work when it falls or swings.

STRAY KERF-(Tree cutting): An unintended cut, or portion of a cut, in the tree that results from error or misalignment and whose presence presents the possibility of a problem in properly finishing what you started.

STRIP: The area designated for a timber faller to work in is known as their strip. Generally designated or defined by a flag line (strip line) or some geographic features like roads, ridge tops and ravines.

STUMP SHOT-(Tree falling): The difference in elevation between the backcut and undercut is referred to as stump shot. Ample stump shot can prevent a tree or top from kicking or shooting back off the stump. There is much opinion expressed about how much stump shot is proper for any situation.

SUCKER-(Tree growth): Generally speaking, vigorous new growth arising from the stump or main structure of a tree that is cut hard.

SWAY: How a tree moves in the wind is known as sway.

SWEEP: Falling term indicating the presence of a curve in the lower trunk or butt of a tree.

SWING-(Tree falling and cutting the tree): To swing a limb or tree is for it to move laterally or horizontally like a door opening. In contrast to just falling over.

TAG LINE: Rigging term implying any line used for the purpose of controlling the movement of a load and not necessarily its support. The distinction is sometimes indistinguishable.

TAIL HOLD-(Rigging): The tail hold is a ground point anchor for rigging, tools or lines, to "dead end" or run through a block. Usually a stump or tree is used. But a stable vehicle or hand dug ground anchors can also be used satisfactory as tail holds.

TAILING: In rigging, the term tailing is sometimes used synonymously with "butt tying and lowering." Tailing is also a term to describe the technique used by a timber faller to pivot the springboard in the notch by using the toe of one boot under it and hopping the board ahead.

TAKE DOWN: Tree cutting and climbing term used synonymously with "tree wrecking," or the procedures of climbing and taking a tree down in pieces.

TEEPEE: A faller's term uniquely describing the result of hanging a number of trees up in one particular tree that is intended to be knocked down by the rest. But not.

TETHER-(Ropes and rigging): Variable techniques used to control the rate of run and load in a line.

TAUTLINE HITCH-(Climbing): The climber's knot used for adjusting the working length in the climb line and safeties.

THIMBLE-(Rigging and tools): Basically any device used to prevent chafing or wear on a line. Thimbles are used in eye splices for that purpose. In certain applications thimbles can be used to control or ease the bite in a line. The climb-line thimble for example.

THREE POINT METHOD: Climbing style by which the climber uses foot and handholds to get around in the tree. In the true sense of the three point style you use either two handholds and one foot or visa versa.

THROTTLE LOCK: Device used on most larger power saws to partially crack the throttle during cold starts.

THROWING HOOK-(Climbing tools): Specifically a slip hook used in rigging and runs of chain. Also used as a climbing aid to set or fix a line in out-of-reach places.

TIE-IN: Climbing term indicating the setting of a climb line in a chosen crotch or limb.

TIE OFF: Climbing and rigging term implying the fixing or dead ending of a line to hold a load or keep the line from running.

TIMBER: An old term implying trees used for harvesting, logging and lumber making.

TOPPING-(Climbing and cutting the tree): To climb and cut the top of a tree out. A phase in the removal of a tree by wrecking it out. Also a term that is used loosely in the trade when speaking of a style of trimming.

TORQUE: One of the five forces encountered while bucking a tree. It implies that one part of the cut wants to turn or roll during the buck. Also, torque, or torquing, is synonymous with a style of saw handling, usually a negative style that results in misaligned cuts. See also **BUCKING THE TREE** in **Chapter 34**.

TRIGGERING: Cutting the tree. See "tripping"

TRIPPING: A loosely used term implying the act of setting something into motion. In this case it would be the act of cutting the last portion of wood (holding strap) that holds a cut together or keeps a tree from falling.

TRUNK DRAG: Climbing term indicating the undesirable tendency for a climb line to run down an off side of the trunk. This usually results in the loss of some scope from the tie-in when it catches on the trunk.

TWEAKED-(Cutting tools): Pruner heads, loppers and shears. Whenever the mechanism of these tools is sprung from improper use, it is known as such. It results in poor performance in the cutting.

UNDERBUCK-(Cutting the tree, saw handling): Reaching under a log, or limb, with the bar of the saw to sever the lower side is known as underbucking. When underbucking you will be "back chaining" with the saw.

UNDERCUT-(Tree falling): Generally the first cut used in falling a tree is the undercut. In climbing and cutting the tree the term is synonymous with underbucking.

VEER-(Bucking the tree): Refers to the motion of a log, or logs, swinging to the side after being tripped loose and while settling.

VERTICAL GRAIN: Wood fibers (wood grain) running longitudinally true through the trunk or stem of the tree.

VERTICAL WORK-(Climbing and cutting the tree): Refers to the upright, straight and free standing attitude of a tree trunk that will be cut and managed by a climber using various methods and techniques.

VIGOR-(Plant growth): The expression of plant growth. Fast growth is vigorous growth.

WHITTLING-(Cutting the tree): A loose term implying various methods of cutting wood in a tree. When correcting or cleaning out an error or corner in a falling cut you will be whittling.

WIDOW MAKER: Tree falling term indicating broken out limbs and tops hanging in neighboring trees that can fall and strike you dead.

WILD EYE-(Rigging): An eye splice in steel cable made by the wrapping technique in which the set in the strands are mated together to form the eye. Sometimes referred to as a fanner John or Molly Hogan.

WIND CHECK: A longitudinal crack, or more correctly a "split," running through and following the grain in the trunk of a tree.

WIND FALL: During a storm, trees will be blown down and be called wind falls.

WINGING-(Cutting the tree): A loose term indicating a small cut of various depths and angles used to sever the corners of the hinge or holding wood of a particular type or style of principal cut.

WOOD DISTRIBUTION-(Tree cutting and falling): A term indicating the amount and placement of hinge or holding wood in a particular cut.

WOOD PULL: The erratic and longitudinal separation of wood fibers resulting from extreme tension and leverage forces. The term has negative connotations in falling and bucking as "wood pull" can significantly reduce the value and quality of a log or tree.

WRECK OUT-(Climbing and cutting the tree): The take down of a tree by climbing it and rendering it in pieces.

XYLEM: See "sapwood"

Index

C

D

E

F

G

H

J

K

L

M

N

O

P

Q

R

S

T

U

V

W

Made in the USA
Las Vegas, NV
31 May 2024

90549017R00302